EXPERIMENTS WITH EMPIRE

THEORY IN FORMS

A Series Edited by
Nancy Rose Hunt and Achille Mbembe

Experiments with Empire

Anthropology and Fiction in the French Atlantic

JUSTIN IZZO

DUKE UNIVERSITY PRESS *Durham and London* 2019

© 2019 Duke University Press
All rights reserved
Printed and bound by CPI Group (UK) Ltd, Croydon, CR0 4YY

Designed by Matt Tauch
Typeset in Minion Pro by Westchester Book Group

Library of Congress Cataloging-in-Publication Data
Names: Izzo, Justin, author.
Title: Experiments with empire : anthropology and fiction
    in the French Atlantic / Justin Izzo.
Description: Durham : Duke University Press, 2019. |
    Series: Theory in forms | Includes bibliographical
    references and index.
Identifiers: LCCN 2018042312 (print) |
    LCCN 2018057191 (ebook)
ISBN 9781478004622 (ebook)
ISBN 9781478003700 (hardcover : alk. paper)
ISBN 9781478004004 (pbk. : alk. paper)
Subjects: LCSH: French literature—20th century—History
    and criticism. | French fiction—French-speaking
    countries—History and criticism. | Ethnology in
    literature. | Imperialism in literature. | Imperialism
    in motion pictures. | Politics and literature—History—
    20th century. | Literature and society—History—
    20th century.
Classification: LCC PQ3897 (ebook) |
    LCC PQ3897 .I98 2019 (print) | DDC 840.9/3552—dc23
LC record available at https://lccn.loc.gov/2018042312

Cover art: *Aerial View Of Cityscape Against Sky*, Marseille,
France. Photo by Hlne Poli/EyeEm/Getty.

Contents

Acknowledgments

It is no accident that this book traces experimental connections between different ways of knowing the world. My initial interest in this question was quite personal, sparked by graduate work at Duke as an unorthodox scholar who started his career in cultural anthropology and later moved to literature. I am deeply indebted to the people who made this move happen and to all those who supported the work that came out of it.

At Duke, Charlie Piot and Alice Kaplan put their heads together and found a way for a young anthropologist to join the Program in Literature. This switch shaped everything that came after, and I am ever grateful for their ingenuity and determination to keep me at Duke. Charlie and Alice remain inspiring interlocutors alongside other teachers and mentors at Duke who guided me, pushed me, and always excited me with new texts and ideas: Michael Hardt, Fredric Jameson, Rebecca Stein, Ken Surin, and Robyn Wiegman. The late and much missed Srinivas Aravamudan took me in as his research assistant during my last two years of graduate school and, more important, showed me what a book should look like. At all stages of my graduate career, Duke friends supported me, made me laugh, and constantly floored me with their thinking: Lindsey Andrews, Leigh Campoamor, Gerry Canavan, Kinohi Nishikawa, and Ryan Vu.

In France, Philippe Roger and Pap Ndiaye hosted me for a year at the École des Hautes Études en Sciences Sociales. Jean-Paul Alglave and Paul Acker-mann welcomed me into their home in Paris and offered me a warm environ-ment for reading and writing.

At Brown, the Department of French Studies has been an ideal home for me and my work as this project neared completion. My colleagues, graduate students, and undergraduates have been sources of inspiration, encouragement, and good cheer since I arrived. Other colleagues at Brown read chapter drafts or offered valuable advice: Tim Bewes, Caroline Castiglione, Nancy Jacobs, Jennifer Johnson, and Ralph Rodriguez. The Brown community, in French studies and beyond, has been a wonderfully vibrant intellectual home since my arrival in 2012. Special thanks, also, to Giovi Roz Gastaldi and Marley Kirton for helping me take screenshots of a quality I could not produce on my own.

I have been able to give several invited talks that allowed me to test out and refine several of this project's interventions in different settings. Stéphane Gerson and Herrick Chapman welcomed me at New York University's Institute of French Studies; Emmanuelle Saada, Vincent Debaene, and Madeleine Dobie invited me to participate in the "Future of French and Francophone Studies" series at Columbia's Maison Française; and Matthew O'Malley invited me to speak as part of Yale University's "Ethnography and Social Theory" colloquia.

Colleagues and friends were unfailingly generous in the time they devoted to reading parts of the manuscript, answering my questions, and offering feedback about the project as a whole. Gerry Canavan, Vincent Debaene, Sam Di Iorio, Martin Munro, and Ralph Rodriguez all read through chapters at various stages of this book's completion. Michael Dash, Charles Forsdick, and Gary Wilder gave input on matters large and small as the book took shape.

Parts of chapters 1, 2, and 4 appeared early in their life in a different form as the following articles: "Narrative, Contingency, Modernity: Jean Rouch's *Moi, un Noir*," *International Journal of Francophone Studies*, nos. 1–2 (2011): 205–20; "From Aesthetics to Allegory: Raphaël Confiant, the Creole Novel, and Interdisciplinary Translation," *Small Axe* 42 (2013): 89–99; "The Anthropology of Transcultural Storytelling: *Oui mon commandant!* and Amadou Hampâté Bâ's Ethnographic Didacticism," *Research in African Literatures* 46, no. 1 (2015): 1–18; "'A Question to Be Lived': Creoleness and Ethnographic Fiction," *Small Axe* 55 (2018): 137–46.

At Duke University Press, Elizabeth Ault has been steadfast in her support of this project and in her desire to bring the book through to publication while making sure it stayed true to my vision. My two anonymous readers for the press provided sharp and insightful feedback; the book is better for their suggestions and I thank them for pushing me to amplify aspects of the project that I had not initially seen.

A small group of friends has supported me at all stages of this project. I thank them for being hilarious and brilliant fellow travelers and for putting up with me: Aaron Castroverde, Eli and Kelly Gamboa, Nick and Deena Giffen, Hanna Ihalainen, and Brantley, Helen, and Ruth Nicholson. My family has been no less supportive and indulgent: Philip Izzo and Susan Izzo, Whitney and J. R. Johnson, and Bob McCarthy. It is to all these friends and family members that this book is affectionately dedicated.

Introduction

Ethnographic Fictions in the French Atlantic

In a 1963 interview with the journal *Les Cahiers du Cinéma*, the French anthropologist and prolific documentary filmmaker Jean Rouch spoke about his work in the *cinéma vérité* style, the boundaries of realist ethnographic filmmaking, and his investment in what he called "the creation of fiction beginning from the real."[1] For Rouch, fiction had unexpected and paradoxical origins that he explored in improvisational approaches to the conventions of ethnographic documentaries about "real" life. These were cinematic experiments that saw stories created on the fly as amateur actors and research subjects collaborated with the anthropologist behind the camera. By 1963, Rouch had already made several such "ethno-fictions" by creating improvisational filmic narratives from various research projects in preindependence West Africa—namely, Ghana, Niger, and the Ivory Coast. One of the most influential of these films was *Moi, un Noir* (1958), in which a Nigerien migrant to Abidjan speaks about his everyday life as a day laborer and his stint fighting in the French colonial war in Indochina. But he also imagines a new, transatlantic sense of self in relation to emerging African and American popular cultures, extending his identification with modernity beyond the French empire. This improvised commentary was recorded after Rouch's visuals had already been shot. In reality, the actor Oumarou Ganda was Rouch's research assistant at the time of filming.

What drives this impulse to push beyond the boundaries of ethnographic film as a genre and to introduce fiction into the documentary expectations of anthropology? Rouch's initial answer to the interview prompt made in this vein humorously cites his own "laziness": it was far easier, after all, to make up stories with his African friends during the filming process than it was to debate and plan for weeks ahead of time, constructing storyboards and determining in advance how characters' roles would play out on-screen. Continuing with his gentle self-deprecation, he goes on to say that the "state of grace" of fictionalized ethnographic filmmaking caused him to develop bad habits: "It doesn't interest me to make films with a set story to tell, roles to play, and a preparation on paper. I was very impressed by the first Westerns I saw, Westerns that were improvised in the course of filming. Unfortunately, African influences took effect, since Africans are people who improvise wonderfully and who have total spontaneity in front of the camera."[2] Rouch's early ethno-fiction films were thus born from alchemical moments where he followed the improvisational lead of his African collaborators and research subjects. These are moments of cinematic transubstantiation, where anthropology is converted into fiction as improvisation filters through the camera lens.

This book is about anthropology, genre, and empire. It is also about the complex, interdependent, and speculative relationship between textual forms and social forms. It studies experiments between anthropology and fiction as creative ways to process colonial situations and imperial afterlives. As Rouch's example illustrates, it examines how literary writers and anthropologists in the twentieth-century French Atlantic thought through colonial and postcolonial situations by producing works of ethnographic fiction. These are generically hybrid texts, either by anthropologists whose documentary works adopt fictive elements or by fiction writers who integrate social-scientific ways of thinking (and commentary on these ways of thinking) into their artistic production. They also contain disparate formal layers that make paratextual and intertextual connections, drawing us into fields of metacritical, self-reflexive commentary.

Helena Wulff defines ethnographic fiction as "fiction built around real social, political, and historical events and circumstances."[3] The idea of ethnographic fiction I work with in this book owes something to this definition, but it also involves reflexive and speculative dimensions: ethnographic fiction in *Experiments with Empire* disrupts generic categories to think critically about social-scientific and literary ways of knowing the world. But it also imagines new ways of world knowing by rearranging the geographies and histories of imperial social forms. Ethnographic fiction in this book is a concept with speculative resonances, one that links formal experimentation with new epistemological desires.

The ethnographic fictions that feature here attempt to express and negotiate imperial situations across the presumed divide of decolonization. They offer sharp political reorderings of (post)colonial knowledge production. Further, they imagine social forms and ways of knowing that are not beholden to the limited political horizon empire offers. But in so doing they also point to the epistemological challenges and contradictions involved in understanding empire using ethnographic realism and the representative conventions of the social sciences.

Transatlantic and Transcolonial Experiments

Experiments with Empire ties the production of ethnographic fiction in twentieth-century French and Francophone letters to the question of empire as a political, epistemological, and formal problem. This connection, moreover, has geographic and historical resonances: on the one hand, tracing twentieth-century ethnographic fictions reveals a French Atlantic world that links metropolitan Europe, Africa, and the Caribbean. We must begin from an Atlantic perspective to observe how these ethnographic fictions generated and participated in a broader field of thinking within and against imperial situations. On the other hand, analyzing this discursive field uncovers connections between older colonial pasts and the contemporary postcolonial present.[4] It prioritizes experimental ambitions that transcend decolonization as a periodizing focal point.

This book's timeline moves from the late colonial period to the end of the twentieth century. More precisely, it begins in the 1930s, when Marcel Griaule led the Mission Dakar-Djibouti (1931–33) across colonial Africa and Abyssinia, and ends in the late 1990s, as debates about race and immigration in metropolitan France began to prefigure the success of Jean-Marie Le Pen's Front National in the 2002 presidential elections. This arc shows how experiments with ethnographic fiction moved across the twentieth-century decolonizing moment, beginning with the Mission Dakar-Djibouti's "promotion" of both French anthropology and the empire (as Vincent Debaene has shown[5]), and extending into the postcolonial Caribbean and Metropole. This periodization allows us to think the colonial, the imperial, and the postcolonial together as an experimental space-time that can generate new political imaginaries and desires for new social forms.

Jean Rouch was at the forefront of post–World War II documentary filmmaking, but he was not alone in experimenting at the intersection of anthropology and fiction using colonial encounters as raw materials for imaginative textual production. Many other figures from around the French Atlantic during the twentieth century also thought deeply and transculturally about the relationship between anthropology and fiction. Several decades before Rouch began his ethnofictional experiments, for instance, the Haitian physician and ethnographer Jean Price-Mars, who studied both medicine and the social sciences in Paris, wrote his book *Ainsi parla l'Oncle* (1928) in which he urged Haiti's elite to cease idealizing French aesthetic norms (an infatuation he famously referred to as "collective bovarysme") and to valorize instead the creation of literature and fiction that reflected the nation's singularity. His transatlantic argument was based on an ethnohistorical reading of African cultural survivals in New World contexts and on an aesthetic appreciation of the African origins of Haitian Vodou. Also in the Caribbean, in his seminal *Discours antillais* (1981), Édouard Glissant studied social forms left over from the transatlantic slave trade on his home island of Martinique—which had been a French overseas department for nearly four decades when the *Discours* was published—to argue for the social-scientific conditions of possibility of an authentically nationalist kind of postcolonial fiction.

Ethnographic fiction took shape on the other side of the ocean, as well. Dahomeyan author Paul Hazoumé studied at the Institut d'Ethnologie in Paris in the late 1930s, publishing his thesis research as *Le pacte de sang au Dahomey* in 1937 and his ethnohistorical novel *Doguicimi* one year later—as he reminds readers in a brief prefatory remark, this work of fiction has a social-scientific bent since it "deals with the ways and customs of the old kingdom of Dahomey."[6] Michel Leiris unites all the points of the triangle, as it were, since he carried out ethnographic fieldwork throughout colonial Africa on the 1931–33 Mission Dakar-Djibouti during which he wrote *L'Afrique fantôme* (1934), which sees him assimilate himself to a fictional Conradian character out of anthropological frustration. Like Hazoumé and many others, he studied at Paris's Institut d'Ethnologie. He also completed research on race relations in the postcolonial French Caribbean, citing "the poet Édouard Glissant" in *Contacts de civilisations en Martinique et en Guadeloupe* (1955), which he wrote for the United Nations Education, Scientific and Cultural Organization.[7]

Francophone writers working primarily in the domain of fiction also turned to anthropology to forge textually meaningful relationships to the French (post) colonial situation. Writing in the wake of *Ainsi parla l'Oncle*, Haitian novelists such as René Depestre and Dany Laferrière revisited concerns articulated about cultural nationalism by Price-Mars and his contemporary Jacques Roumain, a writer and novelist who studied anthropology under Franz Boas and who co-founded Haiti's Bureau d'Ethnologie with Price-Mars in 1941.[8] Martinican author Patrick Chamoiseau credits anthropology throughout his book *Écrire en pays dominé* (1997), in which he describes his development as a fiction writer and integrates this personal story into a new ethnographic history of Caribbean literary production. Claude Lévi-Strauss and Price-Mars both make cameos in Martinican novelist Raphaël Confiant's *Le Nègre et l'Amiral* (1988), which fictionalizes everyday life on the island under Vichyist colonial rule during World War II.

Working with this experimental archive, this book addresses debates in anthropology, literary criticism, and postcolonial studies. These fields, and the questions I ask of them, offer distinct and interrelated optics through which to consider this project's main arguments. Taken synthetically, they illuminate how imperial complexities opened up stylistic opportunities and prompted experimental forms of generic hybridity.[9] But these questions of form and style are inseparable from questions of epistemology. In the twentieth-century French Atlantic, "knowing" empire was deeply enmeshed in anthropology yet also orthogonal to it: for the literary writers and anthropologists I study here, ethnographic knowledge production had to move outside the bounds of documentary realism if it was to make sense of imperial social forms. Ethnographic realism had to confront, in a productive manner, the stylized free play of imaginative fictionality.

Alternative Anthropologies

Anthropologists famously and provocatively took up questions of ethnographic genre and form during the 1980s and 1990s, when the publication of works such as *Writing Culture* and *Anthropology as Cultural Critique* put self-reflexive experimentation in the service of critiques of anthropological knowledge production. The "writing culture moment," sometimes referred to as anthropology's "textual turn," was characterized by a convergence with poststructuralism and literary theory as anthropologists questioned their authority as knowledge producers as well as the textual conventions of ethnographic representation. In these accounts, documentary authenticity gave way in the face of what James Clifford called anthropology's "partial truths" and "true fictions," emphasizing the discipline's entanglement with fiction's Latin forebear, *fingere*, "something made or fashioned."[10] Scholars have of late reanimated these questions, asking, for instance, what anthropology's literary turn still has to teach us about experimental fieldwork in the age of social media and the digital humanities or, as Michael Taussig wonders, about the underexplored formal links between fieldwork and "writing work."[11]

Addressing this legacy in a different way, this book offers an imperial genealogy of anthropology's textual moment and extends this genealogical relationship throughout the twentieth century. Writing more than twenty-five years after *Writing Culture*'s initial publication, Clifford cites the twin processes of decolonization and globalization as factors that marked the book's conditions of possibility—and he also recognizes Rouch as a "neglected inspiration."[12] This post-1960s moment of upheaval, contestation, and integration was undoubtedly essential for destabilizing the surety of anthropological knowledge claims. But we can trace the twentieth-century relationship between anthropology and fiction back farther, decentering decolonization as a focal point and observing how even in late-colonial contexts writers and intellectuals desired new anthropological epistemologies stemming from experiments with ethnography. "The Poetics and Politics of Ethnography," *Writing Culture*'s iconic subtitle, have unmistakably imperial roots that also speak to postcolonial presents and futures.

This genealogy shifts some of the key terms of anthropology's textual moment. The figures I study here brought fiction and anthropology together during the twentieth century in ways that sidestepped questions of (in)authenticity and truth value. Likewise, although the chapters to come pay close attention to conditions of textual production, the experimental forms that drive this book's analyses go beyond pointing to the constructedness of ethnographic epistemologies.[13] Instead, the experiments with ethnographic fiction considered in this book instrumentalize new generic forms to think orthogonally about empire. Imaginative creativity merges with anthropological approaches to documentary narrative, forging new ways to grapple textually with empire's ideologies and contradictions in the Atlantic world. These become alternative anthropologies of colonial and postcolonial encounters that offer novel epistemological approaches to empire and the history of the human sciences, inventive renderings of ethnographic narrative form, and explorations of fiction's documentary possibilities. Alternative anthropologies are also orthogonal to empire, intersecting with imperial social forms but also veering away from them to imagine new ways of knowing and new political possibilities beyond empire's reach.

In his 1989 essay on empire and "anthropology's interlocutors," Edward Said addresses the writing culture moment and gives a dialogic cast to anthropology's constitutive entanglement with colonized peoples. For Said, the idea of interlocution can be "split quite dramatically into two fundamentally discrepant meanings": on the one hand, in the colonial context interlocution can refer to a quietist form of collaboration (here Said gives the example of so-called native *évolués* in French Algeria) or, with a nod to Frantz Fanon, to a staunch "refusal" that sees "radical antagon[ism]" as "the only interlocution that is possible with colonial power."[14] On the other hand, interlocution can signal "denaturing incorporation and cooptation," a dialogue with the human sciences in which the colonized participate in a depoliticized, "antiseptic" conversation with disciplines that still police the terms of access and debate.[15] This book proposes a third interlocutory mode between anthropology and the (post) colonial world, one that avoids the collaboration-antagonism axis, as well as the overly polite discussion Said describes. The writers and intellectuals I study here mobilize anthropology's imperial roots to establish new epistemologies, generic forms, historical narratives, and political imaginaries. This is both an interlocution with and a "speaking past" anthropology, a mode of address that looks beyond the discipline's representative conventions while remaining attuned to the possibilities ethnography offers for reimagining empire and for thinking beyond it.

In a similar vein, Said goes on to urge anthropologists to focus on "the amalgamation between Europe and its imperium acting together in the process of decolonization."[16] Once again thinking alongside Fanon, he highlights a narrative of inseparability between the West and the decolonized world that encompasses both "a collective as well as a plural destiny for mankind."[17] This model of amalgamation is crucial for understanding decolonial interdependence as humanity's horizon (and for recent historiography positioning France as an "imperial nation-state"[18]), but it does not go far enough: the Said-Fanon formulation misses how empire is also an experimental space-time and how narratives of amalgamation conceal alternative histories, speculative futures, and different ways of knowing the world. Alternative anthropologies call attention to the interplay between amalgamation and reimagination, between the (post)colonial world as a space of variegated integration and one of radical invention.

The experiments with ethnographic fiction taking place in the twentieth-century French Atlantic took an expansive view of this interplay. The figures I study here are invested in generating new forms of knowledge and in creating political and epistemological connections that remained unthinkable within the confines of conventional anthropological rationality or fictional representation. For instance, Malian ethnographer and colonial civil servant Amadou Hampâté Bâ, whose work I examine in chapter 1, uses characterology in his memoirs to advocate for a linguistic universalism that repositions the French language as a decolonized vehicle for the worldwide communication of knowledge about African cultures. Or, to return to Rouch, the characters in *Moi, un Noir* inhabit transatlantic popular cultures in ways that situate them as cosmopolitan knowledge producers as well as late colonial subjects.

Imperial formations imposed new social forms on colonized populations, and the ethnographic fictions I study here seek to understand these forms but also, crucially, to imagine connections across and outside them. They thematize and interrogate their own conditions of possibility and the limitations of anthropological truth claims, but in so doing they generate new political epistemologies that are more than anti-imperial counternarratives. These ethnographic fictions urge us to revitalize our understanding of the relationship between anthropology and colonialism: historically conceived as one of complicity or domination, this relationship is also shot through with politicized and speculative free play, even with utopian desires. It produces illuminatingly self-reflexive texts that offer alternative anthropologies of imperial life worlds. Alternative anthropologies move along the grain of imperial social forms while simultaneously imagining other socialities, histories, and geographies that empire cannot countenance and to which established epistemologies remain blind.

Empire as a Formal Imperative

The idea that ethnographic fictions generate alternative anthropologies requires us to raise questions about literary/fictional form and its relationship to epistemology. More specifically, this involves thinking about how form wrestles with empire in experimental texts that push against the expectations we bring to literary genres.

There is a growing body of scholarship on the history of French anthropology: its relationship to literature, as well as its disciplinary interaction with scientific theories of race and political ideologies of empire.[19] Scholars have also begun focusing more closely on what literature has to tell us about everyday life, often thinking alongside or against anthropological theory.[20] As Debaene argues, twentieth-century French culture experienced an "ethnographic moment" marked by ethnography's rise to prominence as a field science as well as an increasing openness to literary modes of writing that stood alongside more conventional anthropological monographs.[21] This book's scope and stakes, however, are different: first, because I argue that experimental ethnographic fictions signal to us how we can relate literary form to social form without reducing one to the other. My aim is broader, also, because experiments with ethnographic fiction encompass a colonial and postcolonial Atlantic world whose anthropological aesthetic is triangulated and not the exclusive epistemological or artistic purview of the metropole.[22]

From this perspective, what demands does empire make of form, style, and generic experimentation? This book shows how empire pulls literary creativity toward an aesthetics of documentary recording, on the one hand, and toward practices of imaginative textual invention, on the other. Consider Martinican-Guyanese writer René Maran's Prix Goncourt–winning *Batouala* (1921): billed as an "authentic Negro novel" (*véritable roman nègre*) about French Equatorial Africa (AEF), *Batouala* classifies itself according to both its fictionality and the claims it makes to a certain documentary authenticity. As Maran puts it in his introduction, he spent six years "translating" what he lived and saw as a colonial administrator in AEF into *Batouala*: "This novel is thus entirely objective. It does not even try to explain: it observes. It does not express outrage: it records."[23]

Maran's theory of fiction involves positioning the novel as a conduit for "impersonal observation," as a vehicle for the transparent rendering of empire's constitutive violence in narrative prose.[24] In this documentary conception of literature, empire's decadence and exploitative organization of everyday life can be communicated to a broad public in narratives that make a claim to truth value because of the revelatory impulses they express. Authorial stylistic flourishes take a back seat here to a view of fiction as recording—from this perspective the novel comes to resemble a narrativization of field notes. But as helpful as Maran's formulation is in defining the novel as an observational document over and against the stories empire tells about itself, it has less to tell us about the relationship between documentary impulses and imaginative stylization.

Aimé Césaire's *Cahier d'un retour au pays natal* (1939) offers a way to shore up the stylistic elements of empire's entanglement with documentary textuality and creative invention. Césaire's masterful prose poem locates itself at the articulation of imperial geographies and the intensely personal forms of "ruination," to borrow Ann Laura Stoler's processual category, that empire wreaks on its subjects.[25] But we should not read *Cahier* solely in terms of its exquisite anticolonial lyricism. As the surrealist André Breton suggests in his preface written in 1943, in Césaire's poetic persona "human essence is heated to a point of maximum effervescence in which knowledge—here of the highest order—overlaps with magical gifts."[26] Breton argues that epistemology and imaginative creativity both come to constitute the Martinican writer's scathing poetic critique of empire. We can observe how documentary impulses intersect with the "magical gifts" of poetic lyricism in *Cahier*'s opening stanzas, where the repetition of the words "in this inert town" (*dans cette ville inerte*) creates the effect of the poet guiding readers through an urban landscape that could be Fort-de-France, Martinique's capital, or any colonial city at all (and, indeed, Breton develops the metaphor of the poet as guide in his preface).[27] Stirring lyrical intensity is of a piece with a sense of documentary exposition since poetic language can be used to communicate knowledge of colonial conditions of living. For Césaire, then, documentary impulses are stylistic products of imaginative poetic vision.

Maran and Césaire provide two models of what happens when the desire to record and bear witness to imperial power relations confronts the stylized prerequisites for imaginative and fictional creative writing. But these models, one poetic and the other an "observational" novel, also provoke us to make broader points about empire, form, and style. The writers and anthropologists I study in this book conceive of these impulses (the documentary and the imaginative) as always already conjoined features of narratives about empire. Their ethnographic fictions suggest that it is empire's imposition of "contact"—as its originary moment, its foundational violence, and as its enduring and changeable history—that engenders the desire to document the social forms that arise from it, as well as the desire to think beyond it with an imaginative narrative grammar. Focusing on how imperial projects produce these dual desires involves attuning our critical faculties to the ways in which empires are "concrete places" (as Gary Wilder reminds us, reworking Dipesh Chakrabarty's arguments about European universalism[28]) but also formal imperatives, actually existing spaces that demand innovative textual forms that rearrange established geographic and epistemological coordinates.

Imperial political rationalities require modes of knowledge in which empiricism and imaginative invention are inseparable. Making sense of this idea, as this book seeks to do, involves conceiving of imperial projects as constraints, catalysts and, crucially, as stylistic and formal challenges. Salman Rushdie, whose work is devoted to empire's afterimages in literature, echoes this argument and the idea of two intertwined "directions" of style on which it relies. In his memoir, *Joseph Anton* (2012), he describes his search for a style and form adequate to the ideas he wanted to convey in the budding *Satanic Verses* (1988), writing that he wanted to show "not only how the East flowed into the West and the West into the East, but how . . . the imagined world, the location of dreams, art, invention and, yes, belief, leaked across the frontier that separated it from the everyday, 'real' place in which human beings mistakenly believed they lived."[29] For the wry Rushdie, human error causes this porosity between the real world and the world of invention or, to put it in Breton's terms, between the world of "knowledge" and that of "magical gifts." *Experiments with Empire* offers a much stronger version of Rushdie's point that ultimately doubles as a qualitative distinction. I view empire as a stylistic and formal problem not just to signal how distinct literary modes feed into one another, but also to observe how generic experimentation can lead literature and fiction outside of themselves and toward the social sciences. What is more, this book studies how empire provides experimental ethnographic fictions with raw materials for thinking outside of its political and epistemological terms.

(Post)colonial Theory and Imperial Countermapping

These formal challenges and the alternative anthropologies they generate offer new geographic assemblages that in turn suggest new modes of historical connectivity. What do theories of ethnographic fiction have to tell us about how generic hybridity doubles as cartographic praxis, how anthropological and fictional world making simultaneously implies imperial world mapping? Beginning from an imperial and Atlantic perspective, as I do in this book, also means beginning from the ways in which textual experiments rearrange received organizations of space and time. These experiments cut across the actually existing boundaries of (post)colonial territories, mapping transcolonial connections that are at once idealized, spectral, and rooted; they speak to shared historical experiences and at the same time imagine new ones. Orthogonality is again the name of the methodological game: the ethnographic fictions I study here all express real geographies and lived histories, but they also play with their politicized reorganization.

If colonial "common sense" can be reimagined by "map[ping] the multiple imaginaries" that compose and destabilize it, as Stoler writes of the colonial archive, we can also imagine acts of mapping in a more straightforward manner—that is, as imaginative (re)arrangements of the geographies on which imperial formations rely.[30] By making this argument I am urging postcolonial studies to attune itself to the ways speculative epistemologies express geopolitical desires and new historical embodiments. These speculative conjugations of geography, politics, and history are what I refer to as processes of imperial countermapping.

Postcolonial critics have pointed to the slippages and imperfections in colonial cartographies' mapping of imperial space, or to the relativist possibilities opened up by postcolonial confrontations with colonial geographies.[31] Similarly, Chakrabarty points implicitly to geographies of "translation" that "problematize" supposedly universal European analytic categories (a claim Jean and John Comaroff echo in *Theory from the South* [2012]).[32] Thinking about empire as an experimental space-time reveals a different kind of epistemological economy, though—one that is less invested in relativization or provincialization. Césaire once again is helpful here. In *Cahier*, he speaks of a black universalism in geographic terms that extend outward from the centers of the triangular slave trade: "And I say to myself Bordeaux and Nantes and Liverpool and / New York and San Francisco / not an inch of this world devoid of my fingerprint." He later espouses "my special geography (*mon originale géographie*) too; the world map made for my / own use, not tinted with the arbitrary colors of scholars."[33] For Césaire (and for the figures I study in this book), imperial geographies possess creative use value that allows him to redirect their ideologies of world mapping toward new cartographic projects.

But the writers and anthropologists who feature in this book also urge us to theorize generic creativity in relation to very real imperial formations. Textual experimentation is thus caught between acts of freewheeling geographic reconfiguration and markers that endlessly reiterate and actualize empire's presence. This is how we can understand Hampâté Bâ's linguistic universalism that ignores colonial frontiers but is articulated in stories about everyday life in colonial outposts, or how Rouch's characters rearrange signifiers of global modernity as they negotiate the uncertain future of imperial projects in the late 1950s. These are additions to, not replacements of, the geographies traced by imperial divisions of colonized spaces. Or, rather, they are additions doubling as superimpositions. As I see it, generic hybridity puts in place forms of cartographic layering, forging new transcolonial aggregates that do not map neatly onto imperial organizations of space—but neither do they displace or imagine them away. The work of generic experimentation, then, takes place in the push and pull that goes on between these distinct yet interrelated layers of mapping and the "forces" (to borrow Franco Moretti's argument about what maps arrange) they organize and contest.[34]

The speculative knowledge games that give rise to palimpsestic geographies also express new configurations of historical time and new cartographic trajectories of imperial historical narratives. Acts of countermapping redirect imperial histories, uncovering geographies that were unthinkable in their time but also redistributing those histories across differently imagined (post)colonial space. On the one hand, countermapping highlights the geographic dimensions of what Stoler calls colonial "duress," referring to the "uneven, recursive qualities" of imperial formations, their "occluded histories," and the "indelible if invisible gash[es]" they signal in the present.[35] On the other hand, though, it generates a geographic field that is shot through with speculative desires and political possibilities that speak to remixed imperial histories. Countermapping is thus a re-worlding of imperial histories that also seeks to gain purchase on political futurities. This is to give a speculative tenor to David Scott's claim that "the problem about postcolonial futures . . . cannot be recast without recasting the problem about colonial pasts."[36]

It is along these lines that we can read, for instance, Amitav Ghosh's *Ibis* trilogy about the nineteenth-century opium trade and the run-up to the First Opium War (1839–42). These novels are rich with ethnohistorical detail (Ghosh holds a doctorate in anthropology), but more to my point is that his historical anthropology dovetails with fiction to map an Indian Ocean world that converges around opium production and mercantilist imperial ideologies. His narratives and chapters flit among India, Mauritius, and China, constructing in both form and content an Indian Ocean imaginary that takes shape as much through the transoceanic movements of displaced lives as it does in the lived experience of the opium trade's imperial political economy.[37]

To take another example, one that addresses speculative political futures, in chapter 5 I study the crime fiction of Jean-Claude Izzo and show how he maps utopian ideas of citizenship onto the fraught urban terrain of 1990s Marseille.[38] Here, layered forms of belonging in the city gather up French (post)colonial histories, only to disperse them again as radically open challenges to the nation-state in "Fortress Europe." These ethnographic fictions go beyond embracing the kind of "heterotemporality" that Chakrabarty pits against the "empty and homogeneous chronology of historicism";[39] they construct speculative space-times that redirect imperial histories, causing them to veer off course and through reimagined lifeworlds.

Geography and epistemology here intersect with politics and form in textual modes that overlay imaginative space-times on "commonsense" organizations of (post)colonial worlds. New epistemological cartographies in ethnographic fictions push us to liken imperial countermapping to a definition Michel Foucault gives of the statement (*énoncé*) in *The Archeology of Knowledge*, "It is not in itself a unit, but a function that cuts across a domain of structures and possible unities, and which reveals them, with concrete contents, in time and space."[40] Countermapping "reveals," yes, but it also creates and reorganizes. Thus, it signals how speculative knowledge projects help us access what postcolonial studies still has to tell us about new configurations—new "possible unities," we might say—of geography, politics, and history.

Put broadly, this book's chapters focus on (post)colonial encounters as experimental impulses—that is, on the ways imperial social forms motivate textual production and orthogonal creativity. Although the chapters begin from the perspective of empire, its socialities, and its histories, they address varied cultural debates, political situations, and aesthetic possibilities for ethnographic fiction. The first two chapters address anthropology and anthropologists directly and ask how fictional forms and strategies generate speculative documentary thinking about and beyond empire. The next three chapters focus more closely on what literary writers do with anthropology, asking how novels and literary history also create alternative anthropologies that are orthogonal to imperial social forms.

Chapter 1 deals with the problems of style and characterology as they relate to the late colonial Africanist epistemologies of Michel Leiris and Amadou Hampâté Bâ. Jean Rouch's ethnofictional turn features in chapter 2, as I turn to the ways fiction opens up new subject-object relations in anthropological knowledge production. Erstwhile ethnographic objects can become knowledge producers in their own right, I argue, taking my cue from the ways Rouch's characters narrate their lives within and beyond the decolonizing world of the late 1950s. Chapter 3 moves us across the Atlantic to Haiti, from where anthropologist Jean Price-Mars initiated a transatlantic conversation about local knowledge and national literature that later fiction writers remixed and added to as they sought to rewrite the nation throughout the twentieth century.

Chapter 4 draws out this New World intermingling of anthropology and literary history even further, studying how Édouard Glissant and writers from the *créolité* movement read anthropology and the social sciences into histories of Caribbean literary production. Their fictions go on to reference this genealogical cross-pollination in games of intertextuality and paratextuality that reveal the postcolonial novel's anthropological history. Finally, chapter 5 returns us to the postcolonial metropole and explores how the late 1990s crime fiction of Jean-Claude Izzo invents utopian democratic life worlds that coexist with narratives of postcolonial social exclusion and widespread political malaise. The transformations in the crime novel I chart here begin from Jean and John Comaroff's observation that global crime fiction is part and parcel of a "criminal anthropology of late modernity . . . an excursion into the contemporary Order of Things—or, rather, into the metaphysic of disorder that has come to infuse the late modern world."[41] The conclusion continues this outward turn and suggests implications of the book's arguments for twenty-first-century debates about politics, democracy, and postcolonial knowledge production.

My corpus is composed of texts that are representative of an Atlantic-wide engagement with ethnographic fiction, but the texts also all speculate beyond their immediate historical, geographic, and epistemological horizons. Among these diverse optics, a French Atlantic takes shape beyond supposed divisions of metropole and empire, texts by Western or non-Western intellectuals, or colonial versus "decolonized" worlds. More pertinent to my archive are tensions between experimental, self-reflexive works and more conventional texts that sometimes struggle with their heterodox interlocutors. From this perspective, the French Atlantic comes into focus as an epistemological field in which alternative knowledge projects with transoceanic reach intersect with desires for social forms that are orthogonal to empire.

Experiments with Empire is about how generic experimentation produces such intersections and about how writers and intellectuals reimagine the entanglements of anthropology and fiction with empire by pushing them toward imaginative textuality and the social sciences, respectively. But even more fundamentally, it is about how desires to know empire generate new visions of politics and sociality, as well as new textualizations of historical time. The book thinks through these generative possibilities, studying not only how ethnographic fiction uses empire as an experimental medium, but also how anthropology and fiction imply each other in critical reconfigurations of imperial projects in our past and present.

Chapter 1

Ethnographic Didacticism and
Africanist Melancholy

Leiris, Hampâté Bâ, and the Epistemology of Style

Far from cursing my fate, I actually regarded the happenstance that had placed me there as curiously in keeping with what for a long time had seemed to me to be my destiny: the condition of not fitting in, a condition that had already driven me to travel in Africa a few years earlier, and that explains, in a general way, the taste I have for fiction, for memories of periods from which I am separated by time, and for countries other than my own.
—MICHEL LEIRIS, *Biffures*

Michel Leiris wrote the words that I borrow for this chapter's epigraph in *Biffures* (1948), a book he spent eight long years crafting and that comprises the first volume of his *La règle du jeu* tetralogy.[1] He reminisces about being stuck in the Sahara on military duty in 1939, and his frustrated autobiographical reflections prompt him to liken this experience to his work nearly a decade earlier as "secretary-archivist" for the 1931–33 Dakar-Djibouti anthropological fieldwork mission across colonial Africa, work that led to the publication in 1934 of his fieldwork journal as *L'Afrique fantôme*. The existential disquiet

Leiris expresses ties his trip across Africa to a sense of unreality and to a penchant for fiction whose wellspring lies in his deeply felt anxious rootlessness.

At the same time that Leiris was producing his daily reflections that located anthropology within this affective constellation in which discomfiture and fiction feed off each other, the Malian ethnographer, writer, and colonial civil servant Amadou Hampâté Bâ was also traveling around Africa, working for the French colonial state and conducting fieldwork on West African oral traditions in his spare time. He, too, kept a journal: as he moved from job to job in French West Africa during the 1920s and 1930s, he assiduously collected and recorded local cultural histories and observations on the changing circumstances of oral cultures in the face of French colonization. Hampâté Bâ would go on to receive formal training in ethnography, and he later incorporated many of his early anthropological observations into his two volumes of memoirs, *Amkoullel, l'enfant peul* (1991) and *Oui mon commandant!* (1994), in which he recounts his childhood and his early career as an indigenous colonial functionary.

Far from conventional autobiographical narratives, however, Hampâté Bâ's memoirs are at once more novelistic and more ethnographic, first, because in them he deftly shows off his skills as a storyteller, knowingly drawing readers in by developing himself as a literary character;[2] and second, because he uses his sense of storytelling to communicate anthropological knowledge about "traditional" African cultures to an imagined community of non-African readers. I focus here more on *Oui mon commandant!* because in this second volume Hampâté Bâ also communicates anthropological knowledge about colonial ideologies and the inner workings of the French colonial state in Africa, and he does so by thinking through his own relation to the colonial project. Similar to Leiris in *Biffures*, Hampâté Bâ writes that his travels in French West Africa were prompted in part by his awareness of "not fitting in," since he was simultaneously a dedicated civil servant and an educated colonial subject who was fascinated by the local oral traditions French colonialism threatened to eradicate. Hampâté Bâ does not experience his lack of fit in the same uncomfortable terms as Leiris, but it nonetheless also inflects his taste for fiction by promoting his stylized self-development as a literary character.

Spurred by the juxtaposition of two writers whose divergent anthropological relationships to Africa determine the kinds of writing they produce, in this chapter I investigate ethnographic fiction's investment in transcultural forms of knowledge production that emerge from and respond to colonial social relations. Broadly, I focus here on the epistemological cartographies Hampâté

Bâ and Leiris trace as they narrativize their movements across colonial Africa. Their imaginations of imperial space intersect with actually existing imperial formations, as the maps provided to readers in their texts attest. But they also de-realize imperial space, in the case of Leiris, and stretch it far beyond its intended boundaries, in the case of Hampâté Bâ. For the former, African imperial space is haunted by a ghostly, fictive version of the continent that fieldwork endlessly outlines. For the latter, as we will see, the communicability of ethnographic knowledge links imperial itineraries to an epistemological universalism that opens up empire's constitutively restrictive cartographic ideology.

This chapter connects genre, style, characterology, and imperial counter-mapping; it also highlights how ethnographic fiction cultivates and speaks to communities of readers, converting them into willing participants in anthropological knowledge games or, alternatively, trapping them in the occasionally monotonous frustrations and epistemological dead-ends of fieldwork. Hampâté Bâ and Leiris stand in, respectively, for these two directions of the relationship between ethnographic fiction and readerly publics. Hampâté Bâ turns to a form of anthropological storytelling I call "ethnographic didacticism." Leiris, by contrast, forces readers to wade through the affective mire of his difficulties with fieldwork to drive home his growing certainty that the creation of ethnographic knowledge is haunted by the ghostly double of its own imponderability or, worse, its unreality. Both of these figures use ethnographic stylistics to bolster their senses of fiction, but as I explore in this chapter, they do so to contrasting epistemological ends. As I argue here, regardless of how Leiris's *L'Afrique fantôme* and Hampâté Bâ's memoirs call on and communicate with readers, the speculative ties these texts generate with their publics are mediated by their authors' intensely personal relationships to the colonial situation writ large—relationships whose anthropological stakes are expressed in terms of both politics and writerly style.

These late colonial ethnographic fictions, communicating cosmopolitanism, on the one hand, and confusing alienation, on the other, speak to contrasting artistic and political trends in the interwar French empire. As Gary Wilder has shown, after World War I, France tried to "reground itself" in the empire just when imperial projects were newly contested on the world stage.[3] This period saw France adopt reformist and welfarist policies at home and in the colonies; in West Africa, humanist ethnology informed new administrative practices that were characterized by "a dual imperative to protect and to transform native society."[4] But as France anxiously sought to redefine itself in relation to the empire in the interwar period, African, Antillean, and American intellectuals imagined new forms of Pan-African cultural politics based on alternative ways of knowing black experiences in the colonial world: Martinican Guyanese author René Maran published his Prix Goncourt–winning *Batouala* in 1921, for example, and Aimé Césaire, then a student, would begin publishing the journal *L'Etudiant Noir* in the mid-1930s. The Negritude movement and other forms of black internationalism coexisted with metropolitan anxieties about the empire, and the knowledge projects developed by Leiris and Hampâté Bâ situate relationships to readers within the push and pull of national concerns about imperial legitimacy and cosmopolitan projections of Africanist epistemologies.[5] And these projects are embedded in acts of historical layering, as well, since Leiris's paratextual reframings and the posthumous publication of Hampâté Bâ's memoirs situate their late-colonial ethnographic fictions within postcolonial circuits of readership.

The 1931–33 Dakar-Djibouti mission legitimized fieldwork in French anthropology by bridging the epistemological and institutional gap separating those researchers who went to the field and brought home ethnographic data from those who, ensconced in their armchairs, simply interpreted it.[6] Fieldwork was now expected to speak directly to publics at home, too. As Alice Conklin has argued, the highly publicized and lavishly funded Dakar-Djibouti mission tied 1930s anthropology in France to cultural resources that could be extracted from the colonies and put on display back home in an effort to instruct visitors to the Musée d'Ethnographie du Trocadéro about "[all] things colonial."[7] Leiris's journal was always composed with a potential public in mind, but it does not fit neatly into this vein of instructive colonial marketing. The fictionality that occurs throughout *L'Afrique fantôme* is, instead, born of his deep ambivalence toward a colonial situation that made his idealized ethnographic desires possible, and the experience he provides for his readers serves to reveal the fraught underside of what the mission's backers imagined would be the streamlined transmission of anthropological knowledge about African societies under French rule.

Hampâté Bâ's memoirs, which contain an instructive project of their own, allow us to go even further and read this didactic impulse of early French anthropology against the grain: in his work he seeks not only to speak authoritatively to readers about African oral traditions, but also to speak ethnographically about the French colonial state from the inside and from the perspective of a colonial subject.[8] Although his work evinces certain ambivalences with respect to the French colonial project and also offers powerful critiques of colonial epistemologies, it is also deeply invested in developing a different knowledge project entirely—one whose cosmopolitanism recognizes colonial epistemological categories without relying on them exclusively. Leiris and Hampâté Bâ show us how ethnographic fiction thus looks inescapably, and at times in spite of itself, toward colonial strategies of knowledge production and accumulation. However, relatedly and at the same time, reading them together demonstrates how this experimental genre also possesses a distinctly African genealogy, a cultural geography that provokes the adepts of ethnographic fiction to convert colonial social relations into objects of ethnographic commentary via the didactic interchange of storytelling.

Africa, Fictionality, and Generic Legibility

These texts are not works of purely imaginative invention: Leiris and Hampâté Bâ are, of course, real individuals who allow readers to tag along on journeys that actually took place. However, the fact that we as readers never come to doubt the actually existing personal and geographic referents that undergird the narrative relationships these texts establish does not imply that fictionality has fallen by the wayside.[9] For both writers, fictionality serves to stretch their work beyond generic boundaries.

Consider the case of Hampâté Bâ: appended to the text of *Oui mon commandant!* is a several-page defense of the authenticity and veracity of his work written by the executor of his literary estate, Hélène Heckmann.[10] She responds to unnamed literary scholars who have either questioned the representation of certain characters or wondered whether Hampâté Bâ might have fudged or embellished certain aspects of his dealings with French colonial administrators. The very inclusion of such a posthumous defensive appendix should give us pause and alert us to the presence of textual elements that go beyond the conventions of autobiographical narrative. In other words, that Hampâté Bâ's work calls for posthumous reassurances about its authenticity is symptomatic of its relationship to fictionality. The play of fiction in Hampâté Bâ's memoirs does not involve authenticity or clever insincerity, though; it has to do, rather, with the creative forms of distancing that he instantiates between his writerly self and the self that appears as a literary character and storyteller, contained within the autonomous ethnographic world of the text.[11] In this respect, Hampâté Bâ's memoirs call to mind those of J. M. Coetzee, in which autobiographical distancing also introduces fiction into the memoir form (not least because the third volume, *Summertime*, is subtitled "Fiction").[12]

Hampâté Bâ, for his part, does not go so far as to refer to himself as "he" in his memoirs, but his ethnographic and literary *je* has a similar effect on readers. This detachment is playful, and the autobiographical character he creates keeps one eye on the story he crafts while the other seems fixed on readers, impatiently anticipating their enjoyment. As we will see, this dual fixation is part and parcel of his sense of didacticism. These qualities also lend his autobiographical distancing an unmistakable air of "extroversion" which, as Eileen Julien has argued, is a key component of novelistic fiction in Africa.[13]

We could hardly accuse Leiris of excessive extroversion in the relationships he establishes with his readers. Whereas Hampâté Bâ carefully spins ethnographic vignettes for a public that is always squarely in view, in *L'Afrique fantôme* Leiris draws readers into his own introspection to make them feel all the more keenly his frustrations with what he comes increasingly to view as ethnography's broken promises. Fiction for Leiris appears indissolubly tied to what he perceives as the perpetually disappointing inauthenticity of ethnographic objects, a form of epistemological malaise that, by extension, infects and sterilizes his idealized vision of ethnography as offering true "contact" between researchers and the people they study. Anthropology as such was not a dead end for Leiris, though, and *L'Afrique fantôme* is not his personal narrative of the discipline's failure. Leiris was a poet who had recently fallen out with Parisian Surrealists when he met Marcel Griaule and was recruited to join the mission; it was not until years later that he actually received formal training in ethnography.[14] Leiris went on to write *La possession et ses aspects théâtraux chez les Éthiopiens de Gondar* (1958), a properly social-scientific study of spirit possession in which we come across some of the same individuals from rural Ethiopia whom he writes about with such vexation in the pages of his earlier fieldwork diary. Fictionality "happens" in *L'Afrique fantôme* as it reveals itself in the proliferation of events that provoke Leiris to lay bare his existential and epistemological disappointment: bewilderingly fruitless research encounters, his inability to assume the new form of selfhood he left Europe to find, and a constantly threatening sense that authentic ethnographic knowledge production could be happening somewhere else, always wherever he is not. Leiris's skill lies in making these events meaningful for readers, turning us into often unwilling participant-observers in and of his frustration as he gradually unveils ever larger chunks of his tormented interiority—an act South African novelist André Brink has called "a striptease of the soul."[15]

The play of fictionality thus prevents these texts from being immediately legible in terms of the generic classifications that, at first blush, readers might want to bring to bear on them: Hampâté Bâ's memoirs are too extroverted to be straightforward reflections on a life well lived, and Leiris's approval of each new edition of *L'Afrique fantôme*, always in a different series at Gallimard, signals his understanding that the book's eclectic publication history stems from its remarkable ability to sidestep attempts to read it into any one genre.[16] At the same time, the question of generic legibility for Leiris and Hampâté Bâ is of a piece with their understandings of the legibility of Africa in ethnographic knowledge production. Put another way, generic flexibility, the very characteristic that makes these texts such telling ethnographic fictions, springs from the desire to narrativize one's ethnographic relationship to Africa.

This impulse drives Hampâté Bâ's autobiographical extroversion in his memoirs. He recounts his childhood in *Amkoullel, l'enfant peul*, and *Oui mon commandant!* deals with his early career as a colonial civil servant in French Sudan and Upper Volta (now Mali and Burkina Faso, respectively). After several years of French schooling in Djenne and Bamako, he won admission to but refused to attend the prestigious École Normale William Ponty in Senegal, which would have enabled him to become a stably employed administrator or teacher. This refusal so incensed local French administrators that they gave Hampâté Bâ the sardonically menial (in relation to his qualifications) "essentially revocable and precarious position as temporary writer," a role that situated him "essentially precariously" among other indigenous functionaries who complicated colonial social roles, being neither high-level bureaucrats nor "traditional" illiterate indigenous subjects.[17] This administrative role led Hampâté Bâ to shuttle from job to job, outpost to outpost, in both French Sudan and Upper Volta during the 1920s and 1930s, where he spent his free time documenting oral traditions and local cultural histories.

Oui mon commandant! ends before Hampâté Bâ, a devout Muslim, was forced out of the French colonial administration by the new Vichy government and began to receive formal training in anthropology at the Institut Français (later, Fondamental) d'Afrique Noire (IFAN) in Dakar, studying under Africanist anthropologist Théodore Monod (who would go on to write the preface to *Amkoullel* and who also hosted Jean Rouch at IFAN in the early 1940s after he, too, ran afoul of Vichy's colonial bureaucrats).[18] During his career as a professional ethnographic researcher, Hampâté Bâ met, read, and worked with significant figures in twentieth-century French anthropology such as Griaule and Germaine Dieterlen, as well as Rouch, who paid tribute to him upon his death in 1991.[19] He brings this anthropological experience to bear on his autobiography most powerfully in *Oui mon commandant!* a memoir with a decidedly pedagogical bent insofar as it teaches non-African readers, occasionally by addressing them directly, about the cultures of "traditional" Africa and about everyday negotiations of the symbolic political universe of French colonialism.[20]

This second volume of memoirs is underrepresented in scholarship on Hampâté Bâ's work, and yet he puts his penchant for ethnographic storytelling to provocative narrative use in this posthumously published work. Whereas the childhood stories of *Amkoullel, l'enfant peul* transform the text into a colonial-era bildungsroman,[21] I suggest we could give *Oui mon commandant!* the playfully Joycean subtitle "A Portrait of the Anthropologist as a Young Man" owing to the fact that in this memoir Hampâté Bâ not only represents African cultural histories and oral traditions in anthropologically documentary terms but also points to his own incurable habit of conducting fieldwork during his many displacements in French West Africa. For example, on leaving the historic city of Segou on his way to the colonial hinterland of Ouagadougou, he remarks, "I kept myself busy by retranscribing the stories I collected in the large notebook where, day by day, I recorded the elements of oral tradition that I gathered on my journey—just as I would continue to do throughout my life."[22]

At other moments in the memoir, however, he incorporates ethnographic asides and excurses explicitly addressing Western readers who are presumed to lack the requisite cultural fluency to make sense of certain beliefs or traditions. At one point, Hampâté Bâ tells the story of how he spent time working with an interpreter named Moro Sidibé, the great adversary of Wangrin, who was the colonial-era trickster, interpreter, and entrepreneur featured in Hampâté Bâ's prize-winning ethnographic and biographic narrative. Readers of *L'étrange destin de Wangrin* easily remember Moro Sidibé as the hapless indigenous civil servant who fell prey to some of Wangrin's most memorable schemes. Little did the former know, Hampâté Bâ remarks in his memoir, that he would soon be delivering a moving funeral speech for Wangrin in which he would formally forgive his rival and ask him for forgiveness in turn. Hampâté Bâ reproduces this speech and explains, "Such an attitude, with all credit to Moro Sidibé, might seem surprising to Europeans; in reality it was in keeping with an ancient tradition which held that *'death erases all feuds and all disagreements.'*"[23] This pedagogical clarification directly addresses Western readers and allows Hampâté Bâ to step outside the memoir form and play the role of a literary character/storyteller. This explanatory aside also evinces the kind of narrative relationship with an imagined readerly public that emerges through Hampâté Bâ's use of ethnographic didacticism: this relationship is predicated on the virtuosity of the storyteller and on Hampâté Bâ's sense of the fundamental communicability of traditional African cultures and, as we will see in the next section of this chapter, of everyday life under French colonialism in West Africa.

One has little trouble imagining Hampâté Bâ as one of the many indigenous interpreters, clerks, and other civil servants with whom Leiris, Griaule, and their colleagues came into contact as they wheedled their way into the good graces of the colonial administration in French West Africa to facilitate their fieldwork. In fact, maps provided to readers in both *Oui mon commandant!* and the various editions of *L'Afrique fantôme* show significant overlap in the itineraries these two aspiring ethnographers traced. Although Leiris's trajectory in West Africa during the Dakar-Djibouti mission intersects with that of Hampâté Bâ during the latter's career as a civil servant, Leiris's journal chronologically narrativizes a contrasting relationship to Africa and to ethnographic epistemology. For Leiris, the "real" Africa, it seems, always lies somewhere up ahead, such that he continuously bumps up against fictions, ghostly and de-realized versions of what he believes to be authentic people and places that exist somewhere other than where he finds himself. As he puts it after the fact in the introduction he wrote in 1950, in retrospect what the confessional nature of his journal highlights is not anything about the "real" Africa but, rather, simply the feelings of a thirty-year-old European who was surprised "not to escape from himself when he should have realized that the overly personal reasons that convinced him to tear himself away from his loved ones prevented, from the very beginning, things from being otherwise."[24] Thus, the new form of selfhood after which Leiris chases throughout his journey turns out to be just as fictional as the Africa he hoped to find through ethnographic fieldwork.

In the journal, Leiris wrestles at length with the nagging realization that although his political beliefs and anthropological aspirations lead him to condemn colonialism intellectually, he ultimately cannot divest himself fully of the affective ties that connect him to the colonial project and to the ways in which his own subjectivity is bound up in that project.[25] The text of *L'Afrique fantôme* is divided into two parts, the first of which describes the mission's trip to Africa and fieldwork in the territories constituting French West and Equatorial Africa, as well as northern Nigeria and Anglo-Egyptian Sudan. In this first half, Leiris's writing is relatively straightforward, if marked at times by frustrated comments about how certain areas are "too civilized" and about how anxious he is to finally arrive in the "real" Africa. The journal takes a turn, though, just before the second part, when Leiris and his colleagues are forced to wait for several months at the border between Anglo-Egyptian Sudan and independent Abyssinia. The Abyssinian officials put the research team through increasingly ridiculous sorts of bureaucratic rigmarole, and Leiris's journal entries grow more introspective and more disillusioned with the possibilities of a successful continuation of the journey, even though he tries to convince himself that an authentic Africa is still attainable once the mission is finally allowed to move ahead.

Thus, about a third of the way through the journal (right before the seemingly arbitrary break between the first and second parts of the text) when, having reached the Abyssinian border, he declares "Here, finally, is AFRICA, the land of 50°C in the shade, of slave convoys, of cannibal feasts, of empty skulls, of all the things that are eaten away, corroded, lost,"[26] we as readers have long since stopped believing him, our expectations having been frustrated several times already by similar statements made in this vein. It would seem, additionally, that Leiris does not even believe himself, since his use of "finally" (*enfin*) is immediately followed by a romanticizing enumeration that can only serve to construct yet another imagined Africa that is but tenuously grounded in the everyday forms and artifacts of social life that the mission attempts to document and collect.

Quite predictably, then, this declaration falls flat on its face as the rest of the journal (which is given over to fieldwork on spirit possession in rural Abyssinia and a breakdown of relations between Leiris and his informants) is broadly marked by boredom, disillusionment, and listless introspection. Anthropology as an idealized knowledge project for Leiris, one that promises to foster what he calls "contact" between subject and object, is in many ways condemned to unveil fictional ethnographic objects in their very inauthenticity. One of the stories *L'Afrique fantôme* tells is that of Leiris's growing skepticism of his idealized, even utopian vision of anthropology as composed of the mutually constitutive vectors of epistemology and "proximity"—that is, a transformative sense of almost physical communion with the objects of ethnographic knowledge.

This breakdown, not of ethnography as such but of its epistemological idealization, helps to account for the work's generic indecipherability.[27] The proliferation of moments in which fictionality bursts onto the scene, coupled with Leiris's frustrated introspection, make *L'Afrique fantôme* read awkwardly as anthropology. It reads no less awkwardly, though, as the *journal intime* Leiris liked to call it: the confessional intimacy we might expect from a field diary (say, from a work such as Bronisław Malinowski's *A Diary in the Strict Sense of the Term*, published posthumously in 1967) is undercut by the fact that Leiris was always already writing with a public in mind, as we learn in the two drafts of a preface that he includes as journal entries.[28] Much of *L'Afrique fantôme*'s opacity stems from the fact that Leiris was growing aware of these roadblocks and paradoxes at the time of writing, an awareness that the journal form permits readers to experience all the more acutely since it allows us to peek over Leiris's shoulder in the real time of the text. In other words, Leiris felt the phenomenon of generic illegibility occurring while he was creating the text, such that it provocatively infiltrates our experience of reading.

The generic instability created by the unexpected or counterintuitive presence of fictionality in aesthetic forms that, from the outset, would seem to preclude it is a telling component of these anthropological narratives of personal relationships to Africa. More broadly still, the legibility of ethnographic fiction depends in no small part on these breaches of generic protocol. For Hampâté Bâ, ethnographic narrative is easily incorporated into the memoir form, since the distancing by which he renders himself as a literary character allows for the creation of reader-friendly anthropological vignettes. Leiris, by contrast, seems not to want us to read *L'Afrique fantôme* narratively, and the dense, fragmented opacity of the text often allows him to get his way. Yet at the same time, we remain inescapably focused on the chronological organizing structure of this *journal intime*: the temporal progression of the diary entries, coupled with the geographical progression of the mission, whose itinerary we can trace in advance, prevent us from ever drifting too far from the shores of narrative readability.[29] As the next sections of this chapter demonstrate by turning first to Hampâté Bâ and then to Leiris, these personal and anthropological accounts interconnect knowledge production and transmission with stylistic virtuosity and the creation of ethnographic personae. The question of anthropological knowledge, from this perspective, becomes characterological and, as this chapter shows more generally, dovetails with the fraught question of ethnographic fiction's colonial origins.

The Anthropology of Transcultural Storytelling

Hampâté Bâ published his prize-winning *L'étrange destin de Wangrin* (The Fortunes of Wangrin) in 1973, some twenty years before *Amkoullel* and *Oui mon commandant!* appeared. In the foreword to this widely known earlier work, Hampâté Bâ provides readers with a behind-the-scenes look at the conditions of production of his biography of an indigenous trickster and interpreter from the colonial period. This short introduction contains a character sketch of the text's eponymous hero and a brief account of the nightly sessions during which Wangrin, accompanied on the guitar by his griot, told Hampâté Bâ his life story. Wangrin was also careful to stipulate to his biographer precisely how he wanted future readers to receive his life once it made its way to the written page: "Now that you know how to write, you will take down what I will tell you of my life. And when I am no longer of this world, you will make it into a book which will not only entertain people but will serve as instruction for them."[30] Wangrin's directives bespeak both a cleverly framed desire for posthumous literary image management as well as an intimate relationship between the pleasures of storytelling and the pedagogical potential that can be distilled from a good read.

Hampâté Bâ certainly proved to be up to the task: *L'étrange destin* is full of hilarious vignettes and gossip about French colonial administrators and indigenous African functionaries. The "instructional" aspects of the narrative are not necessarily moralizing in nature (although Wangrin's dissolute end certainly has some cautionary merit); rather, they consist of the rigorous documentation and explanation of oral traditions and indigenous customs, in addition to a rich portrait of everyday life under colonial rule in French West Africa.

In his two volumes of memoirs this device becomes a thoroughgoing literary strategy driven primarily by an avowed relationship to foreign readers, a relationship imbued with a strong sense of pedagogy and strengthened by Hampâté Bâ's undeniable prowess as a prolific storyteller. In *Amkoullel*, for example, he discusses how he and his age-mates in his village founded a *waaldé*, an association for young men that had quite intricate governmental rules and whose members had a strong grasp of political rhetoric. Anticipating that readers might be surprised at such youthful sophistication, he comments, "Certain Western readers might be surprised that kids who were on average ten to twelve years old could hold such regimented meetings using this kind of language. It is because everything we did tended to imitate the behavior of adults, and from our youngest ages we were steeped in the medium of spoken language (*le verbe*)."[31]

Likewise, at one point in *Oui mon commandant!* he tells the story of how he and a companion asked a famous religious scholar to pray that they would stay dry during strong storms that threatened to drench them during a trip from Kayes to Koniakary in western French Sudan. Incredibly, the storms passed all around the two travelers and left them dry. "For a Cartesian mind," explains Hampâté Bâ, "our adventure was nothing more than the effect of an extraordinary but random coincidence. For us, it was doubtless that this was a clear manifestation of divine power."[32] *Oui mon commandant!* takes this pedagogical conceit even further than the first volume of memoirs, since here he expands his ethnographic gaze to encompass the French colonial administration for which he worked before turning to anthropological pursuits in Dakar. Hampâté Bâ's strategy, which I refer to as "ethnographic didacticism," allows him to stake out interdisciplinary narrative terrain on which to link his own virtuosity as a storyteller to a more abstract, transcultural and cosmopolitan epistemological project.

My argument here runs deeper, though: studying these memoirs (and the second volume in particular) anthropologically provokes us to consider how, for Hampâté Bâ, the African memoir is a narrative palimpsest in which the writing of one's personal history is also and at the same time an operation of rewriting and writing over, involving the conversion of autobiography into transcultural dialogue and the reversal of the direction of ethnographic knowledge production. Hampâté Bâ's reimagining of the African memoir as a cross-disciplinary palimpsest ultimately encourages us to identify the "Afropolitan" (to borrow the term coined by Achille Mbembe) geographies of anthropological knowledge production by calling forth a practice of reading that is resolutely transcultural in its scope. Thus, Hampâté Bâ's memoirs stand out because they communicate ethnographically with readers while simultaneously paying close attention to the stylistic tenets underpinning ethnographic storytelling.[33]

As a literary strategy, ethnographic didacticism relies on the instantiation in narrative of pedagogical communication between the figure of the anthropologist and his or her curious readers. The scene of ethnographic writing is both rhetorical and epistemological: as Clifford Geertz has argued, the written communication of ethnographic knowledge succeeds by converting the "offstage miracle" of fieldwork into writerly language that persuades readers that one has in "one way or another, truly 'been there.'"[34] Hampâté Bâ certainly has no trouble convincing us that he "was there," but this sense of rhetorical ease is not simply due to the fact that his memoirs are written in the first person; it also has to do with the fact that his virtuosity as a storyteller allows us to assimilate all the more readily the didactic elements of his autobiographical narrative. Virtuosity here refers to a performance of writerly panache that calls attention to itself, drawing the reader in through a sense of stylistic seduction that is immanent to the art and practice of storytelling. When it is coupled with the stylized performativity of virtuosity in storytelling, didacticism as I understand it manages to avoid falling into stilted pedagogy awkwardly or artificially grafted onto a given narrative; from this point of view, far from being an example of simplistic and uninteresting literary "heresy" (*pace* Edgar Allan Poe's thoughts on the matter[35]), didacticism is actually the site of transcultural communication founded on literary and ethnographic intertextuality.

We can observe this didacticism-cum-virtuosity at work in Hampâté Bâ's reflections on and narrations of events and stories dealing with his work as a clerk, accountant, or assistant administrator in the French colonial bureaucracy. As he travels from post to post, he relates significant happenings from early in his career and takes care to situate these major events in the day-to-day life of the colonial administration. This strategy provides readers with a perspective on the French administration as a social space possessing its own cultural logic, one that Hampâté Bâ is in a privileged position to observe since he works for the colonial state while remaining nonetheless a colonized subject. While his job description in reality amounts to that of a clerk and part-time bookkeeper for various white administrators, it also confers on him the status of *blanc-noir* (lit., white-black)—that is, an African who has either made his way in business or gone through enough colonial schooling to enjoy a post in the local bureaucracy. As Hampâté Bâ explains to us in typical didactic fashion, this status is part of a racial taxonomy developed by Africans, what he calls "the indigenous hierarchy" that exists alongside, without mapping neatly onto, juridical modes of classification that separate different types of citizens from different types of subjects in French West Africa.

He goes on to point out, "From the perspective of the 'official' division of classes, I was a *literate French subject*, born in [French] Sudan and not in Senegal, thus just above the bottom category [the *noirs-noirs*, or unassimilated African subjects]. But according to the indigenous hierarchy, I was unquestionably a *blanc-noir*, which, as we have seen, earned us a few privileges—with the understanding that, at the time, the lowest white always came before the first of the blacks."[36] An integral part of Hampâté Bâ's account of his own positioning is his awareness that while his job as a low-level administrator does little to advance his status in the eyes of French officials, his labor racializes him in such a way that he becomes nominally whitened in the eyes of so-called traditional Africans. He is aware, in other words, that his identity is caught between flux and stasis, since his blackness is as much relative, according to the supple indigenous hierarchy, as it is absolute, caught in the ontological fixity of colonial racial taxonomies.

To take an example that amply highlights this productive ambiguity, we can consider the episode from *Oui mon commandant!* titled "An Unexpected Conversion," which describes how Hampâté Bâ, now no longer on the lowest rung of the colonial administration, arrives as a clerk in the Upper Volta town of Tougan and finds that his reputation as an Islamic scholar has preceded him. The other indigenous civil servants, all lapsed Muslims forced by the colonial state to convert to Catholicism, look on him as a marabout, a religious teacher, a designation that displeases our hero since "the title of 'marabout' actually involved more thorns than flowers."[37] He explains that at the time the French considered marabouts to be zealots bent on converting colonized subjects to militant Islam: "thus the colonial administration declared open season on them, especially in the territories where that religion had not yet spread very much. At the time, the Samos, like the Bobos, the Gurma, the Mossi, and almost all the tattooed Voltaic peoples, did not practice Islam."[38] Hampâté Bâ opens his story with a gesture of ethnographic contextualization, but his keen sense of pedagogy pushes him to take his explanatory narrative much further.

The drama occurs when Hampâté Bâ helps the commandant's indigenous interpreter renew his Islamic faith, drawing the ire of local French missionaries who convince the authorities in Upper Volta to open an official inquiry on the interpreter's "conversion." It so happens that, imbued with the spirit of republican secularism, the French commandant in question resents the church's involvement in local affairs and sharply criticizes church leaders in his report, but what is more important for our concerns is the way Hampâté Bâ accounts for his commandant's actions and religious liberalism, which deserves to be quoted at length:

> At the time, no *cercle* [an administrative unit in Francophone Africa] or subdivision commandant could hope to undertake a worthwhile inquiry without his interpreter and his assistant knowing; thus the commandant asked us to be honest with him and to help him lead his inquiry without any biases. . . . In the history of the colonial administration, he was not

the only one who dared adopt this attitude. Such behavior deserves to be pointed out and proves, if such proof were needed, that we must not place all colonial administrators in the same basket. A generalization, whatever it may be, is never a reflection of reality.[39]

Two forms of didacticism emerge in this passage. First, the object of Hampâté Bâ's didactic discourse has a broad political scope, and he comments authoritatively not only on the everyday activities in his own administrative locale, but also on how these activities are representative of certain humanizing and liberal trends in the administrative culture of French colonialism understood in its broadest sense.[40] Second, this ethnographic didacticism is both informative, intended to fill out the cultural knowledge of well-meaning readers, and openly persuasive in that it seeks to disabuse readers of the idea that they might angrily paint all white French administrators with the same brush. Hampâté Bâ is not interested here in offering any sort of naïve apology for certain strains of colonial paternalism; at stake in his commentary is the creation of an anthropological persona who can speak with as much authority about the intricacies of colonial social relations as he does about his own cultural traditions and customs. In this sense, we can view this passage as Hampâté Bâ demonstrating his own ethnographic virtuosity, since he is clearly fluent enough in the culture of French administrative life that he is able to anticipate the potential reactions of imagined anticolonial (implicitly Western) readers and critique them with moralizing ethnographic rhetoric.

The textual creation of this authoritative and trustworthy persona, a character in the work in his own right, allows us to link the virtuosity of the storyteller to didacticism as an epistemological project that, for Hampâté Bâ, is thoroughly transcultural. These memoirs provoke us to add an additional layer of textual complexity to Walter Benjamin's reading of storytelling as pure use value, in which he suggests that "the storyteller is a man who has counsel for his readers."[41] As *Oui mon commandant!* shows, the literary horizons of this didactic use value are expanded when the relationship between storyteller and reader is triangulated through the representation of the storyteller as a character in their own work.

On the one hand, this triangulation promotes a deeper affective investment in the storyteller as a literary character precisely because this character is not embedded in the conventional novel form that, as Benjamin reminds us, actually brings about or requires the isolation of the reader.[42] On the other hand, to return to and transform Geertz's concerns, this investment in the anthropologist as a literary character is what enhances the "been there"-ness of the ethnographic text. The constitutive overlapping among the storyteller, the literary character, and the anthropologist renders didactically meaningful such explanations as the one Hampâté Bâ offers for why his mother's unilateral decision to adopt his newborn daughter and raise her far away from her son and his new wife is neither imperious on her part nor uncaring on his: "Entrusting one's child to another person, generally a relative or very close friend, or to the person whose name the child bore, was at the time a very common custom in our countries. . . . In African society at the time, in which the family milieu was both a site of welcome and sanctuary in all circumstances, a social reference point and a network of alliances and defense, having two families represented an additional opportunity."[43] Here, ethnographic exposition is folded into a story about Hampâté Bâ's young family (a story that does not appear at the outset to be leading toward a broad commentary on "traditional" Africa), and it is driven by a desire to obviate any change in the Western reader's perception of our hero as a character in his own text. Ethnography and literary virtuosity both depend on and foster our affective investment as curious readers.

Toward the end of *Oui mon commandant!* this carefully honed narrative link between virtuosity and didacticism gives way to two brief expository meditations on the history of colonialism in which Hampâté Bâ pulls back from microlevel ethnographic considerations of his relationship to French colonial bureaucracy in favor of a sweeping look at the colonial project writ large. In these essays, titled "From 'Silent Trade' to Economic Colonization" and "Nocturnal Side and Diurnal Side," he lays bare the transcultural and cosmopolitan stakes of his didactic project via broad reflections on the colonial situation and its linguistic legacy. These pages are devoted to Hampâté Bâ's growing awareness of the structural subtleties of colonial social relations,[44] but they do not resemble the other anecdotes that punctuate his narrative and instead are characterized by a loftier, more detached tone. In the first meditation he explains his understanding of exploitative colonial economics, but he shifts his perspective in "Nocturnal Side and Diurnal Side" to account for why he is unable to reject colonialism out of hand: "We must accept and recognize that the colonial era could leave positive contributions, if only, among other things, the heritage of a language of universal communication thanks to which we can exchange [ideas] with nearby ethnic groups and with the nations of the world."[45] For Hampâté Bâ, the colonial era left behind not just a language (French), but also a universal mode of communication that allows for dialogue between different African societies and between former colonized subjects and individuals the world over.

An unstated implication and corollary of this idea is that Hampâté Bâ's vast ethnographic knowledge might not even be available to non-African readers had it not been for the spread of the French language. This linguistic universalism is part and parcel of his broader ethnographic project, begun in earlier works such as *L'étrange destin*, which investigates the ways in which writing remains faithful to orality and oral traditions during the act of transcription.[46] This project sees Hampâté Bâ situate himself as an intermediary in a process of transtextual translation, one involving both linguistic conversion in the conventional sense and translation of and between disparate textual forms that are also distinct forms of textual world making. The historical layering that takes place in the text is what makes this form of translation possible, since Hampâté Bâ's linguistic universalism reroutes colonial histories through postcolonial, utopian imaginations of the global communication and consumption of ethnographic knowledge.

"Nocturnal Side and Diurnal Side" begins with the admission, "Of course, colonization has existed at all times and in all places," a rhetorical gesture that might appear as a curious act of moral dilution if it was sequestered from the principal argument of the meditation. Hampâté Bâ draws this act of recognition back into his larger project and, by extension, back into his didactic relationship with his readers: he ends this opening paragraph by asserting colonialism's legacy of communicative universalism: "It is up to us to put it to its best use and to ensure that our own languages, our own cultures, are not swept aside in the process."[47] From this perspective, what is at stake in the transcultural preservation and communication of African oral traditions is the inevitability of wrestling with the contingencies of French colonialism's linguistic heritage: this is a sort of linguistic *débrouillardise* that opens up the ethnographic potential of universal communication without, for all that, obscuring or explaining away its colonial origins. The didacticism of *Oui mon commandant!* actualizes this "making do" with colonialism's linguistic legacy, and Hampâté Bâ's expository essays on the colonial situation function as methodological expedients, designed to reveal to readers both the goals of his didactic project (i.e., the preservation of local cultures and traditions through their expression in a universal language) and the colonial cultural history of his approach.

Thus, in these meditations Hampâté Bâ uses universalism to highlight the transcultural circulation of his ethnographic knowledge (about oral traditions, to be sure, but also about everyday life under colonial rule) and to unveil his *africanisme* as a global knowledge project.[48] Reading *Oui mon commandant!* palimpsestically allows us to see how the articulation of this project represents the epistemological climax of Hampâté Bâ's gradual movement from more conventional social-scientific research (in works such as the ethnohistorical *L'empire peul du macina* (1955) to a literary anthropology capable of producing the almost novelistic *L'étrange destin* and the stylized ethnographic storytelling of the memoirs. That this project could speak in many ways to Africans and Europeans alike is no accident: Hampâté Bâ's training in traditional African storytelling and European-style fieldwork meant that he was always going to approach writing as a fundamentally hybrid exercise.[49]

Writing ethnographic fiction speaks to a gesture of reconciliation that Hampâté Bâ succeeded in effecting between his personal anthropological research and creative writing and, more abstractly, between disparate forms of textual world making. Intersecting ethnographic fiction with the memoir form affords Hampâté Bâ the richest textual venue for the comingled articulation of his ethnographic *je* with the creation of himself as a literary character. What the palimpsestic perspective I have been highlighting opens up is something of an ethnographic and literary take on the many-worlds interpretation of quantum mechanics, although the rhetoric of interweaving and superimposition implies that distinct textual universes are not necessarily infinitely parallel but can be instead provocatively inextricable and mutually constitutive. The palimpsest "works" because Hampâté Bâ's sense of cartographic layering is both spatial and historical, a coexistence that feeds his alternative universalism.

Hampâté Bâ's knowledge project is an anthropological cosmopolitanism that provokes us to rethink a central tenet of Mbembe's Afropolitanism. For Mbembe, contemporary African cultural production is caught up in what he calls "the circulation of worlds," a phenomenon involving the dispersion and exchange of myriad forms of cultural conflict, migration, trade, and technical savoir faire, both within the African continent and among its various diasporic communities and imaginaries.[50] As he puts it, using imagery that calls to mind a debt to Paul Gilroy's *The Black Atlantic*, the cultural history of Africa "can scarcely be understood outside the paradigm of rootlessness, mobility, and displacement." Afropolitanism is the paradigmatic aggregate of disparate forms of cultural circulation as well as a historical narrative that makes the powerful case that these forms were always already global in their reach and scope, even before our postmillennial moment. Mbembe's formulation is principally concerned with the ways in which aesthetic creativity is fruitfully overdetermined by the intra-African and worldwide displacement of individuals and populations across borders both geographical and cultural-political.

As Hampâté Bâ's theory of transcultural didacticism demonstrates, though, this circulation of worlds is also profoundly epistemological, as it reimagines and renarrates anthropological forms of knowledge production—"making do" with their colonial histories and modes of enunciation—from the most local of ethnographic contexts in what we now call the "Global South." In other words, this is a knowledge project that takes Africa as its point of departure while simultaneously declaring its horizon to encompass modernity itself, although or even because modernity conventionally has been narrated from Europe or the United States.[51] To view Afropolitanism as part and parcel of an epistemological project with universalist aspirations is to displace geographically the very conceptual vocabulary we use to imagine "modernity" or "the universal" as such.

Introspection and Ethnographic Personae

For Leiris, the ethnographer's relationship to the colonial situation prompts far too much introspection to be characterized by the sort of extroverted didacticism, avuncular or otherwise, that we come across in Hampâté Bâ's work or in that of other African writers. In the case of *L'Afrique fantôme*, the very form of the travel journal traps Leiris from the outset in a more intimate and self-reflexive register, but this formal explanation can account only partially for his inward turn, since he remained aware at the time of writing that his journal was a document composed for a community of readers.

We need look no further than the two attempts at a preface Leiris drafted on April 4, 1932, during the mission's seemingly interminable wait to cross the border into Abyssinia.[52] In these two drafts, Leiris explains to his imagined public that the overall thesis of the journal intime (which, he explains, cannot be read simply as a travel diary that would aim at an "objective" literary reconstruction of a trip) is that "it is through subjectivity (brought to its climax) that one touches objectivity. More simply: writing subjectively I increase the value of my testimony, by showing that at every instant I know what to expect from my worth as a witness."[53] Following the logic of this thesis, the truth of the ethnographic text lies much more in what the ethnographer can faithfully record of his own impressions than in what hidden verities anthropology can dispassionately and objectively reveal about other people. From this perspective, ethnography's epistemological premises appear to have much in common with the Delphic maxim, predicated as they are for Leiris on the injunction to "know thyself" and not on a strictly scientific imperative to study others objectively.[54] Leiris would go on to echo his thesis in the essay "L'ethnographe devant le colonialisme" (1950), in which he suggests that the purely scientific pretensions of ethnography are but "a myth" and that ethnographers cannot overlook the policies of the governments who fund their research on colonized populations.[55] These ideas, however, do not receive full analytic treatment in *L'Afrique fantôme*, and Leiris's thesis is instead filtered through an inward-facing, often morose look at the development of his own anthropological persona in relation to a colonial project whose grasp he cannot evade and on whose assistance he must rely.

Leiris's proximity to the French colonial administration is not limited to the financial and other bureaucratic forms of aid offered to Griaule's mission by both the national government and local officials in West Africa. Part of the sense of frustration that emerges in the journal is due to Leiris's growing realization that while he is able to condemn colonialism intellectually, he is unable to sever all affective ties with the colonial situation with the same ease and self-assurance.[56] When in late 1931 the mission must cross an overflowing river separating Upper Volta from Dahomey, for example, Griaule and his colleagues requisition young African laborers and supplies from both sides of the border to reinforce the crossing point with heavy stones. In his entry for that day, Leiris complains of the inefficiency of these forced colonial workers and remarks in his recapitulation of the day's events, "An abrupt flash changes me, for no longer than the time of that flash, into a colonial brute: I hit a tall boy who remains motionless in the line, forever leaving the big rocks in the arms of the smallest boys and not resolving to relieve them."[57] He does not dwell on this sudden transformation or on the sense of entitlement to violence that it entails, and we could hardly bestow on this off-the-cuff comment the rhetorical gravitas of a confession. Its inclusion in the day's entry seems indicative of a sense of disappointment that will only grow for Leiris in the remaining pages of the text: disappointment not necessarily in the fact that he slipped for an instant into the repugnant moral economy of colonial violence, but in the more deep-seated fact that there remains a part of his self that is capable of effecting this shift in the first place.

We can observe a similar sort of ambivalence in a remark he makes the following month, as the mission travels through Cameroon. In one of the first instances of boredom in the journal, he writes, "One grows bored quickly when traveling and, with some exceptions, things and events that pass by are quick to become tedious, just as if one was not moving at all."[58] This observation concerning his growing listlessness and the inherent disillusionment of all voyages is followed immediately, at the beginning of the next paragraph, by a comment that is striking for the fact that nothing in the preceding paragraph seems logically to give rise to it: "I tolerate less and less the idea of colonization. . . . Pacification, medical assistance have but one goal: to soften people up so that they get pushed around and pay taxes. . . . Ethnographic study to what end: to be able to carry out a more clever policy that will be better able to collect taxes."[59] In much the same way as his earlier remark on his banal turn to colonial violence, this comment appears to stem from the cool, matter-of-fact reporting of his mental state: increasing disappointment in the first instance, and sheer boredom in the second. One even comes away with the impression that Leiris thinks about the colonial question only when he has nothing left to think about.

Thus, although Leiris ostensibly articulates these thoughts in response to objective, external stimuli—the inefficiency of colonial labor or the realization that colonial politics turns on base forms of economic expediency—they are more fundamentally prompted by internal and subjective shifts in his self and his relation to ethnography. While in the first passage the discipline is not implicated directly when he becomes a "colonial brute," in the second instance Leiris indicts ethnography as an intellectual tool put in the service of the colonial state. However, this passage serves so well to highlight Leiris's ambivalence because it is thoroughly and curiously unclear whether this indictment of ethnography springs for him from its cozy relationship to colonial policymaking or from his increasing awareness that he is, quite simply, growing tired of fieldwork.

We could certainly cite other examples of Leiris going back and forth on his relationship to colonization and colonial politics. Indeed, this form of affective alternation that provides the journal with no small amount of its narrative impetus, at least on an emotional level, reaches its frustrating crescendo when the mission is whiling away its final days in Abyssinia and the pace of Leiris's journal has long since slowed to a crawl. The dense Abyssinia section, to which he devotes the entire second part of *L'Afrique fantôme*, owes much of its difficulty to the fact that the mission runs up against bureaucratic road-blocks and internal strife in the country, and the resulting inertia infects the text and changes its tenor entirely. Idleness, it seems, is the devil's writerly playmate: with too much time on his hands, Leiris reflects for days on his dissatisfaction with himself, his impatience with ethnography's apparently empty promises of authentic cultural contact, and his increasingly unbearable resentment of the Abyssinian people he nonetheless feels he must try to understand. This complex ethnographic discomfiture comes to an emotional head not during a failed encounter with an informant but when Leiris is ensconced in the relative comforts of the colonial quarter in a small town. Having described the town and his sense of ease with the lifestyle he can finally, if briefly, lead, he ends an entry by observing, "What I will never forgive the Abyssinians for is having managed to make me recognize that there is some good in the colonies."[60] Although the entry trails off at this point, the comment carries something of the weight of a final verdict that Leiris seems to wish he could pass off as a rhetorical afterthought.

Once again, however, we can observe that an opinion on colonialism initially appears prompted by external factors (i.e., the behavior of the Abyssinians) but is quickly redirected inward, since his use of the verb "recognize" (reconnaître) implies that he both acknowledges and admits a state of affairs that another part of his self already suspected to be the case. To recognize, after all, indicates a process of cognitive identification as well as the logical acceptance of a piece of evidence. To admit and accept a state of affairs that runs contrary to what one asserts or wishes to be true, a small part of one's self must already be disabused or unsure of one's original position, in however small a way.

Leiris's introspective reckoning with his anthropological persona takes place in response to a colonial situation whose unfashionable allure he cannot deny yet whose political and epistemological influence on ethnography he wants to repudiate. However, the decidedly ambivalent note on which Leiris appears to want to leave us toward the end of the journal would prove not to be his final word on the matter. He added an introduction and a preface to L'Afrique fantôme in 1951 and 1981, respectively, and both of these documents raise the thorny question of the paratextual production of the textual self. In other words, to what extent can a writer retrospectively amend and reconfigure the versions of himself and the social roles he played, that appear in a given text, in a similar sort of image management that Wangrin demanded of Hampâté Bâ? Taking these two brief pieces chronologically, we can see how

Leiris resituates his own work—and himself in relation to that work—by revisiting and challenging the idea of the anthropological persona.

Leiris's introduction, written in 1950, opens with a citation from Jean-Jacques Rousseau's *Confessions* that begins quite tellingly: "Myself alone. I know the feelings of my heart, and I know men."[61] This epigraph is Leiris's opening gambit, and it serves to situate the now older writer broadly within the thesis with which he was working some twenty years earlier. *L'Afrique fantôme*'s thesis, as we have seen, suggests that scientific (or "objective") knowledge of others, or of "the other" writ large, can begin only once one's own subjectivity, one's own self, is brought to its most extreme point—its "climax" (*paroxysme*), as Leiris puts it. Leiris's recasting of his sense of ethnography in a Rousseauian vein suggests that solitude and its intense ontological experience of self brings with it (or even causes, as the conjunction "and" would imply) a universalist knowledge of mankind.

The rest of the introduction, however, seems to undercut this connection to the earlier journal, since Leiris now establishes a dichotomy between ethnographic observation, understood as dispassionate and detached, and a universalist sense of political solidarity. He writes that "ethnography could not but disappoint me: a human science remains a science and detached observation cannot, by itself, bring about *contact*."[62] We see here the same desire for an authentic experience of the other, but Leiris now seems to despair of ethnography's ever being able to bring it about—a puzzling assertion, indeed, since at the time of writing Leiris was making fieldwork trips to the French Caribbean for the UNESCO study that was published in 1955 as *Contacts de civilisations en Martinique et en Guadeloupe*, and since he would publish *La Possession et ses aspects théâtraux chez les Éthiopiens de Gondar* less than a decade later. Both of these texts are more or less conventional examples of the "human sciences" that seem to frustrate Leiris so in his 1950 introduction. In this earlier piece, he argues that ethnography breaks down before the sweeping social and cultural changes brought about by capitalist modernity and that some more primal form of connection must be forged: "If contact between people born in very different places is not a myth, this is to the extent that it can come about through shared work against those who, in the capitalist society of our 20th century, are the representatives of the old forms of slavery."[63] Solidarity represents a political and ethical imperative that forestalls any possibility of the detachment of subject from object, self from other, that for Leiris is the problematic corollary of ethnography taken as a field science.

Solidarity also allows for a more clear-cut opposition to colonialism, but only insofar as the struggle between colonizer and colonized is subsumed by a larger, color-blind struggle between oppressors and oppressed. "I can only perceive," he asserts, in a formulation highly reminiscent of that of Jean-Paul Sartre in his "Black Orpheus," that "if there are still obstacles, those which are raised between oppressors and oppressed . . . divide them into two camps."[64] In this introduction, then, Leiris accomplishes two moves that are remarkable for their absence from the journal proper: he outlines a form of universalist contact between the self and mankind in which ethnography has no role, and he views this solidarity as a political tool that makes possible the self's effective opposition to colonialism.

The 1981 preface is less rich and impassioned than his postwar introduction, but it adds another layer of selfhood to *L'Afrique fantôme* that puts even more distance between a more current version of Leiris and Leiris the 1930s ethnographer. Whereas the introduction serves to outline a more militant form of political selfhood than that which appears in his ambivalent introspection in the journal itself, in the preface Leiris acknowledges this earlier resituating of his anthropological persona and admits that Africa is even more fictive and ghostly for him than ever. He traces the development of his anthropological self from a naïve collector of objects for museums to a proponent of "an ethnography . . . of militant fraternity" and concludes that had he not republished the original journal or written about the mission over the years, his voyage would not carry any more weight in his memory than "[my memory] of many faded dreams of which only the stories that, more or less from time immemorial, I have endeavored to make from them still have any cohesion."[65] From this perspective, his own journal appears nearly as de-realized, inauthentic, and fictive to him as the continent of Africa did to his younger ethnographic self who produced the journal in the first place. This is a self who barely recognizes the one posited in the journal some fifty years before, and in this respect his preface reads like the opening remarks that an author writes about a text written by someone else entirely.

Thus, both the introduction and the later preface are resolutely external to the journal but cannot be considered separately from it (if only because we as readers must flip past them to arrive at the main text); thus, these paratextual documents force Leiris's original anthropological persona to recede from us, pushing him ever closer to the realm of unreality until we, too, become increasingly unable to recognize this young *secrétaire-archiviste* as more than a literary character tilting at ethnographic windmills. And it is Leiris's sense of historical layering that enables this reading experience, since the de-realized colonial Africa he maps out in the journal is now crosscut with selves who look back from moments after formal decolonization.

These multiple layers of selfhood, each characterized by a "real" Leiris assuring us that the self that came before is somehow but a fiction from which he must keep his distance (all the way back to the inauthentic self Leiris thinks he left behind in Paris when he went off to Africa in the first place), destabilize any sense we as readers might have that Leiris's anthropological persona is simply coextensive with any of the selves he gives us to view in either the journal or its prefatory remarks. All of these instantiations of selfhood, and the acts of distancing they imply, are articulated in relation to the question of colonialism. Even in Leiris's preface, in which he moves beyond the selves he created after the war, he suggests that as much as *L'Afrique fantôme* appears nearly fictional to his current self, it is all the more so to Africans who are struggling to deal with the effects of neocolonialism.[66] Whereas Leiris's anthropological persona appears increasingly fictional and unreliable, Hampâté Bâ's characterological didacticism is predicated on establishing a stable and trustworthy rapport with an imagined reader who benefits from the storyteller's ethnographic virtuosity. This virtuosity, which moves fluidly between and within both the colonial and "traditional" African social worlds, is shot through with a theory of pedagogy that directly engages the (implicitly Western) reader and aims at their cultural edification.

As Hampâté Bâ's interpolated essays on the colonial situation indicate, his awareness of the ambiguities inherent in his relationship to colonialism functions as a methodological expedient, designed to reveal all the more clearly the goals of his ethnographic and didactic project (the preservation of local cultures and traditions through their expression in a universal language). This move stands in stark contrast to Leiris's realization of his own ambivalence toward the colonial situation, which ends up shifting his gaze inward. However, we can read this inward turn as the establishment of a certain kind of relationship to the reader that, if it is not characterized by the joyous pedagogical interest that drives Hampâté Bâ, at least allows us to experience for ourselves something of what Leiris was wrestling with at the time. *L'Afrique fantôme* is a diary whose intimacy was always meant to be exposed, and in this respect, on a purely formal level, Hampâté Bâ and Leiris both begin from an imagined relationship to a readerly public.

In the second part of his journal, though, when he has long seemed fed up with ethnography and its perceived limitations, Leiris makes an impassioned (and oft-cited) statement that yet again marks his frustration and goes a long way toward explaining why the lengthy Abyssinia section of the text is so difficult to read. During fieldwork with a local spirit possession cult run by an older woman and her daughter, Leiris observes that for all the importance he attaches to their words and explanations, the true value of what his informants have to say is always obscured by ethnographic methodology: "I can no longer tolerate organized research. I need to soak in their drama, to touch their ways of being, to bathe in living flesh. To hell with ethnography!"[67] As readers we are used to such condemnations of the drawbacks of ethnography; however, located as this outburst is in the middle of the dense second part of the journal, in which Leiris's disappointment with ethnography becomes definitive, its emotional resonance inflects our reading experience all the more strongly. Just as he laments the fact that he is unable to abandon himself fully to the lives and cultures of his informants, so we, as readers, in this second part of the journal have trouble abandoning ourselves to the text because our narrator forces us to try to keep up with the very intricate and unfamiliar fieldwork encounters that confound him so thoroughly.

For example, several days after making this apparently definitive remark Leiris actually moves in with the two women who run the local spirit possession cult in advance of several ceremonies to be staged for his benefit. During the course of these ceremonies, Leiris changes the form of his journal entries from ex post facto recapitulations of the day's events to impressionistic, up-to-the-minute accounts of the ceremonies' preparations and proceedings. These entries read like unpolished, hastily scribbled notes from the field since they contain no contextualization, reference local words whose meanings are at least partially obscured and involved individuals of whom we are only vaguely familiar. Let us consider some brief notes taken on December 9, 1932, as a sacrifice is being prepared inside the old woman's hut:

> 10:00 am: the family elders return. They are given the bench on the right. Emawayish [the daughter] comes to sit on the ground near me, on a board.
>
> Everyone is served shoumbra and coffee.
>
> The child is taken into the kitchen.
>
> In order to take part in the discussion of family affairs, Malkam Ayyahou [the old woman] becomes *Abbatié Tchenguirié*.
>
> Malkam Ayyahou's brother takes the floor first. He is a plowman, he says, "neither a qagnazmatch nor a fitaorari" [Abyssinian governmental roles]. His sons too will be plowmen, "neither qagnazmatch nor fitaorari."

Emawayish wipes her hands with the grass that is strewn across the ground.

The brother's speech on the family's affairs.[68]

Although we as readers are able to follow Leiris's ethnographic play-by-play on its most basic narrative level, we are as incapable of grasping the social import of the proceedings as our narrator was when he recorded these notes in the first place. For instance, we are not sure what *shoumbra* is, and we do not fully understand just why Malkam Ayyahou becomes possessed at this moment or why this particular spirit inhabits her. We do not exactly know what role her brother is playing, either, and his declarations are entirely unclear. Whereas classically conventional ethnographic narrative places the reader in a foreign cultural environment through more or less careful contextualization and exposition of individuals, power dynamics, and social roles, Leiris's impressionistic account simply plunges us into the scene and obliges us to follow it as he did at the time.

We are clearly a far cry here from Hampâté Bâ's friendly and approachable contextualized vignettes. Unlike the Malian ethnographer, for whom the ethnographic anecdote unites reader and author in a moment of instructive goodwill, in *L'Afrique fantôme*'s second part the reader-ethnographer relationship becomes profoundly negative: Leiris toys with us in the dense, impenetrable notes that continue for several dozen pages, demonstrating that he is capable of alienating us from his ethnographic narrative (such as it is) in much the same way that ethnography, because of its incapacity to foster true contact, alienated him in these moments of fieldwork that are symbolically rich and yet so ultimately frustrating. This is what we might call "negative virtuosity," a sense of style carefully deployed to keep readers at bay, in contradistinction to Hampâté Bâ's ethnographic stylistics that draw the reader ever deeper into the text. Thus, this relationship, which is created when the reader actually steps into Leiris's ethnographic shoes and experiences fieldwork in the real time of the text, is in part one of nonrelation, since Leiris's anthropological persona pushes us away from the content of his journal and seemingly proves his point about the type of distancing that fieldwork cannot overcome and may even exacerbate. From this point of view, then, it is when Leiris's anthropological persona is at its most clearly visible, in the impressionistic immediacy of his field notes, that his sense of fictionality, with its attendant distancing and awkward unreality, is most vividly apparent to readers.

Style, Virtuosity, Epistemology

Part of this book's argument is that ethnographic fiction understands colonial and postcolonial encounters as stylistic opportunities, moments ripe for generic experimentation and cross-pollination wherein the impulse to account empirically for such encounters is swayed by the temptations of creative distancing and the free play of the imaginative or the nonfactual. Aesthetic virtuosity, in other words, is generative ethnographically. As Gérard Genette argues, echoing Sartre, style involves both expressive denotation and the creation of new forms of textual visibility—that is, the way a text makes a place for itself in relation to others. "Style is nothing else," he writes, "but the aspect—let us call it *perceptible*—that constitutes what Roman Jakobson called a text's 'perceptibility.'"[69] Virtuosity, the most nakedly self-aware exercise of style, is from this perspective integral to the organization of ethnographic fiction's perceptibility as a genre and formative in terms of the writer's (or director's) relationship to ethnographic knowledge. Virtuosity and epistemology are enmeshed in Hampâté Bâ and Leiris, although each of these writers, as ever, pushes this stylistic approach to ethnographic fiction's concern with colonial knowledge production in different and contrasting directions. Whereas Hampâté Bâ shows off stylistically for readers so that epistemology and hermeneutics might go hand in hand, Leiris ends up leaving the register of anthropology altogether and entering the realm of the short story to effect through literary fiction the type of subject-object convergence that ethnographic fieldwork is unable to produce.

Turning first to Hampâté Bâ, we can consider an episode he calls "Flag at Half-Mast." This is the story of his relationship with Commandant François de Coutouly, who stands out for our narrator because he was a white French administrator who took a "colonial wife (*épouse coloniale*)," usually a short-term indigenous romantic partner recruited more or less by force; married her legally, forcing administrators and Africans alike always to refer to her as "Madame de Coutouly"; and recognized the children he had with her. The episode relates the death of one of the commandant's biracial children and of his confrontation with a French army officer who upbraids the civilian administrator for daring to put the tricolor flag outside his office at half-mast in recognition of the tragic event. Hampâté Bâ begins his tale in a manner with which we are already familiar: he not only introduces the protagonist but also provides a contextualization designed to enhance the reader's knowledge about the complexities of colonial cultures.

Thus, François de Coutouly is not just the administrator who recognizes his biracial children; he is also "well placed to know that children born from 'colonial marriages' were generally placed by the administration in 'mixed-race orphanages' after the father's return to France."[70] This comment functions both to shed light on a particular character trait and to outline the social stakes of the story in a way that informs the reader of a certain practice that was de rigueur in the colonial period. Hampâté Bâ continues in this vein by linking this embedded story, in which he plays but a minor role, to a broader commentary on the political capital enjoyed by French administrators: "The very day of the child's death there occurred a fairly serious incident which gives an idea both of the character of François de Coutouly, at once noble and of great integrity, and of the power of colonial administrators in the French colonies."[71] The commandant here appears as a consummate ethnographic example, since he stands out precisely because he does not resemble other administrators in either character or actions and because his case is fundamentally indicative of the prestige and power wielded by all French administrators. Before the story proper even begins, then, we as readers are aware of just what Hampâté Bâ would like us to take away from it since it is preceded by its own hermeneutic utility. The establishment of this bond with the reader, in which hermeneutics and colonial epistemology are indistinguishable, allows Hampâté Bâ to create for himself some room for free play.

What stands out in the story that follows is more than the sheer power of the commandant that its primary function is to illustrate; indeed, the army captain who attacks de Coutouly ends up being repatriated to France via a long, sandy trip up through the Sahara, per the orders of the colonial governor in Ouagadougou who knows the commandant well. This narrative showcases Hampâté Bâ's virtuosity at its most engaging, since he deftly moves among several linguistic and dialogic registers in re-creating the incident while downplaying his own role in the affair—he appears only as a passive messenger and bystander, having no dialogue of his own, who takes orders from the enraged de Coutouly.

We can highlight here three linguistic registers that Hampâté Bâ reproduces for us as he recounts how the army officer insults the administrator for bothering to commemorate the death, as the captain puts it, of his "little black boy (*petit négrillon*)." First, we have the standard, highly formal French used by the captain to address de Coutouly before the captain learns why the flag has been lowered: "Mister administrator, why are you crying? What has happened? What misfortune has stuck us that the flag has been put at half-mast?"[72] Once the administrator informs his military colleague of his young son's death, the tone of the scene changes markedly, as does Hampâté Bâ's narrative reportage of its dialogic shift. Incensed, the army captain insults the commandant, who responds with an insult-laden tirade mocking the officer's Germanic family name: "You Johnny-come-lately Frenchman! Dirty kraut! Traitor to his country out of material interest! . . . Get the hell out of here before I give you the round of kicks you deserve!"[73] From correct, polite French we have moved quickly to insults with slang and cultural-political references that our narrator clearly wants us to savor.

Finally, the tension in this scene is dialogically dissolved by a lowly indigenous sentry who has the temerity to intervene and shame the two French verbal combatants while addressing them in the imperfect *français des tirailleurs* (which Hampâté Bâ also refers to as *forofifon naspa*) spoken by many indigenous subjects: "Oh, you two great chiefs! You not have shame fighting before two Negroes who watching you like two roosters fighting hand to hand without bayonets?"[74] This colorful interjection has a specific function in Hampâté Bâ's carefully constructed narrative, since it breaks the immediate drama of the episode by turning the white French men's attention to their linguistic-racial difference from the indigenous bystanders. However, it also permits our hero to take his re-creation in yet another linguistic direction by demonstrating his comfort with the jumbled and marvelously vibrant language of those Africans who occupy the lower strata of the colonial hierarchy.

The linguistic triangulation we encounter in this episode serves to remind us that we are dealing with an adept storyteller character who can both instruct and entertain his readers by showing them that he can easily inhabit the linguistic lifeworlds of any number of characters with disparate social and racial roles in the colonial system. We are, in short, dealing with a narrator who is not only engaged in creating a scene for our enjoyment and edification but who also tells the story of his own virtuosity as a literary entertainer. This metanarrative runs alongside the story told in the episode and the vision of ethnographic didacticism whose function it serves. Further, though, this metanarrative provides the hermeneutic key for the first-order story it accompanies, such that we must pass through Hampâté Bâ's stylistic virtuosity to process the epistemological claims the story wants to make.

For Leiris, by contrast, style is not exactly the handmaiden of ethnographic epistemology. We have seen how for him fiction acts to reveal anthropology's roadblocks that prevent the discipline from proceeding in the way he believes it ideally should—namely, as effecting true contact between subject and object, self and other. Leiris deploys writerly virtuosity to force readers to tackle the concept of authenticity by growing aware of the relationship between the fictional and the unreal, on the one hand, and ethnography as a field-based discipline, on the other. This obligation that Leiris thrusts on us is born from the notion that ethnography for him is a disciplinary ideal type that makes promises of authentic forms of cultural contact it can never actually keep, condemned as it is to chase the "shadows" of culture: people, places, and artifacts that are always more inauthentic than Leiris feels they really should be and that are not readily amenable to the sort of contact that fieldwork ought to offer.

Later on, in the four volumes of *La règle du jeu*, poetry and revolutionary politics join ethnography as additional ideal types that tempt Leiris with promises of authentic contact (with writing, poetic language, socialism, the working class) and in terms of which he must situate himself as a writer. As one of these ever unsatisfying poles, anthropology's ideal objects appear forever epistemologically out of reach—a problem with which Leiris wrestles constantly in *L'Afrique fantôme* but that never prevented him from conducting fieldwork afterward. This imagery, of grasping and reaching, references perpetual movement and pursuit quite intentionally, for it is in this respect that ethnography and travel are conceptually linked for Leiris. ("But why must we stop at Djibouti?" he writes early in 1933. "It would be so simple to continue on to India."[75]) In *L'âge d'homme* (written between 1930 and 1935 and thus overlapping with the African journey), Leiris fleshes out this connection by assimilating himself, among reflections on painting, theater, and women, to Wagner's Flying Dutchman, doomed forever to roam the seas. This figure, he writes, has something to do with "the magical attraction exercised on me— until I indeed made a slow and faraway journey—by the notion of wandering (*vagabondage*), of the impossibility of being attached and, more precisely, of settling down in a specific point in space where one is materially and sentimentally fulfilled, instead of roaming about from sea to sea."[76]

The fact that the "journey" of which Leiris speaks here is the Dakar-Djibouti mission, which he references in his following paragraph, is quite telling and sets restless wandering in this context as analogous to the status of ethnography in *L'Afrique fantôme*: just as *vagabondage* had a wondrous allure for him before he actually made a lengthy voyage, so ethnography held out the promise of authentic contact with other people until he actually began conducting fieldwork. Unfortunately, as he comes to learn in his field journal and as he mentions just after this passage in *L'âge d'homme*, one is incapable of recapturing the magical attraction of anticipation once one has taken the first step, "once that virginity of the initial departure is lost."[77]

Leiris's exercise in writerly virtuosity consists of making readers participate, fully and awkwardly, in the intensely intimate singularity of his personal desire for restless movement, his drive to dive headlong into yet another fruitless departure. Along with Leiris, we experience his self the way John Dos Passos describes the concept in *The Big Money*, as "the bellyaching malingerer so often the companion of aimless walks."[78] This virtuosity produces an uncomfortable anthropological voyeurism through which we begin to identify with Leiris and, like him, hope that contact and ethnographic satisfaction—any kind of epistemological relief—will come in just a few pages' time, perhaps in a week or whenever the mission moves to a new location.

He is able to convey his sense of frustration at ethnography's pursuit of fictional objects to such an extent that it infects the reader's interaction with his journal: we are increasingly aware that the promise of some sort of textual resolution (in which we implicitly believe on opening any book for the first time) cannot be kept, and the fact that the voyage eventually comes to an end is but a meager compensation for our dashed readerly expectations. Even before the journal takes a depressingly introspective turn in its second part, Leiris's pessimism and disappointment link his relationship with ethnography to our own experience as readers. The many weeks he and the other members of the mission spend waiting in British Sudan before being given permission to cross into Abyssinia give our narrator time to reflect on the ways in which ethnography cannot help him escape into another self, a self-possessing authentic knowledge of other human beings. "Why has ethnographic inquiry often made me think of a police interrogation?" he wonders, in a comment that also refers implicitly to Marcel Griaule's characteristic field methodology. "We do not really get closer to people when we study their customs in depth. They remain, after the fieldwork as before it began, stubbornly closed."[79] Although the Africans Leiris studies "open up" to him during interviews and other fieldwork activities, ethnographic encounters for him have such an air of mutual mistrust and inauthenticity that he feels no closer to his informants than before he started his research.

In much the same way, though, remarks such as these, which cast doubt on the possibility of his ever constructing an ethnographic self that would satisfy him, provoke us as readers to reformulate his provocative observation and conclude that "we do not really get closer to people when we study their journals." Having finished *L'Afrique fantôme*, we ultimately feel no closer to Leiris than we did before we opened the text for the first time, even though the very form of the journal intime ought to provide us with the very sort of authentic contact with another person that he hopes ethnography will provide for him. Although Leiris opens up to his readers in the pages of his journal—in much the same way that his informants open up to him but still remain "stubbornly closed"—his failed attempts to create a new self through ethnography tie the discipline to a fictional sort of reading experience that we take away from the text, having come no closer to Leiris the ethnographer despite our good faith attempts to do so.

Leiris's sense of virtuosity, which translates the ethnographic diary into a fictional experience of reading, culminates in a fascinating entry from late December 1932. Here he makes an unexpected move and temporarily abandons his introspective register by turning to literary fiction and more conventionally literary articulations of selfhood. For much of the mission's last few months, Leiris's journal entries contain obsessive musings on his own masculinity, virility, and sexuality (or lack thereof), all with the goal of interrogating what he perceives as his possible impotence and his inability to regard sex as fulfilling a human need as he imagines that other men do. Characteristically, he is also unsure that he even wants to conceive of sexuality as having anything to do with biological drives.

He begins the entry with two terse sentences: "Dreadful depression. Real depression: colonial depression."[80] Struck by this languorous depressive state (which, if anything, is mere boredom), Leiris begins sketching a story based both on his own experiences during the mission and on the plot of Joseph Conrad's 1915 novel *Victory*. "Idea for a story," he suddenly begins, "whose elements would be borrowed, for the most part, from the present reality. A character in the style of Axel Heyst (see Conrad). As much of a gentleman, but less at ease. Much more timid, even more reserved."[81] In much the same way that individuals today joke about which star would play them in a film about their life, Leiris wonders which fictional character would play him in a fictional story based loosely on his journey.

The character is initially called "someone like Axel Heyst," Conrad's protagonist in *Victory*, but Leiris almost immediately dissolves his character into that of Conrad, such that this short story is as much a reboot of *Victory* as it is a tale "about" Leiris. We are dealing here with a sense of fiction that has been curiously doubled: Leiris undertakes not only to fictionalize himself but also to fictionalize his fictional self by rendering his own character indistinguishable from Conrad's Axel Heyst. The plot of the story is straightforward enough and is entirely in keeping with Leiris's reflections on his masculinity and sexuality: Axel Heyst lives alone in a nameless colony, with few friends and no female companionship. He attempts unsuccessfully to kill himself (as did Leiris in the late 1950s, an act on which he reflects at great length in *Fibrilles* (1966), the third volume of *La règle du jeu*) and ultimately allows himself to perish in an epidemic that ravages the colony. His only friend, a local doctor, finds a *journal intime* among Heyst's belongings that reads unsurprisingly very much like Leiris's own journal and that prompts the doctor to track down an African prostitute with whom Heyst attempted to have sex before scaring her away. The story ends abruptly with Heyst's doctor friend writing to a woman in Europe, presumably the protagonist's love interest, to inform her of his friend's death.

In spite of the slippage of naming, Leiris's fictional character is not, strictly speaking, Conrad's Heyst. This new Heyst is less at ease and far more reserved, and Leiris is interested here in re-creating Conrad's character so that he becomes the same sort of "sentimental outcast" that Leiris feels himself to be.[82] What, then, do we make of this sudden literary-fictional interpolation that reads like a retreat back into Leiris's writerly comfort zone in the face of all the disappointments ethnography has caused for him? We can answer this question by turning to a correlative problem it raises—namely, what might this literary-fictional self have to offer that ethnographic selfhood clearly cannot? In this untitled short story, Leiris finally becomes both self and other, Axel Heyst and not–Axel Heyst, by simultaneously assimilating a fictional character to his own self (the writing subject) and by assimilating himself to a fictional personage (the literary object). In short, Leiris effects in a fictional register the very form of contact that ethnography should have provided but failed to so miserably. Whatever its merits as a story, this embedded fiction constitutes a literary utopia, an imagined resolution to a problem ethnography cannot solve for Leiris and an extra-anthropological manner of highlighting all of the discipline's epistemological shortcomings.

This sudden Conradian turn immediately places *L'Afrique fantôme* into conversation with Malinowski's posthumously published *A Diary in the Strict Sense of the Term*, which critics have long mined for its references and similarities to the work of Malinowski's countryman—and, more specifically, to his *Heart of Darkness*.[83] Malinowski saw his personal and professional life as close to Conrad's, and his declaration that "[W. H. R.] Rivers is the Rider

Haggard of Anthropology: I shall be the Conrad!" certainly finds a welcome echo in a request Leiris made to his wife in a letter from 1932: "Reread *Lord Jim* and think of me."[84] Commentators have rightly highlighted the powerful Conradian similarities and reminiscences at play in Malinowski's *Diary*. Leiris's epistolary request and his interpolated short story go even further, though, and hint at a greater degree of fictional indistinguishability. Is Leiris referring to the author of *Lord Jim* or to the novel's eponymous protagonist? Why does Leiris's fictional character need to become Axel Heyst, to the extent that his story outline ends up being little more than literary remixing?

The first of these questions is tellingly unanswerable, but the second provides us with an idea of the role that this interpolation plays in *L'Afrique fantôme*: Leiris needs fiction to supplement ethnography, for it is through the former that he can, by dint of writerly virtuosity and literary fiat, finally effect a self-other reconciliation. What is more, though, he forces the reader temporarily to leave the register of anthropology entirely to glimpse a potential fulfillment of the promises he thinks the discipline holds out to him. In other words, in this final fictional grand gesture we can observe how the detour through fiction is actually constitutive of Leiris's idea of ethnography as it appears in his field diary—constitutive as both a supplement and as a utopian textual interruption.

The exercise of virtuosity, by showing off the range of one's writerly voice or by inhabiting a different voice altogether, organizes ethnographic fiction's relationship to the epistemological claims the genre seeks to make. Reading virtuosity in Hampâté Bâ and Leiris alerts us to the stylized figuration of ethnographic realism such that style becomes the premise according to which epistemology is proffered as well as the hermeneutic playbook that makes textual knowledge games meaningful and communicable.

Expressing Empire

As epistemological fantasy and ethnographic field site, Africa's centrality to the formation of the social sciences as professional disciplines has figured prominently in postcolonial reroutings of the history of anthropology. In France particularly, Africa and the colonies were powerful discursive organizing principles for anthropology as a budding human science under the Third Republic, especially in the 1920s and '30s, when Leiris and Hampâté Bâ were embarking on their fledgling ethnographic careers. France's new social scientists were born from humanist intellectual traditions, though, and they often positioned themselves ambiguously in relation to what were called "the colonial sciences" (such fields as "colonial geography" or "native psychology") and to ideologies of empire which nonetheless called on their ethnographic expertise.[85] As we saw at the beginning of this chapter, interwar colonial humanism was positioned awkwardly between anxieties about colonial legitimacy and emerging Pan-African epistemologies. The coexistence in interwar France of colonial anxiety and new black cosmopolitanisms helps explain why figures such as Leiris and Hampâté Bâ would devise new ways of expressing empire to readers in their ethnographic fictions, whether in alternative universalism or alienating negative virtuosity. And the careful historical layering in their texts ensures that these late-colonial expressions circulate among a postcolonial readership.

These ethnographic fictions situate the question of knowledge production at the point of conjuncture between anthropological imperatives of documentation/preservation and various forms of "contact" and the self-aware free play involved in writing ethnography into a transgeneric imagination. As we recall from the introduction, this argument is one of this book's main interventions. But as I have explored in this chapter, ethnographic fiction also reimagines the epistemological and aesthetic relationship obtaining between colonial-era fieldwork and empire by filtering it through an acutely felt sense of positionality.

For Hampâté Bâ, the question of ethnographic virtuosity is inseparable from the role he plays as an anthropological-literary character and colonial subject. His cosmopolitan didactic project is predicated on the stylized management of his role as one of what Jean and John Comaroff call "those social scientists who argue for the distinctive forms of knowledge yielded by peripheral vision."[86] Peripheral ways of seeing (and being in) the world allow for the dislocation of Western-derived theories of modernity, cosmopolitanism, and ethnographic knowledge, prompting us to conceive of these theories as narratives with African genealogies. These acts of peripheral reinvention and redefinition are predicated on conceiving of empire as both a foundational locus of anthropological expertise, as it was for so many early twentieth-century French anthropologists, and, more radically, as a field site in its own right, where salvage anthropology might be set against the backdrop of communicative universalism.

For his part, Leiris does not deny the first, communicative term of this epistemology: as frustrating and unbearably melancholic as *L'Afrique fantôme*'s introspective entries are, we rarely lose sight of their author's implicit aware-ness of his readers. Leiris's communicative impulse is tethered to singular-ity rather than universality, though, to the breakdown of cultural exchange, and to the untranslatability of moments of ethnographic knowledge creation. (Indeed, he ends up translating such a moment of self-other convergence into literary fiction, where he can better control its outcome.) If the ethnographic encounter is singular and only communicable in its attendant defamiliariza-tion, the same holds true for the encounter with empire: it can only be offered to readers through the irreplaceable uniqueness of its alienating undertow. The colonial encounter here is not so much a field site as an ethnographic attitude, an utterly singular affective positioning whose components can only be recon-structed in hindsight and with difficulty.

As the transgeneric terrain on which a colonial functionary-turned-native anthropologist meets an implacably morose ex-surrealist, ethnographic fic-tion accommodates both communicative universalism and colonial singularity. At the same time, these alternative anthropologies are invested in expressing empire to communities of readers and in constituting publics who, on the one hand, are amenable to cosmopolitan pedagogy and, on the other, are able to bear witness to the ineffable singularity of the colonial encounter. Read to-gether, these ethnographic fictions hold these disparate publics together and facilitate their cultivation by providing a grammar that is at once stylistic and epistemological, indebted to empire and yet not beholden to the constraints brought about by its powers of disciplinary consecration.

Chapter 2

The Director of Modern Life

Jean Rouch's Ethnofiction

As the director of more than one hundred films from the late 1940s until his death in 2004, the French anthropologist Jean Rouch was so attuned to the formal and thematic imperatives of his métier that he could savor the often porous boundaries between documentary filmmaking and the cinema of fiction. Rouch was earnestly committed to formal experimentation across various cinematic genres throughout his sixty-year career as an Africanist anthropologist and filmmaker, but an early move in his work toward story-driven ethnography allowed him to explore playfully how documentary renderings of everyday life might mobilize and require the free play of fiction. Rouch's movement toward ethnographic fiction occurred in the late 1950s, when French colonies in West Africa were gaining independence and when his directorial interests became more intensely focused on modern life in burgeoning postcolonial cities. Rouch had previously focused exclusively on filming rituals and spirit possession ceremonies in rural Niger and Mali. Three films in particular punctuate this ethnofictional expansion: *Jaguar* (1957–70), *Moi, un Noir* (1958), and *La pyramide humaine* (1959). Rouch referred to hybridized films such as these as his *ciné-fictions* (or, humorously, as "science fictions"), and these early works are characterized by the creative rapprochement of improvised narration and collaborative ethnography.[1]

Each of these films deals broadly with the translation into cinematic narrative of emerging relationships between colonial cultures and modernity—its ideologies and its irresistible draw, as well as the attendant anxieties it produces—in Francophone West Africa in the period just prior to independence. Like many of Rouch's films at the time, his ethnofiction grew directly out of fieldwork experiences in Niger and Ivory Coast where, ever the easygoing anthropologist ready to follow a lead, he often prompted his research subjects (many of whom would go on to become his amateur actors) to determine the scope and stakes of a given project. Rouch shot these early films before it was possible to use synchronized sound in the field, and at the heart of his drive to push ethnographic filmmaking beyond its limits as realist documentary was his provocative willingness to incorporate the technical limitations of his time into his experiments with anthropological form and genre. Rouch was as concerned with disciplinary boundaries as he was with cinematic ones: allowing these concerns to resonate with his creative sense of experimentation, he sought to upend the traditional ethnographic project in his films by turning African social actors who had conventionally been considered passive ethnographic objects into knowledge producers in their own right. The argument that I trace here is that for Rouch, ethnographic fiction set in motion two types of narrative. The first of these is resolutely metadisciplinary and recalibrates expectations about the creation of anthropological knowledge and about the representational purview of documentary cinema. The second (which is tied to and emerges from the first) is a broader narrative of modernity itself, communicated on-screen by the actors living it and cinematically staged through improvised anthropological thick description and through often racialized adjustments to modern life in urban colonial West Africa.

Rouch never stopped making more straightforward ethnographic documentaries, and in other nonfiction films, the question of modernity certainly looms large (as in *Les maîtres fous* [1955]). But these late-1950s ethnofictions open up new cinematic avenues: in them, storytelling becomes a filmic category in its own right, prompting modernity to appear not only as a thematic concern but also as a dialogic and narratological creation, one that could be improvised and communicated to nonspecialist cinematic publics. Indeed, many of Rouch's early films were produced by organizations such as the Centre National de la Recherche Scientifique (CNRS) or the Institut Français d'Afrique Noire (IFAN) and thus were intended for narrower, more specialized audiences. Each of the early ethnofictions, however, along with a select few other works from the time, were produced by Pierre Braunberger's commercial outfit, Les Films de la Pléiade, and were destined for much wider distribution and consumption. For comparison's sake, we could consider the film *La circoncision* (1948), Rouch's brief treatment of a Songhay circumcision ceremony in Mali, in tandem with *Moi, un Noir*, which was released ten years later. The earlier film is purely expository, with Rouch's camera acting as narrator in the place of any voice-over or dialogue, and draws viewers into the ritual proceedings through strategic close-ups and engaging low-angle shots. In *Moi, un Noir*, by contrast, ethnographic exposition is inseparable from and dissolves into fictional and improvisational free play, as Rouch's protagonist, Robinson, makes up stories about his everyday life in Abidjan while spontaneously commenting on images of the city captured by the anthropologist's camera. This later film is as much about Robinson's move from rural Niger to the colonial metropolis as it is about his ability to speak on film about everyday life on his own terms. The movement toward fiction thus situated modernity as a narrative problem that could be tackled cinematically by the creative tension and interplay between the documentary exposition of ethnographic realism and fictionally inspired improvisational storytelling.

This chapter explores the development of ethnographic fiction in response to late-colonial encounters in Francophone West Africa, in a context geographically removed from the colonial hinterlands traversed by Michel Leiris and Amadou Hampâté Bâ. While Leiris deplored the inauthenticity of emergent forms of modernity in colonial Dakar, for example, Rouch reveled in the phenomenon of rural-urban colonial migration and in the creative negotiations and appropriations of modern life this phenomenon provoked in ordinary Africans. The nearly postcolonial city became Rouch's cinematic playground as he developed his *ciné-fictions*, whose ludic aesthetics feed off their modern urban settings.

But the films in Rouch's early ethnofictional turn also point us outside their urban contexts and toward decolonizing processes taking place in the French empire and beyond. Indochina gained independence from France in 1954 following a war that serves as an oblique backdrop to *Moi, un Noir*, and the Algerian war for independence was taking place as all three of these films were produced. Closer to home, Guinea voted for independence in 1958 after Charles de Gaulle promised a referendum on the future of France's colonies at the start of the Fifth Republic; by contrast, Léopold Sédar Senghor and other African politicians argued for socialist autonomy within a transnational French Community, as illustrated by the short-lived Mali Federation that broke up into independent Senegal and Mali in 1960.[2] Elsewhere on the continent, although certain former colonies had gained independence by the late 1950s, such as Ghana which turned toward socialism and Pan-Africanism under Kwame Nkrumah, other countries were still thoroughly colonial. South Africa, for instance, expanded Pass Laws in the 1950s that helped provoke the Sharpeville massacre in 1960. In this geopolitical moment characterized by uneven decolonization in Africa and by uncertainty about what, exactly, decolonization would look like in the French empire, Rouch asks not only what decolonization might mean for anthropology, but also how experimental ethnographic forms might decolonize anthropological knowledge production.

In terms of this book's argument, for Rouch modernity at the moment of decolonization posed specific stylistic and epistemological problems for anthropological narratives of empire: documentary forms had to experiment with characterology and fiction to make sense of how colonial subjects positioned themselves in relation to emerging global cultural signifiers (from France, the United States, and elsewhere in Africa) and to pressing anticolonial debates. Rouch's early ethnographic-fictional films generate cartographies of modernity that are at once transatlantic and transcolonial. True to the kinds of orthogonal thinking this book highlights, his experiments with genre not only remix colonial histories through fictional improvisation; they also map speculative narratives of decolonizing presents that extend beyond and across colonial borders.

Ethnographic Formalism and Rouch's Experimental Career

Of *Moi, un Noir* (1958), Jean-Luc Godard wrote, "All of Rouch's originality lies in having made his actors into characters."[3] Godard's *Breathless* (1960) was influenced by Rouch's early work, and although he had only one of Rouch's films in mind when he made this observation, he nonetheless touched on two important formal questions that were to inflect the content of Rouch's work throughout his long ethnographic career: How do actors play characters at the same time that they play themselves? And how does this role-playing imbue with fiction the everyday realities of social life that documentary films are supposed to capture?[4] Many of Rouch's more dramatic and feature-length films, shot primarily in Francophone West Africa and in metropolitan France, can be read on some level as attempts to work out precisely this bifurcated problem of form and genre. Whether they deal with economic migrants in colonial Gold Coast, reverse ethnography carried out by Africans on the streets of Paris, or everyday life in the proletarian quarter of Abidjan, Rouch's early feature-length films function in many ways as meditations on the narrative and fictional aesthetics of visual anthropology. Rouch's movement toward fiction in the late 1950s responds to certain concerns he articulated about cinema—both big-budget and documentary—earlier that decade: on the one hand, as he wrote in 1955, ethnographic film, stripped of the cumbersome technical trappings of classical cinema, could force spectators to encounter "the deeply moving face of reality" without the intervention of technicians or intrusive recording devices. On the other hand, though, ethnographic film was able to produce a cinematic reality that the amateurish documentary films of the day (whose arrival was hastened by the wide availability of 16 mm film) could attempt to replicate only through sensationalism and facile exoticism.[5]

Between the excesses of commercial cinema and the inauthenticity of documentary film in the 1950s, Rouch saw a specific role for ethnographic filmmaking: this new cinema could produce work that was "just as captivating as all the *tarzaneries* in the world" while simultaneously speaking to the experimental desires of the filmic avant-garde.[6] Ethnographic film of the early 1950s in Africa met these twin imperatives through a newfound reflexivity: as Rouch wrote about his compatriot Pierre-Dominique Gaisseau's film *Forêt sacrée* (the first version of which was released in 1953), "For the first time, one is an actual witness to the research, which perhaps was hopeless but nevertheless shows an unbounded respect for African culture."[7] For Rouch, opening up ethnographic film to fiction was a way to move in both of these cinematic directions at the same time. More specifically, improvisational fiction for Rouch placed cinema in a "state of grace" from which it derived this directional flexibility.[8]

As a student, and later as a professional anthropologist, Rouch moved in the same Africanist circles as Leiris and Hampâté Bâ. Although his films were set in several different West African countries, Rouch carried out most of his sustained ethnographic fieldwork in Niger and Mali from the beginning of his career in the late 1940s until his death in 2004. Much like Hampâté Bâ, though from different ends of the colonial hierarchy, Rouch came to anthropology through employment in the French colonial administration: after studies in engineering, Rouch worked in West Africa designing bridges during World War II and grew interested in possession ceremonies in Niger.[9] He wrote up notes after attending these ceremonies and sent them back to Marcel Griaule and Germaine Dieterlen in Paris, with whom he had been studying before entering the colonial civil service. During these early days as a budding ethnographer in Niger, Rouch consulted the only two books he had taken with him to Africa: Hegel's *Phenomenology of Spirit* and Leiris's *L'Afrique fantôme*.[10] Leiris's text may not have provided Rouch with a viable ethnographic model to follow, but this early work of ethnographic fiction was nonetheless an intellectual presence during his formative years in the discipline.

Rouch was connected both intellectually and personally to this book's other Africanists who worked with ethnographic fiction. After running afoul of the Vichy authorities in Niger, Rouch, like Hampâté Bâ, was invited to conduct fieldwork at the IFAN in Dakar under the auspices of Théodore Monod and arrived just several years after his Malian colleague. Rouch admired Hampâté Bâ's research and writing, commenting in an interview on the radio station France Culture after Hampâté Bâ's death in 1991 that "there wasn't a single tic of those colonial governors, who were sometimes marvelous and very often ridiculous, that escaped him. . . . Among all the people at the IFAN, he represented the Fulani. He spoke to everyone with such simplicity that one inevitably became friends with him."[11] When he returned to France, Rouch pursued a doctorate in anthropology under Griaule, and he returned to West Africa after the war to descend the Niger River with two friends by canoe. Rouch shot his first ethnographic footage with an old Bell and Howell 16 mm camera on this trip. Leiris, along with Griaule, Claude Lévi-Strauss, and Dieterlen, attended a screening at the Musée de l'Homme in Paris of some of this silent footage, and all agreed it showed promise. From his earliest days in the profession, then, Rouch was in touch with figures who were deeply invested in thinking through and writing in terms of anthropology's literary and fictional aesthetics.

Many of Rouch's shorter films from the 1940s and 1950s depict intricate spirit possession ceremonies and hunting rituals in remote villages in Niger among the Songhay and in Mali among the Dogon. As Paul Stoller has pointed out, in these films Rouch is primarily interested in the ways in which collective historical experience is embodied, performed, and re-created through ceremony.[12] In the early 1960s, Rouch spent time in both Africa and France while making what would become his best-known film, *Chronique d'un été*. Shortly thereafter he began conducting intensive fieldwork among the Dogon, working closely with Dieterlen to shoot important ceremonies and other rituals. The 1960s and '70s saw Rouch among the Songhay once again, shooting films with synchronized sound and long takes, and at this time he began making more feature-length narrative films, including many in the characteristic ethnofictional style whose early development I examine here, such as *Petit à Petit*

(1968–69), *Cocorico! Monsieur Poulet* (1974–75), and *Madame L'Eau* (1992).[13] In these longer films, Rouch often appears to take a different tack, turning his camera on bustling colonial and postcolonial urban centers and focusing on how young, usually male, Africans cultivate and negotiate complex and paradoxical relationships to labor and (neo)colonial capitalism, technology, and modernity.[14] Since these latter films are both organized around narratives and driven by storylines (however loosely defined or interpreted), they afford Rouch the opportunity to experiment explicitly with the ways fictional elements impinge on and reshape the techniques people deploy to produce meaningful accounts of their subjective experiences. He continued with these feature films into the 1990s, shooting in both France and West Africa, while still producing more conventional ethnographic documentaries in Niger. Of Rouch's prolific directorial output only a handful of films have been distributed in the United States. Since his death in a car accident in rural Niger in 2004, however, his work has garnered increasing scholarly attention in the Anglophone world, in both anthropology and film studies.[15]

Jaguar, Moi, un Noir, and *La pyramide humaine* occupy a privileged place in Rouch's oeuvre not only because they successfully and provocatively encapsulate his enduring commitment to formal experimentation or his enthusiasm for the production of new cinematic realities through the creative intrusions of his participating camera in the lives of his filmed subjects. Were these our only evaluative criteria, it would be nearly impossible to bracket just one set of films for critical attention to Rouch's formalism. What is especially striking about these three films is that, in turning to ethnographic fiction as a filmic genre, Rouch places his sense of formal experimentation and his anthropological vision of *ciné-réalité* (i.e., a reality that, upon filming, becomes a new type of cinematic truth) into conversation with an ethnography of the colonial encounter writ large that is thoroughly enmeshed in a narrative reconceptualization of modernity.

The Serendipity of Technical Difficulties: Rouch as Thinker of Modernity

These films represent Rouch's move toward dramatic, plot-based cinematic storytelling, a shift that begins with *Jaguar*, continues in *Moi, un Noir*, and culminates in *La pyramide humaine* (1959), the last film he shot before beginning to film with fully synchronized sound in *Chronique d'un été* (1960). The matter of (non)synchronized sound was no small technical issue for Rouch, however, and I argue that it is crucial to our understanding of his vision of anthropology's relationship to fiction, as well as to his theorization of modernity. In the 1950s, Rouch was commissioned to undertake more sociological and quantitative research on Nigerien migrants in the British Gold Coast which led to the rather dry monograph, *Migrations au Ghana* (1956), and to the comparatively richer *Jaguar*, a composite fictionalization of the results of Rouch's research starring three young Nigeriens (Damouré Zika, Lam Ibrahima Dia, and Illo Gaoudel) who had once served as conventional ethnographic informants but had since become amateur actors and Rouch's lifelong friends. The film charts the migration cycle of three Nigeriens who travel on foot to the Gold Coast as their warrior ancestors once did, end up starting a small business in the vast market at Kumasi, and return to Niger with tall tales and gifts to give away to friends and relatives. *Jaguar* has an extended production history that spans and surpasses Rouch's early ethnofictional movement: the majority of the film was shot between 1954 and 1955 when Rouch was in the Gold Coast, and his protagonists improvised commentary over the rough cut of the film in 1957 and 1960 before Rouch finalized the soundtrack in 1967.[16]

Several years after completing his fieldwork Rouch undertook similar research on Nigerien migrants in Abidjan. When he showed footage from *Jaguar* to his ethnographic informants in Ivory Coast (including Oumarou Ganda, who would go on to become *Moi, un Noir*'s protagonist), he was urged to make a film about Treichville, the Abidjan slum where the migrants had settled. Thus, even though *Jaguar* was not completed until much later, we can think of it as a precursor to *Moi, un Noir*. Rouch also viewed the film's genealogy this way.[17] *Moi, un Noir* became a "week in the life"–style film about modern life in Treichville and Ganda's increasingly keen awareness of economic marginalization and the deep despondency he experiences after returning home from the French war in Indochina. Thus, "one film gave birth to another," as Rouch himself characterized his approach,[18] and in keeping with his ethnographic method—what he called *anthropologie partagée* (shared anthropology)—he conceived and shot these two films in rigorous collaboration with his informants-cum-actors.

Rouch remained in Abidjan for the shooting of *La pyramide humaine*, but in it he approaches colonial modernity from above, as it were, by turning to the relations and emerging friendships between white Europeans and Africans at an elite French school in the Ivoirian capital. *La pyramide humaine* represents Rouch's response to critics who saw his work, and especially *Moi, un Noir*, as overly concerned with the African lumpenproletariat.[19] He deals here with race- and class-consciousness at the end of French colonial rule in Ivory Coast, a fraught transitional moment that looms thematically large in the film while remaining only obliquely referenced by the characters. Rouch and the students came up with the film's plot in response to a question that serves both as the film's organizing principle and as an anticolonial thought experiment with a utopian, postracial affective tenor: what would happen in West Africa if blacks and whites established genuine friendships, "without any racial hang-ups"?

This question leads *La pyramide humaine* into different thematic territory from that which Rouch covers in his two previous ethnofictions. However, *Moi, un Noir* is very much the conceptual and anthropological sequel to the earlier *Jaguar*.[20] A brief sequence from *Jaguar* helps illustrate how Rouch sets forth a narrative of modernity and allows it to be provocatively revisited and elaborated in his subsequent filmic project. At the end of the film, as the three migrants make their way back to their home village in a rickety truck, Rouch refers to his protagonists as "the heroes of the modern world." In a film of many boastful pronouncements, Rouch does not make this rather grand claim simply for dramatic effect. His statement instead bespeaks a relationship among cinema, anthropology, and modernity that underlies many of his films and that is curiously doubled. On the one hand, the ciné-réalité created at the interface of Rouch's camera and the situations of everyday life in which that camera necessarily participates links ethnographic practice to the formal experiments of artistic modernism. On the other hand, moving beyond experimentation, we can understand Rouch's claim in narratological terms— that is, as highlighting how his amateur protagonists are the heroes of their own filmic restagings of their relationships to modernity and modern life in colonial West Africa. While this idea lurks below the surface in powerful ways only to burst forth with Rouch's declaration near the end of *Jaguar*, it emerges in full narrative force in *Moi, un Noir* and becomes the structuring principle of the film, both because the film's subject matter lends itself to more explicit iterations of these restagings and because the technological limitations with which Rouch was forced to contend at the time obliged him to give his actors' narratological relationships to modern life pride of place in the story.

In interviews, Rouch enjoyed claiming that *Moi, un Noir* was the first film in which an African spoke on camera about his everyday life in his own words, and while such an assertion may or may not be true, it nonetheless allows us to grasp some of the important aspects of Rouch's early ethnofic-tional style (of which *Moi, un Noir* is such a striking example). To be sure, in *Jaguar* Rouch's Nigerien protagonists do provide commentary about their lives and their travels; however, while the film was shot in 1957, it was not finished until ten years later, when Rouch and his actors finally added the post-synchronized dialogue. Rouch's ethnofiction, a cinematic genre blending fictionalized commentary and narrative flourishes into ethnographic docu-mentaries, came about thanks to the serendipity of "technical difficulties." At the time, no noiseless 16 mm cameras existed that could shoot synchronized sound—and yet, Rouch made creative and loyal use of his 16mm Bell and Howell camera to create his ambulatory and Vertovian shots. Dziga Vertov's style, best captured in his film *Man with a Movie Camera* (1929), sought to organize the perceptible world by creating a filmic realism in which the cam-era becomes a mechanical eye (and not simply a vehicle for the human one) capable of deciphering reality and creating a specific type of filmic truth proper to the cinema.[21] For Vertov, the camera possesses its own conscious-ness and, for this reason, allows us to consider the ways in which lived experi-ence is constructed both by and through filmic observation. This dual sense of the filmic construction of everyday life is crucial to Rouch's understanding of the potential of documentary film making, and he found himself forced to reconcile the Vertovian influence on his shots with the frustrating inability to shoot with fully synchronized sound.

Taking advantage of this technical setback, Rouch and his amateur Niger-ien actors in *Jaguar* and *Moi, un Noir* improvised scenes based on a mutually agreed-on storyline that were shot silently. Next, during postsynchronization Rouch showed his actors the rough cut of the film, and his participants impro-vised a dialogue and a narrative that more or less corresponded with the im-ages on the screen but that, provocatively, was not necessarily determined by the images in advance. Not beholden to any a priori primacy of the visual over speech, the participants were free to comment on the images as they saw fit, and this sort of freewheeling retrospection often forces the postsynchronized dialogue in Rouch's ethnofiction to shift uncomfortably from accessible hilar-ity to brooding, haunting introspection. In this way, though, semifictionalized filmic lived experience was produced spontaneously through purely contin-gent narratives that hinged on whatever the actors felt like saying about their visual selves and the characters they were supposed to be playing. Rouch's strategy changed somewhat in *La pyramide humaine*: the film contains certain scenes that were shot with synchronized sound but were improvised on the spot. He accomplished this by placing the actors around a large, heavy stationary camera. The more characteristically Rouchian shots in the film were created through silent shooting and postsynchronization, very much akin to what we see in *Jaguar* and *Moi, un Noir*.[22] However, this time his actors did not improvise their retrospective voice-overs: these were written by Rouch and reflect the fictional basis of the film, unlike the earlier two ethnofictions which were at least partially based in reality and documentary research.[23] Like *Moi, un Noir*, *La pyramide humaine* contains actors playing characters who are often uncomfortably close to themselves, but in the later film this role-playing serves an entirely fictional thought experiment. Thus, even though an awkward sort of synchronization was possible, Rouch's approach still privileged the fictional possibilities opened up by improvisation and storytelling.

Rouch's amateur actors certainly do have much to say about their own lives and experiences, but, as Godard rightly observes, his protagonists are portraying characters as much as (and, importantly, at the same time as) they are playing themselves. Although Rouch's dramatic assertion that Damouré, Lam, and Illo represent the heroes of the modern world comes at the very end of *Jaguar*, this authoritative voice-over retrospectively inflects the viewer's engagement with the film up to that point. Put another way, to take Rouch's claim in narratological terms is to posit in hindsight that the film is constructing a narrative of modernity through an investigation of its characters' adaptations to urban life and in terms of the thoroughly modern(ist) tropes of travel, migration, and displacement.[24]

Jaguar opens with another voice-over by Rouch, in which he interpellates an unknown, unseen character, saying, "Adamou, we are going to tell you a story (*histoire*)." Like Hampâté Bâ's memoirs, Rouch's ethnofiction links anthropology to transcultural storytelling: his voice-over apostrophizes an unknown African character but, at the same time, is also directed at uninitiated spectators. From the outset, the film moves in two narrative directions. On the one hand, it is the improvised, fictional distillation of Rouch's quantitative research in the Gold Coast and, thus, storytelling understood in its conventional sense. On the other hand, though, playing on the dual meaning of the word *histoire* in French as both "story" and "history," Rouch is careful to mention at several points throughout the film that what the spectator is seeing is also a sort of cultural history of the present: Nigerien migrants, like the three protagonists, reenact and retrace the southward migrations of their warrior ancestors, but in so doing, they endow these seasonal movements with new historical meaning. Of these modern migrants, Rouch remarks: "They do not

FIGURE 2.1 Damouré looking like a cool jaguar on a walk through downtown Accra.

bring back captives, like their ancestors from last century. They bring back luggage, they bring back wonderful stories, they bring back lies." Following their director's lead, these characters traffic in transcultural fictions, earning prestige at home in Niger by virtue of the stories they concoct about their travels abroad and the social and economic diversity they learned to navigate in another colonial context. This new cultural history, in which migrants follow the cartographic movements of their forebears while simultaneously resignifying them, is thus what enables Rouch's characters to produce fictional stories in the first place.

This cinematic production of concurrent nods to and divergences from historical trajectories is part and parcel of a broader sense of simultaneity that the film creates through narrative. The characters partake in a modernist experiment uniting a fictional story and an ethnographic documentary. At the same time, they negotiate and reshape their own cultural history by forging relationships to modernity and modern life through travel to the Gold Coast, whose twin urban centers of Accra and Kumasi are imagined by migrants and represented by Rouch as cosmopolitan metropolises. The Ivoirian capital, Abidjan, appears in much the same light in *Moi, un Noir* and *La pyramide humaine*. More specifically, though, as Damouré (the *primus inter pares* of Rouch's protagonists in the film) boastfully reminds us, becoming modern in Anglophone West Africa means becoming a "jaguar," that is, embodying and artfully displaying a sense of colonial cool that highlights the extent to which one is in touch with the cosmopolitan currents of colonial urban life.

We get a glimpse of what this means in the middle of the film, when Damouré defines "jaguar" for us as Rouch's camera follows him on a walk through town in a series of low-angle shots that make his protagonist's stylized sense of the modern African flaneur loom ever larger.[25] As we watch him carefully hang a cigarette from the corner of his mouth, Damouré tells us in postsynchronized voice-over, "A jaguar is an elegant young man, who has his hair done right, who smokes, who walks around. Everyone looks at him, and he looks at everyone, he sees all the beautiful girls, and he calmly smokes his cigarette. That's what 'jaguar' means." Modernity here is thus understood as a stylized, aesthetic imperative as well as a concept produced through geographical displacement: modernity does not exist solely in the metropole, the film suggests, but is created in the cosmopolitan routes leading to and from its privileged position.

Mobility and displacement are also thematic concerns raised by Rouch and his actors in *Moi, un Noir*, however in this film modernity takes a somewhat different spatial and geographic form. As the film's title indicates, the story is centered on the narrative voice of one young man, Oumarou Ganda, who plays himself yet goes by the name of Edward G. Robinson (in a conscious nod to US filmic ascendency) since he is fearful of revealing his real identity as an undocumented Nigerien migrant in Ivory Coast. The other major character in the film, Robinson's roguish friend, goes by the name Eddy Constantine or, alternatively, Lemmy Caution, a self-styled "*agent fédéral américain*."[26] During the week the migrants look for work and do whatever odd jobs they can find, and on the weekends, we see Rouch's protagonists going to the beach, practicing boxing, and flirting with girls in Treichville's bars and nightclubs.[27] The film presents the colonial city of Abidjan as a metropole in its own right and as a logical destination for young economic migrants from other French colonies: in the voice-over that opens the film, Rouch explains, "[These young people] have abandoned school or the family domain in order to try and enter the modern world. . . . These young people, caught between tradition and mechanization, have not given up their beliefs but are devoted to the modern idols of boxing and cinema."

FIGURE 2.2 A modern American cowboy adorns the wall of a neighborhood bar in Treichville.

Rouch and his narrators, though, are careful to remind us that city life for these migrants also draws heavily on French and US modernities. Thus, for example, Robinson presents Treichville as "the Chicago of black Africa," and Rouch's camera makes a quick succession of cuts to various storefronts whose names link Treichville's modernity to French and American cultural referents: we see the Chicago shoe repair shop, a restaurant called A la Ville de Paris, a clothing store called Aux St. Germain des Prés and another called the Boul' Mich, a hair salon called Hollywood, and a cowboy painted as a mural on the wall of a local business.

In a similar vein, when we see Robinson at boxing practice, the name on his training jacket reads "Edward G. Sugar Ray Robinson," in a humorous concatenation that has absorbed the name of the American boxer Sugar Ray Robinson. Thus, the "modern life" to which Robinson and his compatriots must adapt themselves is simultaneously local, in that Abidjan is a cosmopolitan metropole in its own right, and always already triangulated, since the ideas and ideals of modernity travel transatlantically among West Africa, France (specifically,

Paris), and the United States. The inclusion of an idealized America here in addition to France is telling, for it signals the imagination of modernity both in terms of and beyond the colonial relationship. Robinson captures this ideational triangulation in his introspective postsynchronized narrative, which offers a mixture of ethnographic thick description and impressionistic reflections on his return from Indochina where he fought and lost with the French army.

In *La pyramide humaine*, modernity appears less as an object of cinematic wonderment than as one of narrative wish fulfillment. The film presents its social and political context with an immediacy that we would be hard put to recognize in either *Jaguar* or *Moi, un Noir*. At Rouch's behest, his high school students adopt personas that are accompanied by divergent positions on racial integration and the colonial situation writ large: the Europeans grow more or less racist according to the demands of their roles, and their African classmates in turn become stridently anticolonial or, alternatively, more willing to engage in dialogue with the French and move beyond the racial tensions that have long prevented the two groups from socializing outside of school. Rouch provokes this role-playing by asking his question about the possibility of postracial friendship and by introducing the character of Nadine, a wide-eyed ingénue fresh off the plane from Paris with whom all the boys fall in love and who tries to bring her fellow students together while negotiating complex new social relations in an Africa where the colonial edifice has already begun to crumble.

As the European and African students attend parties together and develop closer ties, the film opens up the story of Nadine's initiation into the cultural politics of late-colonial modernity: ethnographic didacticism surges to the thematic forefront here as Denise, the most outgoing of the African students, teaches Nadine about how colonial racism operates in everyday life. Thus, she explains to Nadine that when Europeans off-handedly use the familiar *tu* form with Africans they do so derisively, and Nadine ends up remarking, "I learned that there's racism in Abidjan, too." Denise links this initiation to broader discussions of apartheid and colonial ideologies in Africa, and the film's political context intersects with the specifically cinematic social life created by Rouch's camera. In this respect, as Rouch points out early in the film, *La pyramide humaine*'s documentary imperative is not to "reflect" reality but to "create another reality" through cinema, one that would end up becoming meaningful in the nonfilmic real world. In *La pyramide humaine*, then, modernity refers both to the fraught actuality of the late-colonial period and to the possibilities for thought experiments this historical moment creates and that enable the film's characters to imagine themselves beyond it.

Rouch's theory of modernity and his protagonists' struggles with and adaptations to modern life are elaborated most provocatively on the level of filmic and ethnographic narrative. The sort of modernity these films enact is not limited to the geographies Rouch traces in the peripatetic shots he constructs while following his actors around the dusty streets of Treichville or the bustling market at Kumasi, teeming with prospective vendors and consumers. The kind of modernity at play here is instead characterized by how Rouch's protagonists locate themselves within the cultural space that they occupy along with the ethnographer. While in *Jaguar* modernity is conceptually linked to adventure, storytelling, and the aestheticized adoption of colonial urban chic, Robinson's translation of US and French modernities into the cultural idiom of cosmopolitan colonial Abidjan in *Moi, un Noir* is anything but uncritically celebratory. The thrust of Robinson's commentary is to highlight his isolation and despondency despite modernity's undeniable appeal. Likewise, in *La pyramide humaine* modernity straddles the film's tense political backdrop and the imagined, idealized, and experimental social relations produced within the bounds of Rouch's ciné-réalité. In all these cases, modernity depends on how Rouch's characters account for themselves narratively according to storylines prompted, but not entirely determined, by the ethnographer's interests.

Modernity in these early ethnofictions holds together several disparate emotional registers. To take one example, on several occasions Robinson proudly and jokingly suggests ways in which Treichville's residents are modern like Americans (in relation to the number of cars wrecked regularly in both places,[28] or in his observation that nightclub dancers are just like cowboys), but these rather ambitious assertions are undercut by his almost obsessive references to his sadness at his proletarian status and to his desire to consume the products of a capitalist modernity that, he realizes, must keep him on the outside looking in. On the contrary, in *Jaguar* the heroes dabble in the cosmopolitan colonial capitalism that attracts migrants to the Gold Coast from throughout West Africa, only to return home to Niger penniless and happy, having either sent home all their earnings or given them away in the form of presents. In this earlier film, the question of proletarianization, which plays such a prominent narrative role in *Moi, un Noir*, is for the most part unthinkable. Robinson's distress, by contrast, is compounded by the fact that he understands all too well that he is more acutely aware than others of his relegation to the very margins of the colonial economy.

The vision of modernity produced within and among these three films is thus different from Paul Gilroy's notion of a modernity that travels throughout the black Atlantic world and relies on a Du Boisian double consciousness that holds in tension national identities and transnational (read, transatlantic) modes of subjectivity.[29] Although Rouch's modernity does look at the black Atlantic world from intensely local perspectives in West Africa, his sense of the modern is predicated on a different idea of the transnational from the one Gilroy developed in his well-known theory of overlapping racial ontologies expressed in the "roots/routes" formulation. The modernity created in Rouch's ethnofiction fosters affective forms of transnational and transcultural identification, in which the modern is less linked to the problem of national identity. Instead, it does double duty as both a triangulated ideational beacon and as the referent for a fraught cultural present wherein the truly modern remains within reach only as a cinematic ideal type.

The complicated historical present of Rouch's modernity is certainly echoed in *The Black Atlantic*'s analysis of black political culture as in but not necessarily of the modern West (and we can read Robinson's distress as expressing the same concern); however, his broader theory has more in common with a later formulation of Gilroy's, one that he elaborates in *Against Race*. "Although it is not acknowledged as often as it should be," Gilroy suggests, "the close connection between 'race' and modernity can be viewed with special clarity if we allow our understanding of modernity to travel, to move with the workings of the great imperial system it battled to control."[30] This later idea is not so caught up in questions of national identity and "roots" and instead, like Rouch's theory, urges us to conceive of the modern as a concept whose racialization depends on its ability to shift and travel within an imperial/colonial network in which West Africa is an important node. In Rouch's case, this even holds for *La pyramide humaine*, which does not thematize travel as such but allows modernity to move from the actually existing present to a cinematically utopian alternative present—this shift is inseparable from the types of reality Rouch declares his film to mobilize. Where Rouch diverges from Gilroy is in his highlighting of the transnational and the transcultural as primarily affective categories, whether in the case of cosmopolitan colonial cool or in that of friendship ties forged beyond the strictures of colonial racial tensions.

Ethnographic fiction traces modernity's spatial and affective cartography through storytelling, and as such Rouch's films offer a narrative unpacking of modernity similar to the ideological unpacking of the concept that Fredric Jameson has performed. Jameson begins from the elaboration of four maxims that place modernity as a concept in a seemingly endless dialectical series of alternating breaks and periods that elucidate both contemporary repackagings of the modern and the narrative gears that keep the concept of modernity running. In so doing, his project is as much revelatory (insofar as it unveils the narrative underpinnings of modernity) as it is methodologically prescriptive, since it functions as a "recommendation to search out the concealed ideological narratives at work in all seemingly non-narrative concepts."[31] In the context of Rouch's ethnofiction, Jameson's second maxim of modernity is especially illuminating, since his critical work leads him to consider modernity a rhetorical effect and a trope that is inherently susceptible to rewriting, dislocation, and defamiliarization.[32] According to this maxim, modernity "is not a concept, philosophical or otherwise, but a narrative category."[33] This formulation dovetails with the theory of modernity that Rouch develops in his early ethnofiction, since what Jameson calls the rewriting of the trope of modernity is recast in these works as filmic restagings of everyday negotiations of the modern through purely contingent forms of improvisation and fictional free play.

A Rouchian rewriting of Jameson's maxim might take the form of another methodological question: if modernity is a narrative category, what happens when we place it simultaneously in the service of documentary and fictional narrative imperatives that bring together both realist exposition and spontaneous invention? This phrasing rightly conjures up images of playful experimentation, since so much of Rouch's oeuvre consists of cinematic thought experiments developed and carried out collectively with the people he filmed. Thus, the narrative staging of modernity we see in these films is produced at the point of conjuncture between narrative improvisation (including a dialectic of narrative voices) and collaborative participation in ethnographic praxis conceived of as a shared knowledge game. Rouch's restaging of the modern is an often racialized narrative operation of rewriting (or "refilming," as it were) that is created experimentally and improvisationally and relies on a geographic triangulation of modernity's spatial coordinates. For Rouch, this rewriting operation is also inseparable from his method of shared anthropology, a sort of mise en abyme of ethnography and of its epistemological projects and aspirations that proceeds through feedback loops between ethnographer and subject such that anthropological authority is continuously and dialogically displaced.

Critical work on Rouch's cinema has remained sensitive to the convergence in his filmmaking of the seemingly divergent impulses of fictional cinema and conventional documentary realism.[34] The blank canvas offered by fictionality (or the fictionalization of reality) is what allowed Rouch to use ethnography to gain critical purchase on the most pressing issues facing post–World War II West Africa—namely, emerging social forms produced by increasing urbanization, the end of European colonial rule, and the still very real instantiations in everyday life of colonialism's attendant racist ideologies. Even though Rouch was not a militant filmmaker in the same way as René Vautier, for example, this critical purchase is also political purchase. What lends these films the pressing, immediate import that is lacking in his earlier and shorter films on spirit possession or hunting is the fact that modernity here is not only thematized but narrativized, such that the modern becomes an object of anthropological-political inquiry by banding together with fiction.[35] These are narratives of modernity that serve simultaneously as documentary exegeses of colonial encounters. This twofold enterprise is a profoundly collaborative undertaking for Rouch, and since his experiments with genre provoke us to engage with him as a thinker of modernity (the "director of modern life," we might say, à la Charles Baudelaire and Walter Benjamin[36]), we must also view the production of narratives of the modern as of a piece with the development of collective forms of participation in what, following Pascale Casanova, we might call the "world republic of anthropology."[37]

Improvised Narratives and the Powers of the False

The collaborative impetus in Rouch's ethnofiction seeps into the level of the films' conditions of production, moving from the thematics of modernity as a broad cinematic plotline to the construction of individual shots and scenes. It is on this level that Rouch and his actors create cinematic experiences of the modern in everyday life, provocatively deploying and rearranging filmic narrative building blocks that inflect the sense of fictional storytelling that underpins Rouch's initial approach to ethnofiction generally. His scenes are permeated by this collaborative aesthetic, which lends them a playful, often joyous cast, imbued as they are with off-camera laughter, good-natured ribbing, and humorous asides. And yet, just as often, they pleasurably disorient viewers and dislodge expectations about the straightforward communication of ethnographic narratives. Improvisation and postsynchronization do crucial work for the rapprochement Rouch effects between anthropology and fictional filmmaking. Additionally, such cinematic elements as camera movements, voice-overs, and improvised commentary betoken the ways in which fiction and ethnography for Rouch rely to a large extent on the proliferation of voices within a film, voices that often challenge, misdirect, or outstrip that of the professional anthropologist. This polyphonous filmmaking thus acts as a conceptual hinge linking Rouch's ethnographic methodology to the turn toward a fictional aesthetic in his own cinematic oeuvre. Put another way, this hinge appears to serve a provocatively paradoxical function in his early ethnofiction: it allows fictional elements to sustain each film as an ethnographic documentary at the same time that it forces the spectator to acknowledge the ways in which fiction can be born of the very messiness of everyday life that conventional ethnographic realism takes for granted.

In *Jaguar*, the fictional imperative goes far beyond the simple fact that, although they are playing themselves, Lam, Damouré, and Illo are characterological distillations of the Nigeriens Rouch met while undertaking his more quantitative research in the Gold Coast. This tension allows for a good deal of improvisational play in the film, and the three heroes incessantly switch back and forth between the characters they are playing on screen and their post-synchronized commentary or metacommentary. These moments of narrative slippage occur throughout the film and highlight how the ethnographic and the fictional slide into one another and become indistinguishable. In other words, by endlessly reiterating the founding tension of the film, the protagonists point at all turns to the fluidity of the generic categories with which Rouch is concerned.

These reiterations begin quite early in the film, once Rouch has introduced his characters via voice-over and set the stage for the long journey from rural Niger to the Gold Coast. Rouch's camera follows Lam the cattle herder around the market in the Nigerien town of Ayorou as he goes to meet Damouré who is sitting under a tree filling out tax forms for illiterate townspeople. Continuing his voice-over, Rouch tells us that it is under this tree that they all decided to leave for the Gold Coast. As Lam and Damouré shake hands, they verbally greet each other in "real time," as in conventional filmic narrative ("How are you doing, Lam?" Damouré inquires of his friend.). Immediately thereafter, however, Damouré begins explaining to the viewer what he is doing in the scene, thus departing from the very narrative conventions he has just established: "Now we're writing . . . So, I read over the tax form and I earn ten francs, fifteen francs . . . Look, for example, at this family man. He has to pay a fifteen thousand eight hundred-franc tax. Well, man, he's rich! He has a lot of cattle!"

The narrative has shifted here from real-time filmic dialogue to descriptive commentary that explicitly takes advantage of postsynchronization in order to formulate observations about the footage on the screen.

Another shift occurs in quick succession, since after voices from the crowd around Damouré grumble that there is no money to pay taxes, Rouch's voice-over returns to confirm these remarks before nudging the narrative along: "But, next to our tree are the card-players," he observes as the camera cuts to a card game going on nearby. "[These are] young people who have left for Kumasi. The ones we dream of imitating . . . we, too, must leave." On the face of it, the return of Rouch's voice-over at this early moment does not come as a surprise, since he has been providing introductory commentary (albeit with little in the way of general contextualization, which is not his style) since the beginning of the film. What does surprise the viewer, though, is that Damouré responds to Rouch without missing a beat: "Oh yeah, we have to go, right? To the Gold Coast, we have to go, right?" he interjects, insistently and excitedly. The anthropologist's voice-over, which often preserves its authority by standing above and beyond the filmic narrative, is drawn into the immediacy of the scene when Damouré responds to Rouch and agrees with him.

In just under a minute, then, the film's mode of narration has moved between several different registers. What begins with a more or less "objective" introduction, in which Rouch sets the scene for his viewers without giving too much away, shifts to the narrative real time of the film as two of our heroes greet each other before Damouré takes it upon himself to engage in a bit of ethnographic commentary of his own—he does so by retrospectively discussing the scene via postsynchronization. Rouch's voice-over returns, only this time his ethnographic authority is undercut: not only because he uses "we" (nous) and so includes himself among the group of travelers, but also because Damouré actually responds to him and bridges the gap between filmic real time and postsynchronized commentary which takes place in a different filmic present altogether. An important way in which the fictional imperative operates for Rouch is by confronting the viewer with a proliferation of filmic presents that are all equally valid but that cannot fit together seamlessly, and the viewer cannot help but register this curious narrative simultaneity. For Rouch, fiction enters the ethnographic film through these temporal seams.

In *Moi, un Noir*'s opening sequence, just before the opening credits, the camera locates Robinson at night, standing beneath a sign marking the entrance to Treichville, and Rouch's voice-over explains that the film deals as much with Robinson's self-discovery as it does with any ethnographic portrait of everyday life as an economic migrant in Abidjan. Like many of Rouch's voice-overs in this and other of his films, it exudes a matter-of-fact narrative authority that cannot but be self-effacing when compared with the far more engaging richness and thoroughness of his characters' reflections.[38] Robinson's improvised and contingent narration takes place not only in an introspective tone, however; it is actually tripartite: in addition to looking inward, especially when referencing his profound sadness concerning his precarious condition as a day laborer at Abidjan's docks (yet another fictional element of the film, since Oumarou Ganda was employed full-time as Rouch's research assistant at the time of shooting), his narration is also dialogic—or apostrophic—and ethnographic-descriptive, such that the viewer wonders who the "real" anthropologist in the film actually is. *Moi, un Noir* revels in and thrives on this constitutive uncertainty.

These intertwined narrative registers make their presence felt in two of the film's early sequences: in the first, Robinson returns to Treichville by ferry, unsuccessful in his search for work, crossing the river that divides this newer neighborhood from the city's relatively wealthier commercial districts. Robinson begins by telling viewers that he is getting into the boat to return to "his" side of the river, in perfect, one-to-one narrative correlation with the footage running on the screen. During the ferry trip, Rouch juxtaposes a close-up shot of Robinson's face with a wider-angle shot of a modern, two-story building from the side of the river our hero has just left. In the transition between these two shots, Robinson improvises and comments on how hard his life is because he has so little money and cannot afford to live "closer to God" in a multistory building. The shift in this early sequence is striking: at the beginning Rouch's images appear to provide Robinson with easy content for his narrative (i.e., he is boarding the ferry and narrates accordingly), but in the juxtaposition of the close-up and the shot of the modern commercial building there is nothing that inherently lends itself to Robinson's commentary on class and labor in colonial Abidjan. This sequence unites our first and third narrative registers, the introspective and the ethnographic-descriptive. What is more, the spectator does not experience moments like this one as simple concatenations of technical minutiae, for sequences such as these pull spectators in two directions at once: one is drawn into Rouch's rich documentary footage while being called on, at the same time, to process a narrative that corresponds to those images without necessarily arising organically from them.

A second early sequence illustrates the dialogic and apostrophic register: it features three- or four-second shots of other Nigerien laborers who, we learn, are Robinson's friends. In these shots Robinson greets his friends and says a few words to each in turn—however, Robinson himself is nowhere to be seen. In fact, he is taking advantage of postsynchronization to apostrophize friends who are "present" only in filmic instantiations, and even then only after the fact. This narrative register is inseparable from the problem of *Moi, un Noir*'s temporality: if Robinson uses his narration to produce ex post facto dialogues that are in no way given by Rouch's images, when exactly is the narrative present of the film?

Such a temporal break between represented filmic space and the narrative strategies that only appear to coincide with it is part and parcel of what Gilles Deleuze (in a chapter of his second volume on cinema, in which Rouch's work plays no small analytic role) calls "crystalline narration." Deleuze repeatedly deploys the figure of the crystal (crystal-image, crystalline description, etc.) not only to illustrate the collapse of various organic sensory-motor linkages in the cinema, but also to point to the indistinguishability of the actual and the virtual, the real and the imagined, in the direct, pure presentation of time. The types of spaces that correspond to crystalline narration "cannot be explained in a simply spatial way. They imply non-localizable relations. These are direct presentations of time."[39] These direct presentations are not, for all that, straight-forward; on the contrary, in the direct time image "we no longer have a chrono-logical time which can be overturned by movements which are contingently abnormal; we have a chronic non-chronological time which produces move-ments necessarily 'abnormal,' essentially 'false.'" What this assertion implies for Deleuze's broader argument is provocative and helps to unearth another layer of fiction in Rouch's work: since crystalline narration implies that time is "out of joint," it is a form of narrative that relies on what he calls "the powers of the false."[40] This implies not the existence of different types of truths but, rather, in a nod to Leibniz, the proliferation of presents coupled with the multiplication of undecidable alternatives for the past.[41]

Thus, to return to Robinson's second short sequence, although he and his Nigerien friends are objectively real individuals, they exist in presents that are incommensurable, the one visual and the other purely verbal, and the nar-rative that holds them together is ultimately "falsifying" since it functions to preserve this incommensurability. The same can be said of the sequence from the beginning of *Jaguar*: in less than a minute, and with only one cut, the purely visual present of the film (i.e., the immediate visual image, insofar as it can be considered in isolation from the types of sound that complement it) is crisscrossed by any number of spoken presents that approach each other, cut each other off, and advance the story of the film without any one of them ever taking the narrative reins for good. Aside from the obviously fictional elements in the stories of these films writ large, the shots and scenes are constructed from falsifying narration whose fictional powers make it difficult to decide between present and past and difficult to determine whether Rouch or Robinson controls narrative progression.

These powers of the false rely to a great extent on such contingent audiovisual linkages, and the same holds true for Rouch's characters' relationships to their own blackness and the ways in which colonial subjectivity appears as a narrative-ontological category inflecting their relationships to modern life. Even in the more properly anthropological aspects of these ethnofictions, Rouch's protagonists make scant mention of their relationships to France and their status as black colonial subjects or, in the case of the European students in *La pyramide humaine*, to their privileged positions in the upper reaches of the colonial social hierarchy—in *La pyramide humaine*, it is precisely Nadine's bewildering naïveté in the face of the colonial encounter that serves as one of the principal narrative problems to be resolved. The characters often refer only obliquely to French colonization as such, but the tumultuous, almost postcolonial context of these films nonetheless weighs heavily on their documentary storylines. The presence of the hexagon and the colonizer-colonized relationship haunts the symbols of modernity that make up the characters' most immediate experiential referents—for example, when Robinson and one of his friends are shown loading sacks of coffee on a ship bound for France, the former matter-of-factly remarks that the products are destined for metropolitan consumption and then proceeds into a more personal ethnographic commentary, saying, "For us, this is what life is like: sacks. The life of sacks." These sacks of coffee stand in synecdochically for the inevitably racialized colonial relation par excellence, but Robinson's frustrated utterance encourages us to take him strictly at his words and observe his acute awareness of the relationship between his own alienated labor and his participation in the increasingly globalized networks of modern colonial capitalism.

Likewise, this curiously detached or depersonalized relationship to colonial capitalism appears in *Jaguar* when Lam leaves Accra to sell robes in the countryside and meets a friend, Douma, who works with other West African immigrants in one of the country's many gold mines. The narrative of the film is bracketed at this point in favor of a roughly five-minute sequence in which the three heroes, with the help of Douma, comment on footage Rouch has taken from a ramshackle mining village and from down in the mine itself (footage also used in *Les maîtres fous*), before the story abruptly resumes and we learn that Lam has convinced Douma to work for him as a porter instead of risking his health and life in the mine. During this interlude, in which Rouch's characters fully assume the roles of ethnographic commentators, we observe Douma and other miners descending into the mine, where workers produce gold ingots to be exported to Britain. Damouré remarks that the gold is destined for safes in London, and Lam interjects, exclaiming, "It's to screw you over (*couillonner*)!" As Rouch's camera cuts to a wide shot of the mine and the lush countryside, Damouré continues in the same register: "Exactly, the English have screwed over the Africans. They come to take away their gold and then that's it, they bring it back home."

Thus, although the protagonists engage in a direct critique of colonial exploitation, this rhetorical move is accomplished through several degrees of remove: the characters are not commenting on a scene in which they are involved personally (indeed, during the entire sequence none of them appears on screen), and because of this it is rhetorically impossible for them to engage in a critique of specifically French colonialism, even though decolonization was just beginning when the commentary was recorded. Further, they do not insist that this economic relationship is necessarily cast in an explicitly racialized mold and instead allow the spectator to infer colonial racism from their damning treatment of the transnational gold economy.

Lam, Damouré, and Illo do not suffer direct encounters with colonial racism in *Jaguar*, despite the fact that British colonization and Ghana's transition to independence (complete with shots from political rallies and from Kwame Nkrumah's swearing-in ceremony as leader of the newly independent state[42]) punctuate the otherwise playful and adventure-filled narrative. A rather incongruous improvisational moment does bring blackness and racism to the forefront, however, and serves as an ephemeral contextualizing reminder that, in spite of the freewheeling innocence that characterizes much of the film's storyline, we are dealing with social actors and social relations that cannot be extricated from colonial histories and structures of power.[43] The question of how to produce context and, by extension, of how to formulate an ethnographic narrative with the spectator explicitly in mind is one Rouch tackles only occasionally, and even then he often does so through subtle winks, jokes, or half-truths. Brief moments of contextualization in Rouch's work are thus always overdetermined.

After the three adventurers arrive in the Gold Coast, they go their separate ways, and Damouré takes a job with a timber firm in Accra. He starts as an unskilled laborer, but thanks to his quick wit and literacy, he is swiftly promoted to the rank of *chef d'équipe* (foreman). From one shot to the next, Damouré goes from pushing wagons and counting planks to donning ridiculous oversize sunglasses and letting what little status he has go straight to his head. He is beginning to "play the gentleman" (*faire le galant*), he explains (an important step in becoming a thoroughly modern jaguar), and Rouch's camera cuts to him upbraiding a group of workers who are standing around instead of loading wood into a wagon. He sarcastically shouts, via postsynchronization, "It's me who's in charge! Look out! This cart isn't loaded, it's impossible, my God! What! You can't work with Negroes!" The smiles on the workers' faces in Rouch's footage contrast sharply with Damouré's racialized improvisational remarks, and it is not entirely clear whether he is voicing European colonial bosses or African *évolués*, or perhaps both at once. This distinction, though, is less important than the observation that this brief moment pushing racism and blackness to the thematic foreground links an act of narrative contextualization to the improvised production of affect (i.e., mock anger and mimetic silliness).

This moment acts as a sort of narrative catharsis, since it finally allows the film's colonial context to burst forth from where it had been lurking just beneath the surface.[44] The racialized production of affect, which for Rouch ties improvised narration to the colonial encounter, takes on a more explicitly political tone in *La pyramide humaine* and a darker and more intensely personal tenor in *Moi, un Noir*. Toward the end of *La pyramide humaine*, some of the students leaf through the day's newspaper in their classroom and their discussion of current events prompts Denise to comment again on the South African situation and on the fact that nobody in Abidjan seems to be talking about recent repressive violence in the country.

Rouch's camera focuses on Nadine at the beginning of this scene, panning upward across the top of her downcast head while she intently reads the article about apartheid violence. With her characteristic inoffensive innocence belying her role as catalyst of discord in the film, she asks her friends how the Ivory Coast government is going to respond to the situation. Nadine's question initiates a frank conversation about colonial politics, the only moment in the film in which the narrative of postracial friendship intersects with the colonial situation on its broadest level.

In true ethnographic-didactic fashion, Denise begins by explaining to Nadine that Ivory Coast is represented by France at the United Nations and that both France and Britain deem the state-sponsored violence in South

FIGURE 2.3 The Abidjan high school students discuss the colonial situation while Nadine takes in the debate.

Africa an internal matter. Denise loses her trademark even-temperedness at this point and remarks that France should vehemently condemn the South African government's crackdown on protests against pass laws, to which another of the African students, Bacchus, replies that the violence the French colonial state is currently perpetrating in Algeria precludes them from doing so. Denise continues by sketching the history of colonial racism in South Africa for Nadine before Elola, an African student standing behind her, makes a more synthetic pronouncement about the situation: "The Europeans who came to Africa, they applied a principle: divide and conquer—you all know this." The Africans shout down Alain's critique of their Pan-Africanism ("Take an interest in your country first," he says) before the scene abruptly shifts away.

It would be all too easy to conclude that we as viewers should take away from this scene the idea that angry outbursts of political affect have somehow frayed the students' nascent friendships. However, the rather utopian idea of postracial friendship that constitutes *La pyramide humaine*'s experimental point of departure is not intended to function as an apolitical idyll. The new forms of friendship on display here make the production and, crucially, the communication of political affect possible in ways that (we are given to understand) might not be thinkable outside the confines of the film's thought experiment. In fact, since this is the moment in Rouch's early ethnofiction in which colonialism as a political and philosophical strategy is put forward most nakedly, imaginative cinematic wish fulfillment becomes the only vantage point from which blunt contextualization of these films' colonial backdrops can be expressed.

The narrative confluence of race and affect becomes more troubled in *Moi, un Noir*. At first glance, it may seem odd that the protagonist of a film with such a title does not describe his relationship to his own labor (e.g., at the docks in the sequence discussed earlier) in explicitly racialized terms. *Moi, un Noir*, however, was not the original title of the film. Ganda and Rouch originally intended to make a film called *Treichville* (or, according to Paul Henley, *Le Zazouman de Treichville*[45]) and later agreed to change the title.[46] This anecdote about the post hoc racialization of the film's title throws into stark relief the moment late in the film when Robinson actually does assume his blackness as a narrative and ontological category. Given the highly localized nature of the film's subject matter, it is perhaps unsurprising that Robinson's encounters with colonial racism writ large are few and far between. Indeed, the only significant incidence of racism occurs toward the end of the film, when a white Italian man (played by André Lubin, Rouch's French sound technician, and postsynchronized with the voice of the Italian ethnographic filmmaker Enrico Fulchignoni, in yet another playful fictional move by Rouch[47]), full of promises of cash, moves in on the beautiful Dorothy Lamour while Robinson is wooing her at a nightclub. The Italian leaves with Dorothy after racially abusing Robinson, leaving Robinson to sulk in front of his beer until he runs out of money. The next morning Robinson, still visibly drunk, pounds on the door of Dorothy's house, only to be chased away by the Italian after more insults and after the two men exchange blows in the dirt, a fight scene characterized by extremely short point-of-view shots in which Rouch's camera and Robinson's narrative consciousness are momentarily fused together for the only time in the film.

This sequence does not so much illustrate a coming to (racial) consciousness, as the film's title might have us suggest, as it acts as a vehicle for the creation of affect: this is the moment in the film in which Robinson's blackness explicitly occupies his narrative consciousness, and it is surely no coincidence that after this moment, for the remaining ten minutes of this seventy-minute film, his narrative becomes noticeably angrier. It is as if the emergence of blackness as Robinson's narrative focal point offers him a moment of catharsis: it is only after this encounter with European racism that he is able, in the final sequence of the film, to speak about his childhood in Niger and the violence of the colonial war in Indochina, where he fought with the French. The French were ungrateful for his service and left him in the most precarious of positions in Abidjan.

In short, while blackness does appear in the film as a narrative category that is contingent on Robinson's chance encounter with the Italian, this contingency appears inextricably tied to the affective register of his narrative, in which expressions of anger and sadness at being left out of modernity's idealized grand narrative of progress (which he desperately tries to consume, to which his Americanized moniker attests) have been present since the beginning. In a similar vein, the moment in *Jaguar* in which Damouré tries to "play the gentleman" and mock colonial racism by performing whiteness and making a spontaneous joking remark about "*les nègres*" allows the colonial context of the film to unveil itself while remaining congruent with the affective tone of the three migrants' humorous improvised ethnographic commentary. Race and affect appear to mediate and hold contingency and necessity together, without letting either pass over into the other, as two sides of the same narrative coin. In other words, treating race cinematically and improvisationally as an affective question functions to balance contingency and necessity in productive narrative tension. The narrative give-and-take that produces and relies on such profound moments of filmic collaboration also raises a significant question concerning methodological approaches to fieldwork and ethnographic filmmaking: in what ways do methodological meditations resonate, determine, and intersect with restatings of modernity as a contested narrative category?

Shared Anthropology and Collaborative Productions of the Modern

Ethnographic fiction for Rouch is resolutely improvisational in its spontaneous embrace of contingency; it is also a self-consciously collective enterprise. Rouch's documentary film making more generally is an aesthetic venture that always already implicates thorny matters of cinematic representation and

FIGURE 2.4 Rouch watches footage with his high school students in Abidjan.

politically tinged problems of anthropological knowledge production. To bring these problems to the fore, Rouch places the question of collaboration at the methodological and thematic heart of so many of his films. Indeed, *Chronique d'un été* and *La pyramide humaine* actually contain scenes in which the informants/actors informally discuss with Rouch how various improvisational roles will be played, how sociological and anthropological fieldwork might be represented on-screen, and, at the end of the films, which improvisational approaches worked for the actors and which worked less well.

In *La pyramide humaine*, Rouch appears on-screen meeting with both European and African students before roles are distributed and experiments in postracial friendship begin.[48] This reflexive impulse takes an especially striking metafilmic form later on, just after the students debate Pan-Africanism and colonial politics in the classroom: as Alain struggles to get his critique across amid the shouts and angry dismissals of his African peers, the sequence suddenly cuts to Alain watching himself on-screen, visibly disconcerted by and absorbed in his own performance. The students and Rouch are now in a darkened room watching the rough cut, and Rouch's voice-over returns at this point to explain that at the screening each student "discover[ed] an un-known image of himself. Fiction thus becomes reality." The camera pans around the room, focusing on each student in turn, as well as on Rouch sitting among them, as his voice-over continues, reminding us that the friendships that began as cinematic thought experiments have now extended into the real world: "Now, everything is possible." The cinematic and fictional creation of real relationships provokes Rouch to throw a final spanner in the works—he decides to have Alain drown in the ocean—and he reminds viewers that this make-believe dramatic turn becomes all the more real once it is filmed. This is the case precisely because *La pyramide humaine*'s collaborative ethos has filtered through into the extra-filmic everyday life that shooting has created.

Collaborative and metafilmic techniques such as these both enable and encourage us to link Rouch's treatment of modernity and modern life in his early ethnofictional films to his relationship to the *auteur* figure in cinema. In the 1940s and 1950s, this term was deployed as a way to aesthetically paper over the multiple forms of expertise that went into making films, as well as the stylistic flexibility of the best directors. From this point of view, the auteur is an imaginary figure (or, at the very least, an overblown and overdetermined one) concealing the collective conditions of production and possibility of cinematic texts.[49] Rouch's films, and especially his ethnofiction, both allude to the auteur figure (who adopts the role of the European ethnographer exercising his authority through such techniques as voice-overs) and thoroughly undermine his heuristic efficacy by highlighting their intensely collective conditions of possibility. To view Rouch's relationship to the auteur this way is to translate into filmic language his methodological commitment to shared anthropology, a polyvocal ethnographic undertaking that sought to redefine the hitherto passive role that conventional ethnographic "objects" played in anthropological knowledge production.[50]

Thus, while the manifold types of contingency at work in *Jaguar*, *Moi, un Noir*, and *La pyramide humaine* illustrate Rouch's playful, improvisational, and carefree approach to filmmaking, they also raise the related methodological question of this doctrine of shared anthropology and its implication in the production of a narrativized modernity. Two photographs that appear in a collection of Rouch's newspaper writings from his first three research trips (1946–51) offer pictorial representations of his collaborative ethnographic methodology: in them, Rouch has his back to the camera, facing a group of Nigeriens of all ages from the village of Wanzerbé, and is filming the slaughter of a young white bull.[51] The photographs were taken by Damouré Zika, who was Rouch's informant and research assistant at the time and who would go on to star in *Jaguar* and appear in many of Rouch's films as the two developed a lifelong friendship. He would also publish a diary, serialized in 1956 in *La Nouvelle Nouvelle Revue Française*, recounting his travels and work with Rouch throughout West Africa in the early 1950s, in another example of Rouchian-inspired reflexivity.[52] These pictures, then, not only represent a collaborative imperative in research and fieldwork, according to which ethnographic "others" can produce anthropological knowledge. They also represent a mise en abyme of anthropology as such, since the research practices of the (Western) ethnographer are always already caught up in feedback loops that subject these practices to the scrutiny of those (non-Western) objects of the ethnographic gaze.

Another anecdote—one Rouch loved to recount in interviews—is especially poignant in this regard: in 1951, Rouch shot *Bataille sur le grand fleuve* (1952), a film about Sorko hippopotamus hunters in Niger, and inserted a traditional hunting song that played at the moment of the great chase. Two years later, when he returned to the village where the film was shot and screened it for its participants, the chief of the hunters demanded that the music be removed on the grounds that hippopotamus hunting must take place in absolute silence. Rouch duly complied and cut the music from the film.[53] Thus, even an "authentic" aesthetic flourish was undercut by this imperative to allow Rouch's research subjects to determine the form taken by the filmic knowledge produced about them.

Such a formative moment early in Rouch's career evinces the extent to which he was able to depart from Dziga Vertov's conception of the camera as an apparatus capable of absorbing and making coherent the entirety of social life. Vertov's 1920s Soviet film collective was called the Kinoks, from the Russian *kino-oki* (cinema-eyes). In an early manifesto, Vertov defined these Kinoks as "organizers of visible life."[54] Rouch's vision of shared anthropology, by contrast, does not grant the same kind of organizational priority to the camera lens. If for him the camera is an ethnographic agent provocateur in the sense that its presence is capable of setting off social situations that might not otherwise occur (in fact, this is in some ways the central cinematic premise of *La pyramide humaine*), then it does not follow that the camera alone is able to organize and capture social life taken as a totality. As Rouch explained about his relationship to the Soviet master, Vertov's cinéma vérité directly implicated film in the creation of Truth, whereas his rereading of Vertov relativized

Vertov's absolutism, seeing cinema as designating not a totality but "the particular truth of the recorded images and sounds—a filmic truth (*ciné-vérité*)."[55] What Faye Ginsburg has referred to as Rouch's cultivation of a "parallax effect" in his productive process forestalls any easy totalizing perspective.[56] Rather, Rouch's experimental and improvisational style wonders what kinds of representations might be produced if the anthropologist's camera divested itself of some of its authority and entered into dialectical and dialogic relationships with the people being filmed. This emphasis on relationality is why the camera must never remain hidden, as it was for Vertov, as Rouch told the Dutch filmmaker Philo Bregstein in the documentary *Jean Rouch and His Camera in the Heart of Africa* (1986).

Scenes from *Jaguar* and *Moi, un Noir* offer provocative filmic instantiations of how these relationships operate within a commitment to anthropology as a shared epistemological enterprise. In the first, Rouch's characters take on the roles of ethnographers as they journey on foot to the Gold Coast and create a parody of anthropological representations of so-called exotic cultures. This sequence is in keeping with Rouch's ongoing fascination with reverse ethnography, in which traditional ethnographic others become ethnographic knowledge producers or study Western societies in ways that caricature conventional anthropological research methods. In the second, the compelling final sequence from *Moi, un Noir*, Robinson finally vents his spleen at his treatment by the French army and at how he feels abandoned after returning home from Indochina. These scenes open up a productive avenue for illustrating how Rouch's ethnographic fiction, as a hybrid genre composed to no small degree by narrative negotiations of colonial encounters, reorganizes participation and belonging in anthropology as an academic discipline.

As we have seen, the characters played by Lam, Illo, and Damouré make their way southward to the Gold Coast as much for modest economic gain as for the possibility of adventure and the collecting of experiences to be recounted upon their eventual return to Niger. Their postsynchronized commentary allows for the narrative production of micronarratives, adventurous vignettes the boys make up on the spot to impress their friends and relatives at a later date. This generation of second-order narratives also enables our heroes to play the role of anthropologists who provide ethnographic narrative commentary on the various groups of social actors with whom they come into contact during their travels: these groups range from Hausa merchants from Nigeria in the Kumasi market to members of Kwame Nkrumah's Convention People's Party at a rally in support of their leader. One of the boys' more

FIGURE 2.5 Damouré strips down and "goes native" on the boys' journey down to the Gold Coast.

poignant encounters, though, occurs early in the trip when they cross into northern Dahomey (contemporary Benin) and enter the lands of the Somba. As Rouch's camera cuts to a group of huts with tall, conically shaped roofs, Lam exclaims, "They've got houses like mice there!" Damouré jumps in to explain that he learned in school that the Somba do not wear clothes, and the three protagonists dissolve into hysterical laughter when Lam walks up a ladder to meet an elderly man and remarks with embarrassment, "I see something down there, white white white," in reference to the man's white penis sheath. This exoticizing commentary reaches its high-water mark when Damouré tells Lam that the bloody bones attached to the huts are fetish objects, finally prompting Lam to say that although he has heard about the Somba, now that he sees them, he "isn't sure that they're people."

Imputing a conscious critique of Western colonial ethnography's often dehumanizing rhetoric to the improvised comments of the film's three heroes risks engaging in our own sort of retrospective anthropological wish fulfillment. Nonetheless, the parodic effect of this sequence is hardly lost on viewers, since Rouch's footage and its accompanying commentary see his ethnographic "others" negotiating an encounter with their own others. The sequence undergoes a marked shift in tone, however, and what began as an exoticizing set of observations morphs into a primer on cultural relativism: as Rouch's footage of his protagonists meeting the naked Somba continues, the three suddenly agree that "when you arrive in a country, it's the country that changes you. It's not you who changes the country." This is a reversal of the colonial process. As Damouré finishes explaining this principle, Rouch's camera cuts to a shot of him nearly naked: always the showman, he has stripped down to his underwear to accommodate himself to his hosts' culture.

Several shots of varying length follow of dancing at a Somba market before Damouré closes the discussion on relativism: "Lam and Illo, you see, it's not because they're naked that we should make fun of them. God wanted them to be like that. Just like where we live, God wanted us to wear clothes. . . . They're brothers like us." The fraternal note on which this sequence ends encourages us to read it as a narrative of what an idealized anthropological encounter might look like to Rouch, since skepticism and dehumanization make way for the expression of transcultural affect. Such an approach would certainly be consonant with Rouch's propensity for filming improvised idealizations of fraught social relations, as the utopian premise of *La pyramide humaine* indicates so well. Overemphasizing this perspective, however, risks obscuring the fact that his filmic representation of an idealized anthropological encounter involves the transformation of ethnography's traditional objects into active, knowledge-producing ethnographic subjects.

This question of how anthropology films itself is a crucial one for Rouch, even if it is not always explicitly thematized. In many of his films, it is inseparable from the question of ethnography understood as a collaborative enterprise that often requires Africans looking back at the Westerners who have traditionally studied them. In *Petit à Petit* (1971), a sequel to *Jaguar*, for instance, a much older Damouré flies to Paris to conduct a crudely caricatured sort of fieldwork to ascertain how Parisians cope with living in skyscrapers, in moves inspired by Montesquieu's *Lettres persanes*.[57] Thus, naturally, he accosts passersby in the street, taking cranial measurements and counting teeth, in a hilariously awkward parody that harks back to colonial anthropology's roots as a racist pseudoscience while reminding contemporary viewers of the best (or worst) of reality television.

Manthia Diawara, for his part, imagines himself to be reenacting Damouré's fieldwork trip as he flies to Paris and meditates on reverse ethnography from a meta-anthropological point of view in his documentary *Rouch in Reverse* (1995).[58] In a similar vein, some of Rouch's African friends from Ivory Coast join him in Paris for the filming of *Chronique d'un été* and provide reverse ethnographic commentary on French modernity while working with a research team interviewing ordinary Parisians and asking the question, "Are you happy?" What these examples have in common with the sequence from *Jaguar* is that they demonstrate how, for Rouch, the filmic representation of anthropology is both framed by and in dialogue with the ethnographic gaze of those whom anthropology has hitherto conceived as passive objects to be studied. Visual anthropology, then, "succeeds" as an epistemological endeavor only if it produces its own mise en abyme at the same time that it purports to document the everyday lives of social actors through the medium of film. Whereas the sequence from *Jaguar* elucidates this process at the level of content, the compelling final sequence from *Moi, un Noir* addresses this complex anthropological relationship through the dialectical relationship of narrative form between Rouch and Robinson that reaches its dramatic crescendo at the end of the film.

In this closing sequence, it emerges that Robinson's friend Eddy Constantine, the *agent fédéral américain*, has been thrown into prison for three months for fighting with the police. After paying him a visit, Robinson and his friend Petit Jules stroll along the shore of Abidjan's lagoon. Robinson asks Petit Jules to imagine the lagoon as the Niger River passing through the country's capital, Niamey, and after a fictionalized flashback (which doubles as an ethnographic dream sequence, since Rouch has obviously spliced in footage shot in Niger[59]), he reminisces about fighting in Indochina in a narrative turn that is suddenly grim and dark. He remarks bitterly, "I've done everything, everything, everything, everything, everything, but nothing has helped me." The scene progresses with Robinson acting out the part of a soldier, launching imaginary grenades, crouching in imaginary bunkers, and going into graphic detail about the carnage he has witnessed. "I've seen blood flow," he tells Petit Jules while running his hand across his neck; he has seen comrades blown to pieces two meters from him (he mimics the explosions); and he mentions how he has killed Vietnamese. Whether this commentary is intended as a sort of confession or as so much on-camera braggadocio is impossible to discern and, at any rate, is unimportant relative to the broader point that both the form and content of his rhetoric in this sequence are not consonant with his narrative style before the intensely racialized encounter with the white Italian

FIGURE 2.6 Robinson plays dead on an imaginary battlefield during his walk with Petit Jules.

man—an encounter that was provoked by Rouch, who always enjoyed playing the directorial gadfly.[60]

The scene is crucial because in it we can observe quite clearly the narrative dialectic that makes *Moi, un Noir* such a profound collaborative experiment, a dialectic whose terms (Robinson's spoken narrative and Rouch's cinematic-technical narrative) are held together in uneasy tension in the totality of the sequence. Once again, it is entirely unclear just who is taking the narrative reins here: on the one hand, Rouch himself has remarked that for much of this sequence he was shooting without any cutaways or connecting shots, which gives viewers the impression that he is trying to catch up to his protagonist and follow his narrative lead.[61] On the other hand, when Rouch finally does cut away to a shot of a European water-skier whizzing by in the lagoon, affording viewers precious respite during a remarkably tense sequence, Robinson interrupts himself to catch up to Rouch's image and comments on it accordingly.

Between these two narrative moments that more or less bookend the sequence in question, Robinson's narrative and Rouch's technical flourishes coincide for several seconds with the introduction of gunfire and explosion sound effects (seemingly out of place in an ethnographic documentary) that match up with Robinson's description of shelling and battle in Indochina. Taking into account that the only other moment in the film when Rouch uses artificial sound effects is when he overlays shootout-style gunfire—akin to what we find in Western and gangster films—onto his early shot of a cowboy mural on the wall of a Treichville storefront, Robinson's "performance" in this sequence is of a piece with the forms of modernity that function as such important cultural referents for all of *Moi, un Noir*'s protagonists. Similarly, the only moment in *Jaguar* in which Rouch incorporates sound effects is during a long point-of-view shot from the perspective of Damouré, who has hitched a ride on a truck as he makes his way to Accra. Already showing signs of the cool, jaguar persona he will soon be adopting, Damouré triumphantly looks out as he stands in the bed of the truck while Rouch cuts to footage of Ghanaians on the side of the road (another moment of spliced-in wish fulfillment) and we hear the sounds of a raucous crowd fade in as a sort of imaginary welcome for his protagonist. From this perspective, the artificial sound effects, coupled with the point-of-view shot taken from atop a truck, liken Damouré to the modern politician who travels around his country currying favor with the populace.

In the important final sequence of *Moi, un Noir*, Robinson is not only (or not simply) rewriting the trope of modernity in his image. Such an observation undoubtedly has merit, but it does not tell the whole story; we must go further and posit the question of the relationship between cinematic modernity, which Robinson both consumes and produces, and anthropological knowledge production, of which Robinson (the research subject) is the object and (as improvised narrator) the subject. Rouch's theory of shared anthropology is preoccupied with converting notions of co-authorship, reflexivity, and self-criticism into the epistemological sine qua non that allows anthropology—understood as a circular process of knowledge production—to take place. In fact, these were important components of Rouch's ethnographic methodology long before they took center stage in ethically tinged debates about the politics of representation and anthropology's disciplinary complicity with colonialism that were played out in significant texts such as the now canonical *Writing Culture*, edited by James Clifford and George Marcus, or the earlier collection, *Anthropology and the Colonial Encounter*, edited by Talal Asad.[62]

To speak of fictional restagings of the narrative of modernity in the same breath as anthropology conceived as a collective epistemological enterprise is to posit the question of disciplinary belonging in much the same way that Pascale Casanova raises the problem of literary belonging in her "world republic of letters." World literary space is a realm that contains forms and structures of domination that are wholly proper to it, a zone that is semi-autonomous from, yet inextricably linked to, actually existing political and national spaces. One consequence of this semi-autonomy (which is also a semi-heteronomy) is that there is often some degree of overlap, especially in countries that have experienced colonialism, between literary domination and linguistic dependency. "Literary domination" here refers to enforced aesthetic distance from the norms established by a literary center that holds the powers of consecration and defines what is "modern."[63]

Complicating this model would involve teasing out certain possibilities for consecration in this relationship of literary domination and would involve writers from dominated literary spaces engaging in a form of translation or conversion, transforming their aesthetic dependence into legitimacy and recognition. "To criticize established literary forms and genres because they have been inherited from colonial culture," argues Casanova, "misses the point that literature itself, as a value common to an entire space, is not only part of the legacy of political domination but also an instrument that, once reappropriated, permits writers from literarily deprived areas to gain recognition."[64] The observation of this striking ambiguity, which goes some way toward accounting for how writers from spaces with few literary resources force their way into world literary space, opens up a provocative parallel with Rouch's method of shared anthropology. This shift takes shape, for instance, in the number of Rouch's actors and research subjects who went on to work in African cinema, including Oumarou Ganda, who helped to internationalize West African cinema, had his first feature shown at Cannes in 1968, and completed four films before his death in 1981.[65] Other Nigerien associates who made names for themselves in African film include Moustapha Alassane, who made the first African-produced western, and Moussa Hamidou, who trained in sound recording in Paris and subsequently worked on films by both Alassane and Ganda.[66]

In Rouch's own films, his anthropological method simultaneously evinces narratives of cultural difference as well as metanarratives that reveal the blind spots of these first-order ethnographic knowledge claims. This occurs both during significant moments of critique, such as when Rouch's actors demanded the removal of music from his film about hippopotamus hunting or when our protagonists from *Jaguar* take a parodic look at the anthropological encounter, and in more subtle instances of dialectical back and forth, as in *Moi, un Noir*'s dramatic crescendo or during the film screening scene in *La pyramide humaine*. Thus, one implication that arises from the analogy established with Casanova's formulation is that just as writers from literarily (and often politically) dominated spaces, writing in dominant languages, struggle to earn what she calls "literary capital," so do individuals in anthropologically dominated spaces (such as French colonial Abidjan in the 1950s, or even Africa more generally) earn what I would call epistemological capital. They do so by using ethnographic fiction to become anthropological knowledge producers—for example, in how Robinson narrates in tandem with Rouch to create a film about his and his friends' lives in Treichville and to discuss angrily his war exploits, and in how Damouré explains to viewers precisely what it means to be a modern "jaguar" in colonial West Africa. What becomes clear, then, is that this production of epistemological capital by ethnographic "objects" through narrative techniques such as the ones developed in Rouch's ethnofiction serves in effect to determine what kinds of knowledge a European ethnographer may produce about them.

Although Rouch's shared anthropology allows for the production of new filmic reiterations of the trope of modernity, his approach does not offer any methodological panacea that would finally settle venerable and thorny debates within anthropology about the politics and ethics of "responsible" fieldwork. Inasmuch as shared anthropology became an explicitly elaborated research strategy for Rouch, it still leaves important problems unaddressed. For instance, in his writings on the subject, Rouch does not adequately tackle the loaded problem of authorship in collaborative anthropology; however, he does point out that the medium of film contains radically democratic possibilities that would allow the Third World to speak back to the West using the West's own technical innovations.[67] In this respect, ethnographic film for Rouch contains within itself the prospect of a visual and epistemological utopia to which fiction affords him special access. There remains, in addition, the matter of thinking through Rouch's own entanglement with colonialism: he began his career in West Africa as a colonial engineer, overseeing indigenous African laborers, and Ousmane Sembene famously critiqued what he saw as Rouch's entomological approach to African social life. Rouch and Sembene loved to have a go publicly at each other: while for Sembene Rouch's documentaries ended up "insecticizing" Africans, for Rouch the Senegalese master was a vulgar Marxist whose politics ideologically blinded him to the realities of everyday life. Yet, as Diawara has suggested, Sembene's socialist realism relies on the convergence of documentary and fictional perspectives (we need only consider his early short film *Borom Sarret* or the aerial shots of street scenes in *Xala* as examples of this point), so the two filmmakers share more generic and aesthetic common ground than either perhaps would have cared to admit.[68]

Whatever the blind spots that contemporary narratives of the history of African cinema have highlighted in Rouch's work, they are not necessarily at odds with Casanova's formulation that has such strong analogical ties to his vision of anthropology's disciplinary space as one that can be occupied via the creative reappropriation of the very tools used to erect the boundaries of that space in the first place. As an extension of Casanova's metaphor, if we can follow her model and speak of a "world republic of anthropology," we can also observe how Rouch's ethnographic method allows for the development of citizenship in this republic through the accumulation and use of epistemological capital by those who traditionally have been only the objects of anthropological forms of knowledge production.

In a passage from *Cinema 2* dedicated to the fictional poetics of the invention of collectivities in Third World cinema, Gilles Deleuze writes, "It may be objected that Jean Rouch can only with difficulty be considered a third world author, but no one has done so much to put the West to flight, to flee himself, to break with a cinema of ethnology and say *Moi, un Noir*."[69] Although I have not sought to propose that Rouch be rehabilitated or retrospectively integrated into histories of Third World or African cinema (or written into narratives of its modernity, to stay within the idiom of this chapter's approach to ethnographic fiction), the context of this passage is entirely consonant with the avenues I have explored in this chapter. Deleuze is concerned here with the ways in which both Rouch and his "real" characters become other in a seemingly endless proliferation of stories—an observation that incorporates Godard's praise of Rouch's work, and specifically *Moi, un Noir*, into Deleuze's conceptual universe.

Although it is characteristically provocative, there are two ways in which Deleuze's comment appears to be only half correct. On the one hand, Deleuze does not account for the ways in which the narratives in Rouch's ethnofiction belong in many ways as much to Rouch's amateur protagonists as they do to the professional ethnographer himself. As I have argued in this chapter, this collaboration, which occurs on the level of narrative form as well as on that of narrative content, is what allows Rouch and his actors to restage the trope of modernity by imagining a decolonized anthropology at an uncertain historical moment when the meaning of decolonization in the French empire was up for grabs. This operation of restaging relies on geographic forms of identification that are always already triangulated among the US, France, and Africa (cultural repositories, places to be borrowed from selectively and strategically in a playful syncretist free-for-all) and on reimaginations of histories of France's decolonizing present. Restaging decolonizing modernity for Rouch is thus a provocative exercise in imperial countermapping that results in ludic documentary forms that reshape the geographies and histories of empire.

On the other hand, making our way back to Deleuze, his comment misses the notion that this operation of restaging, which relies on an improvisational aesthetic, creatively decenters the production of anthropological authority. This does not occur because Rouch "breaks" with ethnographic cinema, in strict terms. His turn to ethnofiction was anything but a rupture; it was, instead, a way to identify anthropology's fictional potentiality and draw it out as far as he could using the language of documentary narrative.[70] The creative decentering of authority occurs because, for Rouch, fiction allows ethnographic cinema to sow the seeds of its own creative reappropriation. In other words, this gesture asks: How does anthropology look when its documentary thrust traffics in transcultural fictions? In what way is fiction deeply enmeshed in ethnographic realism, and how does this immanence expand realism's epistemological purview? Finally, why do anthropological narratives of colonial encounters call for extra-anthropological aesthetic strategies that come to function as representational reinforcements for the documenting of those encounters?

These are central questions Rouch's ethnofictions raise that reflect and inflect the broader interventions I make in this book. For Rouch, anthropology's transcultural fictions require a passage through visuality: in his visual imagination, fiction creatively distorts and subverts the expectations that viewers bring to screen-based ethnographic narratives. It does so by visualizing and narrativizing collaborative ethnography—as I have shown in this chapter, this is one way in which ethnographic realism may reveal its relationship with fictionality. Collaborative approaches to empire accommodate both terms of this relationship and allow us to refocus ethnographic film in terms of orthogonal narratives that imagine themselves both within and beyond the confines of imperial polities. In Rouch's ethnofiction, then, the classic representative tenets of visual anthropology, with its neat distribution of knowledgeable ethnographic subjects and passively photogenic ethnographic objects, give way to a speculative, decolonized ethnographic fiction that blends collaborative documentation with cinematic storytelling, and playful dissimulation with realist epistemologies.

Chapter 3

Folklore, Fiction, and Ethnographic Nation Building

Price-Mars, Alexis, Depestre, Laferrière

For just as the unsettled appearance of this Haitian valley conceals numerous habitations, cultivated fields, and hard-working inhabitants, so the frenzy of Haitian religious rites is but a gloss upon disciplined ceremonialism, and the relatively placid everyday existence of the Haitian peasant but a mask behind which is waged a spiritual conflict that is his heritage from the dual sources of his traditions.
—MELVILLE HERSKOVITS, *Life in a Haitian Valley*

[The nation] is that part of the historically derived cultural repertoire that is translated in political terms. . . . The nation is not a political fiction; it is a fiction *in politics*.
—MICHEL-ROLPH TROUILLOT, *Haiti: State against Nation*

The Haitian anthropologist Michel-Rolph Trouillot wrote the words with which I open this chapter in a book on state power under the dictatorships of François Duvalier and his son, Jean-Claude, tracing the origins of Duvalierism back into the nineteenth century and through the nineteen-year American occupation of Haiti, from 1915 to 1934.[1] Trouillot conceptualizes the nation (distinct from the state) as the outcome of a conversion, as the aggregate of those elements of cultural production that can be rendered communicable only according to a political grammar. His subsequent claim revises a key point made by Benedict Anderson and holds that the nation is not inherently a political community. Rather, it becomes one in the actualization of its imaginary underpinnings.[2] We can understand Trouillot's two interrelated ethnographic claims in a way that is both more literal and more literary. First, to view the nation in these translational terms is to adopt an approach that is at once ethnographic and aesthetic—rethinking the nation as the political expression of culture does not necessarily detextualize it. Second, we can take Trouillot's formulation literally and see the nation as bringing literary fiction into the ambit of politics. This chapter takes these two observations and draws out their generic resonances and implications, investigating how Haitian ethnographic fiction is inscribed within aesthetic and anthropologically inspired debates on the nation and its imagined futures.

Writing just over fifty years before Trouillot, the American anthropologist Melville Herskovits published his thoughts on the unexpected syncretic complexity of Haitian folklore and religious traditions in the introduction to his ethnography *Life in a Haitian Valley* (1937).[3] Herskovits was fascinated by African cultural "survivals" in the New World, and at the behest of the Haitian ethnographer, physician, and diplomat Jean Price-Mars, with whom he had been in touch since 1928, he carried out fieldwork in the village of Mirebalais, east of Port-au-Prince, in the summer of 1934.[4] Herskovits was deeply influenced by Price-Mars's book *Ainsi parla l'Oncle* (1928), in which the Haitian scholar argued for the valorization of his country's folk traditions (in particular, peasant Vodou religious practices) and for the uniqueness of its blend of European and African cultural influences, the latter of which could be identified and analyzed through careful Africanist ethnohistorical investigation and critical dialogue with European anthropology. As we will see, *Ainsi parla l'Oncle* was a major theoretical force behind the development of Haitian ethnographic fiction.

The remarks on the concealed complexity of Vodou traditions that constitute this chapter's first epigraph are significant in two respects: first, they point toward an abiding interest in the early twentieth century among European and American ethnographers and travel writers in Haitian folk religion, interest captured in books ranging from the luridly primitivist (e.g., William Seabrook's infamous *The Magic Island* [1929]) to the scholarly and serious (e.g., *Life in a Haitian Valley*; Zora Neale Hurston's *Tell My Horse: Voodoo and*

Life in Haiti and Jamaica [1938]).[5] Second, at the time that Herskovits was undertaking his field research, the Haitian government and officials representing the US occupation had been trying for years to eradicate so-called superstitious practices among the peasantry in campaigns that paradoxically fueled ethnographic interest in Vodou.[6] This latter point reemerges later in the context of my reading of Jacques Stephen Alexis's novel *Les arbres musiciens* (1957).

Read together, Trouillot's and Herskovits's comments trace links between fiction and folklore, between popular religion and aesthetic nation building. These two anthropologists did not have Haitian ethnographic fiction in mind at the time of their respective reflections, but the constellation of issues they identify also preoccupied writers who experimented between anthropology and fiction throughout the twentieth century. This chapter examines how twentieth-century Haitian writers (Alexis, René Depestre, and Dany Laferrière) transformed the nation into a self-reflexive epistemological project, creatively distilling prescriptivist experimental impulses from more conventional early texts that interrogated the boundary between ethnography and fiction. From this perspective, Price-Mars's early transatlantic ethnohistory comes to spur new national epistemologies expressed by and in the novel. More broadly still, the chapter examines how anthropology can be used to reassemble the nation in fiction and how alternative ethnographic knowledge can be translated into literary form. It situates the postcolonial nation as a product of orthogonal thinking about imperial histories and lived experiences and beyond the epistemological terms those histories and experiences can offer.

Studying Haitian ethnographic fiction in a transatlantic context requires a different kind of historicizing work from what we saw in the first two, Africanist chapters of this book. There, ethnographic fictions were enmeshed in late-colonial social forms that were beginning to give way to early decolonizing upheavals. This New World context, however, forces us to confront imperialism on different terms: twentieth-century Haiti was a French postcolony, but for figures such as Price-Mars, France remained present through the elite's undue deference to French and European cultural norms. This more insidious imperial presence coexisted with the American occupation, which was eventually followed up by dictatorships of Duvalier *père* (1957–71), tolerated by the US for his anticommunist politics, and Duvalier *fils* (1971–86), who spent a quarter-century in exile in France after his ouster in 1986. The ethnographic-fictional conversation begun under the occupation by Price-Mars posed the question of how to textualize and aestheticize national renewal within and beyond this historical matrix of domination (imperialism, postcolonialism, and state repression). For several of the writers I study here, this involves tapping into the creative potentiality of exile. As Martin Munro highlights, exile has served as a powerful literary impetus for extending the space of Haiti beyond its geopolitical boundaries.[7]

In this chapter, ethnographic fiction is part and parcel of projects of national (re)writing. National literature appears here not only as the epistemological endgame of the geographically triangular perspective Price-Mars sought to valorize; it is also a continuous interdisciplinary project that historicizes itself through anthropology. This historical and cartographic extension imagines the relationship between national literature and anthropology as one of radical naturalization: in its historicizing gestures it hypothesizes this relationship as given but goes on to remix and defamiliarize its key terms to raise questions of national futurity. Thus, what begins as anticolonial transatlantic anthropology expands and morphs into novelistic projects that embrace and transform the histories with which they converse.

Jacques Roumain's *Gouverneurs de la Rosée*

Although Price-Mars's *Ainsi parla l'Oncle* set in motion a century-long conversation about national renewal, anthropology, and fiction in Haiti, this is not the only text that serves as a touchstone for Haitian ethnographic fictions. Jacques Roumain's *Gouverneurs de la Rosée* (1944) is also invested in rewriting the nation in terms of ethnographic knowledge.

Roumain's posthumously published *Gouverneurs* is one of the most impactful and best-known Haitian novels of the twentieth century. Its focus on national renewal via an idealization of folkloric collective identity makes it a foundational text of Haitian ethnographic fiction. Roumain studied at the Institut d'Ethnologie in Paris in the late 1930s and continued his ethnographic and literary training at Columbia University before returning to Haiti and founding the country's Bureau d'Ethnologie in 1941 in collaboration with Price-Mars, who created the teaching-focused Institut d'Ethnologie that same year.[8] In addition to *Gouverneurs*, Roumain wrote ethnographic studies and collections of poetry (which, Depestre has argued, deserve to be included in Roumain's anthropological oeuvre[9]). Fascinated by peasant folklore and Vodou, he helped the Swiss anthropologist Alfred Métraux conduct fieldwork on Vodou that led to Métraux's study *Le vaudou haïtien* (1958) and published the results of his own fieldwork as *Le sacrifice du tambour-Assôtô(r)* (1943). The first edition of Roumain's short "peasant story," *La montagne ensorcelée* (1931), contained a preface by Price-Mars, and a later edition carried one by Alexis. Indeed, Alexis would go on to fictionalize Roumain as the character "Pierre Roumel" in his novels. Thus, during his short life (1907–44), Roumain moved between ethnography and fiction—although he did so less playfully and more overtly politically than Jean Rouch, as we saw in chapter 2—in ways that resound in the work of later Haitian writers.

Gouverneurs thematizes a humanist (and Hegelian, in Jacques André's reading[10]) renewal of the nation through a narrative retreat to the Haitian countryside, to which the protagonist, Manuel, returns after working on a plantation in Cuba, to find his family and their fellow villagers struggling to survive during a severe drought. Ecological catastrophe meets demographic disintegration as rural villagers begin to leave for larger towns, threatening the future reproduction of this agrarian community. Manuel is murdered by a jealous romantic rival but succeeds posthumously in mending old feuds and converts the atomized peasant community back into the organically collective society it should always have been, facilitating an ambitious community irrigation project, to the consternation of the local authorities.[11]

Roumain's rural Haiti exists both inside and outside history. On the one hand, it is connected to the global forces of production of the time: the isolated peasant community acts as a reserve of cheap labor for enterprises outside Haiti, such as the American-owned Cuban plantation where Manuel works. Labor migration here generates networks of transnational solidarity, as Manuel returns home full of inspiring stories about striking sugarcane workers that help galvanize the Haitian peasants' resolve. On the other hand, though, Roumain's rural community is contained in a timelessly and transhistorically pastoral village essence: before Manuel's arrival and his importation of socialist humanism, the only event that seems to periodize the lived history of his community is the deforestation undertaken by the villagers that exacerbates their ecological crisis. Before this crisis set in, communal work among the peasantry reproduced the community's cultural and social cohesion.

Roumain's narrative sets this historical ambiguity alongside cultural exposition. He punctuates the novel with dialogue in Creole and descriptions of folk beliefs and Vodou ceremonies. On several occasions, he interrupts his ethnographically realist narrative to address an imagined foreign reader in ways that echo Amadou Hampâté Bâ's ethnographic didacticism, examined in chapter 1: "Friend, you do not know the Mahotière spring? That's because you aren't from these parts, brother. . . . You leave behind the huts and the gardens and following the gentle slope, you arrive at the gully."[12] Roumain's sense of ethnographic realism calls attention to itself when he highlights the phenomenology of peasant folklore and religion and when he breaks the fourth wall of the text. But these moments appear ancillary to the broader socialist concerns that drive Roumain's realism: ultimately, he is too interested in creating a politically prescriptive narrative to allow his ethnographic interests to outshine the novel's collectivist thrust.

Thus, in spite of Roumain's didactic impulse, his text is not written in the experimental vein that characterizes so many of this book's most striking ethnographic fictions. Although it mobilizes local knowledge, this epistemological drive feeds into the novel's socialist prescriptivism so directly that it does not interrogate its own ethnographic conditions of possibility in the same way that later, more reflexive Haitian novels will. For this reason, in spite of its political desires, the novel lacks the speculative edge of many ethnographic fictions (and even of the earlier *Ainsi parla l'Oncle*).

We could phrase this point differently, though, and argue that while *Gouverneurs* does contain a measure of speculation, it points to political futures rather than to alternative knowledge projects that reimagine both textual and social forms. Roumain's novel ends just as his villagers' collective action returns water to their community, and we as readers are given to understand that this event inaugurates a new sense of socialist historical time for the peasantry. But by the same token, the return of water marks the community's return to itself, its social reproduction assured now that ecological damage and individualist atomization have been reversed. Political futurity here means Roumain's Haitian peasantry coinciding with what it always was, and this circularity or restoration allows his realism to remain self-identical in the end. In short, Roumain's ethnographic realism inspires socialist futures without the more thoroughgoing kinds of alternative anthropologies that I privilege throughout this book.

As we will see, later writers often return to or nod toward Roumain's seminal work of Haitian ethnographic fiction, at times knowingly remixing its thematic concerns. The more obviously experimental and speculative Haitian ethnographic fictions require this kind of referentiality, since the operation of rewriting loops literary production back into past narratives of the nation and into older anthropological knowledge projects. This acute sense of continuity allows writers to pose the nation as a reflexive ethnographic assemblage without thereby fetishizing a discourse of exceptionalism.[13] For Price-Mars, though, to whom I now turn, the early twentieth-century nation was already an ethnographic assemblage—one created from the alternative anthropology he sought to trace.

Price-Mars's Haiti: The Nation as Ethnographic Public

Haiti had long since been under American occupation when *Ainsi parla l'Oncle* was published in 1928. But by 1917, Jean Price-Mars was giving talks that traced US imperial domination in Haiti back to slavery, tying life under American "pseudo-colonial" rule (as J. Michael Dash puts it) back to Haiti's integration into the French empire.[14] Price-Mars broke up this transcolonial continuity in striking fashion in *Ainsi parla l'Oncle*, which seeks to convince the Haitian elite to divest themselves of their uncritical preference for all things French in matters both aesthetic and racial—what he famously called the elite's "collective bovarysme." In this broad ethnohistorical study, Price-Mars rewrites the nation in terms of an alternative anthropology of black cultural practices.

During the rule of François "Papa Doc" Duvalier, Price-Mars disavowed the authoritarian Negritude that composed the racial-political nucleus of the dictator's ideology. He also repudiated his youthful intellectual development as a member of the Griot movement in Haiti; this movement offered an authoritarian current of black cultural nationalism that emerged from indigénisme.[15] Yet it is easy to see how Price-Mars's ethnographic nationalism might have been steered toward rigidly dangerous political ends. Price-Mars viewed himself as the intellectual heir to the late nineteenth-century Haitian scholar Anténor Firmin, whose *De l'égalité des races humaines* (parenthetically subtitled *"anthropologie positive"*), published in 1885, refuted the pseudoscience of the French writer Arthur de Gobineau's *De l'inégalité des races humaines* (1853–55) and argued for "real, effective, civil, and political" liberty for the black race, "in Haiti and elsewhere."[16] Price-Mars's *Ainsi parla l'Oncle* was also a transatlantic refutation, this time of the French sociologist Gustave Le Bon and his social-psychological study of racial typologies *Les lois psychologiques de l'évolution des peuples* (1894). Le Bon actually suggested to Price-Mars that he write a book about Haiti in an admission that his racist conclusions might have been erroneous.[17]

Price-Mars made his name during the American occupation, and his book *La Vocation de l'élite* (1919) takes Haiti's ruling classes to task for lacking the necessary nationalist will to prevent any loss of autonomy. *Ainsi parla l'Oncle* further develops this argument and seeks to cultivate a national sense of self that would draw the elite away from cultural identifications with France, pushing them toward an appreciation of local cultural and religious practices and their African antecedents. In the opening lines to the collection of ethnographic essays, Price-Mars reveals that he has "long since harbored the ambition to raise, in the eyes of the Haitian people, the value of its folklore."[18] Such a didactically nationalist goal sets the tone for this sweeping study of the African roots of Haitian Vodou and folk traditions. Although "the people" appear as the object of Price-Mars's ambitions, his book is primarily concerned with offering the elite an ethnographic way out of their cultural aping of French and European values. Anthropology, from this point of view, functions as an epistemological antidote to the "collective bovarysme" that prevents local knowledge from fostering national cohesion. Further, anthropology is capable of creating a public—an ethnographic community of readers and writers—that understands and appreciates the singularity of the Haitian people and Haiti's cultural indebtedness to Africa.

Price-Mars's thinking ultimately constructs an ideal literary public that could respond productively to an ethnographic theory of literature, and his anthropological and nationalist goals depend on the very materiality of the book he set out to write. The written text plays a role that is at once generative and intermediary: it calls on the nation as a community of readers (even though this community is largely imagined) and simultaneously constitutes the nation as object and subject of ethnographic study, over and against the epistemologically dubious accounts written by American travelers for eager audiences back home. Beyond the valorization of folklore, the existence of the published book makes space for the post-slavery nation, on its own epistemological terms, in what in chapter 2 I called the "world republic of anthropology."

In elucidating the main epistemological goal of his ethnographic study, Price-Mars explains that "all the material in this book is but an attempt to integrate popular Haitian thought into the discipline of traditional ethnography."[19] This work of integration is as much an exercise in didactic nationalism (i.e., anthropology put to the careful pedagogical task of demonstrating why national unity should exist) as it is a reasoned corrective to the lurid pseudoscientific travel accounts of Haiti and Vodou and to early American interest in zombie tales.[20] Following the anthropological goals Price-Mars sets for himself at the outset of his book, then, we can observe that Haitian nationalism is for him a particularly powerful social-scientific assemblage. From this perspective, it is

not enough to locate the epistemological roots of the nation in folkloric practices, although Price-Mars's ethnohistorical analyses do precisely that. What
he ultimately points to is the textual construction of Haiti on the scene of ethnographic writing (a strategy similar to the one used by Édouard Glissant in
his appropriation of the social sciences in *Le discours antillais*, as we see in
chapter 4). Thus, the valorization of Haitian folklore in *Ainsi parla l'Oncle* is
of a piece with the imagination of a literary public that is, at the same time, a
national public and an anthropological one.

Just as interesting as Price-Mars's main chapters, which present a rich set
of back-and-forth movements between the religious tenets of Vodou in Haiti
and the African social practices he holds are their Old World referents, is
Ainsi parla l'Oncle's introduction, which, like any ethnographic text worth its
salt, sets forth a methodology. Price-Mars tellingly refers to this as a "comparative ethnology" that identifies certain Haitian religious practices and seeks
out their African analogs. These comparisons are set in an evolutionist theory
of culture, as "older" religious practices from less civilized societies made their
way across the Atlantic during the slave trade and survived into Haiti's syncretic present. What does this evolutionary perspective mean for Price-Mars's
anthropology? The genealogical imperative he establishes, regardless of how
we might evaluate it from a contemporary perspective, highlights how Haitian Vodou is both unmistakably African and uniquely autochthonous. This
methodology is invested in grand comparisons between civilizations perceived to be at different and unequal evolutionary stages, situating Price-Mars
closely in relation to nineteenth-century English and American anthropologists (such as E. B. Tylor or Lewis Henry Morgan) who sought to account for
how "primitive" peoples might represent so many living fossils displaying the
stages of development of Euro-American civilization.

At the same time, however, this methodology is bent on highlighting the
indigenization of practices whose African heritage accentuates rather than
diminishes their uniquely Haitian constitution. For René Depestre, this indigenization of African survivals is what makes Price-Mars "the first Haitian
innovator of the movement of ideas that was to take the name of *Negritude*."[21]
"Survivals" constitute singularity. The methodology also points to how Price-
Mars strives to endow Africanist epistemologies with localized referents, putting down roots in the Caribbean that other Negritude writers missed in favor
of a much broader perspective—this is one critique of Negritude made by
Martinique's *créoliste* writers, to whom I turn in chapter 4. The fact that Price-
Mars ties together comparison and indigenization allows him to go beyond

anything concluded by his nineteenth-century ethnographic forebears. Comparison ends up doing double duty, then: initially, it locates Price-Mars in an anthropological genealogy that looks backward, one concerned with civilizational hierarchies and evolutionary chronology located in embodied and verifiable cultural traits.

This sort of comparativism, however, has more pressing and immediate ramifications, since it resolutely seeks to put anthropological knowledge of Africa in the service of developing an understanding of Haitian religious phenomenology and lived experience. As Price-Mars reminds us time and again, such a comparativism is unthinkable for the Haitian elite. And this distinction is crucial for his focus on Haitian oral traditions. As he points out, his anthropological project responds to (and, in many ways, is written for) Haitians who are poised to make the most productive use of his comparative ethnographic knowledge. The figure of the "native anthropologist" looms large here and stands as a social-scientific foil to untrained foreign travelers who might write sensationally and "authoritatively" about Haiti.[22]

Acknowledging what he calls a "struggle" between different sectors of society (which turn out to be ordinary Haitians in opposition to the European-facing elite), Price-Mars writes that his interest in folklore stands in dialogue with the minds of the masses. "Those on the bottom," he suggests, "adapt themselves with the utmost simplicity to the juxtaposition of beliefs and to the subordination of the most recent beliefs to the most venerable and thus manage to obtain a most enviable equilibrium and stability."[23] He goes on to write that the upper classes, by contrast, are too stunned and humiliated by African-based folkloric genealogies to appreciate how they both determine and evince distinctively Haitian cultural practices. Here Price-Mars seems to take the onus of the development of Haiti's "national character" off the elite and locate it in the everyday syncretic beliefs of ordinary people. This is the closest Price-Mars comes to being the Marxist that Depestre, writing in *Bonjour et adieu à la négritude* (1980), wants to find in him but who in the final analysis is not really there.[24]

This class division, or class "struggle" if we want to play on Depestre's perspective, facilitates what Price-Mars imagines as the potential consumption of the anthropological knowledge he produces: the syncretic ethnographic public he both calls on and wants to create can for him be only the most ordinary Haitians. Hence, a fundamental tension runs through Price-Mars's work: in texts such as *La vocation de l'élite*, he addresses Haiti's ruling classes, appearing to write for and in terms of their weaknesses and blind spots while simultaneously iterating and reiterating the argument that the question of national identity lies outside their grasp.[25] In *Ainsi parla l'Oncle*, national unity is folded into an ethnographic public that exists only as pure potentiality.

It follows from this constellation of folkloric and class-based concerns that Creole-language folktales are for Price-Mars of inestimable richness. The Creole language displays the same syncretic qualities of adaptation and assimilation that he finds in everyday religious practices, so it is unsurprising that he characterizes it as possessing a "power of creation."[26] This creative linguistic impetus, imbued with the ethnographic powers of syncretism, is what bridges the gap between folk beliefs and traditions, on the one hand, and literature, on the other. Indeed, one of the founding questions of the text has to do with what we might call the ethnographic axiology of such a connection: "If . . . this folklore exists, what is its value from a dual literary and scientific point of view?"[27]

In terms of language, Price-Mars expresses this mediating function in a series of opening questions that deserve to be cited in their entirety for the way in which they allow him to arrive at an ethnographic conception of Haitian fiction. He asks, "Is Creole a language from which we might extract an original literature by which the genius of our race could be consecrated? Must Creole become one day the Haitian language like there is a French, Italian, or Russian language? Starting now, can we use it for pedagogical applications the same way, in solving a problem, we use known terms to arrive at the discovery of other terms in operation?"[28] We can describe this confluence of race, language, and literature as actualizing a powerful didactic immanence, since Price-Mars wants to legitimize all its constituent terms in the eyes of the Haitian people, instructing them in the inherent value of such cultural elements as they already possess.

However, as Dash has pointed out, this tripartite conception of Haitian literature, to which Price-Mars turns in a concluding essay titled "Folklore and Literature" before devoting the rest of *Ainsi parla l'Oncle* to reproductions of academic talks given in April 1922, uncomfortably ties what Price-Mars calls the "Haitian soul" to a national community grounded, literally, in a shared experience of national territoriality. This formulation is unmistakably reminiscent of the far-right literary nationalism of Charles Maurras.[29] Certainly, to speak of "the earth" (*le sol*), as closely and (crucially) aesthetically linked to "spiritual unity" and "the days of glory and sacrifices" bespeaks an intellectual relationship with French far-right conceptions of literature in the interwar period.[30]

Without denying or otherwise downplaying this philosophical and political connection, though, what I want to highlight here is how, at the same time, Price-Mars's vision of Haitian national literature and fiction is fundamentally ethnographic. For one thing, if it is indeed born of an innate rootedness in national territory, this rootedness is grounded in the everyday lived experience of the American occupation. He refers to the historical conjuncture that informs his thinking when asserting that "nothing can, finally, prevent the fact that, at the moment of transition and uncertainty that we are living currently, the same imponderable elements [of our collective self] act as the mirror reflecting most faithfully the worried face of the nation. They constitute in an unexpected and stunning fashion the materials of our spiritual unity. Where, thus, would we find a more sincere image of our community?" The "imponderable elements" of which Price-Mars speaks here are actually "tales, legends, songs from far-off lands or created, transformed by us."[31] This is a definition of syncretic fiction that privileges creative importation and repurposing alongside and in tandem with more conventional forms of literary invention. Syncretic fiction appears here as bound up in a transformative mimesis, acting as a mirror that reflects reality while also rearranging and reimagining its constituent elements to do justice to the "moment of transition and uncertainty" opened up by the colonial encounter.

Taking this passage in its entirety, I think, demonstrates that the national literary community Price-Mars seeks to cultivate is certainly Maurrassian in one sense, in that "the people" appear as a passive collective body inheriting and passing on the qualities and literary traditions that remain immanent to their national soil. However, this passive "Haitian soul" also stands in tension with the image of active literary creation or transformation—what Price-Mars does not refer to as "creolization" but that we might recognize as such—against the backdrop not of a timeless and dehistoricized national territory but instead amid the "transition and uncertainty" of foreign occupation.[32] From this perspective, he appears torn between a passively pastoral Maurrassian literary nationalism and a national literary community composed of fraught transitions, conflicts, and creative appropriations and revalorizations. Ethnography for Price-Mars moves in both of these directions at once: it attempts to account for imagined and idealized forms of national belonging and collective unity just as it simultaneously points to a sense of fiction that has actually existing referents and that relies on the active negotiations and transformations of folklore by ordinary social actors in everyday life.

A concluding remark Price-Mars makes in the 1922 conference speech appended to the main text of *Ainsi parla l'Oncle* intensifies the sense of syncretic flux residing in the anthropological link he establishes between fiction and nation. In the context of a discussion of marriage rites and the composition of the Haitian family, he points out that since the 1804 Revolution "through a confusion of mores, beliefs, and customs" there "slowly emerges a new social form. It is perhaps now only a chrysalis that provokes anger, mockery, or causes to blush the impatient people, the myopic, and the ignorant, but that philosophers and big-hearted people behold, made tender and interested. What will it be in one hundred, two hundred, five hundred years?"[33] This revitalized national community, projected far into the future, is not a static idealization but one best described through syncretically evocative metaphors of metamorphosis and transformation, a "social form" that, it would seem, is constantly caught up in a process of emergence. The vestiges of Maurrassian nationalism that appear so clearly elsewhere in Price-Mars's formulations seem here to give way to a modernist ideology fetishizing perpetual newness in an unfolding, endlessly transforming narrative of the nation.

In his *Formation ethnique, folk-lore et culture du peuple haïtien* (1939), a study published about a decade after *Ainsi parla l'Oncle*, Price-Mars opens his reflections on race, folklore, and national identity with a citation from another Haitian diplomat, writer, and ethnographer, Louis Joseph Janvier (1855–1911): "Haiti is a field of sociological experimentation."[34] While this statement proved true for many American travelers to Haiti who experimented with pseudo-ethnographic sensationalism in their accounts of Haitian folklore in the first half of the twentieth century, in *Ainsi parla l'Oncle* Price-Mars reconceptualizes Janvier's assertion as a social-scientific tenet of Haitian national renewal, one that has transatlantic epistemological underpinnings. This sense of experimentation also characterizes his ethnographic axiology, what he perceives to be the literary value of social-scientific approaches to Haitian folklore and to the fictional potentiality of syncretic realism. These two gestures of valorization are inextricably linked and, indeed, mutually constitutive in ethnographic-fictional reappraisals of national futurity. They are echoed and adopted by other Haitian writers, as well, from Roumain (so closely linked, both anthropologically and personally, with Price-Mars) to later writers as we will see first with the case of Jacques Stephen Alexis's *Les arbres musiciens*.

Ainsi parla l'Oncle is emblematic of the kinds of alternative anthropologies this book traces: it redirects accepted anthropological knowledge toward a new epistemological grounding of the nation over and against both French and American imperial projects. But at the same time the book's sense of experimentation does not go as far as it seems to want for itself. Price-Mars actualizes new, transatlantic ethnohistorical perspectives, to be sure, but he does so by harking back to an older comparativism and never manages to articulate a clear sense of what a renewed national literature might look like beyond its anthropological underpinnings. Roumain's *Gouverneurs de la Rosée*, as we saw, relies on local knowledge but eschews speculative thinking. *Ainsi parla l'Oncle*, by contrast, delves into speculative epistemologies but lacks the experimental self-reflexivity that later novelists will embrace when they rewrite Price-Mars's concerns in new literary contexts. In short, Price-Mars generates an anti-imperial anthropological counternarrative that will allow later writers to displace conventional ethnography in more reflexive literary works. These novels become alternative anthropologies, as well, but they do so in creative tension with Roumain's and Price-Mars's earlier texts, finding in them impulses toward experimentation that they did not originally express.

Local Knowledge and Folkloric Humanism

For Jacques Stephen Alexis, national renewal or rejuvenation entails a concurrent written refashioning of the category of the human. His novel *Compère général soleil* (1955) is an expression of longing for a reattachment to national soil (that evinces his deep intellectual debt to Roumain) accompanied by the cultivation of socialist-humanist solidarity, a universalist gesture mitigating what, at first glance, we might all too quickly read as ecological nostalgia. Alexis's hero in the novel, Hilarion Hilarius, is thus at once "a true face of Haiti, and also a face from anywhere (*un visage de partout*)."[35] His second novel, *Les arbres musiciens* (1957), makes the same double movement and privileges national grounding or rewriting via a more abstract humanism. But whereas *Compère* thematizes consciousness-raising and Marxist didacticism through Hilarion's emigration to the Dominican Republic and experience of the massacre of Haitian workers sponsored by the government of Rafael Trujillo, *Les arbres musiciens* turns to local knowledge, folk traditions, and Vodou to reimagine national belonging through the fictionalization of humanist desire.[36]

This text narrativizes the Catholic Church's violent attempts to eradicate Vodou from the Haitian peasantry, the notorious *campagne anti-superstitieuse*, which was intensified around the middle of the twentieth century, amid an encroaching American presence in the Haitian countryside.[37] It also dwells at some descriptive length on folkloric traditions and Vodou practices, introducing the ethnographic more fully into a narrative universe in which it had hitherto played a much less significant role—in *Compère*, folklore and religious traditions are subordinated to political pedagogy. Alexis thus adopts and adapts the anthropological concerns articulated by Price-Mars in *Ainsi parla l'Oncle*, translating them into a narrative of national transformation that depends on a narrative renewal of the human.

From this perspective, I think we can read the ethnographic impulse of *Les arbres musiciens* as a fictional continuation of a claim Price-Mars makes in a 1939 speech appended to the text of his *Formation ethnique*. The collective aspects of folk culture and religion (such as dances and spirit possessions) constitute what he calls the "Message" of Haitian cultural singularity: "This Message is the stockpile and the symbol of our Haitian culture, based on the human aspirations of our people for more justice, more fraternity, and more compassion among men."[38] Alexis takes up Price-Mars's more conventionally rooted concerns with folklore and places them in the service not only of national renewal but of a new universalist vision of political humanity, a socialist *anthropos* that the novel feeds with local epistemologies.

Alexis strengthens the connection between the human and the collective aspects of Haitian singularity in this implicit conversation with Price-Mars. His debt to Jacques Roumain, however, is avowed and well known, and he incorporates Roumain into his universalist humanism. In his panegyric "Jacques Roumain vivant" (1957), for example, Alexis uses the words "Mankind" and "Humanity" several times each in just the opening paragraphs, going so far as to rebaptize Roumain as *"gouverneur de la rosée humaine,"* master of the human dew.[39] In terms of this chapter's focus on ethnographic nation-building, Alexis's word choice suggests that he sees Roumain's ethnographic fiction as both compatible with and generative of his own folkloric humanism. As we will see in *Les arbres musiciens* he moves beyond Roumain's grounding of the nation in a dehistoricized rural indigenism toward a rurality that holds folk traditions in place while indexing their relationship to far broader forces of social transformation. In my reading, then, ethnographic fiction for Alexis narrativizes a valorized folklore and religiosity while simultaneously writing their diffusion into a new humanism. This dual action of writing is part and parcel of how Alexis imagines Haitian marvelous realism, which owes as much to Roumain as it does to the Cuban writer Alejo Carpentier: it mobilizes a literary witnessing of Haitian syncretism in everyday life and expresses, on a different yet still visible level of abstraction, an idealized political solidarity that encompasses all of humanity.[40]

The narrative of *Les arbres musiciens* turns on the fortunes of the three Osmin brothers: Diogène, a Catholic priest; Edgard, a military officer; and Carles, a dilletantish bon vivant. Diogène and Edgard find themselves swept up in political matters of national importance, as the Haitian government and President Elie Lescot collaborate with the United States to open Haiti's country-side up to American business interests (Alexis has Lescot declare, "My policies are the faithful reflection of the policies of the United States of America!"[41]). In return for supposedly friendly terms on an international loan deal, the Haitian president confers on a US company, the Société Haïtiano-Américaine de Développement Agricole, rights to "develop" the country's agricultural sector by logging and producing rubber. This economic modernization involves the expropriation of land either held by local landowners or worked by peasants who cultivate the land in the owners' absence. Edgard and the newly frocked Diogène are sent to the countryside to help smooth the way for the Americans' arrival: the former to help prepare for the expropriations and the latter to lead an anti-Vodou campaign to forestall peasant recalcitrance, the idea being that Africanist folk spirituality might breed and bleed over into political resistance.

This realist framing is inlaid with more impressionistic and phenomenolog-ical descriptions of Vodou ceremonies, as priests and adepts of the La Remembrance sect seek to prevent temples and ritual objects from being confiscated and destroyed. Alexis tells their story, complete with footnotes explaining ritual terms and religious offices, capturing how folkloric beliefs push back against the French-backed clergy and the Haitian representatives of American business interests.

One embedded narrative emerging from Alexis's valorization of folk tradi-tions is that of a young boy named Gonaïbo, who lives on his own in the wilderness and is feared by the local peasantry for his otherworldly connection to Nature. Yet in a theme running through the novel, sociality exists as the con-stitutive flip side of this connection and vitiates the would-be timelessness of the unadulterated rurality that Gonaïbo appears initially to embody. He must live in isolation, his dying mother tells him, "Until the little calabash tree under the hill blooms. . . . Then, you will go down toward the town, among men, yourself a fully-formed man."[42] Sociality does not so much supplant Nature as it references the inevitable end of its usefulness; or, to put it in Marxist philo-sophical terms of which Alexis might approve, sociality marks the exhaustion of abstract Nature's idealized use-value.

Gonaïbo's hesitant first steps into the world of men signal a grand transition that also functions as an underlying tension pushing Alexis's narrative along: folk traditions are rooted in relationships to Haitian rurality and the land (relationships of which Gonaïbo's is an originary and foundational example), and yet they exist only uneasily with the immeasurably broader forms of humanist solidarity that the novel wants to narrativize and valorize at the same time that it highlights the richness of local knowledge. Ethnographic fiction as folkloric humanism follows Price-Mars's recommendations while imagining social relations that supersede the localized context of their articulation: national rewriting via folkloric valorization is caught up for Alexis with its own surpassing as it points toward new political understandings of the human.

Thus, against the backdrop of looming expropriation and more or less forced renunciation of the peasantry's belief in Vodou, the text sways like a pendulum between the two poles of indigenist rootedness and expressions of desire for participation in an abstract humanity. National rewriting for Alexis occurs between these shifts and in the narrative tension they evoke and that pushes the story forward. The first, indigenist pole is characterized by a pastoral mysticism that would not be out of place in Roumain were it not for Alexis's penchant for tying descriptive verve to characterological development in a way that clashes with the former's terser characterological realism. We might consider, for example, a speech Léonie Osmin delivers to her two sons, warning them of the risks they run by interfering in the lives of the peasantry: "If what they say is true, you will be ordered to strike at things that are part of the soul of this country. . . . Remember, this land has secrets, values, customs that no one may desecrate without being severely punished! . . . If you think you can lay a sacrilegious hand on what is the heart of this people, the mysteries of this country will cancel you out, will show you to be vulgar puppets, if they don't just kill you outright."[43]

Léonie comes close here to the Maurrassian literary nationalism of Price-Mars as she outlines an innate spiritual link between the Haitian people, a national "soul" literally grounded in the land, and an immanent religiosity that demands valorization. She confidently ends her admonishment by declaring that, as a "woman from Guinea" (*nègresse de Guinée*) she alone is capable of managing their risky attempts at social mobility—a formulation that indicates how an Africanist sense of self bespeaks intimate types of local knowledge emerging from the Haitian people.

Predictably enough, Diogène and Edgard do not heed their mother's request to proceed with caution (although each has his doubts at times), and the church's antisuperstition campaign sweeps through the region, resulting in burned temples and confiscated ritual objects that await destruction. Once Carles Osmin learns that Diogène has sacked and burned three temples (*hounforts*), he rushes to his brother's rectory and stands nonplussed, in confused contemplation, before a pile of confiscated statues and other religious objects. Picking up a statue representing a woman standing in profile, he loses himself in "this perfect piece, witness to an ancient art." Further still, his mind detaches itself from its corporeal container and embarks on a transhistorical journey set off by the apprehension of the work of art:

> Carles drifted, further away than the slave trade (*Traite*), further than the conquistadors, he bathed in the happy ages of the primitive community of the Arawaks (*Chemès*) of Haiti. . . . Strength and grace, mystery and wonder, the dream and the harshness of life in a shimmering nature, this is what the artist wanted to offer the Arawak gods that he believed to be the guides of life. The knowledge of the Carib *butio* [priest] had enriched the *zambo* [people of mixed black and Amerindian descent], also the heir to eternal Africa. The little statue had passed from hand to hand, the gods had been modified over time, taking on other colors and other qualities.[44]

Here, Kant's noble sublime meets Proust's madeleine, as the wonder of aesthetic contemplation produces a series of transhistorical associations that pass through tactile contact with the object. Carles finds himself unexpectedly inserted into the line of succession to Haitian cultural patrimony, as ahistorical essences ("eternal Africa" or the pre-Columbian community) fuse with historically generative processes of religious syncretism, repurposing, and *métissage*. This is indigenism as transhistorical and transcultural desire—questions to which we return in chapter 4 with Martinique's créolistes and their ethnographic approach to Caribbean literary and cultural history. For now, though, it is enough to highlight how Alexis's character stands outside of himself and bears witness not only to the transmission of national identity but also to cultural and religious practices that are under threat and at risk of disappearing. Fiction functions in this moment as an exercise in salvage ethnography.

The mystical ecstasy of this scene, its expression of deep ontological presence on the entire timeline of Haitian history, finds an echo in a short story (a fictional folktale) titled "Le Sous-lieutenant enchanté," published in Alexis's *Romancero aux étoiles* (1960). In the story, an American soldier, ridiculously named Earl Wheelbarrow, moves to Haiti to search for buried treasure supposedly located by a deceased uncle, posing as an archeologist to avoid arousing suspicion. Under this social-scientific cover, he looks fruitlessly for the treasure in the remote mountains until one night he is bewitched by a beautiful woman before him, "standing like an antique statue from bygone times . . . whose forms and traits remained Indian despite the apparent fervor of the blood of Ham."[45] Besotted by this pre-Columbian siren, Lieutenant Wheelbarrow visits a *papaloa*, a Vodou priest and seer who may tell him how to possess the mysterious woman. The priest warns him against continuing to look for the treasure and has him solemnly profess his love for Haiti: "I no longer know anything but this land and the people of this land!"[46]

As soon as he makes this declaration, the "immemorial splendors of the Haitian land" open themselves up to him, and the beautiful woman reveals herself to be the guardian of Haitian patrimony, as well as the guarantor of future abundance: "The land will open up one day to give its treasures to all the sons of this land. Today we must watch over them."[47] The lieutenant and his indigenous lover end up being captured and put to death by American occupation forces, and the thrust of Alexis's folktale involves precisely writing mystical indigenism (rendered all the more powerful since a white American is initiated into it) into the colonial encounter. And in a parallel with Carles Osmin's contemplation of the confiscated statue, a transhistorical national identity dovetails with the preservation of Haitian cultural patrimony and folk traditions—all captured by Alexis in the form of the folktale.[48]

These moments of folkloric indigenism in *Les arbres musiciens* are caught up in a different yet complementary movement that travels away from an ever deeper grounding in the Haitian soil and toward a politics of national renewal mobilizing an abstract humanism that detaches from or even eschews the valorization of intensely local knowledge. National rewriting sees Alexis pulled in both of these directions at once, since he pragmatically understands the stakes of fostering connections to Haiti's cultural and religious patrimony while idealistically hoping for the supersession of these links in a turn toward socialist solidarity. The boy Gonaïbo embodies this tension, for he passes from an ahistorical rurality in which folk knowledge is indistinguishable from immersion in Nature to an understanding of his own ontology as always already destined to actualize new forms of sociality.

Further, this shift that he accomplishes in the novel involves becoming the living repository of Vodou spirituality upon the death of the region's most renowned priest, Papa Bois-d'Orme. The two join forces to recover ritual objects stolen during raids on Vodou sanctuaries, and Gonaïbo finds himself conflicted, internally divided between a desire to preserve his bucolic idyll and a growing awareness that his ties to other Haitian peasants point toward a humanist futurity: "Tomorrow will reveal that all our destructive madness, all our wild agitations, our confrontations, our ancient hatreds as well as the most modern ones, were but the expression of the barren age, the age of human animality, the moment of passage from sheep-like frenzy to true intellection. . . . And when enlightened man (*l'homme-lumière*) leaves his cocoon of hatred, of wool, of blood and silk, of steel or of dreams, life will be an eternal childhood, passionate, happy, always pleasant."[49]

Gonaïbo's internal monologue converges here with Alexis's moralizing narrative voice, and this passage stands in marked contrast to the immersion in Haitian cultural and religious singularity that is highlighted elsewhere. Whereas this latter movement appears creatively transhistorical, thinking beyond "the age of human animality" is resolutely futuristic and implies a new form of historical periodization that folkloric valorization, almost by definition, cannot countenance.

Gonaïbo's vision of a new, enlightened man finds a complement in another of Alexis's characters named Carméleau, a peasant who left his community to find work in the city and who returns to find himself disillusioned by the La Remembrance Vodou sect to which he once adhered. Carméleau's presence not only serves to mark an urban-rural divide, though; he also prefigures a new political subjectivity that turns away from folk religious traditions in favor of "modern" forms of abstract solidarity. As he puts it during a long conversation with Papa Bois-d'Orme about his loss of faith, referencing Jean-Jacques Dessalines, the leader of the Haitian Revolution,

> I can no longer resign myself and repeat that God is good, that the *Loas* are our fathers and La Remembrance is eternal! . . . Me, I know that one day Dessalines will return to the Haitian land, he will come back to put an end to the groans, the lamentations and he will fight at the head of his children. He cannot not come back! He will emerge from the depths of the earth! And that will be the day of vengeance, the day of justice, the day of dirty men, the day of barefoot men, the day of mountain-men, of forest-men, of true men [*nègres-nègres*]. . . . While he waits for the sovereign people, Carméleau Melon earns his living, he cuts down trees, he saws wood and boards, he gets insulted, he works for others, but wherever he goes he gives the word of Dessalines to the people. In a hushed voice, out loud, everywhere he tells the children of Dessalines to unite in silence, to prepare *lambis* and torches, so that one day the cry of 1804 will break out again among a people who are upright and gathered together.[50]

Carméleau's Dessalinian messianism certainly draws on history, but it does not do so in the same way as those passages in the text that superimpose national belonging on transhistorical affective identification: to affirm the recurrence of 1804 is to reperiodize the revolutionary moment and integrate it into a modern ethics of labor and a collective refashioning of the Haitian people. This declaration also blends messianism with materialism, as the new "sovereign people" to come is no longer formed through deeply felt experiences of indigenist spiritual ecstasy such as the one that occurred unexpectedly to Carles Osmin.

On the eve of the great expropriation, some peasants take false hope in a slight delay of the proceedings and arrange collectively to clean the local cemetery, crying out, "Honor to the dead!" At this moment, the voice of Alexis's omniscient narrator cuts in with a personal intervention: "Honor to the dead, I say, because this is the only guarantee for all the values that have been born and that are being born. It is the only guarantee that, in all of its renewals, a young nation (*patrie*) keeps the wisdom without which there is no people, no race, no humanity. Honor to the dead!" Coming as it does at the end of the novel, this interjection might at first glance be read as Alexis effecting a kind of synthesis between a valorization of folk traditions and a national renewal that leads into a new vision of humanity. However, it loses its synthetic value and gains in ambiguity once we take into account the fact that the local knowledge that would ground new values and a young nation comes from the dead, to whom the people are connected and from whom they are cut off at the same time. Open-ended national renewal thus occurs through a dual act of preservation and detachment, one that short-circuits the continuity of transhistorical indigenism while nudging its epistemological resonance into the future.

Les arbres musiciens leaves us on this ambiguous note and does not offer a definitive working out of the tensions at play in the concept of folkloric humanism that underpins Alexis's approach to ethnographic fiction. Gonaïbo takes over for Papa Bois-d'Orme as the living repository of folk knowledge and Vodou spirituality, and he decides to join Carméleau at a work-camp where the latter has become a logger. Indigenism and Vodou spirituality enter the "modern" world as remainders and reminders, as what is left over in local memory after the end of the La Remembrance sect. Once the two characters meet up, the novel ends on the words "Life begins."[51] The final sentence of "Le Sous-lieutenant enchanté" expresses a similar ambiguity: "In any case, it is a great and beautiful thing for a people to keep [*conserver*] their legends alive."[52] The use of the French *conserver* here is key, I think, to identifying the endgame of

Alexis's folkloric humanism as a literary strategy in which fiction articulates an ethics of conservation according to which local knowledge contributes to, but does not actively participate in, a thoroughly modern humanism.

In the wake of such a creative continuation of the ethnographic conversation begun by Price-Mars, Alexis's final (dogmatic) sequestration of cultural singularity might not satisfy us, especially given how he situates Haiti in an open, transcultural Caribbean cartography in his later novel, *L'espace d'un cillement* (1959).[53] But a close reading of his folkloric humanism does reveal that ethnographic fiction can rewrite the nation without beginning from the foundational enactment of literary "mastery" over pristine spatiality that we see in Roumain's *Gouverneurs*.[54] The difference between Alexis, on the one hand, and Depestre and Laferrière, on the other, is that for Alexis the self-reflexive integration of anthropology into national literature occurs primarily on the levels of narrative and characterology. The latter two authors, as we see in this chapter's final two sections, bring the alternative anthropology sketched by Price-Mars to bear much more openly on questions of textual form. Price-Mars's ethnographic counternarrative is transformed by these writers into new ways of knowing and organizing the nation in fiction.

Zombisme and Anthropology as Telescopic Realism

In 1972, in the preface to the Cuban edition of Alexis's *Compère général soleil*, René Depestre wrote that in Alexis's work "literature is never a simple illustration or a dull continuation of politics: it is a *creation* that, beginning from the author's Haitian roots, gives at the trial of the human condition a moving testimony."[55] We have seen how for Alexis Haitian folk knowledge "gives evidence" (to continue Depestre's judicial metaphor) in a literary narrative that pushes the nation toward his vision of an abstract humanism. In Depestre's fiction, by contrast, folklore does not bear witness on such a grand scale. Depestre is no less anxious about rewriting Haiti than is Alexis, but the stakes of this operation are intimately mediated by the spatiality of his own distance from the nation—a literary distancing that he inflicts upon the reader, as well. This work bears the mark of Depestre's many decades of exile (in France, Cuba, and elsewhere[56]), such that the nation is fictionally rendered through hazy reconstructions, like when Proust's narrator wakes in the middle of the night, still prey to the impressions that his dream-self has designed.

Folklore (and, more narrowly, zombies and *zombisme*) triangulates the author, the reader, and the nation in Depestre's two novels, *Le mât de cocagne* (1979) and *Hadriana dans tous mes rêves* (1988). I want to focus principally on *Hadriana dans tous mes rêves* since in it the written form of the social sciences creeps in much more clearly and the colonial encounter is more narratively determinative. Unlike Jean Rouch's films in which, as we saw in chapter 2, ethnographic triangulation takes place geographically, Depestre's novels (*Hadriana*, in particular) approach ethnographic fiction by leading author, reader, and nation through formal detours that allow generic hybridity to hold folklore and the novel together.

Le mât de cocagne tells the story of the zombification of a "man of action" named Henri Postel, a former senator in an unnamed tropical country forced by the nation's dictator, the "Great Electrifier of Souls" named Zoocrate Zacharie, to live out the rest of his days selling trinkets and foodstuffs in a stall located in one of the capital's down-and-out neighborhoods. Rather than gunning him down in a state-sanctioned killing and risk turning him into a martyr for the opposition, the reasoning goes, it would be far crueler to break his spirit by reducing his life to the most mundane form of routinization possible. This injection of pure listless banality is intended to kill Postel from the inside out, turning him into a zombie (i.e., one of the "living dead") in whom automation has replaced intellection. The government's plan backfires, though, when Postel decides against pursuing an opportunity to flee to Canada and opts instead to show up the dictator by winning a greasy-pole climbing contest open to all the country's residents. Composed of folkloric narrative building blocks, the novel satirizes dictatorial autoeroticism: as one government poster reads, referencing the greasy-pole competition, "As of twenty-four hours ago, *the permanent erection of the phallocratic State has been declared!*"[57]

Le mât de cocagne both does and does not take place in Haiti. The setting of the text is technically fictionalized, and yet a government official drops the name of "our Faustin Soulouque" (in a reference to the mid-nineteenth century self-declared Haitian emperor Faustin I) on the novel's second page.[58] Even before this unsubtle revelation, though, the text's opening disclaimer sees Depestre playfully overcook his distancing from Haiti as an actually existing national referent. He begins by alerting readers to the fact that the novel "is not a historical account, nor a *roman à clef*, nor a work of autobiographical origin." The "Great Zacharian nation" does not actually exist, readers must understand. But he undercuts what reads as an unremarkably standard prefatory comment just several sentences later: "Any resemblance to beings, animals, trees, living or dead, any similarity, close or distant, in names, situations, places, systems, with gears made out of iron or fire, or with any other scandal from real life, can only be the effect of a coincidence that is 'not only fortuitous, but positively outrageous.'"[59]

Depestre doth protest too much, and his use of scare quotes at the end of the sentence distances him from his own warning and makes for hilarious reading. That said, however, how can we read the novel as being "about" Haiti (i.e., read it without ignoring obvious references) while simultaneously taking Depestre at his paradoxical word here? *Le mât de cocagne* may not be a *roman à clef* but the play of literary distancing is key here, although differently so than it is for an ethnographer such as Hampâté Bâ who steps back from himself to feed his sense of anthropological characterology.

For Depestre, literary distancing is composed of two movements, one of physical separation or breaking off and the other of increased proximity. These movements are coterminous, and their constitutive overlapping in the generation of narrative creates the disorienting effect we encounter in *Le mât de cocagne*'s preface. The first movement indexes Depestre's painfully real absence from Haiti (allowing the novel to be read as an exilic allegory): he left the country in 1946 at age twenty, came back briefly in the late 1950s, and left again ultimately to settle in France.[60] The second movement references his closeness to imagined foreign readers who may have no a priori connection to the country. Narrative triangulation and national rewriting are thus both caused and mediated by literary distancing and its unexpected directionalities.

The author-reader-nation nexus derives more strongly from an ethnographic narrative of zombisme in *Hadriana dans tous mes rêves*. For one thing, although Depestre's protagonist in the novel is named Patrick, the story is told from the first person, and we cannot help but allow the *je* of his character to slide toward that of the author figure. For another, while the novel is prefaced by a disclaimer professing the work's pure fictionality that is similar to but less stylized than the one from *Le mât de cocagne*, this statement is itself preceded by another paratextual framing: the novel is dedicated to, among others, "the memory of André Breton and Pierre Mabille." Breton and Mabille famously wrote ethnographically inspired surrealist travel narratives (such as the former's *Martinique, charmeuse de serpents* and the latter's *Messages de l'étranger*) and poetry on Martinique and Haiti, specifically—Breton visited Martinique in 1941 and Haiti in 1945, where he met up with Mabille who was already in Port-au-Prince.[61] Mabille in particular, as a professor of anthropology, was invested in thinking through the complexities of everyday life in Haiti, over and against the exoticizing thrust of other writers, and his Haitian essays often parody or mimic conventional ethnographic field trips.[62] Depestre ties this ethnographic dedication even more closely to his narrative when he describes childhood boredom in the following way on the first page of the text: leaning over the balcony on days off from school, "I watched out for the incident that would put my imagination on some trail of everyday surrealism."[63]

This "everyday surrealism," in many ways synonymous with the marvelous realism on which Depestre, like Alexis, also wrote, contributes to the magical folkloric backdrop of *Hadriana*.[64] The novel turns on the sudden death in the late 1930s of a beautiful young French girl, the eponymous Hadriana, who expires immediately upon saying "I do" at her wedding to a local Haitian boy in the town of Jacmel. Her death instantly becomes the stuff of local legend, caught up in tales of a boy-turned-butterfly who deflowers girls at night and a wedding procession that turns into a carnavalesque wake. Hadriana's parents are liberal French expatriates: "With respect to the matters of vaudou, they had far fewer prejudices than Jacmelian patricians they rubbed elbows with at the Excelsior club" and were closer to individuals who "in the vein of a Price-Mars, [had] undertaken precious research on the Haitian national religion."[65]

Nothing prepares Patrick and the townspeople, who all held Hadriana in reverent awe, for what happens next, as she disappears from her grave, which is found to contain nothing but quickly evaporating rainwater. Patrick and his family immediately suspect that her body has been stolen for zombification, and the novel proceeds to flash forward and back to the present as Depestre's protagonist tries to make narrative sense of Hadriana's hauntology (if I may repurpose Derrida here in this discussion of the undead). Indeed, just as Derrida, in his reading of Hamlet and Marx, poses the question of haunting spectrality as "repetition *and* first time," so does Patrick seek to narrativize the singularity of Hadriana's zombification and its continuation of a much longer, deeper history of zombisme in Haiti.[66]

This is why Patrick, as an adult, wants to write up a realist account of Hadriana's disappearance but finds himself slipping into the social sciences. Patrick's uncle Féfé explains that they broke the news to Hadriana's family while tactfully avoiding the matter of zombisme, which Féfé argues would have been ridiculed by the French parents precisely because for outsiders it is such a stereotypical referent of Haitian cultural singularity. Astonished that an adult could take zombisme so seriously, Patrick breaks into a short, four-chapter narrative arc titled "Ainsi parla mon oncle Féfé," in which Féfé adopts the Price-Marsian didactic role to explain to his nephew how zombification occurs and how it is related to Vodou.

This section of the novel simultaneously parodies anthropological accounts of zombisme and engages seriously with the valorization of local knowledge for which Price-Mars argued more than a half-century before the publication of Depestre's novel.[67] Féfé's commentary ranges from the ethnographically pseudoscientific to the entertainingly anecdotal. As Patrick explains,

> For uncle Ferdinand, a zombie—man, woman, child—was a person whose metabolism, under the effect of a plant poison, has been slowed down to the point of offering the coroner all the signs of death: general muscular hypotonia, rigidity of the extremities, undetectable pulse, disappearance of respiration and ocular reflexes, lowering of body temperature, paleness of the face, and negative mirror test. Despite these symptoms of death, the zombified subject retains the use of its mental faculties. Recognized as clinically dead, placed in a coffin and publically buried, it is, in the hours following the burial, taken from its tomb by a sorcerer in order to be subjected to forced labor in a field (*zombie-jardin*) or in an urban workshop (*zombie-z'outil*).[68]

This detailed breakdown is followed by another chapter, called "Codex of the Zombie-maker, or Zombirific [*Zombifère*] Pharmacopeia," in which the drugs used by the *houngan*, or Vodou priest, are outlined in a rhetoric whose scientific detachment matches the blank automation of the possessed victim. Uncle Féfé proceeds to recount two anecdotes to whose truth he can personally attest, since he heard the first of them from the same informant who worked with William Seabrook while Seabrook was writing *The Magic Island* and since the second involved a wealthy young girl with whom Féfé had a tryst a week before she "died" and was taken from her grave. Luckily, the girl was spotted in the countryside months later and sent to America where psychiatrists managed to pull her out of her zombified state. As further proof of the story's authenticity, Féfé provides Patrick with the woman's most recent letter to him—the two still keep in touch long after the former zombie has decided never to return to Haiti—which the narrator reproduces in full at the end of this section of the novel.

Some thirty years after Hadriana's disappearance, spurred by an article on Jacmel's decline published in the French newspaper *Le Monde* (also reproduced in full) and by an imaginary interview he conducts with its author,

Patrick, now based in Paris, resolves to return to a study he began in the 1960s in which Hadriana's story dissolves in a much broader examination of zombisme in Jacmel. "Might my native land not be a collective zombie?" Patrick wonders about Haiti. He groups his writings into a series of nine propositions on zombisme as an ethnohistorical Haitian phenomenon: these propositions include the arguments that Vodou is tied to other agrarian religions around the world and that nocturnal zombification rituals have cultural analogs not only in historically distant societies such as sixteenth-century Lithuania but in far-flung locales such as Siberia, Tibet, and the South Pacific.[69] Further, he speculates that contemporary zombie mythology may derive from the ontology of slavery according to which the forced reduction of Africans to pure corporeality was internalized by Haitians over time.[70]

Other observations follow about zombie phenomenology (inasmuch as a zombie could ever be conscious of such a thing) that lead Patrick to several questions that he leaves unanswered, including, "Why the zombie—and *zomberie*—in the Haitian imaginary?" and "In a society with such a weak coefficient of law and freedom, is the absolute insecurity of the zombie equivalent, on a mythical level, to the extreme distress of the human condition that characterizes life on my half of the island [of Hispaniola]?" Patrick does not bother to sketch out potential answers to these questions, although their very articulation is enough to evince a link among the social sciences, zombie mythology, and the project of national reconstruction, and he washes his hands of the whole study, dismissing his ethnographic considerations as nothing but "pseudo-Sartrean jargon" and "kooky and vindictive Third-Worldism."[71] For all his detours through, and allusions to, the discipline (Patrick name checks Lévi-Strauss just one page before his chapter-long enumeration of propositions, for instance), anthropology falls short and fails to satisfy on representational, rhetorical, and political levels.

Why, then, write ethnography into this fiction if only to arrive at its insufficiency? As we saw in chapter 1, this is a question that Leiris very well could ask. For Depestre, though, anthropology allows him to pay homage to Price-Mars and to a certain idea of indigénisme and functions as a formal marker of literary distancing. That is, anthropology as form facilitates the immanentization in fiction of the writer's distance from the nation. Both of Depestre's ethnographic excurses in *Hadriana* drift away from the main narrative while nonetheless pointing back to it via social-scientific signposting. But they also intellectualize Haitian culture and folklore in ways that do not befit the much more personal tone that drives the rest of the narrative forward. In other words, taking the nine abortive propositions on zomberie as a point of reference, Patrick's *je* that introduces readers to the folkloric universe into which Hadriana is incorporated after her death is not the same as the *je* of the expert who seeks to make analytic and ethnographic sense of the larger cultural stakes at play in Hadriana's zombification. We can thus read Patrick's frustration at the end of this section as exasperation at his failure to provoke the narrative coincidence of one *je* with the other, of ethnographic savvy with the intimacy of fictional storytelling.

Nevertheless, Depestre writes this noncoincidence into the novel to index his own authorly distance from the nation. (Bear in mind that he published *Hadriana* after roughly forty years abroad.) This indexing goes beyond the fact that he playfully does not allow us to assimilate him to his character Patrick, despite the biographical similarities that the two share. Anthropology provides Depestre with a telescopic realism, a discursive mold into which he can pour a distant Haiti but that ends up offering an intellectualized country that is no less far away. Telescopic realism is not necessarily an aesthetic failure, however; the ethnographic, in its parodic, representational, and citational guises, effects an optically charged rapprochement here between author and reader. We as readers have the sense of peeking over Depestre's shoulder and looking down the lens along with him, not necessarily experiencing the same frustration but certainly feeling keenly the constitutive overlapping of epistemological perception and personal or political separation.

For Depestre, the Haiti of anthropological intellection only maps onto Haiti as actually existing national project in the realm of fiction. (And again, as with Leiris we arrive at a working out of anthropology's shortcomings via the transference of anthropology to fiction.) The success of anthropology as telescopic realism in the novel rests on the fact that readers have access to the same telescopic lens as the author who creates it. But to telescope in *Hadriana* is also to triangulate, for anthropology optically arranges reader, author, and nation in such a way that all three elements occupy the same field of visibility while simultaneously remaining in a state of suspension.

Depestre's anthropological telescoping is set off by a colonial encounter whose resonance in the novel is partially allegorical. This encounter has to do with Hadriana's Frenchness and with her family's rather incongruous presence in Haiti (and, by extension, in a French-language Haitian novel) long after the 1804 Revolution. While Hadriana reemerges in Patrick's life by the end of the novel (we learn that she managed to resist the effects of Vodou sorcery) for much of the story she figures as a zombie—that is, one of the living dead, an absent presence who haunts, intrigues, and frustrates Patrick. Reading Hadriana and Patrick as allegorical figurations of the France-Haiti relationship requires us to bear in mind the fact that Depestre is in fictional dialogue with Price-Mars and his ethnographic rejection of the Haitian elite's bovaryste attachment to France.

The novel's allegorical potential is not fully developed or resolved, but certain aspects of it speak to a desire to work through the "undead" French presence in contemporary Haiti: Hadriana and Patrick romantically reunite, for instance, but only outside Haiti once Patrick has taken a teaching job in Jamaica; Patrick travels to Paris, and it is from there that he feels spurred to reconsider and rework his ethnographic theses on zomberie; and he inserts a 1972 article on Jacmel from *Le Monde* into the text and then proceeds to follow this cut-and-paste with an imaginary interview with the article's author.[72] Yet even though this allegorical potential is not tackled head-on or in full, it stimulates the novel's ethnographic fictionality and its telescopic view of national belonging.

Dreamed Countries and Ethnographic Wish Fulfillment

In his novel *Pays sans chapeau* (1996), Dany Laferrière both reverses and goes beyond Depestre's citational and formally mimetic adoption of anthropology, writing the discipline more seamlessly (but, at the same time, more critically and in a more ghostlike fashion) into the fictional text. Like Depestre, Laferrière writes from exile (in Montreal) and telescopes a literary relationship to a nation from which he is absent. Laferrière took up journalism critical of Jean-Claude Duvalier in the 1970s and, like his father, who fled to New York, decided to leave the country in response to the murder of a colleague.[73] However, whereas for Depestre ethnographic fiction functions like a lens through which an astronomer observes a permanently distant planet, for Laferrière the ethnographic telescope is more akin to a spyglass installed in the crow's nest of a ship: this is an optic through which one peers in the hope of viewing land where one might actually arrive, and it does not act simply to document an insurmountable separation.

Pays sans chapeau is the narrative of such an arrival, as it marks the culminating point of Laferrière's ten-novel "American autobiography" arc that thematizes the childhood, exile, and ultimate return to Haiti of Vieux Os, Laferrière's autobiographical self-fictionalization that mobilizes a bit more literary distancing than the characterology of Hampâté Bâ, whose ethnographic-literary separation from himself I explored in chapter 1. His character's return to Haiti taps into documentary desires that speak to Laferrière's personal history as a journalist and to mythologized renderings of everyday life (such as the tradition of "primitivist" painting in Haitian art that his character appreciates and that call to mind his self-characterization as a "primitive writer").[74] It also adds a speculative ethnographic dimension to the broader tradition of Caribbean writing on return exemplified by such figures as Aimé Césaire and V. S. Naipaul and by more contemporary authors such as Julia Alvarez and Edwidge Danticat.

Laferrière's return to Haiti thus reverses Depestre's ethnographic evocation of a seemingly unbridgeable gap between (exiled) writer and (remembered) nation—or, at least, it effects a certain reconciliation that Depestre cannot envisage without returning to the past (*Hadriana*'s main narrative impetus takes place in the late 1930s, after all). But *Pays sans chapeau* also sets in motion a social-scientific reckoning of Laferrière's character with Haitian folklore and anthropology such that in the novel, the ethnographic opens up narrative space for the play of fantasy, for a sort of literary wish fulfillment that relies on generic hybridity.

Pays sans chapeau deals with the return of Vieux Os from a twenty-year sojourn abroad in Montreal, but the novel opens with paratextual nods to folk culture that almost elide the question of writerly distancing in advance. As we have seen (and as we will continue to see in this book), ethnographic fiction often proceeds from paratextual generic markers that confound our expectations of what is to follow when we might wish for generically indicative moments of prefatory framing.[75] Laferrière begins by warning that the Creole proverbs at the head of the novel's chapters are translated literally, such that their true meaning will always remain buried beneath the overeager exactitude of word-for-word renderings in French. Yet, he goes on, what is hidden by translations that are too faithful "will allow us to appreciate not only popular wisdom, but also the rich Haitian linguistic creativity."[76]

This comment linking folk wisdom with linguistic innovation finds an echo on the next page in Laferrière's epigraphic citation of a "folkloric chant," given in Creole and French, that reads as follows: "Three leaves / three roots oh / he who discards, forgets / he who gathers, remembers." Given the novel's theme of return we can surmise that this epigraph points to a constitutive relationship among memory, exile, and writing, but when we take these two paratextual passages together, they point to a more fundamental question of ethnographic genealogy: they are intertwined gestures of popular valorization and folkloric invocation, and as such they return us to the opening words of Price-Mars's *Ainsi parla l'Oncle* in which the indigenist ethnographer sets out to "raise, in the eyes of the Haitian people, the value of its folklore."

Like a sample of an old song in electronic music, Laferrière borrows a snippet of Price-Mars for literary repurposing—that is, he brings ethnographic indigenism into the contemporary moment to force it to coincide with his return to and rediscovery of the nation. Laferrière thus places himself in a position analogous to that of the Haitians exhorted by Price-Mars to turn a fresh, inquisitive eye toward their country's folklore and cultural singularity. Indeed, this is how Vieux Os reencounters Haiti after twenty years' absence, with the eyes of an outside observer attempting to come to terms with the social changes that have taken place in a country with which he is still nonetheless strangely familiar.[77]

This sense of the ethnographic *unheimlich* pervades *Pays sans chapeau*, as Vieux Os, a self-styled "primitive writer," sets himself up outside his mother's house "in order to speak about Haiti calmly and at length. And even better: to speak about Haiti in Haiti. I do not write, I speak."[78] "Speaking" on his typewriter, he explains that his writerly primitivism comes from transmitting that which he sees around him directly onto the page. This strategy yields the seemingly endless division of chapters into subsections, often headed by a single word or short phrase, that organize everyday life into digestible, if not always immediately comprehensible, textual units—hence, sections titled "A Taxi," "A Jehovah's Witness," "Hygiene," "The Beggar Woman," and "The Young Nurse." Vieux Os writes/speaks his rediscovery of Haiti by organizing experiential data points into a literary spreadsheet that reads like a narrative list of whatever he comes across as he revisits Port-au-Prince.[79]

This enumerative ethnographic realism does not make up the only narrative layer of the text, though. Aside from the first and last sections of the novel (both titled "A Primitive Writer"), the chapters fall under one of two headings: *Pays Réel* (Real Country) and *Pays Rêvé* (Dreamed Country). This division is, first of all, citational, as it calls to mind Édouard Glissant's collection of short poems, *Pays rêvé, pays réel* (1985).[80] Unlike Glissant, though, Laferrière's two countries have less to do with Nature. They point instead to a sort of national overlapping, to a vision of the nation as a palimpsest whose layers can be discerned and juxtaposed by a writer who is no longer as close to his country as he once was.

The Pays Réel chapters proceed from narrative enumeration and group observations and conversations under the subheadings mentioned earlier. The Pays Rêvé chapters, by contrast, jettison such narrative hyperorganization and flow without the aid of enumerative signposts. Vieux Os gestures toward a deeper characterization of the distinction between the two when he writes, "Nighttime exists in this country. A mysterious nighttime. . . . One might say that two countries walk side by side, without ever meeting up. An ordinary people struggles to survive during the day. And this same country at night is inhabited only by gods, devils, and men turned into beasts. The real country: the struggle for survival. And the dreamed country: all the fantasies of the most megalomaniacal people on the planet."[81] The narrator's mother and aunt begin referencing zombies and *bizangos*, undead beings who pass from one country to the other and who are virtually indistinguishable from the mass of ordinary Haitians living in poverty. Vieux Os wonders whether the real world has not already become a grotesque afterlife (*au-delà*), and he resolves to investigate—using the French word *enquête*, which conjures up images of field research—how the world of the folklorically fantastic might actually be bleeding into the world of mundane struggles.

Who better to help the formerly exiled writer undertake this research than an anthropologist? Vieux Os makes his way to the anthropology department at the university to meet up with a professor named J.-B. Romain. Jean-Baptiste Romain (1914–94) was a physical anthropologist and former head of Haiti's Faculté d'Ethnologie. He published a lengthy synthetic study titled *L'Anthropologie physique des Haïtiens* in 1971, but he was also interested in updating Herskovits's research on African survivals in Haiti, work Romain published in 1978 as *Africanismes haïtiens: Compilations et notes*.[82] Vieux Os asks Romain about a mysterious army of zombies his mother has mentioned, and the professor explains that in the arid northwest of the country, where rainfall is exceedingly scarce, peasants revolted against a local landowner who controlled the distribution of water—an anecdotal parallel with Roumain's *Gouverneurs*.[83] The landowner called in soldiers to quash the uprising, but the peasant army could not be gunned down and kept advancing on the gendarmes. One soldier recognized a long-dead individual among the peasants, signaling to the state that they were indeed dealing with zombified rebels. Vieux Os follows up by asking whether there is any truth to rumors that the president has raised his own zombie army to combat American forces occupying parts of the country, to which Romain replies only cryptically and evasively.

Romain the anthropologist does not exist in the Pays Réel chapters of the novel, which renders his presence in the "dreamed" chapters all the more ghostlike and heightens the reader's awareness that Laferrière is conversing across time with the anthropologist. Or perhaps more accurately, given the novel's themes, we might say that Laferrière is in dialogue with Romain's "undead" presence in Haitian fiction.[84] Connecting the J.-B. Romain character with the image of a zombie army fighting off a US occupation certainly locates the narrative genealogically and folklorically as a continuation of the indigenist ethnographic fiction opened up by Price-Mars. As we will see with the end of the novel, however, this is an avenue that Vieux Os ultimately opts not to pursue. The ethnographic encounters that take place with Romain in the "dreamed country" also function as moments of anthropological wish fulfillment, as Laferrière writes Romain into the novel on his own terms even though, as he put it in an interview in 1998, he sought to distance himself stylistically from earlier forms of indigenist nationalism (more specifically, from the work of Roumain).[85] Stylistic distancing does not preclude ethnographic proximity. This meeting of minds, then, is the stuff of ethnographic fantasy, but Laferrière goes further by writing this question of social-scientific wish fulfillment into a broader thematic of contemporary approaches to Haiti's folkloric patrimony.

Romain sends Vieux Os to speak with a well-known psychiatrist, who explains to the narrator that the occupying Americans have discovered that the residents of the small northwestern town of Bombardopolis have been turned into zombies. They stumble upon the situation while undertaking a secret census of the country and immediately send in US experts to examine the mysterious Haitians who go months without eating or drinking. The psychiatrist's information here harks back to the days of American and European pseudoscientific accounts of Haiti's irreducible singularity, a country both eminently knowable yet also and at the same time utterly unassimilable to extant Western social-scientific categories. The novel's climax returns us to the question of ethnographic indigenism, though, as Vieux Os finds himself invited to visit the afterlife by an old peasant man, the godfather of his aunt Renée. Romain encourages Vieux Os to take the man up on his offer to guide him into the *pays sans chapeau*, which takes its name from the fact that no Haitian is ever buried wearing a hat, as Laferrière explains in an initial paratextual note. In the penultimate chapter, which takes its name from the novel's title, the man wakes Vieux Os from a dream just before dawn and accompanies him to the entrance to the other world.

As Vieux Os wanders around the (literally) otherworldly terrain of the after-life, he crosses paths with the Vodou deities Ogou Ferraille, Erzulie Dahomey, and Marinette, and he realizes that the man who guided him to the threshold of the *pays sans chapeau* is none other than Papa Legba, the *loa* who acts as the spiritual go-between linking ordinary humans with members of the Vodou pantheon. Vieux Os returns home unimpressed by the gods' mundanity, a feel-ing he communicates to Romain in a debriefing that sees the anthropologist vehemently defend the religious merits of Vodou over and against European Catholicism. Romain becomes heated and defensive during this exchange, pointing out that the country's "reputation is at its lowest point. And we ask all the sons of Haiti to make an extra effort to honor once again our roots and our gods."[86] This intransigent indigenism causes Vieux Os to realize that what the professor wants is for the narrator to write up a literary-ethnographic puff piece, a bit of social-scientific image management woven into the accessible personal narrative of a writer returning home.

When Romain takes his leave, Vieux Os recognizes in his "swaying gait" the god Damballah, who is associated with serpents: "That morning, [Dam-ballah] took on the traits of the respectable professor J.-B. Romain to come and personally try to convince me to write a book on the curious country where no one wears a hat."[87] The figure of the anthropologist shifts in this penultimate scene of the novel, moving from an indigenist nationalist à la Price-Mars (or, indeed, à la François Duvalier[88]) to a trickster fused with a deity, a rather weak and easily manipulated mouthpiece for an outmoded eth-nographic ideology. Although Vieux Os does not offer any satisfying alterna-tive to the professor's proposition, it is enough for our purposes here to read this scene (and, indeed, the entire series of interactions with Romain) as a meta-ethnographic send-up of the kind of ethnographic-literary nationalism espoused by Price-Mars. This is a critique of Haitian ethnographic fiction *qua* indigenist nationalism that still manages to write ethnography into the fic-tional text, a departure that is nonetheless an anthropological homage.

Pays sans chapeau opens, as we have seen, with a clever paratextual sam-pling of ethnographic indigenism that functions as a genealogical generic marker. Laferrière takes his writerly distance from this genealogy, but he does not disavow it entirely—ethnographic fiction as anticolonial ideology remains present in the novel, even if only as a moment of generic negativity, as a for-mal and ideological foil against which Laferrière writes his own narrative of ethnographic rediscovery. But which of the two countries written into the text does he actually reencounter? We can answer this question inclusively and conclude that Vieux Os sets foot in both the "real country" and the "dreamed country" only if we read this question as first and foremost a historical one. This might appear unexpected at first glance, for the novel foregrounds the contemporary overlapping of imagined and actually existing geographies and mythographies of the nation. Yet his rediscovery of Haiti passes through his imagined encounter with the ethnographic literary history of the nation, such that to revisit the former is to conjure and reimagine the latter.

Even though Laferrière does not seem to offer a thoroughly political vision of his homecoming, his engagement with Haitian ethnographic literary history—he writes in terms of this history, if not exactly alongside it—involves mobilizing the nation as a "fiction in politics," to return to Trouillot, that speaks to contemporary narratives of national rediscovery. Anthropology as an anti-colonial and transatlantic aesthetic ideology is thus still generically resonant, even if it is less generically urgent or immediate than in the days of Price-Mars, Roumain, and Alexis. Trouillot's claim about the nation, with which I opened this chapter, speaks more broadly than he even might have intended: in the context of this chapter, it amalgamates and dissolves into anthropology, literary history, genre theory, and folklore. Fiction here acts as the agent of this dissolutive process, provoking a sense of "unsettledness" akin to what Herskovits references in this chapter's first epigraph. And it is this unsettledness that propels the conversation about ethnographic fiction, begun by Price-Mars, through the Haitian twentieth century, since anthropological nation building elicits anxious fictional activity. Fiction takes on dissolutive powers, then, and allows for imaginative forms of national rewriting that sample, collaborate, and engage in dialogue with literature's ethnographic antecedents.

But as I have highlighted in this chapter, the incorporation of anthropology into literary rewritings of the nation was not a self-identical practice in twentieth-century Haiti. Anthropology functioned first as a transatlantic counternarrative that suggested new, anti-imperial literary epistemologies of the nation in its cultural singularity. Later novelists kept in touch with this Price-Marsian anthropology, first by writing its valorization of folklore and local knowledge into narratives of socialist humanism in the novel. More experimental writers, however, saw anthropology as provoking new fictional forms that could historicize their sampling of Haitian ethnography while, at the same time, offering new ways to encounter the nation from the distance of exile.

Laferrière ends up gesturing toward and ultimately departing from Price-Mars's anthropology and its undercurrent of indigenist nationalism. He leaves indigenism behind for a more critical appraisal of the nation as a site of ethnographic wish fulfillment, where the fantastic coexists with the everyday, thanks to experimental textual forms. Thus, in twentieth-century Haiti, anthropology moves from epistemological counternarrative to a vehicle that expresses formalist fantasy as a new way to know the nation. The question of narrativizing and historicizing anthropology in literary fiction is one to which I return in chapter 4 with the Martinican créolistes Patrick Chamoiseau and Raphaël Confiant. As both of these Caribbeanist chapters suggest with respect to this book's broader argument, such narrative projects rely on an integrative conception of both literary history and anthropology, and they endow both of these terms with transatlantic genealogies.

Chapter 4

Creole Novels and the Ethnographic
Production of Literary History

Glissant, Chamoiseau, Confiant

In a short 1992 article on Michel Leiris, Martinican poet, novelist, and philosopher Édouard Glissant finds in the work of the French Surrealist ethnographer
a desire to forge a relationship to "the other" by investigating the particular
and incomplete truth of his own self.[1] As we saw in chapter 1, this desire leads
Leiris into the realm of fiction and provokes him to effect self-other contact
by rewriting himself as a Conradian antihero. In his essay, Glissant indicates
to readers that he wants to give analytic priority to Leiris's early novel, *Au-
rora* (written in 1926–27 and published in 1946), but his most powerful claims
emerge from his readings of Leiris's anthropological work in *L'Afrique fantôme*
and *Contacts de civilisations en Martinique et en Guadeloupe* (1955), a study of
France's Caribbean departments written for UNESCO.

For Glissant, Leiris's anthropology resists totalizing claims and epistemological universals since studying cultural contact via self-interrogation precludes any easy distillations or the confirmation of ready-made hypotheses.
Drawing on Leiris's experience of everyday life in the French Caribbean,
Glissant suggests that "what interests Leiris is not the essence of this reality
(to discover or 'understand'), but primarily the complexity itself as essence."[2]
This is an "ethnology of *Relation*" that also contains a poetics dedicated to

"insert[ing] the cadenced rigor of writing into the shapeless mass of lived experience."[3] The question of Relation is a touchstone of Glissant's philosophical work on Caribbean literary and cultural production, and his reading of Leiris both establishes intellectual camaraderie and highlights the complicated role anthropology plays in his own thought. Ethnography and the social sciences recur throughout Glissant's work, but he rejects the reifying, totalizing thrust of traditional ethnography's colonially tinged conventions. As he writes in *L'intention poétique* (1969), "We hate ethnography: wherever . . . it does not fertilize the dramatic vow of relation."[4]

In his short piece later published as a section of his *Traité du tout-monde* (1997), Glissant brings Leiris's ethnography and ethnographic fiction into the ambit of his Poetics of Relation, "in which each and every identity is extended through a relationship with the Other."[5] In *Contacts de civilisations*, Leiris moves in the opposite direction, though, and identifies the ethnographic in the Caribbean writers of his day. Richly detailed, if dense at times, the book offers an account of race relations (with a special focus on education) in Martinique and Guadeloupe, former colonies that had become full-fledged French departments in 1946, nearly a decade before the work's publication.

Leiris made two research trips to the Caribbean while preparing his study: the first, in 1948, included Haiti and was intended to discern what remained of "African civilization" in Caribbean folklore while making contacts with local intellectuals. The second fieldwork trip, in 1952, stuck closely to Leiris's contract with UNESCO, which stipulated that he undertake a "critical examination of the means used to integrate human groups of non-European origin into the life of the national community."[6] Examining primarily relations between white Creoles and the extraordinarily diverse *population de couleur* (composed of Africans brought to the region during and after slavery, East Indians, and Chinese, among other ethnic groups) and occasionally citing Aimé Césaire as a "native informant," Leiris's study focuses broadly on how a uniquely Caribbean culture might coexist with and even potentially enrich postwar ideas of Frenchness.

At the end of a chapter on French culture and education in the two overseas departments, Leiris includes a section titled "The Problem of a Specifically Caribbean Culture." After surveying the work of the Martinican surrealists and Césaire's Negritude, Leiris turns to a schematic overview of a "new generation" of writers and intellectuals influenced by Césaire, of course, but also by the Haitian ethnographers Jacques Roumain and Jean Price-Mars (see chapter 3). Leiris does not cite any of these new literary figures by name—although "the poet Édouard Glissant" makes an appearance several pages earlier[7]—but points to "the birth of a specifically Caribbean spirit (*esprit*)," in implicit contrast with the Negritude and Surrealism of earlier writers.[8] This new literature reflected a clearer understanding of the French Caribbean's complex racial calculus, and Leiris argues that a new generation of writers grasped "the entirety of their identity (*personne*)," which was forged "in a milieu where, syncretically, multiple [cultural and racial] factors are at play of which none . . . could be radically excluded without the most serious blow being dealt to that which constitutes, precisely, the originality of the part of the world where these men grew up."[9]

Leiris thus recognizes an ethnographic thrust in the literary work being produced in the French Caribbean at the time of his research, work that he views as concerned with articulating the historical, geographic, and racial particularities of the region. Likewise, the Martinican writers from the *créolité* movement, working in the 1980s and '90s, adopt a similar characterization for a literature they define as Creole. "Neither Europeans, nor Africans, nor Asians, we proclaim ourselves Creoles," write Jean Bernabé, Raphaël Confiant, and Patrick Chamoiseau in their famous manifesto *Éloge de la créolité* (In Praise of Creoleness [1989]).[10] They go on to declare that their words "are not merely addressed to writers, but to any person of ideas who conceives our space (the archipelago and its foothills of firm land, the continental immensities), in any discipline whatsoever, who is in the painful quest for a more precise expression, for a truer art."[11] For the créolistes, aesthetic truth value is tied to the desire for a linguistic and artistic expression of Caribbean spatiality that is also always already a history of Caribbean raciality, an account of what Leiris refers to as the region's constitutive syncretism.

The créolité movement was an attempt to found a literary practice, a theory of Creole language politics, a literary-cultural history, and, as this chapter discusses, an anthropological rendering of Caribbean fiction. Indeed, Leiris's ethnographic instincts were on the mark. As J. Michael Dash has argued, ethnographic travelogues written by French surrealists who traveled in the Caribbean during the 1940s had a significant impact on the post-Negritude "new generation" of writers Leiris observed. Works such as André Breton's *Martinique charmeuse de serpents* (1948) and Pierre Mabille's "Souvenirs d'Haïti" (1951) "arguably launched a new anthropological discourse that would mark the major innovative tendencies in Caribbean writing in French from the 1950s onwards."[12] This chapter explores how the créolistes extended and transformed this influence, developing a theory of Creole literature that was also a theory (and practice) of ethnographic fiction.

Leiris undoubtedly had Glissant in mind when he described the new generation of Caribbean writers. Shortly after the publication of *Contacts de civilisations*, Glissant began studying ethnography under Leiris at the Musée de l'Homme in Paris.[13] Although Glissant was a profound influence on the créolistes, he did not always espouse their arguments and conclusions.[14] In a similar vein, we need not dwell uncritically on the celebratory tenets of *Éloge* to grasp the créolistes' incorporation of anthropology into their reworking of Caribbean literary culture.

Both the early Glissant of the *Discours antillais* (which features in this chapter) and the créolistes were embedded in social and political contexts that echoed, respectively, their critiques of postcolonial departmentalization in the French Caribbean and their desires for a Creole cultural politics that extended beyond national spaces. The 1970s and '80s saw renewed challenges to France's postcolonial integration of overseas territories: critiques, social movements, and violence arose in the Caribbean, the Indian Ocean, and the Pacific. Indeed, Glissant had already been critical of the dashed hopes of Caribbean decolonization *qua* assimilation in the 1960s.[15]

These challenges took a key form in the 1970s in condemnations of France's Bureau pour le Développement des Migrations Intéressant les Départements d'Outre-mer (BUMIDOM), an agency founded in 1963 to facilitate migration from overseas departments (DOM) to the metropole. The agency was hotly accused (by Césaire, among other critics) of funneling thousands of DOM migrants into low-status work while promising upward mobility, and the BUMIDOM was likened to a new slave trade that siphoned off cheap postcolonial labor to the benefit of metropolitan corporations.[16] Chamoiseau references BUMIDOM and its attendant population drain in Martinique in his novel *Chronique des sept misères* (1986).[17] The early 1980s saw bombings in Guadeloupe and metropolitan France that were linked to nationalist movements on the island, violence that seemed to prefigure separatist attacks in the Pacific territory of New Caledonia later that decade. These contestations of postcolonial dependence would find an echo in the general strikes that took place in Guadeloupe and Martinique in 2009 in response to the high cost of island living (*la vie chère*) and, more broadly, to entrenched racial and class divisions.

It was in this context of large-scale economic migration and social unrest that Glissant published *Discours antillais* (1981) and the créolistes published

Éloge eight years later. On the one hand, Glissant analyzed Martinique's postcolonial dependence on the metropole, decrying the economic and cultural stagnation and sterility that resulted from assimilation into French political life. He turned in this text to the social sciences and the category of national literature to work through the relationship between political-economic dependence and cultural production. On the other hand, the créolistes looked outward, beginning from the Caribbean (and Glissant's influence) and using anthropology to imagine historical and cultural kinship with creolized peoples the world over. This is a perspective that is more reminiscent of Glissant's later work on Relation and the category of *tout-monde*.

The early Glissant and the créolistes imagined relationships among the social sciences, anthropology, and fiction not just to critique lived experiences of postcolonial departmentalization but also, more fundamentally, to imagine new ways of knowing local lifeworlds that would speak to new histories of cultural production alongside but orthogonal to national narratives of postcolonial integration. This intellectual relationship is not without tension, however: in *Poétique de la Relation* (1990), Glissant signals his "departure" from créolité as a concept, preferring instead the more processual, open-ended idea of "creolization."[18] But in spite of this tension, the new histories these figures studied expressed desires for (post)colonial kinship that were both more localized and more diffuse than what the unidirectional ideologies of departmentalization could hope to offer. Literature and literary history could not do this expressive work on their own, though. Thus, for these Caribbean writers and intellectuals, anthropology and the social sciences do more than just "inform" literary history; they function as motors internal to it and provoke experimental theories of fiction and the novel. Literary history, from this point of view, becomes an experimental anthropology in its own right that views ethnographic knowledge and histories of form as both mutually constitutive and mutually transformative.

The créolistes reposition the world-making possibilities of Caribbean fiction as emerging from transcolonial forces of countermapping that intersect with anthropological readings of Creole raciality and (post)colonial sociality. We began to trace the connections between anthropology, imperial cartography, and genealogy in chapter 3 by examining how Haitian writers after Price-Mars returned to and transformed his transatlantic ethnographic project in their later fiction. In this chapter, though, I offer a different version of this conceptual linkage, since créolité styled itself as a bona fide literary movement possessing its own manifesto and a novel mapping of Caribbean literary history.

I refer to the créolistes' project as "ambiguous" because, in seeking to reroute the colonial encounter through a narrative of literary hybridity, they often find themselves re-rooting their textual relationship to this encounter in the forms of ontological fixity their project is bent on skirting.[19] Alongside this ambiguity, though, is an exercise in aesthetic equivalence that seeks out a suitably hybrid genre that would be commensurable with the forms of linguistic and racial hybridity the créolistes highlight and valorize, their operative initial proposition being that "Caribbean literature does not yet exist."[20] Following from such a proposition, this chapter discusses how creolized ethnographic fiction is caught up in a feedback loop of creative generic determinism: the "shapeless mass of lived experience" in the postcolonial Caribbean, of which Glissant writes, fosters and nourishes generic hybridity as so much ethnographic raw material for fictional literary production. In turn, this new generic hybridity renders lived experience aesthetically meaningful and legible in textual form.

My archive here consists of the theoretical, fictional, and literary-historical works written by the créolistes (principally Chamoiseau and Confiant) in the years surrounding the publication of *Éloge*. What I want to examine are the ways in which the ethnographic theoretical tenets of créolité are translated and converted into fictional practice while these writers show Creole literary history dovetailing with anthropology. First, however, I turn to Glissant and the *Discours antillais* (1981), published less than a decade before *Éloge*, to discern how for him Caribbean cultural production mobilizes the social sciences. The créolistes adopt a similar line of reasoning in their genealogies of Creole letters and in their fictions, as we will see, but they move between programmatic calls for hybridity and more experimental forms that speak to new ways of knowing and historicizing the decolonized world. Amid these tensions, ethnographic fiction and créolité invite transgeneric prose to intersect with transcultural and transhistorical desire in a series of open-ended connections that call to mind the way in which a character in the Chilean novelist Roberto Bolaño's book *2666* speaks of Mexico: "Every single thing in this country is an homage to everything in the world, even the things that haven't happened yet."[21]

Glissant and the Social-Scientific Scene of Caribbean Writing

Glissant easily makes intellectual elbow room for Leiris and the ethnographic in his theory of Relation, but ethnography and the social sciences also figure in his earlier work on "Caribbean discourse" in *Le discours antillais*, the créolistes' most significant explicit or implicit textual interlocutor in their 1989 manifesto.[22] Romuald Blaise Fonkoua sees a "fascination for the human sciences" in Glissant's work, especially once ethnographers ceased to view the French Caribbean as simply an extension of Europe (and, hence, as scientifically uninteresting in its proximity), seeing the region instead as culturally singular and, by extension, as anthropologically viable.[23] Although Glissant expressed a measure of skepticism in *Poétique de la Relation* about the human sciences' ability to take in, as a "whole," the "rhythms" between societies and cultures, his early work suggests that social-scientific epistemologies can offer new ways to think about literary-fictional production outside metropolitan ideologies of dependence. Later, the créolistes would refine Glissant's engagements with broadly social-scientific categories into more focused intersections with anthropology specifically.

We can locate the ethnographic in Glissant in such an early work as the impressionistic prose-poem *Soleil de la conscience* (1956). Resembling at first blush a series of essays, the text offers poetic meditations on geographies of selfhood written in terms of the author's experiences away from home, in France and Europe. Looking back at the Caribbean from metropolitan France, Glissant observes that "we can say that a people is positively constructing itself. Born from a flow (*bouillon*) of cultures, in this laboratory of which each table is an island, here is a synthesis of races, of customs, of knowledges (*savoirs*), but which extends toward its own unity."[24] Acknowledging that the causal link between synthesis and unity is precisely what remains to be developed, Glissant points out that these issues are of interest to the human sciences at the same time that they represent the most deeply personal of existential questions. "Thus, I am the ethnographer of myself," he concludes, using phrasing that recalls Leiris's particular brand of anthropological introspection considered in chapter 1. In *Soleil de la conscience*, geographic distance fosters ethnographic proximity, just as the poetic word points outside of itself toward empirically inflected discourses that cut across it but do not determine it exhaustively.

Although a quarter-century separates the two texts, *Discours antillais* also raises questions of generic legibility similar to those I highlighted in chapter 1. If Caribbean discourse is multiform, then a corresponding generic eclecticism should characterize theoretical attempts at its definition. Glissant's text wends through seemingly innumerable analytic registers, including linguistically inspired reflections on Creole orality in Caribbean writing, interviews drawn from conference proceedings, enumerations of maxims on folklore in Caribbean theater, and extended poetic epigraphs (called *Repères* [Landmarks]) that introduce each section of the lengthy work.

Two sections in particular, however, are decidedly social-scientific in tone and content and serve as interdisciplinary points of departure or frames of reference for *Discours*'s more specifically aesthetic considerations of literary production in the Caribbean and the Americas more broadly. These sections, titled "Le vécu Antillais" (Caribbean Lived Experience) and "Sociologies," fall within the part of the text titled "The Known and the Uncertain."[25] In the English version of the *Discours*, "Le vécu Antillais" is translated only partially and is rendered as "The Caribbean Experience"; the "Sociologies" section is not included.[26] This rendering certainly captures Glissant's French, but the translation I offer highlights the generic shift in this part of the text by endowing the English with the properly social-scientific category of lived experience. It also responds to an assertion Glissant makes in one of the *Discours*'s several introductions, titled "From *Malemort*," in reference to his 1975 novel of the same name. "What can writing do?" he asks at the end of this fourth introductory essay on suggesting that Martinicans are caught up in a process of "erasure" following a "successful colonization."[27] By way of a tentative answer, he offers: "What remains is to speak (*crier*) the land in its true history."[28] Bracketing temporarily the thorny question of authenticity, Glissant's prescriptive response ties together Caribbean writing with the empirical thrust of lived experience in a way that prefigures the social-scientific reflections to come.

"Caribbean Lived Experience" deals primarily with a sweeping analysis of Martinican social structures, family dynamics, and the impact of French integration on community self-awareness and the political economy of everyday life. Glissant begins from the proposition that Martinican "space-time" is fundamentally artificial because it was imposed forcibly from without during slavery and the consolidation of colonial rule. Social groups in Martinique are thus fractured and fragmented precisely because they do not internalize and experience their collective history as immanent. This diagnosis, which sees in Martinican society a pathological lack of cohesion and solidarity, effectively sidesteps the question of nostalgia for community authenticity (posed here in its negative form) by highlighting this question's inconvenient temporality. "Within this system that is Martinican society," Glissant asserts, "no solution [to social tensions] will ever be viable if it does not allow Martinicans to define, first and for themselves, their own systems of values."[29] If anything, Glissant is nostalgic for the very futurity he militantly ascribes to cultural self-definition in Martinique.

Upon surveying family structures in the 1970s (born from the "antifamily" that was the social structure par excellence of the plantation), as well as the effects of economic heteronomy on the formation of "empty" social classes that lack positive definitions of their social roles, he arrives at an observation that reveals what the rhetoric and categories of the social sciences do for his diagnostic analyses: what characterizes contemporary Martinican sociality is "*la non-maîtrise du quotidian*" (the non-mastery of everyday life).[30] Lived experience and the everyday function as heuristic markers of generic flexibility for Glissant because they allow for the expository interpretation of the cultural present while simultaneously, in the broader context of *Discours* as a whole, bridging the discursive gap between the social sciences and written cultural production.

Glissant makes this connection clearer in the "Sociologies" chapter. "Culture" and cultural production become full-fledged analytic objects here, and although his considerations evince no small degree of economism (e.g., "non-productivity" generates and determines "non-creativity"), their formal impetus opens up a social-scientific scene in which Caribbean writing can occur. Glissant once again denies that his cultural sociology is an attempt to mourn a primordial unity that, because of the trauma of the slave trade, could never have existed in Martinique. Instead, he grounds his call for a renewed identity politics in the rhetoric of an economistic cultural ethics: "This is the demand for a balance between the structure of a system of production and the responsibility of the community within the framework of that system."[31] Cultural "responsibility," understood in the sense of self-definition and -determination, is also a form of adequation in an imperative that links the militant valorization of local identities with the horizon of autonomy on the level of relations of production.

Glissant expands on this argument in reflections on the use of Creole folklore: by turns co-opted by the state in hollow celebrations of authenticity and deployed entirely negatively as a tool for cultural resistance, folklore has been drained of all use value in everyday life and is no longer ingrained in the life cycles of individuals. Similarly, using the same understanding of local color as cultural and political spectacle, the Creole language in this analysis ends up quaintly "folklorized" as a communicational language containing only a bare minimum of cultural capital.

The culmination of Glissant's cultural sociology is a final section, called "Literature and Production," in which he explores why Creole oral popular culture, born from the constraints and forced proximity of the plantation, failed to feed organically the history of French Caribbean letters. Referring to Martinican writing as a "literature in suspension," he makes the transhistorical claim that, unlike the normative history of all other national literatures, oral traditions never initially bled into written textual production on the island.[32] Glissant attributes this to Martinique's fragmented postslavery transition from plantation economy to, eventually, an economy based primarily on importation. The corresponding phenomenon in the world of letters, then, saw Creole orality left by the wayside as writers imported modes and forms from Paris, paying only cursory lip service to Creoleness as quaint aesthetic window dressing.

Negritude represented one way out of this nonproductive impasse, and Glissant calls for the renewed aesthetic vigor of *Antillanité*, the confluence of multiple forms of textual "re-rooting" throughout the Caribbean, as a way to deepen the aesthetic resonance of Negritude by multiplying its geographic, linguistic, and racial referents.[33] Of course, he goes on later in *Discours* to give Antillanité fuller treatment. However, it is not so much the definition of this well-known concept that interests me here as the social-scientific terms from which it emerges: Glissant urges French Caribbean fiction writers to continue and broaden the work of figures such as Derek Walcott, Nicolás Guillén, and V. S. Naipaul, and he does so by "sociologizing" both the historical discontinuities of Martinican letters and the sense of momentous literary futurity born from their surpassing.

This reading of Glissant and the social sciences relies as much on the content and form of the "Sociologies" chapter as it does on the much more stylized and poetic paratextual framing he provides in the "Landmarks" section that precedes it. Subtitled "The Three Discourses," this brief yet evocative opening reflection outlines three discursive phenomena—"traditional oral discourse," "elitist discourse," and "frenzied [or wild, *délirant*] discourse"—without elaborating exactly how they map onto the social-scientific analyses that have come before or that immediately follow. "Entangled in the same real, following each other and superimposed on each other, and distinguishable through analysis," these discourses make claims on everyday life while still falling short of any meaningful correspondence with it.[34] The first, traditional, discourse is one with which we are familiar, as it refers to the oral popular culture of the plantation that has been marginalized in its folklorization, thanks to Martinique's culture of nonproduction. Glissant refers to this discourse as "broken." The second discourse, that of the elite, is both banalized and de-realized—hence, its characterization as "empty." The third, qualified as "tragic," indexes in true dialectic fashion the insufficiencies and inadequacies of the first two.

But it is a parenthetical, fourth discourse that should catch our eye here: a "literary" discourse that runs through the first three while seeking in vain to effect a "surpassing synthesis." As Glissant explains, "Most often it happens that it inherits their lacks, without shaking loose their significations."[35] Despite the parenthetical framing, this last discourse is anything but an afterthought; nor does it play the role of a synthetic *deus ex machina*. This definition of literary discourse is, on the one hand, the performative discovery of a literary countercurrent running against the forms of discursive alienation he has just enumerated—to articulate this discourse is to enact its encompassing potentiality. On the other hand, though, this potentiality remains unfulfilled for the moment, and the definition of a discourse then doubles as proleptic wish fulfillment, a call for a literary language that no one can as yet speak fluently. From this point of view, the function of Glissant's social-scientific investigation is both archeological and anticipatory, since it serves to unearth a form of literature and to call forth writers who can make use of it.

In the interplay between this stylized introductory section and the essays surrounding it, the social sciences and literary fiction express each other without watering each other down or becoming indistinguishable in the creative feedback loop in which they participate. The social-scientific register Glissant adopts allows for the staging of the literary-fictional discourse he excavates and foresees. The image conjured up here is less one of the social sciences "grounding" fiction than it is one of fertile rhetorical soil that both preserves and nourishes fiction amid what Glissant identifies as the discontinuous productive histories of French "monocolonialism." In this respect, then, Glissant deploys the social sciences to restore and renew Martinican literary production while simultaneously using them to examine everyday histories and experiences of colonial and postcolonial nonproduction. In this formal climate, the Caribbean artist grows indifferent to the traditions of generic division (what Jacques Rancière, in a different context, refers to as a hierarchical distribution of genres and the subject matter to which they correspond), becoming at once "an ethnographer, a historian, a linguist, a painter of frescos, an architect."[36] This is creative generic indifference cast as productive generic hybridity.

Our passage through *Discours antillais* reveals that, for Glissant, the social sciences stage not only a new form of Caribbean writing but also a new type of artist who can measure up to it. As he goes on to write in the "National Literatures" chapter, which immediately follows "Sociologies," what is involved here is "the expression of a new man" who is not beholden to the literary constraints of old.[37] This vision of Caribbean literature understands written praxis as generative of a new *anthropos* at the confluence of multiple discursive/generic registers. It also enables us to make a broader point that intersects with the argument of this book as a whole: Glissant's generic shifts trace an ethnographic fiction that is also an anticolonial humanism, becoming a genre that creates and renews its author in the act of writing. Ethnographic fiction here places the interaction between literature and the social sciences in the service of a new anticolonial anthropos, a reanimated vision of man or the human that reinvests the concept of production (central to Glissant's analyses, as we have seen) with aesthetic vigor.

Créolité and Caribbean Literary History as Ethnographic Teleology

The experimental form of the *Discours antillais* allows social-scientific categories and ways of knowing to help reimagine literary production outside ideologies and lived experiences of (post)colonial dependence. Thus, for Glissant, lived experience, *le vécu*, crosses the social-scientific terrain that feeds the futurity of Caribbean fiction, extending into the realm of letters and revitalizing the figure of the Caribbean writer in the process. The créolistes take their cue from Glissant on this point, since they are also invested in a sort of writerly humanism—to wit, the foregrounding of the Creole author whose writing would ideally be representationally and linguistically coterminous with all of humanity. But they also refine and focus Glissant's perspective, distilling his broader concerns with the social sciences writ large into more pointed borrowings from and observations about anthropology. Their vision of créolité mobilizes a language politics that embraces linguistic multiplicity in a "polysonic vertigo" eschewing narrowly conceived Creolophone defensiveness; despite many pronouncements along these lines, though, Chamoiseau and Confiant always err on the side of French, the primary language of their novels and literary studies.[38]

Like Glissant, their project involves reckoning literarily with lived experience, and they approach Creoleness as "*a question to be lived*" and not definitively resolved.[39] The créolistes write this ethnographic impulse into the literary genealogy of their movement, opening up a teleological perspective that reads créolité back into the history of Francophone Caribbean writing and that gives lived experience aesthetic pride of place in the work of their forebears. They include well-known figures such as Césaire and the Guadeloupean-born Saint-John Perse, as well as the Haitian ethnographers examined in chapter 3, but

Glissant remains a towering transitional figure in this rewritten literary history. In their genealogical *Lettres créoles* (1991), for instance, Chamoiseau and Confiant proclaim, "*Voilà*, at the end of these trajectories of Creole letters . . . we arrive at the solitary and unifying (*solidaire*) Marker. It is he who . . . builds today, it seems to us, the future of Creole literature. This Marker of world echoes (*échos-monde*), you understand, is Édouard Glissant."[40] The unifying vision they see in Glissant appears somewhat ironic, given his departure from the créolité concept mentioned earlier.

As we see in what follows, by situating themselves in the futurity opened up by this reading of Glissant, the créolistes also adopt and transform his engagement with the social sciences, often turning specifically to ethnography and anthropology in their writing of créolité as lived experience. But the filiation they want to establish with Glissant is only partial: the créolistes' writing seems caught between programmatic approaches to literary production and identity and the more experimental forms that Glissant espoused.

In *Éloge*, the créolistes use anthropology to think the question of identity both transcolonially and extracolonially, eventually moving outside the postcolonial relationship with metropolitan France to establish new forms of political and aesthetic proximity. The trans- or extracolonial production of affect mobilizes what they call a "double solidarity"—with other postcolonial populations from across the Caribbean, on the one hand, and with culturally or racially hybridized people from across the globe, on the other. The first of these is a "*Caribbean solidarity with all the peoples of our Archipelago*," experienced primarily through geographic contiguity and, implicitly, through intertwined histories of colonial rule. The second, however, is a "*Creole solidarity with all African, Mascarin, Asian, and Polynesian peoples who share the same anthropological affinities as we do—our Creoleness*."[41] The latter formulation points toward certain shared experiences of hybridity, or métissage, to be sure, but the ill-defined "anthropological affinities" also seem to instantiate a fictive kinship that sidesteps the colonial encounter in favor of a politics of analogy in which anthropological proximity proceeds from local experiences of cultural contact (to borrow Leiris's term) that may be geographically distant but nonetheless correspond to one another.

The créolistes go on to suggest, problematically and somewhat overambitiously, that their vision of Creole literature could fully encompass both directions of the political-aesthetic affect they describe. If this were so, how could Creole literary expression avoid being coextensive with prefabricated ideologies of authenticity and reiterating the a prioriness, as it were, of the cultural analogies they proclaim? It is important to identify such blind spots in their manifesto, as critics have rightfully done;[42] nonetheless, doing so is of ancillary concern to my broader point that this vision of Creole literature generates and relies on anthropological claims to self-knowledge.

Likewise, once again adopting a rhetoric of authenticity based on the presumed fullness of literary expression, the créolistes insist that Creole writing "must look for our truths," but "these realities ought not to be described ethnographically, nor ought there to be a census-taking of Creole practices after the fashion of the Haitian indigenists, instead we ought *to show what, in these practices, bears witness to both Creoleness and the human condition.*"[43] This assertion swaps one definition of ethnography for another, rejecting a narrow ethnographic scientism (in the form of dry enumeration, perhaps) in favor of the more expansive understanding of "anthropological affinities" described earlier, in which writing actualizes proximity and kinship in ways that were hitherto unthinkable. Creole writing contains an ethnographic epistemology that recognizes the ways in which local knowledge necessarily intersects with a universal humanism.

Ethnographic epistemology here is recast as a textual strategy of literary perception that is bent on making visible (and hence, thinkable) aspects of lived experience that past generations of Caribbean writers deemed unworthy of attention. In a formulation blending Glissant's social-scientific analyses with his anticipatory definition of literary discourse, the créolistes describe and prescribe the task of the writer, whose "vocation is to identify what, in our daily lives, determines the patterns and structure of the imaginary."[44] In conjunction with the writer's immersion in everyday life, the key word in this prescriptive characterization is "our," since it distinguishes créolité from Negritude, seen as insufficiently rooted due to its preoccupation with transcolonial blackness and exoticist regionalism, which appropriates a metropolitan literary register and brings a colonial gaze to bear on the French Caribbean.

The drawback or pitfall of such a perspective is that, in democratizing the representational objects of Creole writing, it risks veering off into celebratory quaintness. Thus, in another literary imperative, "Our writing must unreservedly accept our popular beliefs, our magico-religious practices, our magic realism, the '*milan,*' '*majò,*' '*ladja,*' and '*koudmen*' rituals."[45] It is difficult to see here precisely where literary ethnography ends and localized essentialism begins. As I show in the sections that follow taking up the novels of Chamoiseau and Confiant, respectively, one way out of this troubling indistinction is to put local knowledge in the service of a critique of metropolitan-derived narratives of political integration. This approach critically stresses the contemporaneity of the colonial encounter while simultaneously drawing an epistemology (a "literary knowledge of ourselves"[46]) from such instances of literary confrontation.

Créolité as a literary knowledge project also emerges from perspectives on Caribbean literary history—genealogical narratives that establish intergenerational affinities and endow the movement with an air of aesthetic inevitability. For both Confiant and Chamoiseau, genealogy involves writing ethnography into the literary history of créolité. Confiant, for his part, locates the roots of Creoleness in the ethnographic travel writings of Lafcadio Hearn, the Greek American journalist known especially for his descriptive accounts of Japanese culture near the turn of the twentieth century. In the late 1880s, though, following a cruise to the Caribbean, Hearn arranged to spend two years in Martinique, and in 1890 he published accounts of both his trips as *Two Years in the French West Indies*. Confiant wrote the foreword to the 2001 edition of Hearn's book, and in his brief introductory comments he proclaims Hearn to be "one of the most modern writers of the second half of the nineteenth century" whose cosmopolitan personal trajectory and intellectual drive allowed for the creation of Creoleness, defined as "the assumption in daily existence, throughout the most common of actions, of various cultural, racial, linguistic and religious components of oneself."[47] Confiant insists that Hearn's descriptions of colonial Martinique lack the exoticizing foreign gaze of an artist such as Gauguin (who traveled to the island around the same time), stressing instead that his descriptions of Martinique's colors and sensitively detailed literary portraits of the population evince an "instinctive relationship" with the colony and its cultures.[48]

Two Years in the French West Indies is not quite as free from exoticism as Confiant would have it, but this observation should not prevent us from noting the cosmopolitan richness of Hearn's ethnographic sketches. The text holds together a travelogue of the cruise and fourteen chapters serving as ethnographic snapshots of folklore, women, race, dress codes, and occupations.[49] To take just one example, we could consider the chapter "Les Porteuses," about the "female carriers" who transport food and goods atop their heads in heavy yet efficiently packed cases. Hearn opens his reflections by likening the town of St. Pierre with its volcano (Mont Pelée would destroy the town in 1902) to a dreamscape from ancient Rome. However, he undercuts this idyllic assimilation of Martinique to European antiquity by revealing that the "hallucination is broken by modern sounds" of port life and bustling transportation. One grows aware, he goes on, that the language being spoken on the streets is "neither Hellenic nor Roman: only the beautiful childish speech of French slaves."[50]

Although these descriptions appear at first to give the lie to Confiant's triumphalist declaration, Hearn follows this remark by asserting that Creole raciality prevents Martinicans from being categorized using conventionally narrow ethnographic taxonomies. Against implied claims that social scientists could seek out atavistic African traits among Martinique's Creoles, he wonders,

> But what slaves were the fathers of this free generation? Your anthropologists, your ethnologists, seem at fault here: the African traits have become transformed; the African characteristics have been so modified within little more than two hundred years—by inter-blending of blood, by habit, by soil and sun and all those natural powers which shape the mould of races,—that you may look in vain for verification of ethnological assertions . . . No: this is a special race, peculiar to the island as are the shapes of its peaks.[51]

Hearn's thinking here reveals a special concern for the singularity of Creole hybridity, which Confiant and his co-authors would revise and describe as radically open nearly a century later. Equally important, though, is his use of ethnographic observation to critique the scientific standards of the anthropology of his day: this is a relativist approach to Creole singularity that, for Hearn, conventional ethnography is taxonomically and epistemologically ill equipped to handle. This line of argumentation lends crucial ethnographic weight to Confiant's genealogical claims.

Confiant and Chamoiseau had already paid homage to Hearn and his creolized personal history in their history of Creole literature, *Lettres créoles* (1991). But they push the ethnographic component of Creole literary history in other directions, too, redirecting créolité through anthropology and ethnographic fiction. Thus, the Martinican writer Vincent Placoly's novel *Frères volcans* (1983) is an example of "a literature articulated in the ethno-text of speech (*la parole*) and which, in speech, creates for itself a language subject to the ambivalences of creolization."[52] Jean Price-Mars's *Ainsi parla l'Oncle* (1928), with its denunciation of "bovarysme" in Haitian literature (see chapter 3), forges a new path in this literary history in which the valorization of Creole popular culture serves to decolonize Haitian fiction. They reference Claude Lévi-Strauss's time in Martinique in 1941 (fictionalized by Confiant in *Le Nègre et l'Amiral*) and point out that Césaire sought out Africa "in the study of ethnographers (the German Leo Frobenius, the French Maurice Delafosse, not yet stricken by the thought of the One, who can still discern the richness of the Diverse, and who describe Africa in admiring terms . . .)."[53] The literary history of créolité is meandering, spanning several centuries and multiple national-colonial traditions, and Chamoiseau and Confiant highlight its productive ethnographic digressions as they write the history of their own movement.

Chamoiseau makes ethnographic teleology intersect with literary autobiography in *Écrire en pays dominé* (1997), his account of his emergence as a writer that doubles as a Creole *Künstlerroman*. Here, the kinds of writerly imperatives that take the form of prescriptive injunctions in *Éloge* or in *Lettres créoles* become experimental narratives whose sense of form relies on creative citationality and speculative literary history. Woven into Chamoiseau's personal narrative is an imagined conversation with a fictional "old warrior" who discourses to the author on the question of artistic production in the peripheral spaces of what we would now call the Global South. The text is also punctuated by aphoristic statements evincing the many intellectual debts Chamoiseau has accrued to figures from world literature and beyond (Proust, Swift, Fanon, among many others). The first of these figures interrupting his narrative is Ogotemmêli, the "old Dogon sage" who was Marcel Griaule's famous ethnographic interlocutor in his *Dieu d'eau* (1948): "From Ogotemmêli: Dreamer, dreamer, still a dreamer, always a dreamer, terrible dreamer."[54] Despite the impressionistic and often opaque tone of these personal adages, the individuals they reference constitute a conversational bibliography of Chamoiseau's aesthetic trajectory—and the fact that Ogotemmêli is given pride of place reveals the extent to which he imagines his writerly *je* as a literary character and as an ethnographer.

Accompanied by an epigraphical nod to sociologist Edgar Morin, the title of the second part of the book alludes at once to Saint-John Perse, Glissant, and the social sciences: "Anabase, *In Digeneses according to Glissant*: Where the Ethnographer becomes a Word-Scratcher (*Marqueur de Paroles*)." Here, Chamoiseau impressionistically inhabits Martinique's constituent racial groups (colonizers, Africans, Amerindians, etc.), imagining the island's cultural history from the perspective of each in turn. This dreamscape—referred to as "my dream-land" (*mon rêver-pays*)—projects Chamoiseau's writerly self ethnographically back into the past so that he might experience the manifold cultural trajectories (what he calls the "anthropological magma"[55]) composing his composite aesthetic present. This is créolité as transhistorical ethnographic phenomenology. For instance, imagining himself as Pierre d'Esnambuc (1585–1636), the founder of the first colonial settlement in Martinique, he writes:

"I hear the first impact of my boot on the sand; it prolongs the sepulchral echo of that of Columbus."[56]

Later, inhabiting both his own self and that of a precolonial Carib Indian, he plays out the same scene in reverse, observing the arrival of d'Esnambuc and the first French settlers with an "eyewitness" account that is also tinged with an artificially constructed literary-historical voyeurism. Predictably enough, wandering imaginatively through the traumas of slavery and colonial indentured servitude, he arrives at a contemporary *moi-créole* whose "anthropological densities" were presaged by the oral culture of the plantation storyteller, and they clamor for writerly attention in the *je* who now recognizes Martinique as a creolized land.[57] This moment of recognition, an ethnographic epiphany, allows for the coming of age of Chamoiseau as a writer who must now produce "the leitmotif of the world" on the written page, a world "that reflects its Diverse in our diversities."[58] In other words, Chamoiseau's transhistorical imagination causes him to realize that converting créolité and experiences of creolization into writing involves the literary actualization of the ethnographic teleology he has just sketched. In fact, the two movements are inseparable.

For Chamoiseau and Confiant, créolité is not so much a genre in itself as it is an aesthetic disposition, a writerly positionality that instantiates an attitude toward and appropriation of literary history. This "mood," as it were, determines the writer's relationship to extant literary forms—especially the novel, as I show in the final two sections of this chapter—and allows for the identification and creative mobilization of hybridized genetic and generic material to which these forms had hitherto remained blind. In other words, to continue with the case of the novel, the créolistes' approach to literary history promotes the discovery of the novel's recombinant DNA, the differentially derived generic elements capable of making this form speak to Creole lived experience. Although créolité is not a genre, Creole fiction is ethnographic fiction because of the generically recombinant claims ethnographic fiction makes on literary history. Chamoiseau and Confiant filter these claims through a teleology that generates créolité historically while simultaneously opening up other discursive (i.e., ethnographic) avenues that lead to and determine the literary history into which they write themselves. But Chamoiseau's solo work on this history calls to mind Glissant's sense of formal experimentation more readily than the more rigidly prescriptive texts on which he and Confiant collaborate, and more readily still than Confiant's own novels. The chapter's next two sections examine what this divergence means for ethnography in the Creole novel.

Ethnographic Realism as Translational Allegory

Whereas Patrick Chamoiseau is concerned with playing intertextual games of referentiality within the realm of the novel, Raphaël Confiant is more explicitly focused on the entanglement of genre, representation, and what we can now recognize as an ethnographic aesthetic in Caribbean fiction. Although this constellation of questions allows him room for free play within the space of the novel, it is also something of a trap: Confiant's focus on representation ends up feeling conceptually narrow, especially in comparison with Chamoiseau's fiction. Although Confiant's work is self-reflexive in many of the ways that matter to this book, the problem of representation ultimately prevents him from imagining in fiction experimental ways of knowing that owe a debt to anthropology.

I focus here on Confiant's novel *L'allée des soupirs* (1994), but the question of ethnography goes back further in his oeuvre. His 1988 novel *Le Nègre et l'Amiral* (1988) was his first work written in French instead of Creole. It deals with everyday life on Martinique during World War II and contains a humorous cameo appearance by Lévi-Strauss, who was indeed stranded on the island on his way to New York in 1941.[59] This cameo sees the budding ethnographer (along with André Breton, who accompanies him in the text) interact with several of Confiant's characters, who are eager to discuss with the two writers the potential merits of the novel for aesthetically capturing the daily realities of Martinican social life.

Although an unexpected plot device, Lévi-Strauss's appearance is much more than narrative window dressing, as it signals a concern on Confiant's part for ethnographic modes of representation, bent as they are on burrowing into the cultural minutiae of everyday life, and for the ways in which the ethnographic writ large might be brought into the realm of the Creole novel. As we have seen, these broad concerns are echoed in *Éloge*, and they receive even fuller treatment in *L'allée des soupirs*, a sweeping reconstruction of daily life in Martinique during the bloody riots that gripped Fort-de-France in 1959. One of the major stakes of this novel involves the definition of a literary form capable of rendering the complex messiness of Martinican life, and Confiant approaches this problem by translating the aesthetic precepts of créolité into a Creole novel that ethnographically allegorizes its own conditions of production.

Confiant deftly transitions from the tenets of literary créolité outlined in *Éloge* to a fictional project with ethnographic aspirations, but at its most basic level *L'allée des soupirs* fictionalizes the story of the riots in the island's capital, Fort-de-France, in December 1959, which began after a European man knocked over a black man's motorbike and initially refused to apologize. Once the French riot police (the notorious Compagnies Républicaines de Sécurité [CRS]) intervened, ordinary residents of the island fought back for several days in clashes with the police that left several young Martinicans dead.[60] Confiant's novel approaches the riots through a multitude of narrative perspectives and subject positions, since his characters occupy a number of social roles and racial categories—not to mention disparate racial(ized) ideologies in a newly postcolonial context in which decolonization for Martinique meant assimilation into the political life of the metropole. The riots thus do not so much "happen" in the novel as they are written into existence via an ever expanding multiplicity of narrative subjectivities, and from this point we can make the observation that, while the text does contain several central characters, it lacks a hero understood in the conventional sense as an organizing or totalizing narrative perspective.[61]

Confiant's sense of plot alone is enough to provoke us to read *L'allée des soupirs* as offering an ethnographic reconstruction of a significant event in Martinique's postwar history that also doubles as a rewriting of the event into the everyday cultural life of the city. However, an important leitmotiv in the novel obliges us to take this observation even further: also at stake in the text is the search for a mode of expression capable of capturing the linguistic, cultural, and racial characteristics of créolité in literature. Confiant encourages us to read his novel as an ethnographic allegory of its own literariness since two of his principal characters, Jacques Chartier (a white Frenchman and amateur novelist bent on aesthetically tapping into Martinique's Creole culture) and Monsieur Jean (a black former teacher who loses his position after minor acts of collaboration during the war and who turns to poetry), occupy divergent aesthetic positions in a debate on poetics that takes place throughout the novel concerning just how Martinique's créolité ought aesthetically to be represented.

The terms of this debate, in addition to the way in which it plays out in Confiant's creolized French, intersect with several major thematic concerns: in Chartier and Jean's debate (and in the novel more generally) the related questions arise of what Creole subjectivity looks like, what kind of modernity a valorized créolité would produce ("Modern man will be Creole or he will not be at all, I tell you!" exclaims Chartier at one point, echoing phrasing used by André Breton and Suzanne Césaire[62]), and how créolité might constitute a cultural utopia coexisting with the decidedly dystopian and disastrous cultural present of the text. In less abstract terms, though, this debate turns on the more obviously anthropological questions of how Creole culture in its hybridity and the everyday life of Martinique can be translated into literature, and it is in this respect that we can allow these major concerns of Confiant's novel to dovetail with his sense of ethnographic fictionality.

As James Clifford has reminded us, allegory as a rhetorical device encourages us to observe how anthropology and literature have a common cause and how questions of anthropological import, such as those addressed by Confiant, might be approached through literary modes of representation.[63] If the ethnographic approaches literature and storytelling via allegory, though, can we not claim that the reverse also holds true? If, as Clifford argues, allegory allows ethnographic writing to acknowledge its debt to literary modes of representation, it also allows fiction to inhabit ethnographic writing and concepts, evincing its own debt to another disciplinary representative logic. From this perspective, allegory is a fundamentally translational concept that fosters and facilitates creative exchanges between the fictional (and hence, the novelistic) and the ethnographic understood in its broadest sense.

Ethnography is particularly amenable to translation because as a genre it already represents a sort of conversion from the rich messiness of everyday practices, beliefs, discourses, and struggles to the polished ethnographic text as organized by the anthropologist, who appears as a translator in their own right. As Lawrence Venuti puts it, translation is "scandalous"—but productively so— since it unavoidably creates new practices of reading and writing as well as novel disciplinary configurations.[64] Confiant's passage from theory to practice is thus doubled by a concurrent postulating of the translational relationship between ethnography and fiction, a relationship that endows *L'allée des soupirs* with its representational power.

As I have stressed throughout this book, since purely fictional texts enjoy the privilege of engaging in translational and disciplinary free play, they are able to set in motion ethnographic thought experiments that more conventional works of anthropology, concerned as they need to be with the preservation of a certain documentary empiricism, must generally avoid. Confiant puts this privilege to good use when he allows two of his major characters, Monsieur Jean and Jacques Chartier (who stand in, respectively, for poetry and prose, the sensuous, Third Worldist Negritude of Césaire and a more specifically Creole critique of such earlier forms of black consciousness in the Francophone world[65]) to stage a debate about literary representation in the Caribbean against the dystopian backdrop of a Fort-de-France in the grip of extreme forms of social violence. Both of these characters are outliers of a sort, since no one in the proletarian neighborhood of Terres-Sainville where the novel takes place understands precisely why Monsieur Jean has been blackballed from teaching or why the white Frenchman Jacques is so interested in Caribbean vernacular cultures to the point where he can joke in Creole for hours over glasses of rum in a local bar.

In fact, the two men remain strangers to each other until they find themselves alone at a bar one night, forced to drink together and to acknowledge each other's presence. This forced proximity initiates the debate that will continue throughout the novel and that begins with the Frenchman critiquing Monsieur Jean's poetic style and, by extension, what he perceives as the defects inherent to all hitherto existing poetry in the Americas: "My dear man, poetry in the Americas only knows how to talk about rocks, the sea, the sun, mountains, and open spaces. It is incapable of evoking the American grotesque.... Your poets prefer the pure air of nature, how should I put it, untouched, yes, untouched by man, rather than diving into the foulness of everyday life."[66] On the one hand, Chartier indicts what he perceives to be poetry's overly pastoral representation of nature, and, on the other hand, he points out that poetry is largely unconcerned with the social drama of everyday life. Poetic language, it would seem, is insufficiently humanist in that it neither seeks to respond nor offers an alternative to everyday struggles in the postcolonial Caribbean. From this point of view, poetic language is "untranslatable" insofar as it cannot be converted into a language-based account of lived experience.

This exchange continues with Monsieur Jean challenging Chartier to consider Césaire's *Cahier d'un retour au pays natal*, whose aesthetic merits the white novelist is quick to recognize and whose shortcomings he discerns with equal speed: "Great art, very great art! But the grotesque of the Americas does not appear in it at all. We only see a very universal misery and the Fort-de-France Césaire describes could be any South African township, any African shantytown or North African casbah. Nothing very specific in spite of the literary genius of the author."[67] Negritude's universalizing conceptualization of black racial particularity dissolves cultural and geographical specificities such that, as Chartier seems to imply here, a universal framework for political solidarity supplants a documentary aesthetic imperative that would represent créolité and Martinique as ethnographically unique cultural imaginaries. "My dear Jean," Chartier concludes, "I think that only the novel has the power to capture this grotesque, I mean, prose."[68] For Chartier, then, the novel is capable of doing what poetry cannot—namely, capturing the specificities of Martinican cultural life in fictional form. However, up to this point the Frenchman's defense of the novel proceeds negatively, through a critique of poetry as beautiful yet fundamentally untranslatable, and does not offer a clear picture of exactly what this fictional and novelistic capture of Martinique might entail.

We can begin to tease out the crux of Chartier's point when we consider what "the grotesque" or "the American grotesque" means for the Frenchman who, despite his linguistic pretensions and affinity for Creole cultures, is still an outside observer of Martinique's social life—a quasi-fieldworker figure, we might say. The two characters continue their conversation several pages later, which gives Chartier the chance to expand on his idea of the grotesque: "Let it be understood: 'grotesque' in no way has a pejorative meaning for me. Let us say that it designates a certain excess of the reality of island life. It is the disproportion between this permanent excess and the smallness of the island that creates this grotesque."[69] Paradoxically, the grotesque seems to gesture at once to the everyday realities of life in Martinique and to the ways in which those realities exceed and travel beyond the geographical confines of the island. Chartier puts this sense of disproportion (*démesure*) more humorously when he observes a pack of semi-wild Creole dogs who spend evenings running around the neighborhoods of Fort-de-France and who seem to follow their own secret, hidden logic: "This is what people must try to write . . . this organized wandering, this madness that is not the ordinary madness that European books describe."[70]

What these abstract and formalist remarks describe is a sense of ethnographic realism that would grasp Fort-de-France and Creole culture more generally in its specificity, but that would also have to account for events, situations, and formal devices that are outside of realism's traditional representative purview. This type of realism is itself a certain *démesure* of conventional literary realism since it must keep track of an "organized wandering" that both characterizes everyday life in Martinique and is difficult to render in strictly realist terms.

Chartier later announces, "We must invent . . . a new form, a diverse architecture that would be able to . . . that would tie together the meanderings of reality without pretending to be able to exhaust it. We need to build the Creole novel with the help of unfinished sections. Let a heterogeneous world be read, a bit like the style of your Creole houses."[71] Chartier's ethnographic realism seems capable of succeeding only to the extent that it makes itself known thoroughly to be constructed, a realist bricolage composed of disparate patches of the social existence of ordinary human beings whose lives are sewn together in such a way that the seams are always intentionally left showing. This is a realism that is at once up to the task of translating everyday life on the island into literature and highly conscious that this form of translation must always remain imperfect, since realism cannot claim to totalize Martinique or Creole culture in any simplistically holistic manner.

Incredibly enough, entrenched as he is in his faith in poetry, Monsieur Jean comes around to his literary foil's mode of thinking, not by deciding to become a literary fieldworker but by realizing that his reticence to share his poetry with those around him stems from his awareness that his poetic rhetoric does not measure up to the "excès de vie" of his compatriots: "He always knew . . . that celebrating the mineral, the vegetal, the sky and its colors, was to flee, a shying away from Creole reality and its train of grotesquenesses."[72] This excess is also what makes for Martinique's cultural specificity, as Chartier indicates: "He had just understood that Western literary heroes such as Lancelot, Werther, or Thérèse Raquin, could not take shape in this universe. They were at the same time too simple and too pure, or rather they were superior to their own personal history whereas the Creole hero was everybody and anybody."[73] This characterological ordinariness comes from realism, of course, but when taken in the context of the créolité project, we can see how it gestures toward a literary ethnography of everyday life.

Although by the end of the novel Monsieur Jean ends up refusing to adopt Chartier's approach, Confiant himself coyly indicates that the very text we are reading constitutes an attempt to represent this new type of literature. He does this by having Monsieur Jean realize that the people with whom he interacts each day are always already Creole literary characters, "tout le monde et n'importe qui": "It's Rigobert, the chief of Morne Pichevin. Or Ancinelle Bertrand, his beloved fiancée. Or Fils-du-Diable-en-Personne, or even that nobody Eugène Lamour. For them, the eventful moments of existence, entangled with crazy inventions or beliefs, weigh more heavily than their meager selves."[74] Jean's list of Creole heroes is composed of none other than other characters in the novel, and Confiant's narrative continually (and even confusedly, at times) jumps between them; the reader cannot help but recognize at this point, along with Monsieur Jean, that the novel itself calls on all these ordinary heroes as so many subjective perspectives on the events of December 1959, and that the cohesiveness of Confiant's story comes from the fact that he refuses to choose from among all these "heroic" points of view.

It is at this significant moment in the text, as well, that we become aware of the ways in which the novel has allegorized its own conditions of production via the ongoing debate between Chartier and Monsieur Jean: in addition to the multitude of subjective perspectives constituting the narrative and a valorization of the Creole language (which Chartier refers to as a "verbal elixir"[75]), the text is interspersed with poems, some of which are Monsieur Jean's own venerations of nature and others of which appear at the beginning of each of the five sections into which the novel is divided and that explicitly take everyday life in the city as their subject. Thus, even though Monsieur Jean assures Chartier near the end of the novel that he will never stray from the poetic word, we as readers come away from the text with the idea that *L'allée des soupirs* is precisely the novel he could have written had he taken up Chartier's theory of Creole fiction and blended it with his own predilection for poetry.

L'allée des soupirs is significant because it stages a debate on Creole literary production that is shot through with the imperatives of ethnographic fictionality and because it actually enacts the terms of this debate in the very form and narrative organization of the novel. In addition, the text is in dialogue with a broader set of questions concerning Caribbean writing from within and beyond the French nation that Confiant himself helped to draft in *Éloge* and that offer a provocative theoretical framework for thinking about ethnographic representations of Creole hybridity and métissage in the Francophone Caribbean imaginary.

As I have argued here, these ethnographic representations, which lead the novel deeper into a narrativization of everyday life, also lead the novel beyond itself into a metatextual allegory that relies on the inherent suppleness and translatability of the ethnographic, characteristics that have subtended my discussion of Confiant's text.[76] But *L'allée des soupirs* reaches its limit at just this point: Confiant's focus on representation ultimately situates his novel too closely to the prescriptivism of *Éloge* to offer the kind of experimental epistemology that animates the work of many figures in this book. In short, the foregrounding of representation causes the novel form to remain too identical to itself. Chamoiseau, to whom I now turn, departs from this set of concerns by bringing the question of documentation into the novel. This move not only allows him to speak more directly to anthropology but also to echo the formal eclecticism of Glissant's *Discours antillais*.

Intertextuality, and Literary Documents

Two novels by Chamoiseau illustrate this departure: *Solibo Magnificent* (1988) and *Texaco* (1992). The former is a Martinican crime novel of sorts, although it is much more poetically stylized and metafictionally invested than the more hard-boiled crime fiction Confiant has written since the early days of créolité.[77] It is also less concerned with adopting or reconfiguring the generic conventions of crime fiction, a question to which I turn in chapter 5 with the detective novels of Jean-Claude Izzo. *Texaco*, Chamoiseau's best-known and Goncourt Prize–winning book, is an ethno-mythography of Martinican history that takes up the question of Creole storytelling through the narrative of the novel's eponymous shantytown.

Much has been written about these two texts, especially *Texaco*, including work that ties ethnography to characterological considerations of the relationship between the storyteller and oral popular culture in the French Caribbean.[78] What I want to stress here, however, are the ways in which metafictional moments of intertextuality—where Chamoiseau narratively hints at or gestures toward discursive and disciplinary interlocutors—are generically productive, creating ethnographic fiction from redirections and refractions of the novel through constituent layers of documentation.

Chamoiseau writes himself into *Solibo Magnificent* as an ethnographer who is distracted from his fieldwork on day laborers in Fort-de-France's marketplace by the supernaturally mysterious death of the novel's eponymous Creole storyteller.[79] This characterization harks back to Chamoiseau's *Chronique des sept misères*, a novel about these day laborers whose annex contains a "Note from the Ethnographer" lamenting their disappearance.[80] Running parallel to the police investigation of the presumed murder is a subtextual narrative of the contemporaneity of colonial social relations in Martinique, as the police (both metropolitan and local) struggle and fail to create a coherently linear account of Solibo's demise in the face of conflicting eyewitness reports and increasingly implausible magically realist circumstances. The plot of the text thus hinges on a critique of state-based hyper-rationality over and against the folklorically imbued everyday life of the postcolony. Likewise, the novel allegorically laments the marginalization of Creole popular oral culture, as Solibo's skillful storytelling attracts only a small coterie of devoted old-timers, as well as Chamoiseau, whose literary bent is not exhausted by his ethnographically characterological representation of himself.

Ethnography constitutes the founding premise of the novel in the sense that it is because of fieldwork that Chamoiseau *qua* narrator finds himself at the scene of the crime. But by the same token, it is relegated to the textual background because of its perceived discursive and representational insufficiencies. Much like Leiris's frustration with ethnography's preventing authentic cultural "contact" on his trip through Africa, Chamoiseau's first-person narrator finds himself losing his anthropological focus as he grows closer to the "jobbers" and ordinary people hawking merchandise in the marketplace. "Once a pretend-ethnographer," he explains, "now I dispensed with all distance, living through the torpor of the warm hours by collapsing in the barrows of the jobbers, or by stiffening myself . . . like old women vendors waiting for the return of a fresh wind."[81] Unlike Leiris, of course, who can only imagine a fictional self shaking off ethnography's limitations, Chamoiseau's fictionality begins from the notion that his characterological instantiation can flit in and out of anthropology as he so chooses—truly a Leirisian fantasy if ever there was one.

Despite this fictionalization allowing the narrator to dispense with ethnography's drawbacks, his critique of his fieldwork echoes Leiris's in his most frustratedly morose moments: "Though I tried during lucid moments to picture myself as a *participant observer*, like the doubtful Malinowski, Morgan, Radcliffe-Brown, or Favret-Saada with her Norman sorcerers, I knew that not one of them had seen himself dissolve thus in what he wanted oh so rigorously to describe."[82] Solibo "rescues" Chamoiseau's *je* from ethnography when, like all the other townspeople, he asks him, "What's the use of writing?" Although it occurs early in the novel, this question marks a point of transition for the author/narrator because it pushes him to consider writing outside of scribbled field notes and more in terms of the literary production of the very social worlds Solibo's storytelling speaks to and calls on. This latter understanding of the written word nonetheless shares kinship ties with ethnographic textuality, which is why Solibo's question refers to both kinds of writing simultaneously.

This conception of writing, derived from but not limited to ethnography, enacts the confluence of a variety of intertexts that emerge from the nucleus of the novel's main narrative (of Solibo's death and its increasingly farcical investigation) like spokes from the hub of a bicycle wheel. *Solibo*'s prologue is a dry police report written up in cold, administrative French by the chief investigator. This is counterbalanced by a series of eyewitness accounts related via free indirect discourse, extracted more or less forcibly by the police, in which the members of Solibo's audience on the fateful night of his death deny any involvement in the presumed killing by losing themselves in hilarious shaggy dog stories that do little more than waste the police investigators' time. Two other intertexts are made present primarily by allusion. The first of these allusive intertexts is, of course, the ethnographer's study, which sets *Solibo* in motion as a literary narrative and determines the first-handedness of its constituently divergent directions, prompting us to read the texts that accompany and supplement the primary narrative as so many field notes recorded diligently by an anthropologist who cannot keep his mind on his actual project—an anthropologist, in other words, who turns to ethnographic fiction. The second is Solibo's monologic narrative, interrupted by his death at the moment he enigmatically exclaims, "PATAT' SA!"—to which his audience responds "PATAT' SI!" as if the former interjection were part of a traditional Creole call-and-response pattern. The novel refers constantly to Solibo's soliloquy, but this is given to us only paratextually, in a coda that forces readers to engage with this primary document as an appendix that cannot be integrated into the narrative proper.

The monologue is not a story in the strict sense of the term but, rather, a dramatization of storytelling's relationship to the cultural landscape of Martinique. Calling on his audience for confirmation of his assertions or to guess at the answers to riddles and word games (all of which are Martinican place names), Solibo proclaims the autochthony of Creole storytelling by narrativizing its origins in Martinique's cultural and geographic imaginary. This is an origin story that eschews essentializing authenticity, however, for although Solibo uses words and phrases such as "fundamental," "primordial," or "the beginning of the first the beforall," he also returns time and again to the image of the plantation as if to underline the contingent artificiality of Caribbean créolité. Creole storytelling, from this point of view, takes root in the richly fertile but unstable ground of contingent indigeneity: "and if they tell you who gave Solibo words? who gave Solibo words? you say no yes no because if one day someone gives Solibo words all you plantashun blackmen hear me if someone gives Solibo words Solibo has no more words ain't no mo' words?"[83]

The form of this appended text resembles Molly Bloom's wandering, unpunctuated late-night thoughts in the final "Penelope" episode of *Ulysses*, with Solibo's "no yes no" destabilizing and equivocating (to use this verb transitively) Molly's famous closing affirmation, "yes I said yes I will Yes."[84] For Solibo, the word (*la parole*) cannot be given, but neither can it be set up as the cornerstone of a timeless ontology; it is instead affirmed in the continuous, spoken oscillation between external imposition and internal embodiment.

What is behind Chamoiseau's inclusion of this "authentic" (albeit still fictional) oral text in the novel's appendix? Its simultaneous paratextual and intextexual nature reminds us that we are dealing with a work of fiction that is still grounded in ethnography: as a supplement, it gestures toward the French anthropologists of the first half of the twentieth century (such as Marcel Mauss and Marcel Griaule) who regularly quoted or reproduced indigenous literature in their ethnographic publications. As Vincent Debaene has shown, indigenous literary documents allowed these French ethnographers to communicate something of the "ineffable" nature of the societies they studied, since authenticity could compensate for what the stylistic shortcomings of ethnographic writing could not reproduce.[85] Similarly, at the close of the novel Chamoiseau refers to his ethnographer-storyteller character as "a pathetic gatherer of elusive things . . . a scratcher of uninscribable words" and ends up positioning himself in the same vein as those early French social scientists who leaned on indigenous literature to render textually present the "atmosphere" of the society under study: "So then, friends, I decided to squeeze out a reduced, organized, *written* version, a kind of ersatz of what the Master had been that night; it was clear now that his words, his true words, all of his words, were lost for all of us—and forever."[86] The authentic literary document here is restorative insofar as it gives readers something of Solibo's essence, and it is a marker of an irretrievable loss, involved as it is in a practice of textualized mourning.

Ethnographic intertextuality is more overtly characterological in *Texaco*. There, figures, registers, and intertexts vie for pride of place (and for readerly attention) in Chamoiseau's fictionalized history of Martinique told through the biography of Marie-Sophie, founder of Fort-de-France's Texaco settlement on the city's periphery. One writerly figure among several in the novel is the urban planner modeled after the real-life Martinican urbanist Serge Letchimy, who would go on to succeed Aimé Césaire as mayor of Fort-de-France in 2001.[87] The planner is sent by the local administration to Texaco to gauge how best to raze the shantytown to make room for a sleek highway connecting Fort-de-France to the interior. Struck down by a stone hurled by Julot the Mangy, a resident annoyed by the prospect of losing his shack, the planner is taken to Marie-Sophie's hut to recover. While recuperating, he becomes enthralled by the history of Texaco as told by the matronly Marie-Sophie, and their ensuing conversation provides the narrative backdrop for the progression of the text. However, this progression does not take place in a linear fashion, for the narrative floats in and out of the past and among several speakers, always haunted by the presence of Marie-Sophie's youthful interlocutor, who earns a messianic moniker by helping administratively facilitate Texaco's urban integration.

Crucially, though, the urban planner never speaks; rather, he is written into existence by a series of notes to the Word Scratcher, in a continuation of Chamoiseau's game of writing himself into his fiction. These notes are interspersed throughout the text and contain ethnographic observations about everyday life on the margins of Fort-de-France (referred to as L'En-ville, or "City" in translation) as well as increasingly critical remarks about the role of French centralization in its overseas department. In *Solibo Magnificent*, Chamoiseau the character is both an ethnographer and a literary "word scratcher," and, as we have seen, by the end of the novel he has begun transitioning from the former to the latter. In *Texaco*, however, this characterological split is much neater, and the ethnographer figure is assimilated to the urban planner (the outside observer par excellence) while Chamoiseau's character now fully inhabits his literary role. Even though this transition is more complete or visible in the later novel, the ethnographic eye of the fictional text is no less present; it is just somewhat displaced.

The urban planner's confrontation with the chaotic networks of alleys and shacks of Texaco is also a critique of the careful rationality of French universalism and its inability to cope with the logics of cultural, racial, and linguistic difference:

> In the center [of City], an occidental, urban logic, all lined up, ordered, strong like the French language. On the other side, Creole's open profusion according to Texaco's logic. Mingling these two tongues, dreaming of all tongues, the Creole city speaks a new language in secret and no longer fears Babel. Here the well-learned, domineering, geometrical grid of an urban grammar; over there the crown of a mosaic culture to be unveiled, caught in the hieroglyphics of cement, crate wood, asbestos. The Creole city returns to the urban planner, who would like to ignore it, the roots of a new identity: multilingual, multiracial, multihistorical, open, sensible to the world's diversity. Everything has changed.[88]

What this passage from the urban planner's note alerts us to is not simply a binary between reason and unreason that is actualized by the growth of the Creole city, or even a multicultural hybridity that flourishes where metropolitan urban life meets the tropics. Instead, what we encounter in this note is an "open profusion," a cartography that indicates both the bricolage of the built environment and a linguistic multiplicity that traces a line of flight from the ordered and rigidified logics of City and points toward a culture and people "to be unveiled." This excited sense of futurity echoes the tone of Glissant's social-scientific setting for Caribbean writing examined earlier.

It is in this sense that the hieroglyphics of Creole urban grammar can be seen as expressive and not merely as descriptive. To express a different potential community is not to lay out blueprints for an entity that might arrive fully formed; it is, rather, to open a path for a new consciousness and sensibility. As the urban planner puts it in another note to the Word Scratcher, "The Lady [Marie-Sophie] taught me to see the city as an ecosystem, made up of equilibriums and interactions."[89] The Creole city's community is constituted by innumerable micro-equilibriums that form and dissolve without ever congealing into a stable shape. Chamoiseau translates this urban ecology into a textual aesthetic formed by layering distinct yet interrelated intertexts on top of one another, such that the ethnographic and the literary-fictional balance each other out. Ethnographic fiction is composed in this case of an equilibrium that generates narrative progression.

Marie-Sophie, founder and protectress of Texaco and repository of Creole oral culture, writes another textual layer into the novel. Driven by necessity to erect a hutch on land owned by the American oil giant and faced for the first time with City's "millennial *no*" (in an interesting displacement and reversal of the Nietzschean eternal recurrence),[90] she redirects her desire for City away from its seemingly impenetrable boundaries and toward an urban space that is included in the state's political calculations only through its exclusion. By inhabiting this liminal site Marie-Sophie asks what kind of sociality can be generated within this inclusive exclusion, this "would-be City" that is subject to police raids and the *békés*' (white Creoles') rage yet always manages to rebuild itself differently each time. As she says of the residents' efforts to reshape their lives continuously, "We were determined to live our exclusion, relentlessly, no matter how many times the *béké*, the France-whites or the seyaress [CRS] barged in and emptied our hutches."[91] In other words, the acts of destruction, rebuilding, and transformation that Texaco underwent during Marie-Sophie's lifetime served as the fluctuating foundation for the Creole community "to be unveiled," as the urban planner puts it.

Texaco is driven by Marie-Sophie's personal autobiographical narrative, but this first-person account is actually a literary reconstruction composed by Chamoiseau the Word Scratcher. The author-character (referred to by the heroine as "Oiseau Cham," in another moment of literary nicknaming) be-seeches Marie-Sophie to write her memoirs and to deposit the resulting note-books in the Victor Schoelcher library in Fort-de-France. The Word Scratcher constructs *Texaco* from this archived material, which is supplemented by in-terviews conducted with Marie-Sophie at the end of her life. In fact, in a con-cluding section of the novel, he refers to her as his "Informant" (*Informatrice*), a choice of vocabulary that sees Chamoiseau the literary artist slip back toward his ethnographic persona.[92]

The act of writing remains a constant struggle for Marie-Sophie, whose words "undo the alphabet" and who wrestles endlessly with "the holy inex-pressible" as she attempts to inscribe her life on the page.[93] As we have seen with the "authentic" (but always already imperfectly recorded) document at-tached to the end of *Solibo Magnificent*, the sacralization of the ineffable is a key component of Chamoiseau's sense of ethnographic intertextuality. Simi-larly, the written word in *Texaco* functions both as a site of redemption where the sufferings of ordinary people take on a tangible meaning beyond their localized context and as an imperfect mode of expression that by definition cannot ever fully restore the fullness of its mystified object.

Marie-Sophie's dilemma, then, is to reconcile these two contrasting dimen-sions of the sacred in her written memoirs. As she points out, however, to unite forcibly the desire to write with the impossibility of fully restoring the object of one's writing (in another literary reprise of the problem facing early twentieth-century French anthropologists) is to enact a type of violence on the object of writing that creates not only distance but also death. Writing for the heroine means finding the memory of her father, Esternome, amid her scattered recol-lections, but she finds that the act brings her no closer to her former slave fore-bears: "With the notebooks piling up, I felt they were burying him once again. Each written sentence coated a little of him, his Creole tongue, his words, his intonation, his laughs, his eyes, his airs, with formaldehyde."[94]

In *Solibo Magnificent*, Chamoiseau's character included the storyteller's literary document out of ethnographic self-loathing—as a "pathetic gatherer of elusive things," he could not possibly hope to re-create the atmosphere in which Solibo delivered his final words. Marie-Sophie's reflections as a writer and ethnographic informant take these earlier intertextual concerns even fur-ther: where writing once was merely deficient, it is now deadly. "I was emp-tying my memory into immobile notebooks," she writes, "without having brought back the quivering of the living life which at each moment modifies what's just happened."[95] Memories expressed in writing lack the power to enliven their referents; writing drains memory of its signifying powers (its "living life"). For all that, however, the two remain co-dependent, since writing relies on memory for its content and memory takes shape through writing, only to be subsequently effaced.

Marie-Sophie expresses the ethnographer's awareness of his shortcomings in *Solibo* on a higher level of abstraction. Writing—or, to be more specific, the interpolated literary document—is linked to betrayal, distance, and death while still retaining its role as a redemptive site that offers hope through textual inscription. For Chamoiseau, if ethnographic intertextuality in the novel actually causes this double-bind, it offers a way out, as well. The characterological layers of intertextuality in *Texaco* introduce different levels of fictionality: Marie-Sophie's notebooks and the urban planner's archived commentary are firsthand fictions, as it were, whereas Chamoiseau's narrative constructs a second-order fictional novel from this first-order raw material. The novel as second-order (but not ancillary) fictional work acknowledges the perceived pitfalls of ethnography and allows for their imagined resolution within the totality of the text. Thus, the Word Scratcher can write the redemption of Texaco while the constituent intertextual—and always fictional—notebooks on which he draws point ethnographically to the same textual problems raised in *Solibo*. To draw a comparison with Leiris's efforts from chapter 1, whereas he settles his stomach by fictionalizing his autobiographical quarrels with ethnography, Chamoiseau uses ethnography to tie together disparate fictional intertexts, drawing anthropology ever further into the realm of the novel. Put another way, we are dealing here with the difference between an act of conversion (the self made fictional) and a mise en abyme.

In a final section of *Texaco*, messianically titled "Resurrection," Chamoiseau brings his ethnographically intertextual approach to the novel full circle. Referring parenthetically to the Word Scratcher as the one "who tries to write life," he begins the chapter by mentioning that he found Texaco by accident while looking for a local mystic (a *Mentô*) who could illuminate him on how best to render Solibo's final monologue as a literarily worthy written text. This is a case of fieldwork breeding fiction, and the anecdote is accompanied by a bibliographical footnote sending readers back to the earlier work. (This is not the first time Chamoiseau cites himself. In *Solibo*, for instance, he sends readers back to his play *Manman Dlo contre la fée Carabosse* [1982].) Chamoiseau breaks with the game he has been playing in two ways. First, locating the genesis of *Texaco* in the field research thematized in *Solibo* has the effect of erasing the distinction between the ethnographer and the literary Word Scratcher that Chamoiseau initially wanted to instantiate. Second, to refer bibliographically and with publication information to the earlier novel breaks with Chamoiseau's intertextual precedent that hitherto had used ethnography to weave together distinct registers of fictionality. Here, however, the Word Scratcher brings ethnographic fiction back into the extratextual "real world," completing the circuit created by Leiris in *L'Afrique fantôme*.

Anthropology, Insularity, and the Novel

One critique we could make of the way in which Confiant stages debates on ethnographic realism is that his approach reduces ethnography (and literature's borrowings from it) to mimesis, thereby ascribing to ethnographic fiction the dully replicative task of narrativizing, more or less richly, an empirical referent. We could lay a similar charge at the feet of Chamoiseau, for in spite of his constant reframing of layers of ethnographic fictionality, he remains fascinated by the ethnographic novel as representative of Creole history in Martinique—or, at the very least, as representative of literary attempts to compensate and mourn for historical loss. From this mimetic perspective, ethnographic fiction in the Caribbean novel "repeats" the island (to give a representational spin on Antonio Benítez-Rojo's well-known formulation) in the insular and closed textual world of the novel.[96] This novelistic insularity would be inescapable, and the main goal of ethnographic fiction would be to measure up, in a well-translated realism, to the impingements of insularity on aesthetics, to an ever more communicable adequation of the novel to its subject matter.

To overstate these critiques, or to press these charges, would be to miss the Glissantian influence on the créolistes, as well as to skirt one of the major arguments of this book—namely, that ethnographic fiction as an experimental generic formation is more concerned with expressing new relationships to textual histories, social forms, and speculative world making than it is with describing, in anything asymptotically resembling holism, the empirical kernel at the heart of the realist novel. As these two Caribbeanist chapters have shown, the types of imaginative cartography on which ethnographic fiction relies express and create new literary genealogies that foreground Caribbean fiction's anthropological historicity. And as I have argued in this chapter more specifically, the relationship between these processes of expression and creation, on the one hand, and genealogical foregrounding, on the other, is a constitutive feature of the créolité movement's approach to fiction.

This sense of expressive openness gets to the heart of the theory of insularity suggested by my readings of Glissant and the créolistes. Glissant's project, as we begin to see in *Soleil de la conscience* and *Discours*, involves thinking insularity in terms of an open totality, in opposition to the universalizing desires of Lévi-Strauss's structuralist anthropology.[97] Relatedly, by thematizing and allegorizing their productive processes, novels such as *Solibo Magnificent* and *L'allée des soupirs* break open their own literary insularity and come to resemble unfinished texts, never as "closed" as we might expect them to be. *Texaco* takes a different tack with similar results, connecting fiction to intertextual documentation and extratextual circuitry in a clever game of open-ended referentiality. Insularity in the novel (and the novel's insularity) exists in tension with a variety of textually mediated desires—for a transcolonial Creole aesthetic, for a space of writing that extends beyond the directions of French national integration, and for a vision of anthropology as a prime mover of an expansive literary history. At its broadest, then, anthropology both expresses literary insularity and turns it inside out, converting it into geographical and historical extension. Ethnographic fiction comes to perform a balancing act for the créolistes, since it sits perched, as if on a tightrope, between representationally mimetic logics of insularity and the manifold forms of desire that think beyond them.

Chapter 5

Speculative Cityscapes and Premillennial Policing

Ethnographies of the Present in Jean-Claude Izzo's
Crime Trilogy

A book of philosophy should be in part a very particular species of detective novel.... By detective novel we mean that concepts, with their zones of presence, should intervene to resolve local situations. They themselves change along with the problems. They have spheres of influence where ... they operate in relation to 'dramas' and by means of a certain 'cruelty.' They must have a coherence among themselves, but that coherence must not come from themselves. They must receive their coherence from elsewhere.
—GILLES DELEUZE, *Difference and Repetition*

Michel Leiris opened this book's twentieth-century trajectory when, aboard the *Saint-Firmin*, he left Bordeaux for Africa on May 19, 1931. Around the same time, as we have seen, Amadou Hampâté Bâ embarked on his career in the French colonial civil service and moved throughout French West Africa as he worked his way up the ranks and carried out ethnographic fieldwork on the side. This study began, then, by situating ethnographic fiction in relation to colonial encounters that took place "vertically" and "horizontally," as it were: these encounters involved moving downward from the metropole to the colonies and, simultaneously, moving laterally and transcolonially across African imperial space. This chapter brings us back to metropolitan France in an organizational move that is less concerned with going full circle than it is with identifying remnants of the colonial experience in the postcolonial cartographies of French ethnographic fiction. I examine Jean-Claude Izzo's 1990s crime fiction trilogy, a group of novels set in postindustrial and postcolonial Marseille and starring the disaffected detective Fabio Montale.

Geographically speaking, this chapter is set at the point of conjunction where the French Atlantic world, in the broad form of the metropole, meets the Mediterranean, in the form of postcolonial Marseille. I take advantage here of France's positioning within both geographies to return to the metropole at a very different moment from the late-colonial period when Leiris set off for Africa. But turning to Marseille also allows us to look outward again from a different vantage point, one that situates the former French empire alongside contemporary challenges to late twentieth-century democracy. Izzo's crime trilogy gathers up colonial experiences and histories and scatters them in premillennial Marseille, a city cast as the virtual capital of the Francophone postcolonial universe.

Jean-Paul Colleyn points out that "the voluntarily imaginary character of artistic fiction does not, for all that, exclude it from the realm of the human sciences."[1] As I have argued throughout this book, experimentation across genres creates a principle of inclusion allowing fiction and anthropology to confront and negotiate ideologies and histories of empire simultaneously and complementarily. This principle of inclusion is also one of cartographic extension, since transgeneric experimentation sets in motion "special geographies" (to return to the Césaire quote from this book's introduction) that map out alternative (post)imperial lifeworlds and literary genealogies. But how does popular French fiction generate narratives of ethnographic observation that participate in these acts of inclusion and extension? And why are narratives of crime and criminality privileged sites for negotiating anthropology's disciplinary marker of fieldwork in the realm of the novel? These questions orient this chapter's reading of Izzo's crime trilogy, and I address them by positioning the detective as a fieldworker, a figure who moves through, analyzes, and links often fractured social spaces and makes narrative sense of them without aiming for a holistic impression of totality.

From this perspective, fieldwork in the novel produces imaginative postcolonial cartographies, realms of creative spatiality that map onto and transform
ethnographic fiction's realist documentary desires. Izzo's detective observes
and explicates social transformations in postcolonial 1990s Marseille but he
also imagines utopian geographies of belonging that gesture toward empire's
political logics and move beyond its contradictions and inherent instabilities.
And this imaginative thrust transforms the crime novel as a form: social observation is accompanied here by narrative defamiliarization, creating an effect
that anthropologist Jean Jamin, in his reading of William Faulkner's novels,
identifies as "the anthropological experience" in fiction. This is a sense of *un-
heimlichkeit* created by the narrative negotiation of recognizable social worlds
and the imaginative invention of new ones, an interplay that for Jamin mirrors
the defamiliarizing aspects of ethnographic fieldwork.[2]

More pointedly still, for anthropologists Jean and John Comaroff global
crime fiction feeds into what they call their "criminal anthropology of late modernity . . . an excursion into the contemporary Order of Things—or, rather,
into the metaphysic of disorder that has come to infuse the late modern world."[3]
Contemporary crime narratives are symptomatic of new anxieties about
the present and future, but as the Comaroffs point out, while contemporary
crime fiction generates ethnographies of the fraught present, even classical
nineteenth-century detectives in Poe, for instance, or in Sherlock Holmes
novels functioned as anthropologists and fieldworkers who "insisted on the
nonobvious significance of obvious facts" in everyday life.[4] They go on to argue
that in the current moment, "conventional genres . . . are challenged by a
new noir that, playing on the prevailing mood of our times . . . when old
sureties unravel, when abstraction, alienation, ambivalence, undecidability,
and il/legality appear to become endemic to 'life itself,' when new truths demand
to be probed."[5]

Izzo's crime fiction resonates with this claim since it situates phenomenologies of fieldwork within overlapping, "undecidable" narrative worlds in ways
that bring imperial histories into anthropological experiences of contemporary
insecurities and uncertainties. As we saw in chapter 4, Patrick Chamoiseau's
crime novel *Solibo Magnificent* makes similar moves and ties political uncertainty to multilayered narrativizations of Caribbean literature. Izzo's noir trilogy ultimately proceeds in a different direction, though: it asks how narratives of political urgency and postcolonial criminality can actually rewrite the
Metropole.

Urban Renewal and Speculative Citizenship

It is tempting, when thinking about Izzo's "new noir" fiction, to take the statements that punctuate his novels about Marseille as a utopian site of métissage in an increasingly fragmented France for idealizations that lead us away from the gritty interplay among policing, citizenship, racism, and immigration that serves as the textual prime mover in the Fabio Montale trilogy. This temptation, however, should not draw our attention from the ways in which Marseille as an imagined postcolonial utopia (an urban space with purposefully ill-defined boundaries that for Izzo has always been ground zero for immigration to France) might be properly coterminous with the Marseille he indicts as being home to far-right politics, police racism, and the kind of urban *ghettoïsation* that made headlines during the riots in French suburbs of 2005, nearly a decade after the trilogy was completed. As Minayo Nasiali points out, Marseille did not "burn" during the riots, but the city's fractured social space has a longer history that fuels Izzo's utopian imagination.[6]

When Izzo's trilogy was published during the 1990s, Marseille's image was changing. The city had long been viewed with "contempt" as a corrupt, working-class port city whose industries had collapsed after colonial independence spelled the end of captive foreign markets; the 1980s and '90s, however, were marked by intense gentrification as local officials and property speculators sought to "reconquer" the city center.[7] Emblematic of these desires for urban renewal is the ongoing Euroméditerranée (Euromed) project that began in 1994, a revamping of the city's docks area designed to court Parisian investment by building slick office buildings, apartments, and parking lots.[8] Gentrification projects such as Euromed and Marseille's renewed cultural cachet masked deepening social divisions. As Alèssi Dell'Umbria shows, the mid- to late 1990s saw major electoral gains for Jean-Marie Le Pen's far-right Front National (FN) in and around Marseille, and the party continues to outperform national averages in the region.[9] The Fabio Montale trilogy tracks these changes and tensions but, at the same time, also thinks beyond them.

It is this narrative simultaneity that characterizes Izzo's ethnographic fiction and distinguishes it from the other kinds of ethnographic fiction that feature in this book: although all the works I study sketch out speculative, alternative knowledge projects, Izzo's trilogy communicates a more thoroughgoing set of utopian aspirations. In his ethnographic fiction he constructs a utopian Marseille as a palimpsest, a layering of urban desire written over more recognizably realist and noir descriptions of social problems in the postcolonial metropolitan city. He does so by arriving ultimately at an innovative form of dual citizenship that relies on the relationship between an imagined form of political and cultural belonging, on the one hand, and intensely fraught conceptions of actually existing French citizenship and its attendant social exclusions, on the other.

I make my way to this point through a broader discussion of the relationship between policing and ethnography that obtains in Izzo's trilogy. Reading Fabio Montale's detective work as an ethnography of policing serves less to illuminate the rhetoric of law as a function of the state apparatus (if for no other reason than Montale is no longer on the force after the first volume) than to ask what distribution of urban spaces, racialized social roles, and (in)visible citizens is generated and reiterated by policing in Izzo's Marseille. Izzo ends up writing a utopian Marseille into the city's premillennial cultural present, superimposing an alternative urban spatiality that functions as a spotlight on and imagined response to the political problems that, for him, policing both attempts to solve and endlessly reinstantiates.

Urban Palimpsests and Noir Characterology

"The site was a palimpsest, as was all the city, written, erased, rewritten," writes Teju Cole about Ground Zero and New York in his novel *Open City* (2011).[10] Cole's observation gestures toward the thematic thrust of this chapter, but only partially. Whereas his palimpsest is a spatial metaphor, mine is an ideational diagnostic, an estranged sense of spatiality that nonetheless proclaims its coextensiveness with more recognizable spatial forms. The palimpsest I describe here is different from the other forms of cartographic layering I have highlighted in this book. This chapter draws out the utopian dimensions of (post)imperial countermapping, a textual feature that has lurked below the surface in previous chapters but that comes to the fore in Izzo's crime trilogy. Somewhat paradoxically, though, these texts articulate utopian reorganizations of (post)imperial geographies from within the metropole. Utopian cartographic desires thus extend outward from the metropolitan space that gave birth to the kinds of imperial mapping this book has sought to reshape and reconfigure.

Izzo's trilogy saw him rise from a career in relative literary obscurity to publication in France's famous Série Noire (SN) and a position at the forefront of what

Michel Peraldi and Michel Samson remind us is now called the *néopolar marseillais*, crime fiction written into the landscape of France's second city.[11] Born and raised in the working-class *centre-ville* of Marseille, Izzo wrote the novels that compose his trilogy (*Total Khéops*, *Chourmo*, and *Solea*) between 1994 and 1998, finishing *Solea* only two years before his death in 2000. The sudden success of *Total Khéops* (which was adapted in 2001 into a three-episode television miniseries starring Alain Delon) came toward the end of a literary career that hitherto had been remarkable: he spent the 1970s and '80s as a minor journalist based in both Marseille and Paris, although, as I argue here, his crime fiction turns away from a narrative politics that we might identify as journalistic. Izzo worked into the 1990s trying to get various literary and screenwriting projects off the ground before writing an early version of *Total Khéops*'s first chapter for the magazine published by the Étonnants Voyageurs literary festival. Patrick Raynal, then the director of the SN, encouraged Izzo to write a manuscript that was quickly accepted for publication in the well-known collection.

In the trilogy, Izzo's hero, Montale, confronts the mafia, corrupt cops with ties to the far-right FN, and forms of social marginalization in the *banlieues* (a formerly generic term for "suburbs" that now tends to connote low-income housing and immigration) where he has his beat as an officer and social worker with little actual authority. As is often the case in noir fiction, the crimes Montale investigates are both set against and involve more painful aspects of his personal life: in *Total Khéops*, for example, Leila, the young Algerian girl with whom Montale is romantically linked, is raped and murdered by FN members (connected to the police and the mafia) who want to use dirty money to fund gang wars in the banlieues as a way to scare Marseille's residents into voting the FN into power. In *Chourmo* (a title that cites the Provençal word for the French *galère*, referencing a miserable situation or struggle), Montale is charged with tracking down his cousin's missing son, Guitou, who came to Marseille to visit the Arab girlfriend his racist parents refused to let him date. Finally, in *Solea* (from the eponymous Miles Davis song), Montale comes face to face with the mafia for the last time after his journalist friend and ex-lover, Babette, returns to France from Italy, having compiled documents that link French politicians to organized crime. Thus, in addition to first-order narratives of crimes that must be solved, the trilogy contains related narrative threads in which Montale makes his peace with figures from the past, such as the two boys turned criminals who were murdered and whom Montale was unable to protect, and the gypsy girl, Lole, with whom they were all in love but who runs away from a relationship with the adult Montale.[12]

In these narratives, the overlapping cityscapes and social spaces of Marseille present a richly developed "texturology," to borrow Michel de Certeau's term: the utopian city for Izzo is a spatial ideal type whose nearly borderless postcolonial topography can be studied as it is narrativized by the roaming detective who probes its actually existing contours.[13] In these crime narratives (which are all tinged with ponderous masculine vulnerability), Montale makes seemingly endless observations about the city's changing demographics and about the cultural and political implications of the forms of urban renewal that Marseille was undergoing throughout the 1990s.[14] What makes my reading of this trilogy possible, then, is that fact that these three texts are not run-of-the-mill police procedurals whose popularity and commercial success would derive from their intense realism or their keen sense of premillennial local color. Marseille, in other words, is more than Mediterranean window dressing for narratives that represent more than conventional detective-story boilerplate.

The same goes for Izzo's characters, especially his protagonist: jaded and faded, like Anny in Jean-Paul Sartre's *Nausea*, the characters in these texts all seem to have outlived themselves; we might also say they have outlived a Marseille that no longer exists. And yet Montale, who expounds for paragraphs on Provençal cuisine and the poetry of Saint-John Perse (intertextual nods to the city's créolité, to return to the questions I explored in chapter 4), is more than another iteration of the gruff and disaffected noir investigator. As I examine here, Montale holds together the narrative imperatives of both the detective and the fieldworker, nudging these two figures toward indistinguishability. An aesthetics of fieldwork intervenes to give the detective story the kind of "coherence" Gilles Deleuze describes in this chapter's epigraph, a certain legibility of the concepts it creates and narrativizes.[15] To put my approach differently, situating it succinctly within this book's broader argument, the expectations these imperatives and interventions generate position the detective as the characterological embodiment of the generic hybridity that fuels this study's analytic range.

Crime Fiction and the Aesthetics of Fieldwork

Reading Izzo's crime trilogy as narrativizing postcolonial encounters in ethnographic fiction involves, first, pointing toward the ways in which the detective and the fieldworker represent figures mobilizing similar methods, the one to solve a case and the other to engage critically with cultural histories and social processes/formations. Montale, for his part, unites both of these tasks. Two formulations of fieldwork in anthropology, set roughly a decade apart, help us work through the convergence—which is at once formal, epistemological, and politico-historical—of the detective and the fieldworker. Let us begin in the late 1990s, around the time that Izzo was finishing the Fabio Montale trilogy: in the introduction to the second edition of *Anthropology as Cultural Critique* (1999), George Marcus and Michael Fischer rework some of the ethnographic cartographies they delineated in the original edition of the book, published in 1986, offering an updated definition of fieldwork that both encompasses anthropology's mode of inquiry in a millennial age of global and postcolonial circulation and draws a compelling parallel with the work of the noir detective. The context of this definition (or redefinition, as it were) is, of course, important for this book's subject more generally, since one aspect of Marcus and Fischer's project was to outline and respond to anthropology's "crisis of representation" precipitated in part by an acute awareness of ethnography's provocatively fraught status as a written genre.[16]

Marcus and Fischer suggest in the revised edition of *Anthropology as Cultural Critique* that "fieldwork should be recognized as a complex web of interactions in which anthropologists in collaboration with others, conventionally conceived as informants and located in a variety of often contrasting settings, track connections amid networks, mutations, influences of cultural forces and changing social pressures."[17] Looking initially at the first half of this formulation, any detective worth their salt must be able to negotiate multiple and complex networks of interactions (with "informants" in the most literal sense of the word) to obtain information, pressure suspects, or follow leads if they are to crack a case and, by extension, resolve a given narrative.

The second half of this definition, though, complicates the first: although detectives from nearly any crime novel move between multiple social worlds to track down information necessary to narrative resolution, readers are not always provided with a clear sense of the "cultural forces and changing social pressures" that impinge on the more immediate context of the investigation. In other words, what this rapprochement points us toward is a shared imperative—namely, the idea that the detective and the fieldworker must be keenly conscious of their embeddedness in history and politics. For Izzo's Montale, however, this sense of social and politico-historical impingement is very present, both because it throws his detective work into relief and because these forces and pressures are also intimately bound up in the investigations themselves. Thus, questions of race, immigration, French universalism, and the changing postcolonial landscape of urban Marseille not only serve to enrich Izzo's narratives but are also part and parcel of the very crimes Montale must solve.

Johannes Fabian offers a second formulation of fieldwork that encourages us to think through Izzo's ethnographic aesthetics. In an essay published in 2007, Fabian gestures toward an argument he made in *Time and the Other: How Anthropology Makes Its Object* (1983) and links the "realness" of contemporary fieldwork to a politics of time. "Research of the kind we anthropologists call fieldwork or ethnography," he suggests, "becomes empirical when it *happens* in or through communicative events occurring in shared time."[18] Fieldwork takes place in the production of shared temporalities or, in the context of my argument here, in the creation of ethnographic narratives in which a shared sense of time is neither an epistemological nor a phenomenological a priori. Not taking this shared convergence for granted, Izzo's novels draw the reader, the detective, and the cityscape into the same textual orbit, and the trilogy's sense of its own empirical real time relies on this triangulated interaction.

Thus, for instance, each volume of the trilogy is preceded by a *note de l'auteur*, a paratextual alert in which Izzo reminds us that while his texts are works of fiction he does borrow from reality (and in *Chourmo*'s note he goes as far as to explicitly request that we not go searching for resemblances between characters in the text and real-world individuals[19]) and from the everyday life of the city. We might consider the following lines from the prefatory comments to *Total Khéops*: "With the exception of public events reported in the press, neither the events recounted nor the characters have ever existed. Not even the narrator, that is to say. Only the city is truly real. Marseille. And all those who live there. With that passion only they have. This story is theirs. Echoes and recollections."[20] This paratextual reminder does more than just spell out to readers that they are encountering a work of fiction—if this were all it did, an author's note would hardly be necessary, since any novel is in itself an immediate signal of fictionality. It also serves as a marker of Izzo's authority—that is, an indication that he possesses the requisite cultural capital to fictionalize the everyday life of Marseille and its "indigenous" residents. Further, it explains to readers that the narratives of investigation the novels contain emerge from negotiations of urban life in the premillennial French port city. As we have seen throughout this book, paratextuality is a catalyst of generic hybridity: here, Izzo's sense of the paratextual highlights how ethnographic fiction narrates shared time as cultural translation.

To read fieldwork in this trilogy is to experiment with and test the limits of ethnographic realism as a narrative mode. Marcus has argued that pushing the boundaries of ethnographic realism involves borrowing aesthetic strategies from literary modernism, particularly to account for the "already constituted relationship that exists between observer and observed" to which conventional ethnographic realism remained blind.[21] Marcus's suggestion is well taken, and to be sure, several modernist figures have already made cameo appearances in previous chapters in the context of, for example, discussions of reconstituted speech in the ethnographic-fictional document (James Joyce in chapter 3) or experiences of selfhood in hybridized ethnographic writing (John Dos Passos in chapter 1). What is more, Izzo's novels gain their ethnographic thrust from the narration in fiction of just such preconstituted relationships: it would be difficult to take Montale's numerous asides and observations about the changing urban environment in Marseille of the 1990s as anything else, since these often moody remarks bespeak an intellectual relationship with the city that precedes the narratives themselves, as Izzo hints in his author's notes.

But to tell the story of ethnographic fiction in the twentieth-century French Atlantic, as this book seeks to do, is to create a narrative of generic convergence and invention rather than one of generic borrowing, for the latter posits discrete entities or parties that need not meet or exceed themselves in the exchange. Izzo's utopia is an indicator of experimental ethnographic convergence; as such, it responds to and moves beyond Marcus's suggestion that ethnography borrow from modernism to "[pose] repressed possibilities documentable on the margins of the cultures studied—to those that seem to be dominant."[22] Fieldwork and fiction must be indistinguishable in Izzo for this to happen—that is, for his detective to highlight the peculiar co-presence of a Marseille that is overrun by the mafia and that threatens at any moment to fall into the hands of the FN with a Marseille that expresses a desire for idealized forms of postcolonial sociality. This is, after all, the city the detective Montale calls "the only utopia in the world."[23] The trilogy thus articulates a stylistics of fieldwork by experimenting with anthro-aesthetic narrative strategies. On a yet broader level, detective fiction opens itself up invitingly to ethnography since investigative narratives proceed by requiring the detective *qua* fieldworker to move through and link disparate, fragmented social actors and social spaces in a cultural politics of textual problem solving.[24]

We can put these ethnographic complexities into further relief by reading the Fabio Montale trilogy in terms of the broad shift in French crime fiction inaugurated by the Série Noire. Toward the end of the first volume of the trilogy, *Total Khéops*, Izzo's hero meets up with a semiretired gangster from the local mafia (often referred to in France as *le milieu*) at a bar near Marseille's

Vieux Port and bluffs his way into coaxing information from the godfather-like figure, Batisti. Batisti's revelations concern the entanglement of highly personal and, more generally, politically volatile questions that serve as the basis for Montale's investigation in the text: Who kidnapped and murdered the young Arab girl that Montale was incapable of loving? Why was Montale's childhood friend, Manu, killed after working for Batisti, and why was another of his friends, Ugo, shot down by the police after he avenged Manu's death by assassinating another local mobster, Zucca? What is the relationship between the police and the far-right Front National in Marseille, and why would the FN go through police officers to establish contacts with young Arab drug dealers in Marseille's working-class banlieues (called the *quartiers nord*)?

Although the actual answers to these questions effectively allow the novel to resolve itself, what is more revealing—both for Montale's consciousness and in terms of Izzo's relationship to the SN—is how the detective describes his reaction on learning that these questions are in fact all interrelated: "Neither could I see myself any longer in the role of the righter of wrongs. I no longer saw myself in any role. Not even that of a cop. I couldn't see anything anymore. I was stunned. Hate, violence. Gangsters, cops, politicians. And poverty as the breeding ground. Unemployment, racism. We were all like insects caught in a spider's web. We might struggle, but the spider would end up eating us all."[25]

Already on the outs with his colleagues for not adopting a hard-line, violence-first approach to policing and relegated by his superiors to meaningless beats in Marseille's quartiers nord, home to many first- and second-generation North African and West African immigrants and plagued by high unemployment, Montale ends up handing in his badge at the end of the novel and for the remainder of the trilogy will work as an independent investigator. This passage is also indicative of the relationship between crime fiction and social life brought about by the SN, France's most famous collection of crime novels.

In a short article written in 1966 in celebration of the one-thousandth text in the series, which the novelist Marcel Duhamel founded in 1945 and directed until 1977, Deleuze writes that, in contrast to the older style of drawing-room whodunits that mirrored French and English philosophy's metaphysical and scientific searches for truth, what was new about the SN was that it showed readers that the activity of policing was hardly concerned with any such *recherche du vrai*. Rather, he argues, "The Série Noire has made us accustomed to the type of policeman that rushes (*fonce*) around on a whim, at the risk of multiplying mistakes, but believing that something will always come of it."[26]

In a similar vein, echoing Deleuze's observation to such an extent that he also uses the verb *foncer*, Montale diagnoses his own shortcomings as a cop: "As an investigator, I still wasn't worth a damn. I rushed (*fonçais*) into my intuition without ever taking the time to reflect."[27] Although it is certainly true that the SN was nudged in this direction by the hard-boiled British and American authors whose translations into French constituted the bulk of early publications in the series, Deleuze's larger point is that Duhamel's new collection helped substitute a literary mirror, in which society sees itself reflected in its police and its crimes, for the metaphysical reflections of earlier crime novels in which detectives discover "true" data points whose existence is taken for granted at the outset.[28]

It is in this vein that we can read Montale's apparent fatalism in the passage cited earlier: although the information revealed to him during his meeting with Batisti has truth value in the sense that it allows both his investigation and Izzo's narrative to come to some resolution, the satisfaction of these formal requirements is thoroughly undercut by the fact that they are dissolved in a larger metanarrative that society has created about itself and in relation to which the detective finds himself powerless. What Deleuze refers to as the SN's mirror effect, then, is actually the dialectical creation of social metanarratives formed via the confrontation and transcendence of first-order narratives of investigation and the formal requirement that these narratives be resolved one way or another.

While this example serves to situate Izzo's work within one fundamental shift inaugurated by the SN, we can also place the trilogy into conversation with a major figure in post-1968 French crime fiction: Didier Daeninckx. The events of May 1968 provided the impetus for younger writers to emerge on the French crime-writing scene, invigorating and politicizing a genre that had become fairly moribund.[29] Daeninckx's novels from the 1980s are especially salient in this respect, since they explicitly seek to upend dominant historical and political narratives by exposing the complicity of state representatives in crimes and scandals. We can elaborate on Izzo's ethnographic aesthetic by highlighting some of the ways in which his work contrasts with that of an emblematic figure such as Daeninckx, whose writing is seen to have problematized in new ways the relationship obtaining between crime fiction and politics.[30] Two textual examples are particularly pertinent here and merit our attention.

On the one hand, this relationship for Daeninckx appears intensely mediated by history and the contestation of prevailing historical narratives through the form provided by the noir novel. Thus, his well-known 1984 novel *Meurtres pour mémoire*, sees Daeninckx's Inspector Cadin investigate the murders of father and son historians who are killed twenty years apart. Roger, the father, is shot point-blank at the October 17, 1961 demonstration in Paris in favor of Algerian independence that was violently broken up by French police forces. We learn later that his death was commissioned by a high-ranking civil servant. Bernard, Roger's son, is murdered in Toulouse after completing research in the local archives while seeking to finish his father's project on the history of Drancy, their hometown. It becomes clear to Cadin that both father and son were killed after having unearthed documents relating to the French state's complicity in the Holocaust—indeed, the civil servant responsible for the killings, André Veillut, is a textual stand-in for Maurice Papon, the wartime prefect of police in Paris who was later convicted of crimes against humanity for his role in deporting French Jews. The figure of Inspector Cadin lends the text a historical conscience at the same time that he demonstrates how the writing of official history is fraught with political choices indissolubly linked to the saving of institutional and administrative face.

Daeninckx's relatively less well-known 1987 novel, *Lumière noire*, sees the author's analytic gaze shift from uncovering alternative historical narratives to exposing state collusion in human rights violations occurring in contemporary French society. In the wake of the 1985–86 terrorist attacks in Paris, policemen shoot and kill a man driving a car in a secure section of Roissy-Charles de Gaulle airport. Yves Guyot, who had been riding in the passenger seat, finds his version of the events dismissed as an official (and questionable) police inquiry determines that Gérard, the car's driver, failed to stop as requested and made threatening gestures toward the police officers through his open window. Guyot is murdered before the findings of his amateur counter-investigation can be revealed, and Superintendent Londrin takes over the case before being murdered, as well, after shedding more light on the police cover-up of the events.

Of more importance than "what actually happened" on the fateful night at the airport, however, is the manner in which Guyot discovers before his death evidence that inculpates the police. While the police feed a story to the press involving two fictional French tourists who happened to witness the shooting from an airport hotel room, Guyot learns that the witnesses in question were in fact undocumented Malian immigrants whom the police had forcefully locked in a hotel room in advance of their deportation by charter flight. Guyot secretly travels to Mali shortly before his murder and records the testimony of one of the witnesses, evidence that eventually goes unused. Although this text does not possess the same sort of organizing narrative conscience that we see in *Meurtres pour mémoire*, it operates according to very similar revelatory logics. The narrative of social exclusion uncovered in *Lumière noire* serves to reveal spaces, people, and transnational itineraries that state policing needs to keep hidden to maintain an appearance of lawfulness and a concern for human rights.

These two examples suggest that Daeninckx's narrative politics might best be described as journalistic, concerned as it is with the ways in which an investigator *qua* reporter follows leads and eventually stumbles on a big "scoop" that takes the form of social wrongs committed by the state that must be brought to light. Such a politics finds its culminating point in the act of revelation, the moment when the detective (and the reader) puts in place the final puzzle piece that illuminates a narrative running counter to official state discourses and through which, it is implied, state wrongs might be redressed.

By contrast, Izzo's narrative universe is entirely postlapsarian, in the sense that institutions, police practices, and the state's rhetoric about itself (especially when this rhetoric concerns political universalism, immigration, racism, or security) are presented as always already suspect. From the opening paragraph of the first chapter of *Total Khéops*, where Montale crouches over the body of his friend, Ugo, recently killed by the police, Izzo makes us aware that his Marseille is one in which the cracks in the foundations of official state narratives are plainly visible: "I bent down before the body of Pierre Ugolini. Ugo. I had just arrived on the scene. Too late. My colleagues had played the cowboys. When they shot, they killed. It was as simple as that. Disciples of General Custer: the only good Indian is a dead Indian. And in Marseille Indians were all there were, for the most part."[31] This is not to say that there are no revelations in Izzo's novels. Indeed, crime fiction as a genre cannot function without revelatory moments, whether or not a given investigation is ultimately successful but rather, that his narrative politics does not rely on the unveiling of fundamental wrongs in the same way that Daeninckx's journalism takes the detective and the reader from a state of ignorance to an ultimately edifying moment of illumination.

Instead, the ethnographic politics of narrative in Izzo's trilogy demands to be understood differently. Fabio Montale appears to be as concerned with examining how the breakdown of official state discourses is negotiated and redefined in the everyday life of the city as he is with investigating the crimes that ostensibly serve as the texts' prime movers. This shift in focus from journalism to ethnography opens up several more distinctions between Izzo and the political, or *engagé*, work of a writer such as Daeninckx. First, the detective's relationship to the city and social space has changed: for Izzo, the city is no longer urban space to be traversed and revealed by a detective following leads. Social space in Daeninckx's work seems to exist only in its blunt instrumentalization—that is, insofar as it is potentially useful to the investigator. By contrast, Izzo's Marseille appears above all to possess a daily life independent of Montale's movements and, in fact, independent of the text itself. This point brings us back to the author's ethnographically paratextual relationship to the city's spatiality. What this means is that urban life encompasses and exceeds the figure of the detective-cum-fieldworker and is not simply written into existence through his organizing and investigative gaze. This textual transformation of social space is, I think, intimately bound up with a second correlative transformation of the detective's consciousness: Montale ceaselessly interrogates and problematizes his real and imagined (or idealized) relationship to Marseille, such that these reflections make up no small amount of his interiority as a character and narrator.

Policing Urban Neighborhoods and Generic Boundaries

Although Montale officially works for the police only in the first of the trilogy's three volumes, in all the texts he remains in close contact with police officers and meditates on the relationship between his own detective work and the marginalized spaces and social actors with whom this work puts him in touch. Montale spends much of his time in Marseille's banlieues because of his personal connections to immigrant families and working-class residents and because, while on the force, he was assigned to these neighborhoods to quell growing social unrest. The textual production of these gritty social spaces that are generally excluded from conventional imaginations of the city are certainly consonant with trends in crime fiction of all types, since detectives display authority to readers in part through their ability to negotiate with some amount of cool nonchalance spaces or city neighborhoods that are marginalized or dangerous.[32]

In Izzo's trilogy, though, Marseille's banlieues do more than shore up our confidence in Montale's street smarts and his management of shady connections that allow him to solve the crimes at hand. Throughout the trilogy Montale crosses through and interacts with marginalized spaces and excluded citizens, implicitly revealing them to readers who might otherwise have no contact with them. This strategy is somewhat akin to Hampâté Bâ's sense of ethnographic didacticism, explored in chapter 1; for Montale, however, his relationship to the reader is characterized less by pedagogical impulses than by the narrativization of investigative expediency—that is, the fact that his cases oblige him to make visible certain spaces and individuals that conventional policing has hitherto kept out of sight. As Didier Fassin argues in a study of policing in Parisian banlieues, ethnographies of policing "[produce] a vision of a world that has been made either invisible or opaque to most of us."[33] Montale's position is in many respects a privileged one, since his work in the banlieues requires him to flesh out how cultural and racial difference is spatialized in republican France and how official police work in marginalized social spaces actually contributes to the kinds of social problems it attempts to eradicate, hardening and reifying deep cleavages in French society.[34]

The detective's relationship to the banlieues deserves close attention, both because these are the parts of the city where Montale the cop is on duty and because, once he leaves the force in disgust at the end of *Total Khéops*, they become more broadly the spaces in the texts where state policing is most visible. To recognize this point is to observe the distinction in Izzo's trilogy between policing and investigation: the former is understood as the racialized and classed ways in which "law and order" is maintained and as the discourses on security that underpin these often repressive techniques. The latter refers to the solving of crimes, to be sure, but also and simultaneously to metanarratives on the social and political viability of the French security apparatus writ large. If the two coincide in *Total Khéops*, where Montale is still more or less on the force, it is because his more personal, off-the-books investigations of Leila's murder and the ties of his friends Ugo and Manu to the mafia boss who had them both eliminated happen to overlap with his beat in the working-class quartiers nord. During this time, he and his team finally manage to pin a crime on a young Arab drug dealer, Mourrabed, that reveals his seemingly incongruous links to Marseille's FN and, in turn, reveals the extent to which the far-right party has infiltrated the city's police force.

In *Chourmo* and *Solea*, however, Montale's investigations take place very much outside the purview of the official police, and the hero takes pains to stay at least one step ahead of his former colleagues, who either hold a grudge against him for his history of insubordination or become exasperated at the way he coyly withholds information from them (and, at times, from the reader). In many respects, then, what holds Izzo's narratives together is this dialectic between the police and the investigation: the fact that Montale mediates between the two elements, makes them antithetical to one another, and prevents their coincidence is what, in formal terms, allows the narratives to "succeed" and reach some resolution. The banlieues are narratively productive spaces in the trilogy because they function as the textual terrain on which this dialectic (whose effects are formal yet whose constituent terms are content-based) plays out.

Montale's initial break from the force, which results in his being "promoted" to a beat in the northern suburbs that offers him less and less actual authority, is thrown back into the prehistory of the text; as readers, we are privy only to his retrospective reconstructions of the break as they pertain to the critiques of policing in Marseille that he elaborates throughout the trilogy. Although Montale never offers us a complete reconstruction of his past as a cop, in the first chapter of *Total Khéops* he creates a distinction between policing and his job in the working-class *quartiers d'immigration*. Brooding and sullen, having returned to his home in the picturesque neighborhood of Les Goudes among the famous *calanques* (steep, ancient limestone cliffs overlooking the Mediterranean) and after reminiscing about his childhood friends Ugo and Manu, who, we have just learned, were both killed in suspicious, mafia-related shootouts, Montale sips wine straight from the bottle and declares it "another one of those nights when I no longer knew why I was a cop."[35]

He goes on to explain that, in the wake of two shootings "accidentally" committed by the police in the banlieues that saw the deaths of a young Arab and a white French boy, he was named as head of a special surveillance brigade whose goal was to prevent further police mistakes and quell popular unrest in Marseille's suburbs. In reality, however, he admits, "That day, I began to *slip*, as my colleagues put it. Less and less a cop, more and more a social worker on the streets (*éducateur de rue*). Or a caseworker. Or something like that. Since then, I lost confidence in my bosses and I made myself a lot of enemies. Of course, there were no more blunders, and petty crime didn't get worse, but the "trophy room" was less than glorious: no spectacular arrests, no big publicity coups. Just the routine, all under control."

Montale is clearly aware that his relationship to the official police becomes more tenuous as he is charged with policing spaces that are outside of the public imaginary—in fact, he appears to be making the case here that he is not actually policing these spaces at all, since he has "slipped" into the role of a social worker, one that his colleagues tell him is antithetical to that of a bona fide cop. He notes that when his superiors have singled him out for critique, "I was reproached for not being firm enough in the projects (*cités*). For negotiating too much with the delinquents, mostly immigrants, and with the Gypsies."[36] Even though these events take place before the narrative present of the text, we as readers are given to understand that Montale was marginalized as a cop because he sought to cultivate constructive relationships with individuals and social groups that the police needed to maintain in exclusion.

The second volume of the trilogy, *Chourmo*, brings this contrast into stark relief when Montale reveals a bit more about his work in the quartiers nord. Although the narrative focus of this novel is Montale's investigation of the murder of his cousin's teenage son, a strong subplot deals with his secondary investigation of the killing in broad daylight of a social worker friend from his work in the suburbs. This killing takes place early in the text, in a housing project just outside the quartiers nord, and Montale happens to be on the scene while following a lead in his main investigation. The police arrive a few minutes after the murder, and the kids with whom Montale has been speaking instantly scatter as the hero sardonically likens the theatrical and caricatured arrival of his erstwhile colleagues to an overly faithful reenactment of a *Starsky and Hutch* episode.

When Superintendent Pertin gets out of the car and asks Montale what he is doing there, Montale introduces Pertin as a political and textual foil. In so doing, he presents another philosophy of policing in French banlieues:

> From the very first days, it was war between Pertin and me. "In these Arab neighborhoods," he repeated, "there's only one thing that works: force." That was his principle. He had applied it to the letter for years. The *beurs* [French citizens of North African descent], you just grab one from time to time and you beat him up in an empty lot. There's always something stupid they've done that you don't know about. You hit 'em, and you can be sure they'll know why, that vermin. That's worth any identity check. It saves you the red tape at the station. And it calms the nerves that these towel heads (*crouilles*) have riled up.[37]

The violent racism expressed in this attitude toward policing is not included in the text for any sort of literary shock value; nor is it necessarily intended to unveil structural racism to readers who hitherto may have been unaware of it. As I pointed out earlier, although crime fiction relies on revelatory moments to hold narratives together, Izzo's work does not attempt to link narrative revelation to political didacticism. What Montale wants to convey in this brief anecdote is the sense that the conventional rhetoric of "law and order" has given way to something more odious. Even though his status as more of a social worker renders him unable to effect any real change in marginalized neighborhoods, the official police are no longer able to right social wrongs and, in fact, appear instead to perpetrate them as a matter of course. Thus, Montale's ethnographic relationship to the reader depends on his negotiation of a certain regime of visibility—to wit, the way in which narratives of investigation highlight the breakdown of ideologies of security and the rule of law.

More striking still than Montale's account of how institutionalized policing fails to provide a sense of justice in marginalized neighborhoods are his descriptions of these social spaces and of the people who live in them. This narrative work helps clarify how, for the detective, social actors participate in a symbolic economy that ties together atomized social space and the imaginative postcolonial possibilities that surpass the depressing immediacy of urban fragmentation. From this perspective, utopian desire (to which I turn in the next section of this chapter) proffers a kind of ethnographic *Aufhebung*.

As an example of this descriptive philosophy, we might consider an early scene in *Total Khéops* in which Montale drives to an Arab housing project, known as a *cité maghrébine*, after receiving a message from Leila's father, who will subsequently inform him of his daughter's disappearance. When he arrives on the scene, he describes the entryway of the decrepit building where Leila and her father, Mouloud, live: "Apartment B7 looked just like all the others. The lobby was disgusting. The light had been smashed with rocks. It reeked of piss. And the elevator didn't work. Five floors. Walking up them, it was sure you weren't ascending to heaven."[38] This type of realist description would not be out of place in many a noir novel, but what stands out here is the way in which Montale goes on to link the visibility of such excluded urban sites to the stories of the ordinary citizens who live there and to broader cultural and political phenomena. "For Mouloud, the dream of immigration was his and his alone," Montale tells us of Leila's Algerian father, who came to Marseille to work on a grand construction project that famously failed before it even began. "He was one of the first to be hired on the Fos-sur-Mer construction site at the end of 1970. Fos was Eldorado. . . . He was proud to participate in that adventure, Mouloud. . . . He never forced his children to cut themselves off from other people. . . . Only to avoid bad company. To maintain self-respect. . . . And to succeed as much as possible. To integrate into society without denying who they were. Neither their race, nor their past."[39]

From the grim description of a dingy apartment hallway grows a narrative about the ideals of immigration gone awry, as seen through the case of an elderly Algerian man who came to France for work, wanted to integrate, and was cast aside when the work dried up: "As the first bar of steel emerged, Fos was already nothing more than a mirage. The last great dream of the seventies. The cruelest of disappointments. Thousands of men fell by the wayside. And Mouloud among them."[40] That Izzo has Montale spend several pages telling the story of an otherwise anonymous Algerian man (who is hardly even a minor character in the narrative) indicates that we are dealing with more than noir realism or a demonstration of the detective's ethnographic dexterity, his effortless ability to navigate any number of social milieus. Mouloud's story is an anecdotal foil, a counternarrative running against dominant anti-immigration discourses emanating from the police and from premillennial French political culture more generally. The centrality of this dominant narrative is posed as early as the prologue to *Total Khéops*: "Republican France decided to wash itself whiter. Zero immigration. The new French dream."[41] In particular, Mouloud's embodiment of "the dream of immigration" is set against this newer, antithetical aspiration of French society and its political and governmental representatives. Montale's political anthropology proceeds through such symbolic sets of oppositions, wherein prevailing French discourses on security and the rule of law receive structural support from individuals positioned as either disposable or, worse, inherently criminal.

The stakes of this series of narratives and counternarratives are high. One of the pressing thematic questions running throughout the trilogy is the very real possibility of urban guerrilla warfare breaking out in the banlieues among Islamist immigrants and "ordinary" immigrant gangs, and between these immigrants and the police (and, by extension, the FN). "It would blow up one day, if we did nothing," Montale muses once he has finished telling the story of how he met Mouloud and his family. "It was a sure thing. I didn't have a solution. No one had one. We had to wait. Not resign ourselves. Wager. Believe that Marseille would survive this new human intermingling (*brassage humain*). Would be born again. Marseille had seen others."[42] Neither Montale nor Izzo delves into political prescriptivism in these novels, but the trilogy's noir realism is predicated on opening up ethnographic narratives that are markers of oppositional cultural difference.

In addition to the vignettes that rely on new forms of investigative visibility in marginalized social spaces, we can read Montale's strategies in these texts as careful negotiations not only of his own position in relation to dominant narratives of policing in France, but also in relation to the forms of criminality and sociality that the more invidious forms of state policing produce. These negotiations take an especially provocative form in Montale's relationship to Marseille's banlieues, where he was assigned to keep peace and through which all his investigations must pass to reach a resolution. In other words, the quartiers nord are presented in the trilogy not only as thematically consonant with the texts' broader critiques of racism and failed discourses of French universalism, but they also paradoxically become, on a formal level, marginalized sites that are narratively indispensable. Thus, in *Total Khéops* Montale cannot avoid passing through the banlieues to investigate Leila's disappearance or to inform her father about her murder, even though this case is off the books. Likewise, in a more official capacity, for the police's relationship with the FN to be sketched out more fully, Montale must travel to the suburbs to arrest a young Arab drug dealer who, we learn, was being funded by the FN under the watchful eye of corrupt police officers doubling as party members.

In addition, in *Chourmo* Montale is obliged to return to the banlieues sometime after handing in his badge so he can track down his cousin's son, who, it is initially presumed, has run off with an Arab girl his racist parents had forbidden him to see. What appear as contingencies of plot (which we recognize after the fact as narrative necessities) allow Montale to link his role as a cop who "makes things personal" to his role as an ethnographic flâneur characterized by a refusal of dispassionate observation or, alternatively, by a critique of the perceived dispassion of others. This is a much more politicized ethnographic flânerie than we saw in chapter 2, since Damouré Zika's stroll through pre-independence Accra in Jean Rouch's *Jaguar* has more to do with showing off local knowledge in an aesthetics of modern African cool than with a hardened critique of colonial politics.

In another example, we can take the ethnographic aside Montale makes early in *Chourmo* as he describes his first trip back to the suburbs since leaving the force: "You had to live there, or be a cop or a social worker, to drag your feet all the way to these neighborhoods. For most of Marseille's residents, the quartiers nord were just an abstract reality. Places that existed but that people didn't know and would never know. And which they would always see through the 'eyes' of television. Kinda like the Bronx. With the fantasies that go with it. And the fears."[43]

His humorous comparison to the Bronx notwithstanding, this short observation appears to move in two directions. On the one hand, Montale implies that the social space of these banlieues is only representable insofar as it can be forced into some kind of discursive consonance with one of the two principal narratives of state policing (the cop versus the social worker) that emerge in the trilogy and at whose intersection Izzo's detective finds himself. On the other hand, however, we also notice that these neighborhoods are not, for all that, entirely invisible spaces. As Montale points out, they become abstractly real as they are converted into visible, mediatized simulacra that residents can passively consume on television. The irony here is that he critiques the consumption of such simulacra via an ethnographic fictional copy of "real" life in premillennial Marseille. At issue, then, is not necessarily the fact that police practices and their attendant narrative logics require certain spaces and citizens to remain invisible, but rather the question of what kinds of visibility these forms of policing generate and regulate, in much the same way that Jacques Rancière speaks of a "distribution of the sensible" and of policing as "not so much the 'disciplining' of bodies as a rule governing their appearing."[44]

We can reformulate this problem and observe how Montale approaches it by returning to a question raised at the beginning of this chapter: what kind of spaces and racialized social roles does policing produce in the trilogy? A lengthy passage from the second chapter of *Total Khéops* provides us with a classifactory enumeration of the sorts of people Montale came across when he first started his beat in the banlieues. This passage offers a rich typology of the social roles created by state policing and the forms of marginalization it fosters. It also allows Montale to show off his ethnographic prowess, to display his intimate knowledge of the difficulties of growing up young (and Arab or black) in these neighborhoods, and to narrativize the police's distribution of disciplined bodies, as Rancière would put it.

He arrives at the suburban cité where Leila's father lives and, after parking his little Renault, remarks, "I remembered that [Charles] Aznavour sang 'La misère est moins dure au soleil.' No doubt he never came here. To these heaps of shit and concrete."[45] He proceeds to reflect on the initial impressions he had of work in the suburbs and of the personalities he encountered there: "When I first showed up in the projects, right away I came up against the gangsters, the addicts, and the drifters. People who don't play by the rules, who cast a chill. Who scare the crap out of people. . . . Armed robbers, dealers, racketeers."[46] Montale shows us, first, that he is as hard as the next cop, rhetorically puffing out his chest in a display of noir bravado. His sense of the field, however, attunes him to a fixed distribution of social types that was reinforced and reified by his predecessors.

This passage takes on a softer, more empathetic tone as Montale speculates on the very uncertain future in store for many of the youths he came across during his work: "Then there are all the other ones that I discovered later.

A mass of kids with no other story than that of being born here. And Arab. Or black, gypsy, Comoran [having roots in the Comoros Islands]. . . . Their adolescence was like walking on a tightrope. Except there was every chance they would fall."[47] Although this passage lacks the personal narrative tone that characterizes Mouloud's story, for example, it serves a similar ethnographic function: here typological stigmatization becomes typological humanism, and a sclerotic distribution of social roles dissolves into "a mass of kids" whose biggest crime was to have been born into a marginalized community. This humanizing gesture, which is born from Montale's intimate knowledge of social life in the banlieues (and effectively conveyed to us in a display of ethnographic virtuosity of which Hampâté Bâ would be proud) is set against a rhetoric of delinquency that we encounter in the initial typology and in remarks such as those made by Superintendent Pertin, who stands in synecdochically for the official police as a whole.

Montale's ethnography of policing succeeds because of the trilogy's generic self-awareness. Crime fiction, like all genre fiction, self-identifies by strategically policing and transgressing its own generic boundaries. Here the conventions of genre are identified as they gesture outward and beyond themselves: Montale is a classic noir figure (a lovelorn and weary cop, he lives hard and drinks harder), but we recognize him as such only insofar as he endows investigative narratives with an aesthetics of fieldwork. As so much of this book's archive suggests, ethnographic fiction encourages and even demands that we account creatively for such transgressive processes of generic identification: as an anthropological meta-genre, ethnographic fiction highlights the discrete forms of textual world making contained within its constituent elements even as it gains conceptual authority by foregrounding integrative moments of generic convergence.

Utopian Desire as Anthropology of the Present

Montale communicates a sense of political powerlessness in the face of urban decay, the breakdown of law and order, and rising institutional racism. Although we as readers are aware of the hero's persistence in assuring us that he has no effective solution to the bleak cultural present he ethnographically critiques, these assurances nonetheless prompt us to read the trilogy attentively, looking out for hints of a response to the disenchantment that hangs over so many of Montale's observations and reflections. Disenchantment is not synonymous with fatalist resignation, however. Even though Montale refuses to offer a politically prescriptive solution to lived experiences of alienation, he does imagine another sort of belonging that is woven into the present, one that rejects disenchantment by positioning Marseille as radically open to the world's diversity. Political antiprescriptivism nurtures speculative ethnographic desire.

The alternative form of cultural belonging for which Montale forces us to search as we engage with his critiques of dominant French discourses on race, immigration, and criminality is an idealized and utopian rendering of the city, one that exists at the same time and in tension with the other Marseille whose present and immediate future appear bleak. Alongside the more conventionally realist representation of Marseille in the trilogy as a fractured social space, marked by exclusions and marginalizations on which the FN constantly threatens to capitalize,[48] is another version of the city whose residents are inextricably linked through generations of exile and (post)colonial immigration. This alternative spatiality begins from an imagined sense of belonging that precludes exclusions of all kinds. Toward the end of *Total Khéops*, Montale makes a brief remark whose ambiguity unites both of these written versions of the city: "Our former colonies were now here. Capital: Marseille."[49] Marseille appears at one and the same time as a colony internal to the French nation-state and, in a more speculative vein, as the de facto capital of the French postcolonial world, uniting people in their movements to and from the metropole.

For Édouard Glissant, whose work we examined in chapter 3, this act of postcolonial gathering positions the Mediterranean as a maritime foil for the Caribbean and its histories of dispersion. He writes, "The Caribbean sea differs from the Mediterranean in that it is an open sea, a sea that diffracts, whereas the Mediterranean is a sea that concentrates. . . . The Caribbean is a sea that diffracts and that brings about the commotion (*émoi*) of diversity." This opposition lends the Mediterranean world a hermetic quality that stands in rather stark contrast with the Caribbean's (post)colonial history as a site of "transit and passages" and of "encounters and consequences."[50] Izzo's Marseille breaks down Glissant's oppositional definition, though, since the city is part of a Mediterranean world whose unity is but a refractive illusion of the monolithic wholeness decried by the Caribbean philosopher; this unity holds together fluctuating, tenuous histories of exilic movements.

We can follow Montale's ethnographic lead and explore the ways in which a utopian reimagining of Marseille is written over his other descriptions of lived experience that situate the city in a corrupt present, where the banlieues allow for the normalization of state violence or, as Étienne Balibar puts it, "the invasion of public space by practices of non-right,"[51] where the police are in bed with the FN, and where the mafia is in bed with just about everybody. However, the utopia that emerges in the trilogy is not set in a spatially or temporally distanced realm; it appears, rather, as an alternative imagining of the present that, while not prescriptive in the sense that it would represent a blueprint for futurity, is diagnostic in the sense that it makes visible the limitations inhibiting collective experience and democratic citizenship in contemporary French society. In a related register, Arjun Appadurai argues that futurity, "a space for democratic design," must respond to an "affective crisis" in the present. More broadly, an "anthropology of the future" must provoke "a full-scale debate about the best ways to design humanity."[52] The idea of utopia as a palimpsest allows us to reorganize this formulation somewhat: the spatiality of hopeful democratic intentionality need not be conceptually soldered to an anthropological futurity or to a forward-looking constructive humanism. Rather, my argument here reads utopian spatiality in terms of an anthropology of copresence and copresents, in terms of contrasting visions of cultural immediacy that generate speculative thought in their competitive contemporaneity.

We can begin with an example from *Chourmo* that amply demonstrates this type of conceptual stratification. Montale wanders into a historic working-class neighborhood called Le Panier and comes across an archeological site that was hastily constructed when plans for an underground parking garage hit a snag after workers discovered they were digging into the fortifications of the ancient port city of Massilia. Recognizing that this site was examined by an Algerian historian who was killed at the same time as Guitou, Montale reflects on how new building projects (especially parking garages) are inexorably paving over Marseille's archeological patrimony: "In the Centre Bourse area, the negotiations were long and hard. . . . The awful concrete bunker won out in the end, though. . . . In the Place du Général-de-Gaulle, steps away from the Vieux-Port, nothing and no one could stop the parking garage from being built. . . . I was ready to bet my nice polka-dot shirt that, here too, concrete would be the big winner."[53] Montale follows up these observations by moving into a different discursive register, asserting, "Everything would be lost except memory. The people of Marseille would be satisfied with that. They all know what lies under their feet, and they carry the history of their city in their hearts. It's their secret, which no tourist can ever steal."[54] What emerges here is an idealized ineffaceability of belonging and being together in the city that exists over and against actually existing attempts to refashion that belonging in postindustrial urban renewal projects.

As Montale's reflections on the archeological strata of Marseille's urban identity show, the utopian gestures in the trilogy do not run parallel to critical appraisals of everyday life but are actually superimposed on them. Following the generic and narrative model that recurs throughout this book, utopia as a palimpsest represents a rewriting that is also a writing over, one that, in the words of Fredric Jameson, throws into relief "the mud of the present age in which the winged Utopian shoes stick."[55] I do not disagree with Jameson's suggestion that the utopian text writ large is often more or less non-narrative, but Izzo's trilogy pushes us to observe that a palimpsestic utopia relies on the noncoincidence of temporal claims on futurity and narrative claims on the ethnographic production of utopian desire.

Even though these claims are not coextensive in Izzo's trilogy, a sense of futurity (a grim future, in fact, that is even bleaker than the real time of the texts themselves) does exist in all three novels that runs parallel to Montale's utopian musings in the present. This point is important, for it helps us to see more clearly how the dystopian near-future that lies just slightly beyond the trilogy's narrative horizon—but that Izzo still lets us glimpse because it is crucial to his sense of plot—represents an indispensable element in the production of the textual present.

The trilogy is explicitly set in the present of late 1990s Marseille, but Izzo's narratives and Montale's investigations rely to no small extent on a foreboding dystopian near-future that moves in two directions. The first of these, which emerges most clearly in *Total Khéops* and *Chourmo*, involves urban guerrilla race warfare originating in the banlieues and provoked by the police (via the FN) or by Islamic fundamentalists trained in North Africa or the Balkans who return to France and recruit an army from the disaffected youth of Marseille's immigrant suburbs. In *Total Khéops*, for instance, we learn that the two cops who shot down Montale's childhood friend, Ugo, and raped and murdered his pseudo-love interest, Leila, were working for the Italian mafia, which had been trying to gain a foothold in Marseille and was using its connections to funnel weapons to drug dealers in the suburbs who, in turn, distributed them to young Arab men. As the local mafia boss, Batisti, puts it when he reveals this information to Montale toward the end of the narrative, "They think they're gonna clean up Marseille. They dream about setting fire to the city. About mayhem beginning in the quartiers nord. Hordes of young people giving themselves over to pillaging."[56] As Montale explains it, "Violence on one side. Fear, racism on the other. And with that, they hoped their fascist buddies would make it to City Hall."[57]

Similarly, in *Chourmo*, during his investigation of the murder of his social worker friend Serge, Montale comes across one of Serge's notebooks containing the names of people involved in Islamist terrorism in the banlieues. This is information the police want kept under wraps, not least because, as it turns out, they were involved in sending Islamist militants to murder Serge in the first place. At the end of this second text we learn that, thanks to information Montale ensured was placed in the right hands, trustworthy police officers were able to break up terrorist cells in the quartiers nord and, in so doing, discover a large weapons cache in a makeshift mosque. By the end of the trilogy's first two volumes, then, we learn that Montale's investigations have narrowly prevented such urban warfare from erupting (indeed, the verb Izzo uses is *exploser*), but this investigative and narrative success does not diminish the texts' sense of futurity. If anything, the possibility of a violent and dystopian near-future, where racial and religious warfare has been ignited and the FN sweeps to power, has simply been deferred until another day.

Whereas this dystopia, in which the state appears to have orchestrated the very urban violence that would see it delivered into the hands of the FN, is imagined in the first volumes of the trilogy in terms of the everyday practices of corruption that could make this possible, the trilogy's final volume, *Solea*, offers a second dystopian direction. This anxiety plays out on the grander stage of the nation-state, global capitalism, and the relationship of both with transnational forms of organized crime. Here Montale must protect his journalist friend and erstwhile lover, Babette, from the mafia, which has learned that she possesses sensitive documents linking many French government officials to organized crime. Neither Montale nor the reader remains unaware that Izzo's characters in this volume are nearly eclipsed by more abstract politico-economic issues. We easily notice how *Solea* is marked by a deep sense of anxiety, since the texts' millennial concerns about the near-future (*Solea*, the final novel in the trilogy, was published in 1998) are also effectively channeled into the narrative present. This occurs through Izzo's extensive "citations" of

Babette's journalistic writings that diagnose the mafia's infiltration of contemporary French political life and, in so doing, sketch a relationship among transnational money laundering, world debt, and economic austerity policies that threaten to plunge the mafia-run Global North into an economic crisis that may be just around the corner.[58] We cannot help but recognize a prescience in Izzo and his detective's anxiety, since *Solea* was finished roughly a decade before the 2008 global financial crisis.

The fact that both of these dystopian directions, as well as the attendant sense of futurity they produce, emerge most forcefully at the end of Izzo's novels (i.e., paradoxically at precisely the moment in which the success of Montale's investigation has ensured their temporary deferral) sheds light on how extratextual futurity is involved in the retrospective creation of narratives of utopian desire in the textual present. Put another way, we might say that in some respects Montale's utopian reimagining of Marseille gains political salience and narrative significance only after the texts' sense of futurity has reached a crescendo that anchors the desire for utopia more fully in the present. To pose this unexpected temporal relationship allows us to move beyond overly simplified distinctions between utopia and dystopia and to conceive of futurity in such a way that it becomes an imperative urging us to rewrite the present in utopian terms. Ethnographic fiction's speculative streak is an imaginative provocation and not a demand for a fully fleshed-out representative logic.[59]

Leaving aside the matter of futurity for the moment, we can notice that these utopian rewritings of the city are both presentist and deeply concerned with the ways in which an imagined, alternative present necessarily puts multiple temporalities into play. A moment from late in *Total Khéops* illustrates this point quite strikingly. Montale has just left his crucial meeting with the mob boss, Batisti, who answers many of the questions that hold the narrative in place. He wanders into yet another bar, where he overhears a conversation among several young Arabs about French national identity and about the fact that Arab youth are "the least French of all French people." When one of them declares that he does not care, that he is Marseillais before anything else, Montale begins to reminisce about his own experiences negotiating belonging in the nation-state and in the imagined space of the city: "They were from Marseille, and were Marseillais before being Arabs. . . . Just as we were fifteen years ago, Ugo, Manu, and I. One day, Ugo asked: 'At my house and at Fabio's we speak Neapolitan. At yours, you speak Spanish. At school, we learn French. But what are we, at the end of the day?'—'Arabs (*Des Arabes*),' Manu replied."[60] The word "*Arabes*" is resignified here and refers not to excluded Maghrebi citizens of the Marseille Montale describes when he critiques police practices and anti-immigrant discourses, but to a universalist and hybridized sense of belonging in a city conceptualized as a utopian melting pot.

Montale proceeds to think about his Italian father telling him that when he arrived in Marseille with his brothers, they hardly ever had enough to eat, but they still managed to make do, thanks to an unspoken sense of solidarity in the city. "That's what it was, the history of Marseille," Montale concludes. "Its eternity. A utopia. The only utopia in the world. A place where anybody, of whatever color, could get off a boat or a train, suitcase in hand, without a penny in their pocket, and melt into the flow of other people. A city where, as soon as one's foot hit the ground, one could say: 'It's here. I'm home.' Marseille belongs to those who live there."[61]

Initially, we might consider this passage as offering a vision of French universalism grafted onto an idealized sense of belonging in the city or as an elevation of French democratic republicanism to the level of narrative fantasy.[62] However, Montale's reflections demand that we pay attention to how different senses of time and history are enmeshed in the production of present-based utopian desires. For one thing, what stands out is the intentional folding of history into a transhistorical utopian fantasy: for Montale, Marseille's past is also always already its "eternity," and it follows from this that the development of such a historical consciousness is part and parcel of an alternative conceptualization of the present.

We can humorously rework Marx's famous dictum from *The Eighteenth Brumaire* here and observe that, although men make their own history under preexisting circumstances, when history and utopia are conceptually linked, men are free to reimagine the present as they see fit. This is exactly what Montale does in this passage, even though his utopian desire is rerouted through a meditation on Marseille's history and the only positive characteristic he gives to his utopia is the idea that "Marseille belongs to those who live there." Returning to Marcus's "modernist" ethnographic strategy discussed at the outset of this chapter, we can note that an anthropological imagining of alternatives to the cultural present need not be concretely programmatic; instead, it should constitute thought experiments by virtue of which one can ethnographically confront the contemporary.[63]

Rather than indicating its imaginative powerlessness, a rewriting of the present that resists a full and positive descriptive program is useful precisely because it avoids spelling out in prescriptive detail what an alternative present must look like. Instead, what we might refer to as descriptive blind spots in the palimpsest can be taken to indicate potential avenues for utopian thought that have simply have not been imagined yet. It is in this sense that the presentist utopian text is both descriptively "closed" and imaginatively "open" at one and the same time. We can approach this copresence from another angle by taking up the question of geography in Izzo's Marseille and thinking through the ways in which its sense of spatiality exceeds the cartographic boundaries of the city itself. Often, an actually existing site in the text affords Montale inspiration for his utopian reflections. The first chapter of *Solea*, for instance, sees our hero shrug off premonitions about his own demise (in fact, the chapter opens with the sentence, "Life reeked of death") by heading out for drinks at one of his favorite watering holes. "I liked it in Hassan's bar," he remarks. "The regulars mingled without any barriers of age, sex, skin color, or social status. We were among friends. Whoever came there to drink his pastis, you could be sure that he didn't vote Front National and had never done so."[64]

This actually existing ideal space opens up a virtual geography for Montale, as he indicates in the observation that follows: "Here, in this bar, each person knew well why they were from Marseille and not from someplace else, why they lived in Marseille and not somewhere else. The friendship that floated in there, among the scents of anise, took hold in a shared glance. An expression of our fathers' exile. And it was comforting. We had nothing to lose, since we had already lost everything."[65] In Montale's pastis-fueled observations, this virtual geography is expressed in two ways that are intimately linked to each other.

The first way this geography is articulated is in an idealized common knowledge, according to which the imagined contours of this other Marseille can be said to extend as far as people are capable of recognizing and affirming the forms of contingency that tie together what Izzo calls the "human minglings" (*brassages humains*) of the port city.[66] The second is in relation to the placeless place of exile that locates Marseille at the virtual center of a multiplicity of displacements from somewhere else. This intense geographical diffusion stands in stark contrast with the spatiality of Thomas More's early conception of Utopia, whose *limes* is formed through geographical scission and relies fundamentally on such manufactured isolation to succeed as an imagined country. As More puts it, "They say, though, and one can actually see for one self, that Utopia was originally not an island but a peninsula. However, it was conquered by somebody called Utopos . . . the moment he landed and got control of the country, he immediately had a channel cut through the fifteen-mile isthmus connecting Utopia with the mainland, so that the sea could flow all round it."[67] Following this origin story, we can understand More's early Utopia as relying on geographic limitations, what we might call the geographic production of utopian autochthony. By contrast, Izzo's utopia begins by precluding the very idea of autochthony, relying instead on flux, expansion, and boundaries that shift, break apart, and congeal again around ever new modes of identifying with exile.[68]

This is a geography that both maps and is constituted by an alternative mode of belonging. Exile allows for a potentially limitless expansion of the fictive borders of this imagined Marseille, since it can accommodate virtually every sort of geographical displacement. As Montale notes during a conversation with his friend Félix in *Chourmo*, "Marseille belongs to exile. This city will never be anything else, the world's last port of call. Its future belongs to those who arrive. Never to those who leave."[69] Yet, when we take this in conjunction with the passage cited earlier, we notice that exile also operates as an assumed ontological category that functions as a criterion for inclusion within Izzo's utopia: if everyone is living the exile of their forebears, then it suffices to recognize this status (in much the same way, for example, that Sartre's Saint Genet chooses to be who he is[70]) to be able to participate in this collective reimagining of the city. Montale himself agrees with this idea of exile as a linchpin holding together geography and belonging: a few dozen pages after his conversation with Félix, he asserts, "I belonged to exile. Three-fourths of the residents of this city could say the same thing. But they didn't. Or not enough for my liking. And yet, that's what being Marseillais was. Knowing that one wasn't born here by chance."[71]

This idealized form of belonging is thus written over what Montale perceives to be a sort of indifference (i.e., a mode of belonging in the city that is thoroughly dehistoricized) on the part of many of his fellow city dwellers. Whether his diagnosis is correct is less important than the fact that his reflections produce two forms of belonging in the city that correspond to the two visions of Marseille that emerge in these introspective field notes. This interaction takes an especially striking form if we resituate it under the rubric of citizenship and observe that what Izzo accomplishes in writing an alternative Marseille over the Marseille that appears in his gritty ethnographic realism is an articulation of "dual citizenship" that is lived in relation to two political communities—one of which is "real," the other of which is imagined—that are always interdependent.

Citizenship offers a particularly provocative lens through which to reckon with these disparate forms of belonging, for although modalities of inclusion and exclusion in the French nation-state are always thematically lurking in the trilogy, the horizon of the political community Izzo outlines is at once "below" and "beyond" the nation-state. It is below the nation-state because the real world of the text is a Marseille presented as a culturally autonomous *polis*, and it is beyond it because the utopian Marseille superimposed on this first one is formed through radical diffusion and is always already imagined as exceeding the geopolitical confines of France. The idea of utopia as a palimpsest implies, as we have seen, a certain simultaneity and coexistence and a holding together of imaginative forms. It is for this reason that the idea of dual citizenship stands out: it maps a bifurcated conception of membership onto a community whose horizon is itself doubled.

This community of citizens is not the result of a zero-sum game that would position political belonging in terms of either an ideal community or an empirical one. As Balibar has argued, the community of citizens contains "a moving historical site that is both sociological and symbolic. . . . its domain is a dialectics and not a constitution, a sociology, or a logic. . . . A dialectic of 'constituent' and 'constituted' citizenship.' [I]t is a contradictory process, fed by permanent conflicts between several types of subjectifications or identities, some cultural or prepolitical, others political."[72] How can we democratize citizenship by rethinking the borders of the community to which citizenship refers? We can begin to answer this question, I think, by conceiving of the political community in the cultural present as holding together boundaries that can be "documented" by the social sciences and imaginative transgressions of such empirical constraints and limitations. This sense of dual citizenship is produced (and is never definitively resolved) in the textual alternation between empirical forms of belonging in 1990s Marseille and the idealized, constitutively transgressive, utopian belonging that Izzo writes over everyday processes of policing, restraint, and containment. Dialectical shifts between fully formed and openly processual modalities of citizenship stand out all the more clearly because Izzo's palimpsest allows for these terms to be grasped and articulated in their aesthetic simultaneity. Utopia, in short, stands at the generic and synthetic crossroads opened up by ethnographic fiction.

It is in terms of this dialectic that we can understand the succession of chapter titles in Izzo's trilogy. With the exception of his brief prologues and epilogues, each chapter title offers a sardonically empirical or, alternatively, an idealized situating of Marseille according to a recurring formula. Examples include "Where even in order to lose, you have to know how to fight," "Where dawns are but the illusion of the world's beauty," "Where you rub elbows with the smallest morsels of the world's filth," "Where it's often secret loves that one shares with a city," "Where it is said that vengeance doesn't get you anywhere, and neither does pessimism," and "Where the question is raised of life's enjoyment in a society without morals." From chapter to chapter, we, as readers, shuttle back and forth among filth, illusion, and decadence, on the one hand, and, on the other, optimistic resilience, a refusal of fatalism, and an awareness of being swept along in a larger, open collective project. These titles, all beginning with "where," are also spatial (re)iterations of the city in which we experience the tension between constituted and constituent citizenship: Izzo's trilogy "happens" in the succession and surpassing of these dialectically organized moments.

The detective as experimental ethnographer must engage in critical thought experiments in which alternative or repressed cultural possibilities go head to head with the dominant political or discursive trends that would otherwise marginalize them. These are moments of speculative confrontation in which ethnographic strategizing in the cultural present takes advantage of fiction as a textual vehicle to seek out utopian potentiality in the face of empirically foreclosed avenues for social transformation.[73] For Izzo, Marseille finds itself "forever halfway between tragedy and enlightenment (*la lumière*)," as he puts it in the author's note to *Solea*. Fictional ethnographic speculation holds social space in hopeful textual suspension, allowing realism and thought experiments to map each other in the novel's multilayered cartography.

In an experimental ethnography on "social belonging and endurance in late liberalism," Elizabeth Povinelli writes that her study of "alternative worlds" turns its back on anthropology's long-standing generic convention of thick description. She instead tips her cap to James Clifford and assimilates her ethnographic writing to "sociography"—that is, "a way of writing the social from the point of view of social projects."[74] From this perspective, speculative projects preclude or obviate the kinds of generic moves that anthropology has long held up as disciplinary markers. As I have argued in this chapter, though, Izzo's ethnographic fiction is generically satisfying because it allows us to have it both ways: it incorporates an aesthetics of fieldwork, allowing us to glimpse disciplinary boundaries through sociographic reading, while also laying claim to speculative desires that encourage us to skirt the ethnographic comfort zones identified by Povinelli. Fiction relies on the imaginative production of lifeworlds and thus traffics in thick descriptions of all kinds, regardless of how loosely certain writers might adhere to them. From premillennial policing to postcolonial forms of utopian desire, this ethnographic fiction transcodes thick description, implicating it in generic experimentation and alternative countermappings of speculative social projects.

Conclusion

Empire, Democracy, and Nonsovereign Knowledges

This book began opening outward in chapter 5, when we studied how Jean-Claude Izzo's crime fiction creates an anthropology of the present by rewriting the postcolonial city as a utopian palimpsest in which new visions of democracy and of a postcolonial *demos* are overlaid onto actually existing anxieties about contemporary life at the end of the millennium. In certain respects, this is a culmination of the moves made by many of the figures I study in this book. Like Jean Rouch and his friends, Amadou Hampâté Bâ, Patrick Chamoiseau, and Jean Price-Mars, Izzo imagines new social forms that arise from formal and generic experimentation. And like many figures from earlier in the twentieth century, his sense of experimentation is rooted in new ways of knowing empire that also gesture beyond imperial organizations of geography, politics, and history. This epistemological intersection with empire that veers away from it at the same time is part and parcel of the kinds of orthogonal thinking that this book's alternative anthropologies have highlighted and textualized.

But Izzo also makes more explicit and more contemporary certain tendencies that are only obliquely addressed by other figures that feature in this study. As we saw in chapter 5, he asks questions of sovereignty and postcolonial democracy by rerouting these concepts through utopian forms of political desire that figures from earlier in the twentieth century might have embraced but did not identify with the same sort of precision or thoroughness. This is where

Izzo's work opens this book's scope further and brings it into the twenty-first century. It gestures toward the textual and social possibilities imagined by earlier experiments with empire but directs them toward neoliberal ideologies, toward new political opportunities for confronting them, and toward new democratic forms of knowledge.

This concluding chapter continues turning outward and suggests that this book's major arguments have implications for—or allow us to intervene differently in—pressing twenty-first-century debates about politics, democracy, and postcolonial knowledge production. The overarching idea here is that if we begin from experiments with genre, empire, and twentieth-century alternative anthropologies, we can arrive at some of the most important debates taking place in twenty-first-century political thought and cultural critique. I want to offer a set of interrelated interventions here, all of which emerge from a series of broad questions. Once we identify the speculative, experimental underside of French imperialism, what conclusions can we draw from this relationship between experimentation and empire for current thinking about postcolonial epistemologies, especially as they relate to "global Africa" and new knowledge forms extending from the continent? If orthogonality is the methodological hallmark of this experimental relationship, what avenues for political thought does orthogonality open up today? And finally, if we accept that contemporary democracy is in "crisis"—whether because of crises originating "from below" on the level of social production that Michael Hardt and Antonio Negri sketch out, or because of crises provoked by neoliberal ideologies of moral/political/economic "sacrifice" as Wendy Brown highlights, or more fundamentally because modern democracy is constitutively entangled with empire, as Achille Mbembe argues—if we accept these ideas, then how do the principles of orthogonality and speculation help us imagine alternative democratic forms?[1] These questions point us toward the political and epistemological resonances of this book's focus on alternative anthropologies and speculative textual/social forms.

The Speculative Atlantic

One key idea of this book, motivating the analysis of all of the texts in my archive, has been that empire is an experimental space-time. From one perspective, this is something we already knew from above, as it were, from governmental and administrative standpoints. As Gary Wilder has shown, for instance, ethnologist-administrators in French West Africa during the interwar period sought to devise new, "humanist" methods of colonial rule that were based on scientifically rigorous studies of the needs and interests of colonial subjects. The development of this "scientific-administrative complex" was intended to solidify reformism in the colonies and contribute to national renewal back home in the Metropole.[2] From this point of view, empire is a pliable political-epistemological project/ideology that allows for the promotion and testing out of new social forms and ways of knowing that bring empire and Metropole together in the same political and social circuitry.

The experimental empire I have been working with in this book is distinct from this administrative model, however. For the writers and anthropologists I have studied here, empire provokes much more intense forms of speculation that take place across the chronological divide of decolonization. Unlike the ethnologist-administrators who embraced new ways of knowing the colonized to refine imperial rule and renew the nation, thereby remaining comfortably ensconced within the ideological and political terms already given by empire, the figures that have featured in this book honed their visions of empire the better to imagine social and textual forms beyond its grasp. Even metropolitan ethnographers such as Rouch and Michel Leiris were acutely aware of, even motivated by, their ambivalent attitudes toward and ambiguous positions within the colonial project.

These forms were driven by alternative ways of knowing the world that promoted new imaginations of extraimperial sociality and, correlatively, experimental modes of textual world making. The Atlantic world that takes shape in this book is thus a speculative geographic and historical venture that imagines new cartographic assemblages and alternative social forms beyond the horizon of empire itself.[3] In this speculative world, empire's power relations and modes of domination do not just appear as eminently knowable; they also function as epistemological raw materials allowing us to imagine what Judith Butler might refer to as empire's "constitutive outside."[4]

This idea of the speculative Atlantic affects how we think about world literature today—or world cultural production, if we can group the ethnographies, novels, and films from my archive under this term. More specifically, it helps us think world cultural production beyond the nexus of translatability and untranslatability that serves as the driving force behind Emily Apter's critique of world literature. For Apter, the institutionalization of world literature risks amounting to an "entrepreneurial, bulimic drive to anthologize and curricularize the world's cultural resources," an impulse that relies uncritically on the neat translatability of texts, contexts, and identities.[5] She argues instead for a disjunctive perspective, "an approach to literary comparatism that recognizes the importance of non-translation, mistranslation, incomparability, and untranslatability."[6] Apter's point is well taken: would it not be ahistorically naïve to conceive of world literary space as fundamentally smooth and built to facilitate conversions of all kinds?

Yet this disjunctive approach to comparatism does not exactly capture the types of experimental world making that took place in the twentieth-century French Atlantic. As I have argued throughout this book, the textual and social forms that anthropologists and literary writers imagined were precisely not "incomparable" with empire and its sociopolitical logics. On the contrary, they emerged from engagements with empire and its afterlives. These engagements were not "translations" of empire, either, however. They were speculative projects that read empire as an epistemological expedient facilitating the imagination of entirely different political, historical, and geographic assemblages. This is speculation as orthogonal thinking, and as such, speculation functions here as a comparatist motor that prompts us to read texts beyond questions of commensurability and instead in terms of alternative knowledges and lifeworlds.

Speculation relates in part to the development of epistemological capital in world textual space, as I argued in chapter 2. Rouch's research subjects, as we saw, rearranged imperial space and thought beyond it by making themselves anthropologically legible as knowledge producers in their own right. Hampâté Bâ, whose work we studied in chapter 1, engages in a similar kind of textual labor. But speculation relates even more fundamentally to the setting in motion of defamiliarized textual worlds that nonetheless bear some resemblance to the social forms and modes of knowledge that we already recognize. Speculation as a comparatist act and ethic relies, then, on the "circulation of worlds" (to borrow Mbembe's phrase from his work on "Afropolitanism").[7] From the perspective of this project, this circulation refers to the interpenetration and separability of disparate textual, social, and epistemological universes that are and that might be. This is a vision of world cultural production that is only superficially interested in (in)commensurability and only insofar as it is an imaginative jumping-off point.

Africa World against Postanthropology

Speculation as comparatism brings us further into the domain of postcolonial knowledge production. For many of the figures I have studied in this book, speculation involves new ways of knowing Africa and global blackness that rely on rerouted geographies and rewritten histories. Recall that this is the methodology underpinning Price-Mars's transatlantic call for a renewed Haitian literature, or that Rouch's research subjects rewrote global modernity in terms of their everyday life in rapidly decolonizing West Africa. If the circulation of worlds is a fundamentally speculative perspective, as I suggested earlier, then it depends on the circulation of alternative knowledge forms.

Mbembe echoes this speculative engagement with global and diasporic Africa when he returns to his "circulation of worlds" thesis (which received full treatment in his book, *Sortir de la grande nuit* [2010]) in an essay titled "L'Afrique qui vient" (The Coming Africa). He takes a planetary view of the continent here and argues for "a politics of opening (*déclosion*) and circulation" that would generate an "Afropolitan public space."[8] This creative opening reveals the "world figure" of Africa in "new assemblages . . . new stylistic forms, or new imaginations of the future."[9]

In another essay from his edited volume *Ecrire l'Afrique-Monde* (Writing Africa-World [2017]), Mbembe gives this thinking an anthropological cast. And it is here that I want to intervene more directly in terms of this book's project. In this piece, "Penser le monde à partir de l'Afrique" (Thinking the World from Africa), Mbembe offers a set of twelve propositions on how "modern regimes of knowledge" can think about Africa today, moving through figures such as Frantz Fanon, Édouard Glissant, and Paul Gilroy to respond to the question, "How can we make the present and African life . . . an *event for thought* for people of African origin, of course, but also for our world?"[10] This planetary and African perspective, the argument goes, can allow us to move beyond ideologies and theories of difference (which appear implicitly linked here, at least by analogy, to the rise of right-wing nativisms across the West) and toward a "politics of similarity" that functions as a "thought of the world."[11]

Mbembe concludes that emerging forms of African and diasporic cultural production (he cites the "postcolonial African novel" as an example) can revamp our understandings of "distance and proximity," self and other, and of Africa's constitutive worldliness. We can read these ideas in terms of a politics of similarity if we adopt what he calls a "postanthropological" perspective on Africa that will push us to "overcome the aporias of discourses on 'difference.'"[12] But is this not too ready an assimilation of anthropology to uncritical fetishizations of "difference?" And why pit anthropology against art, fiction, and literature in this periodization of a politics of similarity? This book's focus on generic experimentation demands that we ask such questions of Mbembe's argument and its critique of anthropological knowledge production.

Although Mbembe does not specify what the "post-" in "postanthropology" signifies (how does it periodize the relationship between artistic production and anthropology?), his critique of a certain kind of anthropology's unreflexive interest in "difference"—before the *Writing Culture* moment, we might say—is well founded. But as I have argued throughout this book, alternative anthropologies are born of creative connections with other forms of imaginative cultural production, and the speculative work they do generates new historical and geographic mappings—precisely the kind of "new assemblages" and "new stylistic forms" Mbembe calls for in his planetary Africanism. The fact that literary writers from the French Atlantic sought out anthropology to think through empire in their fiction suggests that the discipline can offer radical forms of political connectivity. This is why, as we saw in chapter 4, Glissant and the créolistes turned to anthropology to imagine new social forms in the Caribbean and global Creoleness over and against ideologies of integration into the postcolonial French nation-state. A fundamental argument of this book is that anthropology actually implies experimental creativity, that anthropology enhances transgeneric thinking and the production of open-ended, politicized knowledges beyond empire.

What this means is that integrative, planetary perspectives on Africa and the diaspora arise as anthropology interacts with other forms of cultural production—or, better, as we recognize anthropology as a form of cultural production alongside (and constitutive of) fiction, cinema, and other artistic ventures. This awareness is a speculative legacy of anthropology's *Writing Culture* moment that we can recuperate and reactivate today. Even more fundamentally, though, the creative forms of connectivity imagined in this book suggest that alternative political and epistemological desires are not "postanthropological," as Mbembe might have it. Anthropology beyond difference is not necessarily post-anthropology. But it is an alternative anthropology, one that foregrounds anthropology's constitutive openness to other forms of cultural production as key for imagining new political subjectivities and new ways of knowing the world. The Africa world perspective Mbembe espouses thus is not incompatible with anthropology, provided that we remain attentive to the ways anthropological knowledge is embedded in other forms of cultural production. This is a defamiliarization of anthropology, to be sure, but one that does not for all that leave anthropology behind.

Orthogonality as a Political Principle

Defamiliarizing anthropology is another way of naming the kinds of orthogonal thinking that I have studied in this book. The writers and ethnographers who experimented with ethnographic fiction in the French Atlantic embraced anthropological knowledge forms but also turned them inside out, leading them toward new textual and political possibilities. Likewise and relatedly, the figures from my primary archive all sought new ways of knowing empire to imagine new sociopolitical forms beyond it. This even holds for Leiris, if we take a longer view of his career. In chapter 1 we saw him wallow in his ambivalent relationship to French imperialism, but nearly two decades later he published his famous essay "L'ethnographe devant le colonialisme" (1950) in which he imagines and calls for a postimperial anthropology.

These intersections with established knowledges, ideologies, and social forms that also move away from them comprise what I have called orthogonal thinking. In mathematics, orthogonality can refer to perpendicular line segments; similarly, orthogonal curves are defined as "two (or more) intersecting curves that are perpendicular at their intersection."[13] Orthogonality implies intersection and connection but also separation and divergent movement. This is how the figures I study in this book interacted with empire: their ethnographic fictions are orthogonal experiments that imagine political possibilities beyond empire's grasp. But what political possibilities does orthogonality open up in the twenty-first century? And what new relationships between knowledge and politics does it suggest today?

Hardt and Negri implicitly adopt an orthogonal perspective on the constitution of new political subjectivities in their book *Assembly* (2017). This book opens up diverse avenues for thinking about democratic forms of organization beyond sovereign institutions that rely on centralized governance and on the fundamental indirectness of representative politics. Capitalist production today is thoroughly social, they argue: we produce ever more cooperatively, and what is produced are "not just commodities but social relations and ultimately society itself."[14] Because of this, we can imagine new social relations and political institutions that are autonomous from sovereign power. These movements and forms of "assembly" are not purely horizontal in their sense of organization, but neither do they adopt vertical leadership structures. The challenge today is to invent political subjectivities that point to "durable social structures" but that do not rely on the kinds of vertical centralization that are immediately recognizable to the state's sovereign authority.[15] Some examples of "leaderless" movements they cite include Black Lives Matter, the Zapatistas in Mexico, and the Tahrir Square protests in Egypt, not to mention Occupy Wall Street.

But I want to focus on a related type of political geometry that lies below the surface of Hardt and Negri's analyses of social production and emerging modes of assembly. In a chapter on "political realism," they characterize this concept as "treating power as a set of social relationships and basing the potential of political action on the intelligence and capacities of existing social forces, which resist and create, composing and conflicting with each other."[16] Realism refers to the empirical nature of political potential and suggests that the raw materials for alternative political forms are given in social life (but that the outcomes of democratic transformations are not necessarily predetermined). Unstated here, I argue, is the implication that political realism requires new epistemologies, new ways of knowing the social that reveal the political potential that is immanent to it. If we attune ourselves to the rhythms of social production, then we can see more clearly how it signals new experiences of the "common," the wealth we all share and the democratic ways of "managing" it.[17] Hardt and Negri come closer to embracing the epistemological potential of their argument when they ask the following question at the end of the chapter: "Is it still possible today for political knowledge . . . to move within history and take up the project to transform it?"[18]

We can recognize that this question points to orthogonality as a political principle because it is another version of the kinds of questions writers and anthropologists asked themselves throughout the twentieth century as they experimented in their texts with imperial social relations. Textual experimentation in the French Atlantic was certainly grounded in histories of empire, but at the same time, movements between anthropology and fiction sought to reread these histories in terms of what might lie beyond them. The alternative anthropologies these figures imagined were thus deeply engaged in developing forms of "political knowledge," in Hardt and Negri's terms, that could encompass new ways to view and organize social life away from empire.

Twentieth-century experiments with empire suggest that speculative textual and epistemological work can also be seen, perhaps paradoxically, as exercises in political realism.

Orthogonality demands that we make such conceptual linkages. Doing so signals two important implications of the experimental methodologies I have studied in this book. First, we can see how radical democratic thought today intersects with older forms of political, textual, and epistemological experimentation that took place in colonial and postcolonial situations. Orthogonal thinking about and beyond empire during the twentieth century allows us to focus even more sharply on the relationship between social production and political knowledge, a relationship that is more implicit in Hardt and Negri's work but that comes to the fore once we take orthogonality seriously. Second, and more fundamentally, orthogonal intersections with empire point toward the constitutive ordinariness of speculative, even utopian, forms of political desire. As we have seen throughout this book, everyday life demands forms of knowledge whose empiricism can be translated into speculation—it is fitting that this sort of layering and translation reached its crescendo in the previous chapter, as Jean-Claude Izzo wrote one city on top of another, illustrating the palimpsestic qualities of everyday utopias. Orthogonality shows how speculation and realism (in Hardt and Negri's sense) can in fact be thought in terms of each other.

Nonsovereign Knowledges

Adopting orthogonal perspectives on political desires certainly tells us how speculative political projects take shape within, or are derived from, new ways of knowing social life. Political knowledge of everyday life, in other words, furnishes us with creative tools for imagining democratic alternatives. But orthogonality signals a relationship of extension outside of what already exists, and it has less to tell us about what kinds of knowledge circulate in these alternative spaces. To rephrase the point in terms of this book's arguments, orthogonality describes how writers and anthropologists confronted empire to think beyond it, but it has less to tell us about what they thought.

Yet many of the figures that feature in this book offer a sense of the new kinds of knowledge on which their alternative anthropologies rely. These are forms of knowledge that circulate, connect, and historicize beyond empire's constitutive relations of domination. We can think back to Hampâté Bâ's linguistic universalism highlighted in chapter 1: this is an instrumentalization of the French language that gathers up local colonial histories and projects them through a planetary lens (to return to Mbembe's terms) that presumes the global communicability of local knowledges. To return to Rouch, we see his characters nonchalantly cross colonial borders (in films such as *Jaguar*, whose production spans both ends of the decolonizing moment) while they creatively position themselves as both consumers of global popular cultures and producers of knowledge about their reinventions of global modernity. In a similar, albeit more programmatic vein, Jacques Stephen Alexis sought to rewrite Haiti in terms of folkloric knowledge and universal socialist humanism against US occupation and French cultural domination. Finally, Patrick Chamoiseau and Raphaël Confiant imagine new modes of literary and ethnographic knowledge that forge creole connections across both shared and fractured histories and cartographies. This set of examples is internally varied, and in this book's chapters I have pointed out some of the limitations of each. However, on their broadest level they are knowledge projects that reassemble geographies and histories beyond domination.

We can refer to these epistemological projects as nonsovereign knowledges. In doing so, I return to Hardt and Negri and their call for democratic institutions that operate outside the centralized apparatuses of sovereign power. We should not be lulled into thinking of sovereignty as exclusively synonymous with "independence and self-determination," they argue. "In contrast to those concepts sovereignty always marks a relationship of power and domination: sovereignty is the exclusive right to exercise political authority."[19] Hardt and Negri outline the colonial resonances of modern sovereignty (i.e., colonial ideology involves the sovereign making decisions for people who cannot act politically) and argue their way out of the relations of domination that sovereignty or sovereign judgment implies via a critique of Jean-Jacques Rousseau and political representation.

We are left with a call for democratic "nonsovereign institutions" that bypass vertical structures of authority and the stultifying univocity of centralized forms of political action. Moving beyond sovereignty "means leaving behind, on one hand, the sovereign relationship of power and domination and, on the other, the mandate to unity."[20] A key takeaway for the purposes of this book does not come until the very end of *Assembly*, however: this is the idea that since sovereignty implies the unilateral exercise of authority, "it always carries a colonial relation at its heart."[21] As I have suggested, the writers and anthropologists experimenting in the twentieth-century French Atlantic were keenly aware of this proposition. Although they were not necessarily thinking in terms of visible and enduring nonsovereign institutions, they were imagining and enacting nonsovereign knowledges either outside the bounds of colonial authority structures or above and beyond the reach of the postcolonial French nation-state. As the set of examples mentioned earlier indicates, these were knowledges that traveled globally and allowed for unexpected assemblages that were untethered from formal sovereign structures. Even in the case of Haiti, nonsovereign knowledges moved through exile, universalist humanism, or Price-Mars's transatlantic anticolonial anthropology.

The experimental knowledges at work in this book suggest not just that we can understand sovereignty in epistemological terms. For one thing, anthropology's *Writing Culture* moment already showed us this much as it highlighted the (often colonial) power relations inherent in ethnographic knowledge production. But if a key challenge for twenty-first-century political thought is to imagine institutions beyond sovereignty, then the ethnographic fictions in this book demonstrate, first, that nonsovereign desires extend back earlier than our contemporary juncture and, second, that these desires can be expressed in terms of knowledge games that push established disciplines, textual forms, and geopolitical entities outside of themselves. How do we "know" beyond sovereignty, these ethnographic fictions ask? This question implies that nonsovereignty is not just a strictly political imperative; it must be taken as an epistemological one, as well.

Democracy after Empire

Thinking outside empire affects how we think about democracy and democratic futures. The writers and anthropologists in this book rarely use the word "democracy," yet their alternative anthropologies sketch out knowledge projects and social forms that we can recognize as mobilizing alternatives to the entanglement of actually existing political possibilities with (post)colonial ideologies. Empire limits democracy's horizon, in other words, which helps explain why these figures from throughout the French Atlantic sought to experiment beyond it.

Mbembe's book *Politiques de l'inimitié* (2017) helps us flesh out this entanglement and its repercussions for democracy today. He establishes a colonial genealogy for contemporary Western democracy, pointing out, for example, how "civil peace" in democratic colonial powers depended on violence perpetrated outside Western metropoles (from the slave trade to economies of resource extraction), and concludes that we must think colonialism and democracy as overlapping, mutually constitutive categories. "As the offspring of democracy," he writes, "the colonial world was not the antithesis of the democratic order. It has always been its double, or rather its nocturnal side. . . . This is not external to democracy. It is not necessarily situated outside its boundaries. Democracy carries the colony within itself, just as the colony carries democracy, often in masked form."[22] The upshot of this genealogy is that it speaks to a crisis of democracy today: the colonial relation has been "renewed" across the planet as war has settled in as an "end and necessity" of democracy, politics, and culture.[23]

Mbembe suggests that war is the *pharmakon* of our current democratic moment, the "poison and remedy" of twenty-first-century democracy. As such, it has "freed deadly passions that, little by little, push our societies to exit democracy and to transform themselves into societies of enmity (*inimitié*), as was the case under colonization."[24] Enmity is "a force of separation rather than a force that intensifies links," it is a "force of scission and real isolation," as well as a principle of governance that tightens borders and blurs distinctions between violence and law, norm and exception.[25] The rise of Right populisms across the West as well as struggles between cosmopolitanism and "perpetual war," as Bruce Robbins has analyzed, testify to the pervasiveness of enmity. That these forces of separation come to underwrite democracy while capitalist globalization promotes homogeneity on other levels is a feature of what Michael Hardt and Antonio Negri call the "mixed constitution" of empire today.[26]

This makes for rather discouraging reading. We are left with a vision of democracy that owes an originary debt to colonialism, that has reactivated colonial relationships of exclusion, and that links up with a supranational empire of finance capital and globalized relations of production and consumption. Mbembe passes through the clinical work of Fanon and the cosmic perspectives offered by Afro-futurism to propose a planetary scale for democracy in which our "vulnerability" as humans can be held in common and in which "detachment" transcends narrow conditions of primordial belonging and can generate global forms of solidarity.[27] But what kinds of knowledge would a planetary democracy require? And would even this kind of planetary politics leave modern democracy's imperial roots in place? How, in other words, do we imagine new forms of democracy while reckoning simultaneously with its colonial conditions of possibility?

My study leaves us with this set of questions, encouraging us to route democratic futures through older attempts to experiment beyond imperial social forms and ways of knowing the world. Alternative anthropologies and experimental textualizations of ethnographic knowledge blend creative free play with rearrangements of empire's ideological coordinates; as such, they are future-oriented projects. They also suggest political futures that are not postanthropological (*pace* Mbembe) but that may be postimperial.

Taking this observation seriously leaves us with a twofold task. First, if we are to take our cue from the writers and anthropologists who experimented with empire in the twentieth-century French Atlantic, then thinking postimperial democratic futures means rehistoricizing empire itself. It means thinking histories of domination as constitutively linked with experimental opportunities. This is a colonial nexus in which each side receives its analytic due but that also situates empire as a toolkit for new forms of political knowledge. Colonial histories point to real modes of subjugation and exclusion, but they also act as building blocks for different ways of knowing the world. Thus, to rehistoricize empire is to focus intently on how empire generates alternative histories and unexpected geographies, how it fuels speculative desires that it cannot contain, and how it requires future-oriented epistemologies. This methodological imperative urges us to seek out texts and social forms that indicate not just where empire's common sense contradicts itself, but where new political logics are elaborated in its place and how these logics project unforeseen futures.

But democratic futures do not only mobilize new historicizing impulses. Democracy after empire would need to go further. And it is precisely this "after" that signals the second task before us, that of reperiodizing democracy. If empire is modern democracy's original sin, and if empire generates experimental knowledge projects that lead orthogonally away from its circumscribed set of political possibilities, then we can begin to write narratives of democracy (shades of Rouch, once again) that proceed from these experimental moments. Narratives of democracy after empire might privilege nonsovereign knowledges, open-ended universalisms that defy prescriptive modes of knowing and living, or intensely local social assemblages that create new global cartographies. But these are just glimpses, utopian fragments that peek out once we posit democratic lifeworlds after empire. The broader point is that modern democracy may indeed be intimately bound up with empire but that this origin story is neither inevitable nor immutable. Thinking about empire as an experimental space-time shows us how we might go about imagining new, postimperial political desires.

Thus alternative forms of historicization and periodization go hand in hand as they open up reflective space for imagining democracy after empire. Colonial ideologies are still with us, of course. They feature in camps, immigration policies, legal and "exceptional" forms of state violence, and postmillennial populisms driven by enmity. The creative interplay between historicization and periodization allows us to take this lingering presence seriously while also showing how it must be untangled from any viable sort of democracy to come. And at the heart of all these imaginative operations and methodologies are experimental knowledge projects that position new textual forms alongside new social forms as political opportunities that can be thought in terms of each other.

Notes

Introduction

1 Jean Rouch, *Cinéma et anthropologie*, ed. Jean-Paul Colleyn (Paris: Cahiers du cinéma-Institut National de l'Audiovisuel, 2009), 129.

2 Rouch, *Cinéma et anthropologie*, 131.

3 Helena Wulff, "An Anthropological Perspective on Literary Arts in Ireland," in *A Companion to the Anthropology of Europe*, ed. Ullrich Kockel, Máiréad Nic Craith, and Jonas Frykman (Chichester, UK: Wiley-Blackwell, 2012), 538.

4 As Christopher L. Miller has shown, for instance, the tripartite geography of what he calls "the French Atlantic triangle" not only accounts for slavery-era theories and literatures of trafficking and abolitionism. It also allows us to flash forward into the twentieth century and consider "the rise of Francophone literature and film" in the same epistemological and aesthetic conversation: Christopher L. Miller, *The French Atlantic Triangle: Literature and Culture of the Slave Trade* (Durham, NC: Duke University Press, 2008), x, xii.

5 On the Mission Dakar-Djibouti and its marketing of both anthropology and empire, see Vincent Debaene, *Far Afield: French Anthropology between Science and Literature*, trans. Justin Izzo (Chicago: University of Chicago Press, 2014), 34–35.

6 Paul Hazoumé, "Foreword," in *Doguicimi* (Paris: G.-P. Mausonneuve et Larose, 1978 [orig. 1938]), 13. On the publication history of *Doguicimi* and its place in Hazoumé's career, see János Riesz, *De la littérature coloniale à la littérature africaine: Prétextes, Contextes, Intertextes* (Paris: Karthala, 2007), 249–68.

7 See Michel Leiris, *Contacts de civilisations en Martinique et en Guadeloupe* (Paris: Gallimard and United Nations Educational, Scientific and Cultural Organization, 1955), 104.

8 On the history of Haiti's Bureau d'Ethnologie, see Rachelle Charlier-Doucet, "Anthropologie, politique, et engagement social: L'expérience du Bureau d'Ethnologie d'Haïti," *Gradhiva* 1 (2005), accessed July 28, 2014, http://gradhiva.revues.org/313.

9 From this point of view, the theory of genre that I am working with in this book begins from the observation that what Thomas Pavel calls "the instability of generic

categories" is not so much "puzzling" or "frightening," as he goes on to assert, but instead begs for instrumentalization and makes a case for its creative functionality. Generic instability, then, is generic use value: see Thomas Pavel, "Literary Genres as Norms and Good Habits," *New Literary History* 34, no. 2 (2003): 210.

10 James Clifford, "Introduction: Partial Truths," in *Writing Culture: The Poetics and Politics of Ethnography*, ed. James Clifford and George E. Marcus (Berkeley: University of California Press, 1986), 6.

11 On the first example, see Kim Fortun, "Foreword to the 25th Anniversary Edition," in *Writing Culture: The Poetics and Politics of Ethnography*, ed. James Clifford and George E. Marcus (Berkeley: University of California Press, 2011 [orig. 1986]), xvi–xviii. On the second, see Michael Taussig, "Excelente Zona Social," in *Writing Culture and the Life of Anthropology*, ed. Orin Starn (Durham, NC: Duke University Press, 2015), 150.

12 James Clifford, "Feeling Historical," in Starn, *Writing Culture and the Life of Anthropology*, 25, 31. Likewise, James Clifford, *The Predicament of Culture: Twentieth-Century Ethnography, Literature, and Art* (Cambridge, MA: Harvard University Press, 1988), contains chapters on Michel Leiris and Aimé Césaire, further linking empire and the French Atlantic to the writing culture moment.

13 For French perspectives on ethnographic constructedness and the *Writing Culture* debates, see Colleyn, "Fiction et fictions en anthropologie," 150–51; Vincent Debaene, "Ethnographie/Fiction: A propos de quelques confusions et faux paradoxes," *L'Homme* 175–76 (2005): 219–32. Orin Starn helpfully reminds us that these literary-minded concerns with reflexivity, form, and epistemological constructedness were seen as "naval gazing" by critics at the time. See Orin Starn, "Introduction," in Starn, *Writing Culture and the Life of Anthropology*, 3.

14 Edward W. Said, "Representing the Colonized: Anthropology's Interlocutors," *Critical Inquiry* 15, no. 2 (1989): 209–10.

15 Said, "Representing the Colonized," 210.

16 Said, "Representing the Colonized," 224.

17 Said, "Representing the Colonized," 224.

18 See Gary Wilder, *The French Imperial Nation-State: Negritude and Colonial Humanism between the Two World Wars* (Chicago: University of Chicago Press, 2005), 3–23. Wilder later revisits this idea and radicalizes it, revealing its "utopian potentiality": see Gary Wilder, *Freedom Time: Negritude, Decolonization, and the Future of the World* (Durham, NC: Duke University Press, 2015), xiii, 5–7.

19 Alice Conklin has argued that French anthropology made an instrumentalist case for itself as a politically useful disciplinary tool for studying empire and for educating a receptive public about France's imperial projects and aspirations: see Alice L. Conklin, *In the Museum of Man: Race, Anthropology, and Empire in France, 1850–1950* (Ithaca, NY: Cornell University Press, 2013), 189–235. Similarly, Pierre Singaravélou refers to a "tension" and "interdependence" when speaking of the relationship between the "colonial sciences" and imperial politics. Colonial social scientists were not just pawns in a larger imperial game but actively tried to posi-

tion themselves strategically within a growing academic field and an established colonial ideology and administration: Pierre Singaravélou, *Professer l'empire: Les "sciences coloniales" en France sous la IIIe République* (Paris: Publications de la Sorbonne, 2011), 27.

20 See, e.g., Alison James, "Thinking the Everyday: Genre, Form, Fiction," *L'Esprit Créateur* 54, no. 3 (2014): 78–91; and Saikat Majumdar, *Prose of the World: Modernism and the Banality of Empire* (New York: Columbia University Press, 2013), 1–36.

21 Debaene, *Far Afield*, 1.

22 In an interestingly anticipatory moment, Debaene actually calls for an in-depth study of (post)colonial French and Francophone ethnographic fiction: Debaene, *Far Afield*, 286–87. Cultural production in the Francophone Caribbean and West Africa accompanied anthropology's establishment as a viable tool for producing imperial epistemologies and its openness toward literature writ large. West African literature in French came of age at the same time as metropolitan anthropology and was largely aware of this disciplinary kinship. In the Caribbean, ethnographic travelogues written by surrealists such as André Breton and Pierre Mabille strongly influenced post-Negritude writing in French (and Negritude itself was influenced by the anthropology of the German Leo Frobenius, who worked in the early twentieth century). On surrealist ethnography's influence on Francophone Caribbean fiction, see J. Michael Dash, "Caraïbe Fantôme: The Play of Difference in the Francophone Caribbean," *Yale French Studies* 103 (2003): 93–105; see also J. Michael Dash, "Le Je de l'autre: Surrealist Ethnographers and the Francophone Caribbean," *L'Esprit Créateur* 47, no. 1 (2007): 84–95. On the emergence of Francophone black African literature and Negritude in relation to anthropology, see Christopher L. Miller, *Theories of Africans: Francophone Literature and Anthropology in Africa* (Chicago: University of Chicago Press, 1990), 6, 10, 1–30. Miller's study is a key early book on anthropology in the Francophone (post)colonial world. He is particularly and rightly concerned with the ways in which anthropology might contribute to an ethics of Western readings of African texts; he also studies how fiction and anthropology have dealt with divergent yet interrelated visions of Africa. My interest here is indebted to this work but lies elsewhere—namely, in questions and theories of generic creativity set in a wider Atlantic context.

23 René Maran, *Batouala* (Paris: Albin Michel, 1921), 9–10.

24 Maran, *Batouala*, 18.

25 See Ann Laura Stoler, "Introduction, 'The Rot Remains,'" in *Imperial Debris: On Ruins and Ruination*, ed. Ann Laura Stoler (Durham, NC: Duke University Press, 2013), 11.

26 André Breton, "A Great Black Poet," in *Notebook of a Return to the Native Land*, by Aimé Césaire, ed. and trans. Clayton Eshleman and Annette Smith (Middletown, CT: Wesleyan University Press, 2001), xii. I have consulted the French version and quote from this established English translation.

27 Aimé Césaire, *Notebook of a Return to the Native Land*, ed. and trans. Clayton Eshleman and Annette Smith (Middletown, CT: Wesleyan University Press, 2001), 2–3.

28 Wilder, *Freedom Time*, 10.

29 Salman Rushdie, *Joseph Anton* (New York: Random House, 2012), 68–69.

30 See Ann Laura Stoler, *Along the Archival Grain: Epistemic Anxieties and Colonial Common Sense* (Princeton, NJ: Princeton University Press, 2010), 9.

31 Graham Huggan helpfully reviews these arguments in *Interdisciplinary Measures: Literature and the Future of Postcolonial Studies* (Liverpool: Liverpool University Press, 2008), 21–33.

32 See Dipesh Chakrabarty, *Provincializing Europe: Postcolonial Thought and Historical Difference* (Princeton, NJ: Princeton University Press, 2000), 17–20. Jean and John Comaroff adopt a broadly similar rhetoric when they study how "Afromodernity" is "*sui generis*" and not a byproduct of a supposedly universal European modernity: Jean Comaroff and John Comaroff, *Theory from the South: Or, How Euro-America Is Evolving toward Africa* (Boulder, CO: Paradigm, 2012), 19.

33 Césaire, *Notebook of a Return to the Native Land*, 15, 43.

34 See Franco Moretti, *Graphs, Maps, Trees: Abstract Models for Literary History*, (New York: Verso, 2007), 63–64. To my point here, he argues that to work between maps of "real" spaces and "maps/diagrams of fictional worlds, where the real and the imaginary coexist in varying, often elusive proportions . . . [r]eveals [literary] form as a diagram of forces; or perhaps, even, as *nothing but force*." The reading of imperial mapping and countermapping I propose in this book relies on a similar sort of cartographic interplay but emphasizes production and expression rather than revelation. Whereas Moretti is interested in how diagrammatic mapping lays bare relations of force, I argue that we can conceive of geography as the expression of cartographic textual desires. From this perspective, maps are not diagrams but geographic vectors of textual invention and indicators of longing for new configurations of imperial space.

35 See Ann Laura Stoler, *Duress: Imperial Durabilities in Our Times* (Durham, NC: Duke University Press, 2016), 6, 10.

36 David Scott, *Conscripts of Modernity: The Tragedy of Colonial Enlightenment* (Durham, NC: Duke University Press, 2004), 8. Reworking Scott's argument via the category of speculation allows us to decouple experimental epistemologies and the forms of political desire they generate from the "stories of salvation and redemption" that constitute what Scott diagnoses as the utopian "horizon" and "mythos" of the anticolonial narrative writ large.

37 One of the more obviously anthropological passages in the trilogy is the paratextual chrestomathy Ghosh includes at the end of *Sea of Poppies* (2008). It functions as a testament to the hybridized vocabulary of the Indian Ocean world and to the words Ghosh's protagonist "collected" throughout his life. Here anthropology meets didactic etymology in the medium of fiction: see Amitav Ghosh, *Sea of Poppies* (New York: Picador, 2008), 501–43. We could also consider *In an Antique Land* (1992), in which Ghosh dreamily recounts moments from his dissertation fieldwork in an Egyptian village. Here the literary instantiation of himself seems entirely the product of his informants' perception of him—his character goes only by the nickname the villagers give him, "Ya Amitab." This sense of characterol-

ogy links Ghosh to Amadou Hampâté Bâ, whose ethnographic memoirs I study in chapter 1. Inserted within Ghosh's text are chapters devoted to re-creating the life of a twelfth-century Indian slave from Jewish manuscripts found in the Cairo Geniza. The didactic goal of this move (reminiscent of what we see in *Sea of Poppies*) is to deploy ethnography, history, and narrative to demonstrate that Africa for centuries has been an important node in an Indian Ocean cosmopolitan and migratory imaginary. For Ghosh's more explicit thoughts on the relationship between anthropology and fiction, see Damien Stankiewicz, "Anthropology and Fiction: An Interview with Amitav Ghosh," *Cultural Anthropology* 27, no. 3 (2012): 535–41.

38 Despite our last names, I have no known relation to Jean-Claude Izzo.

39 Chakrabarty, *Provincializing Europe*, 239.

40 Michel Foucault, *The Archeology of Knowledge and The Discourse on Language*, trans. A. M. Sheridan Smith (New York: Pantheon, 1982 [orig. 1972]), 87. Rey Chow cites this passage in her analysis of postcolonial "languaging": see Chow, *Not Like a Native Speaker: On Languaging as a Postcolonial Experience* (New York: Columbia University Press, 2014), 54.

41 Jean Comaroff and John L. Comaroff, *The Truth about Crime: Sovereignty, Knowledge, and Social Order* (Chicago: University of Chicago Press, 2016), xiv–xv.

Chapter 1. Africanist Melancholy

1 See Michel Leiris, *Biffures* (Paris: Gallimard, 1948), 141. For the epigraph, I use Lydia Davis's translation of *Biffures*: see Michel Leiris, *Scratches*, trans. Lydia Davis (Baltimore: Johns Hopkins University Press, 1997), 119. Davis translated the first two volumes of *La règle du jeu*, and I will use her rendering wherever appropriate. All other translations from *La règle du jeu* and all translations from *L'Afrique fantôme* are mine.

2 Abiola Irele has written about the "novelistic" style of Hampâté Bâ's *L'étrange destin de Wangrin*, but his assertion (that this ethnographic biography reads in many ways like a novel) certainly holds true for Hampâté Bâ's ethnographic memoirs: see F. Abiola Irele, *The African Imagination: Literature in Africa and the Black Diaspora* (New York: Oxford University Press, 2001), 85.

3 Gary Wilder, *The French Imperial Nation-State: Negritude and Colonial Humanism between the Two World Wars* (Chicago: University of Chicago Press, 2005), 50–51.

4 Wilder, *The French Imperial Nation-State*, 80. On colonial ethnology, see Wilder, *The French Imperial Nation-State*, 63–75.

5 On Negritude and Pan-Africanism, see, e.g., Brent Hayes Edwards, *The Practice of Diaspora: Literature, Translation, and the Rise of Black Internationalism* (Cambridge, MA: Harvard University Press, 2003), 1–68; Wilder, *The French Imperial Nation-State*, 201–55.

6 See Jean Jamin, "Objets trouvés des paradis perdus: A propos de la Mission Dakar-Djibouti," in *Collections passion: Exposition du 5 juin au 31 décembre 1982*, ed. Jacques Hainard and Roland Kaehr (Neuchâtel, Switzerland: Musée d'Ethnographie, 1982), 79.

7 See Alice L. Conklin, *In the Museum of Man: Race, Anthropology, and Empire in France, 1850–1950* (Ithaca, NY: Cornell University Press, 2013), 208. In the late 1920s, Marcel Mauss, Paul Rivet, and Georges Henri Rivière, the early deans of French anthropology, had sold intellectuals and state officials on the usefulness of the discipline for understanding the variety of populations under colonial control, and the exciting new mission promised to demonstrate to the French public just how this emergent field science might enhance pride in the empire by linking it to the collection, display, and categorization of a vast array of colonial objects: see Conklin, *In the Museum of Man*, 200, 206.

8 African writers from the first half of the twentieth century produced ethnographic work for a range of professional or individual reasons, and it would thus be difficult to read Hampâté Bâ's research into narratives of complicity with or opposition to the colonial project. On this point, see Jean-Hervé Jézéquel, "Voices of Their Own? African Participation in the Production of Colonial Knowledge in French West Africa, 1910–1950," in *Ordering Africa: Anthropology, European Imperialism, and the Politics of Knowledge*, ed. Helen Tilley and Robert J. Gordon (Manchester, UK: Manchester University Press, 2007), 165.

9 Fictionality, in other words, is more than doubt or a fundamental sense of disbelief created in the mind of the reader. It is as once suppler and subtler and qualitatively other: it refers more to the imaginative construction of narrative relationships than to the objects of those relationships and thus does not necessarily require or set in motion an originary (albeit at times good-natured) skepticism on the part of the reader.

10 See Hélène Heckmann, "Annexe I, Genèse et authenticité des ouvrages *L'étrange destin de Wangrin* et la série des *Mémoires*," in *Oui mon commandant!* by Amadou Hampâté Bâ (Paris: Actes Sud, 1994), 479–84.

11 Laurent Dubreuil traces the self as character back to Toussaint Louverture, arguing that in his writing that "Toussaint is a character for himself and for others. . . . [I]n many ways, Toussaint Louverture enables the birth of francophone literature": see Laurent Dubreuil, *Empire of Language: Toward a Critique of (Post)colonial Expression*, trans. David Fieni (Ithaca, NY: Cornell University Press, 2013), 93.

12 Critics have highlighted this relationship between distancing and fiction in Coetzee's work: see, e.g., Regina James, "'Writing without Authority': J. M. Coetzee and His Fictions," *Salmagundi* 114–15 (1997): 103–21. See also Tim Parks's review of *Summertime*: Tim Parks, "The Education of 'John Coetzee,'" *New York Review of Books*, February 11, 2010, accessed August 1 2018, http://www.nybooks.com/articles/archives/2010/feb/11/the-education-of-john-coetzee. David Attwell considers the relationship between biography and "estrangement" in Coetzee: see David Attwell, "Coetzee's Estrangements," *Novel: A Forum on Fiction* 41, nos. 2–3 (2008): 229–43. And let us not neglect the words of the man himself. In his opening address to the Worlds Literature Festival in Norwich, United Kingdom, in 2012, Coetzee posed the relationship among autobiography, distancing, and fiction in the form of a characteristically cryptic question. "If we are going to be the

authors of our own life stories," he asks, "are we free to be the authors of their truths as well?" This speech is available on You Tube: see Writers' Centre Norwich, "J. M. Coetzee Gives the Opening Provocation at Worlds Literature Festival Salon," video, YouTube, July 5, 2013, accessed August 1, 2018, https://www.youtube.com /watch?v=1EaxNqutqDk#t=35.

13 See Eileen Julien, "The Extroverted African Novel," in *The Novel, Volume 1: History, Geography, and Culture*, ed. Franco Moretti (Princeton, NJ: Princeton University Press, 2007), 680–91.

14 As Edwards reminds us in his introduction to the English-language translation of *L'Afrique fantôme*, as a poet and writer Leiris was an "unlikely participant" in an expedition like the Mission Dakar-Djibouti: see Brent Hayes Edwards, "Introduction," in *Phantom Africa*, by Michel Leiris, trans. Brent Hayes Edwards (New York: Seagull, 2017), 3.

15 André Brink, *Rumors of Rain* (Naperville, IL: Sourcebooks Landmark, 2008 [orig. 1978]), 5.

16 In his introduction to the latest edition of the text, Jamin takes up this publication history in greater detail: see Jean Jamin, "Présentation de *L'Afrique fantôme*," in *Miroir de l'Afrique*, by Michel Leiris, ed. Jean Jamin (Paris: Gallimard, 1996), 65–66.

17 For a fuller discussion of racialized social taxonomies in Francophone colonial Africa, see Jean-Hervé Jézéquel, "Grammaire de la distinction coloniale," *Genèses* 69 (2007): 4–25.

18 For a more detailed biographical portrait, see Muriel Devey, *Hampâté Bâ: L'homme de la tradition* (Dakar: LivreSud, 1993). Rouch's relationship with Monod and his time in Dakar at IFAN is discussed in Paul Stoller, *The Cinematic Griot: The Ethnography of Jean Rouch* (Chicago: University of Chicago Press, 1992), 32, 39, 41.

19 Devey, *Hampâté Bâ*, 88.

20 Hampâté Bâ's relationship to generic hybridity reflects a broad and diverse engagement with anthropology on the part of twentieth-century African writers. Such figures as Léopold Sédar Senghor and Paul Hazoumé, for instance, graduated from the Institut d'Ethnologie in Paris before turning to political and literary pursuits. Fily Dabo Sissoko, a Malian contemporary of Hampâté Bâ, produced several ethnographic articles before moving on to more autobiographical essays, and the Ivoirian novelist Ahmadou Kourouma, in *En attendant le vote des bêtes sauvages*, borrows from studies of traditional hunters carried out by the Malian anthropologist Youssouf Tata Cissé. On this last point, see Théophiste Kabanda, "Théâtralité et formes parodiques dans *En attendant le vote des bêtes sauvages*," in *L'imaginaire d'Ahmadou Kourouma: Contours et enjeux d'une esthétique*, ed. Jean Ouédraogo (Paris: Karthala, 2010), 257–64. János Riesz has argued that during the interwar period, African authors were "compelled" to write dryer documentary and social-scientific texts before earning enough writerly capital to produce literary works, but the fact that this engagement persisted in the postwar—and, indeed, the postcolonial—period suggests a more meaningful relationship between certain African writers and anthropology than one of instrumental expediency:

see János Riesz, "From Ethnography to the African Novel: The Example of *Dogu-icimi* (1938) by Paul Hazoumé (Dahomey)," *Research in African Literatures* 35, no. 4 (2004): 17. This is doubtless the case for Hampâté Bâ, who not only wrote literary-documentary texts such as his prizewinning *L'étrange destin de Wangrin* (1973) at a time that the prestige and perceived viability of ethnographic scholarship on "tradition" was at a historically low ebb in Francophone Africa, but who also shifted his anthropological and autobiographical gaze onto the colonial situation itself, most notably in *Oui mon commandant!*

21 See Ralph Austen, "From a Colonial to a Postcolonial African Voice: *Amkoullel, l'enfant peul*," *Research in African Literatures* 31, no. 3 (2000): 2.

22 Amadou Hampâté Bâ, *Oui mon commandant!* (Paris: Actes Sud, 1994), 31–32. All translations from Hampâté Bâ are mine. Hampâté Bâ was thus an amateur fieldworker before he was a trained ethnographer. Long before either of these steps in his anthropological trajectory, though, he served in 1912 as a "native" informant for a French administrator and self-styled anthropologist, François-Victor Equilbecq. Equilbecq even credits "Amadou Ba" (and Wangrin, the translator) in the book that resulted from his research. Without overstating how important this very early "research" actually was, its inclusion as a vignette in *Amkoullel* encourages us to attribute to it a certain distinctive formativeness for Hampâté Bâ's anthropological imagination. For just one citation among several, see François-Victor Equilbecq, *Contes populaires d'Afrique occidentale* (Paris: G.-P. Maisonneuve et Larose, 1972), 366.

23 Hampâté Bâ, *Oui mon commandant!* 406. Emphasis in original.

24 Michel Leiris, *L'Afrique fantôme* (Paris: Gallimard, 1934), 14.

25 Later, in the four volumes of *La règle du jeu*, the question of politics and complicity shifts for Leiris. He writes at length (and somewhat repetitively) about accepting revolutionary politics intellectually but being unable effectively to act on those beliefs. Here, complicity is tied closely to a radical sort of political passivity that for Leiris earns its paradoxical nature from the fact that revolutionary politics is fundamentally active—an observation that he embraces but on which, characteristically, he cannot ultimately act.

26 Leiris, *L'Afrique fantôme*, 279.

27 Speaking of the question of narrative rather than of genre specifically, James Clifford refers to *L'Afrique fantôme*'s "inexplicability." I prefer a vocabulary of legibility and decipherability for my purposes here, since it stresses the generic terms according to which we encounter the text rather than its impossibility: see James Clifford, "Tell me about Your Trip: Michel Leiris," in *The Predicament of Culture: Twentieth-Century Ethnography, Literature, and Art* (Cambridge, MA: Harvard University Press, 1988), 172–73.

28 See Vincent Debaene, *Far Afield: French Anthropology between Science and Literature*, trans. Justin Izzo (Chicago: University of Chicago Press, 2014), 180–81.

29 Although Michael Dash views *L'Afrique fantôme* as an "antinarrative," I am more concerned with considering the ways in which incomplete and fictive narratives

of selfhood and ethnographic authenticity are produced and contained within a travel journal that, at its most basic level, does constitute the narrative of a journey: see J. Michael Dash, "Caraïbe Fantôme: The Play of Difference in the Francophone Caribbean," *Yale French Studies* 103 (2003): 95. I would suggest that it does not necessarily follow from the presence of one or more stunted or incomplete narratives in a text that the text in question is an antinarrative. It seems to me, rather, and this is implied in my argument, that the failure of narrative can be captured narratively. In other words, we could take another look at Dash's claim and observe that his assertion misses the ways in which failed narratives might in fact represent constitutive moments of narrative negativity that can be bound up again in another narrative. *L'Afrique fantôme* is, from this point of view, the narrative of a failure rather than a failed narrative.

30 Amadou Hampâté Bâ, *L'étrange destin de Wangrin* (Paris: 10/18, 1973), 8. For a more expansive discussion of this point, see Jean-Marc Moura, "Textual Ownership in *L'étrange destin de Wangrin (The Fortunes of Wangrin)* by Amadou Hampâté Bâ," *Research in African Literatures* 37, no. 1 (2006): 96.

31 Amadou Hampâté Bâ, *Amkoullel, l'enfant peul* (Paris: Actes Sud, 1991), 207.

32 Hampâté Bâ, *Oui mon commandant!*, 290–91.

33 On style and storytelling in anthropology, see Steven Webster, "Ethnography as Storytelling," *Dialectical Anthropology* 8, no. 3 (1983): 200. This is also how the Dahomeyan ethnographer and literary writer Paul Hazoumé frames his novel *Doguicimi* (1938), about courtly intrigue and political culture in precolonial Dahomey. For Hazoumé, the success of *Doguicimi*'s realist narrative depends on readers seeing it as an "important ethnological and historic document" designed to communicate literarily both a sense of exoticism and one of authenticity: see Paul Hazoumé, "Foreword," in *Doguicimi*, by Paul Hazoumé (Paris: G.-P. Maisonneuve et Larose, 1978 [orig. 1938]), 14. Critical perspectives that privilege the African writer as a "native anthropologist" risk reducing African creative writing to communicably "authentic" accounts of cultures whose merits are seen as more ethnographic than properly literary. On this point, see Carey Snyder, "The Possibilities and Pitfalls of Ethnographic Readings: Narrative Complexity in *Things Fall Apart*," *College Literature* 35, no. 2 (2008): 156–57; Eleni Coundouriotis, *Claiming History: Colonialism, Ethnography, and the Novel* (New York: Columbia University Press, 1999), 4. Reading an African text ethnographically, in other words, risks minimizing or even denying the claims that text makes on literature. Keeping in mind this potential trap, my consideration of Hampâté Bâ's ethnographic didacticism has as much to do with literary style as it does with documentary impulses—indeed, reading the African memoir as an ethnographic palimpsest encourages us to bear in mind how literary narrative and anthropological documentation are not only mutually constitutive but also intimately intertwined such that we cannot easily extricate one from the other.

34 Clifford Geertz, *Works and Lives: The Anthropologist as Author* (Stanford, CA: Stanford University Press, 1988), 4–5.

35 For Poe's thoughts on the heretical nature of didacticism, see Edgar Allan Poe, "The Poetic Principle," in *Essays and Reviews*, ed. G. R. Thompson (New York: Library of America, 1984), 75.

36 Hampâté Bâ, *Oui mon commandant!*, 229–30.

37 Hampâté Bâ, *Oui mon commandant!*, 322.

38 Hampâté Bâ, *Oui mon commandant!*, 322–23.

39 Hampâté Bâ, *Oui mon commandant!*, 328.

40 Gary Wilder echoes Hampâté Bâ's thinking here as he lucidly analyzes the development of what he calls "colonial humanism" in French West Africa: see Wilder, *The French Imperial Nation-State*, 43–75.

41 Walter Benjamin, "The Storyteller: Reflections on the Works of Nikolai Leskov," in *Illuminations: Essays and Reflections*, ed. Hannah Arendt, trans. Harry Zohn (New York: Schocken, 1969), 86, 100.

42 Benjamin, "The Storyteller," 100.

43 Hampâté Bâ, *Oui mon commandant!*, 295–96.

44 Hampâté Bâ, *Oui mon commandant!*, 412.

45 Hampâté Bâ, *Oui mon commandant!*, 416–17.

46 For Jack Goody, this act marks a transitional moment in the history of narrative and fiction whose historic import he refers to as "an anthropological breakthrough in storytelling": see Jack Goody, "From Oral to Written: An Anthropological Breakthrough in Storytelling," in *The Novel, Volume 1: History, Geography, and Culture*, ed. Franco Moretti (Princeton, NJ: Princeton University Press, 2006), 3–36. On Hampâté Bâ's abiding concern for the fidelity of writing to oral cultures, see Moura, "Textual Ownership in *L'étrange destin de Wangrin (The Fortunes of Wangrin)* by Amadou Hampâté Bâ," 98.

47 Hampâté Bâ, *Oui mon commandant!*, 417.

48 See Kusum Aggarwal, *Amadou Hampâté Bâ et l'africanisme: De la recherche anthropologique à l'exercice de la fonction auctoriale* (Paris: L'Harmattan, 1999), 98.

49 Aggarwal, *Amadou Hampâté Bâ et l'africanisme*, 233–34. Unlike Aggarwal's reading of Hampâté Bâ's writerly career, my reading relies on conceiving of it as involving more than a transition from a so-called native informant to an African writer whose work was accepted as literature just as certain themes and questions appeared, reappeared, and changed form from one text to another as he found an independent voice with which to speak to European audiences: see Aggarwal, *Amadou Hampâté Bâ et l'africanisme*, 199.

50 Achille Mbembe, *Sortir de la grande nuit: Essai sur l'Afrique décolonisée* (Paris: La Découverte, 2010), 227.

51 But as I stress throughout this chapter, in the case of Hampâté Bâ this act of renarration is fundamentally dialogic, encompassing Western readers as it provides an "Afropolitan" genealogy of ethnographic knowledge and of ethnographic fiction. This dialogic impetus explicitly avoids casting "Europe" (or the West) as what Dipesh Chakrabarty calls a "silent referent" in the creation and circulation of ethnographic

knowledge: see Dipesh Chakrabarty, *Provincializing Europe: Postcolonial Thought and Historical Difference* (Princeton, NJ: Princeton University Press, 2000), 28.

52 See Leiris, *L'Afrique fantôme*, 263–67.

53 Leiris, *L'Afrique fantôme*, 263.

54 Leiris gives this idea a rather morbid spin when discussing the "deep meaning" of suicide in *L'âge d'homme*, the writing of which overlapped with that of *L'Afrique fantôme*, but which was not published until 1939. Reflecting on death and symbolism, he writes that the convergence of opposing symbols reveals "the deep meaning of suicide: becoming at once *self* and *other*, male and female, subject and object, that which is killed and that which kills—the only possibility for communion with oneself": Michel Leiris, *L'âge d'homme* (Paris: Gallimard, 1939), 141. *L'âge d'homme* is also an autobiographical text in which Leiris takes himself as an ethnographic object, in much the same way that he seems to want to do in his African journal, but without the same introspective intensity that he would adopt in the four volumes of *La règle du jeu*. In *L'âge d'homme*, we come across an ethnographic portrait of an aestheticized self (rather than the properly ethnographic self that Leiris seeks in Africa) created through Leiris's consumption of and reflections on painting, music, opera, and theater. In this respect, the Leirisian artistic self that emerges in this text appears close to Proust and his narrator's aesthetic vision of selfhood—a convergence that Leiris eventually denies in the last pages of *Frêle bruit* (Paris: Gallimard, 1976), the final volume of his autobiographical tetralogy. In his extended meditation on the supernatural (*le merveilleux*), in which Proust's name recurs, Leiris differentiates his theories on selfhood and writing from those of the modernist author of *In Search of Lost Time*: Leiris, *Frêle bruit*, 323–79.

55 Michel Leiris, "L'ethnographe devant le colonialisme," in *Cinq études d'ethnologie* (Paris: Denoël, 1969 [orig. 1950]), 86–87.

56 Marie-Denise Shelton places this ambivalent aspect of *L'Afrique fantôme* into conversation with interwar French modernism's obsession with figures of the primitive and highlights Leiris's role as producer of colonialist discourses of primitivism, chiding critics such as James Clifford or George Marcus who in her opinion downplay Leiris's engagement with colonialism in favor of a celebratory focus on selfhood and surrealism. Such an assessment, in my view, forces approaches to Leiris's journal into a rather unsavory zero-sum game in which Leiris is positioned either as a living repository of colonial primitivist ideologies or, alternatively, as a provocative theorist of literary selfhood who we might extricate entirely from his ethnographic context. See Marie-Denise Shelton, "Primitive Self: Colonial Impulses in Michel Leiris's *L'Afrique fantôme*," in *Prehistories of the Future: The Primitivist Project and the Culture of Modernism*, ed. Elazar Barkan and Ronald Bush (Stanford, CA: Stanford University Press, 1995), 326–38. Compare with James Clifford, "Tell about Your Trip," 165–74; George E. Marcus and Michael M. J. Fischer, *Anthropology as Cultural Critique: An Experimental Moment in the Human Sciences* (Chicago: University of Chicago Press, 1999 [orig. 1986]), 122–25. Irene Albers has also argued against such

dismissive approaches to Leiris's journal and suggests instead that we focus on the epistemological underpinnings of his ethnographic exoticism. See Irene Albers, "Mimesis and Alterity: Michel Leiris's Ethnography and the Poetics of Spirit Possession," *French Studies* 62, no. 3 (2008): 271–89.

57 Leiris, *L'Afrique fantôme*, 170.

58 Leiris, *L'Afrique fantôme*, 210.

59 Leiris, *L'Afrique fantôme*, 210.

60 Leiris, *L'Afrique fantôme*, 611.

61 Leiris, *L'Afrique fantôme*, 11.

62 Leiris, *L'Afrique fantôme*, 13.

63 Leiris, *L'Afrique fantôme*, 13.

64 Leiris, *L'Afrique fantôme*, 14. In "Black Orpheus," Sartre argues that black men must divest themselves of their racial particularity to join a color-blind, universalist struggle against capitalism that will ultimately liberate them. Sartre writes, "But there is something even more important in [Negritude]: the Negro himself, we have said, creates a kind of antiracist racism. He wishes in no way to dominate the world: he desires abolition of *all* kinds of ethnic privileges; he asserts solidarity with the oppressed of every color. After that, the subjective, existential, ethnic notion of negritude 'passes,' as Hegel says, into that which one has of the proletariat: objective, positive, and precise." Both Leiris and Sartre argue in favor of a Hegelian-inflected sense of solidarity that gathers up political particularisms into the universalist *Aufhebung* of the proletariat's struggle against capitalism: see Jean-Paul Sartre, *"What Is Literature?" and Other Essays* (Cambridge, MA: Harvard University Press, 1988), 326.

65 Leiris, *L'Afrique fantôme*, 8–9.

66 Leiris, *L'Afrique fantôme*, 9.

67 Leiris, *L'Afrique fantôme*, 436.

68 Leiris, *L'Afrique fantôme*, 469.

69 Gérard Genette, *Fiction and Diction*, trans. Catherine Porter (Ithaca, NY: Cornell University Press, 1993 [orig. 1991]), 113. In a more overtly political vein, Jacques Rancière addresses these questions by filtering perceptibility through the "distribution of the sensible," artistic practices that reform existing "ways of doing and making" by reorganizing what appears to sensory experience: see Jacques Rancière, *The Politics of Aesthetics*, trans. Gabriel Rockhill (New York: Continuum, 2004 [orig. 2000]), 12–19.

70 Hampâté Bâ, *Oui mon commandant!*, 201. Emmanuelle Saada has studied paternity and filiation across the French colonial world, including the phenomenon of orphanages for *métis* children in French West Africa: see Emmanuelle Saada, *Empire's Children: Race, Filiation, and Citizenship in the French Colonies*, trans. Arthur Goldhammer (Chicago: University of Chicago Press, 2012), 4, 31, 73.

71 Hampâté Bâ, *Oui mon commandant!*, 201.

72 Hampâté Bâ, *Oui mon commandant!*, 202. "Monsieur l'administrateur, pourquoi pleurez-vous? Que s'est-il passé? Quel malheur nous a frappés pour que le drapeau soit mis en berne?"

73 Hampâté Bâ, *Oui mon commandant!*, 203. "Espèce de Français de fraîche date! Sale boche! Traître à sa patrie par intérêt matériel! . . . Foutez-moi le camp d'ici avant que je ne vous administre la volée de coups de pied que vous méritez!"

74 Hampâté Bâ, *Oui mon commandant!*, 203. "Ô vous deux grands chefs! Vous n'a pas honte bagarrer devant deux nègres qui regarder vous comme deux coqs y faire corps à corps sans baïonnettes?"

75 Leiris, *L'Afrique fantôme*, 627.

76 Leiris, *L'âge d'homme*, 97.

77 Leiris, *L'âge d'homme*, 125.

78 John Dos Passos, *The Big Money* (New York: Mariner, 2000 [orig. 1936]), 156.

79 Leiris, *L'Afrique fantôme*, 260.

80 Leiris, *L'Afrique fantôme*, 615.

81 Leiris, *L'Afrique fantôme*, 616.

82 Leiris, *L'Afrique fantôme*, 622.

83 See Clifford, *The Predicament of Culture*, 92–113; George Stocking, "Empathy and Antipathy in *Heart of Darkness*," in *Readings in the History of Anthropology*, ed. Regna Darnell (New York: Harper and Row, 1974), 85–98.

84 Cited, respectively, in Clifford, *The Predicament of Culture*, 96; Debaene, *Far Afield*, 56.

85 See Conklin, *In the Museum of Man*, 189–92. On Third Republic colonial sciences, see Pierre Singaravélou, *Professer l'empire: Les "sciences coloniales" en France sous la IIIe République* (Paris: Publications de la Sorbonne, 2011), 13–32.

86 Jean Comaroff and John L. Comaroff, *Theory from the South: Or, How Euro-America Is Evolving toward Africa* (Boulder, CO: Paradigm, 2012), 3.

Chapter 2. The Director of Modern Life

1 See Paul Henley, *The Adventure of the Real: Jean Rouch and the Craft of Ethnographic Cinema* (Chicago: University of Chicago Press, 2009), 74–75. Henley points out that the term "ethnofiction" has been used primarily in secondary scholarship on Rouch's work, suggesting that the concept itself is "ambiguous." However, in the context of this book, "ethnofiction" is not only a quite telling characterization, but one that explicitly situates Rouch as a cinematic theorist of ethnographic fiction as a genre.

2 On decolonization and the Mali Federation, see Gary Wilder, *Freedom Time: Negritude, Decolonization, and the Future of the World* (Durham, NC: Duke University Press, 2015), 218–22.

3 Jean-Luc Godard, "L'Afrique vous parle de la fin et des moyens," *Cahiers du Cinéma* 94 (1959): 19.

4 Following Catherine Russell's work on avant-garde filmmaking and/as visual anthropology, we could reformulate my question and ask how does fiction "[enable] the documentary to be read differently, to be 'displaced' and made ambiguous"? See Catherine Russell, *Experimental Ethnography: The Work of Film in the Age of Video* (Durham, NC: Duke University Press, 1999), 112.

5 Jean Rouch, "Des films ethnographiques," *Positif* 14–15 (1955): 145–49.

6 Rouch, "Des films ethnographiques," 149.

7 Jean Rouch, "The Situation and Tendencies of the Cinema in Africa," in *Ciné-Ethnography*, by Jean Rouch, ed. and trans. Steven Feld (Minneapolis: University of Minnesota Press, 2003), 58.

8 Jean Rouch, "Questions de méthode: Entretien avec Éric Rohmer et Louis Marcorelles," in *Jean Rouch: Cinéma et anthropologie*, ed. Jean-Paul Colleyn (Paris: Cahiers du cinéma-Institut National de l'Audiovisuel, 2009), 131.

9 Rouch met Damouré Zika around this time, when he was just beginning to explore field research and possession cults. Damouré would go on to be a lifelong friend and star of several of Rouch's plot-driven films, including *Jaguar* and *Petit à Petit* (1969). See Paul Stoller's excellent overview of Rouch's early work in anthropology, work that would shape his entire ethnographic career: Paul Stoller, *The Cinematic Griot: The Ethnography of Jean Rouch* (Chicago: University of Chicago Press, 1992), 28–47.

10 Stoller, *The Cinematic Griot*, 31.

11 Muriel Devey, *Hampâté Bâ: L'homme de la tradition* (Dakar: LivreSud, 1993), 88.

12 Stoller, *The Cinematic Griot*, 48.

13 See Steven Feld, "Introduction," in *Ciné-ethnography*, by Jean Rouch, ed. and trans. Steven Feld (Minneapolis: University of Minnesota Press, 2003), 10–11.

14 While we should, of course, beware of establishing arbitrary dichotomies within Rouch's oeuvre, we can nevertheless highlight certain thematic divergences in his work and point to several features that characterize his more plot-driven narrative films. *Les maîtres fous* (1955), Rouch's most controversial film, is an important exception in this regard: it is a short film that deals with a particularly violent Hauka possession ceremony held outside of Accra and with the striking contrasts between the participants' behavior when possessed and their everyday lives as laborers in the Ghanaian capital.

15 See Feld, "Introduction," 11–12.

16 See Henley, *The Adventure of the Real*, 72, 74.

17 Henley, *The Adventure of the Real*, 83–84.

18 Cited in Stoller, *The Cinematic Griot*, 43.

19 Henley, *The Adventure of the Real*, 92.

20 However, the properly filmic sequel to *Jaguar* is Rouch's film *Petit à Petit* (1968–69), which revisits the three heroes from the earlier film as they develop their business into a successful corporation and send Damouré to Paris, in a brilliant example of anthropology in reverse, to investigate how ordinary Parisians live in skyscrapers—the goal being to collect ethnographic "data" in support of the corporation's (unrealized) plan to build a skyscraper in the bush to rival the tallest building in Niamey, the Nigerien capital.

21 Rouch saw Vertov's contribution along these lines, remarking that the Soviet's camera was "a new eye open on the world": see Sam Di Iorio, "Total Cinema: *Chronique d'un été* and the end of Bazinian Film Theory," *Screen* 48, no. 1 (2007): 30.

22 Rouch did not begin shooting with fully synchronized sound until *Chronique d'un été* (1960).

23 Henley, *The Adventure of the Real*, 92–94. Robinson was Rouch's research assistant when he starred in *Moi, un Noir*, but he was acting out his life as a migrant worker before joining the anthropologist's team. Likewise, the three heroes from *Jaguar* adopted the roles of migrants Rouch had actually worked with and who were taking up a long history of southward migration within West Africa. By contrast, the plot of *La pyramide humaine* was entirely fictional.

24 See, e.g., Alexandra Peat, *Travel and Modernist Literature: Sacred and Ethical Journeys* (New York: Routledge, 2010). Sam Rohdie has addressed these issues as they specifically relate to cinema in his *Promised Lands: Cinema, Geography, Modernism* (London: British Film Institute, 2008). Examples from the novel abound here, and we need hardly go further than Bloom's peripatetic relationship to Dublin's cartography in *Ulysses*, Marcel's travels by train in Proust's *In Search of Lost Time* (especially in *Time Regained*), or the spatial displacement of sprawling narrative points of articulation in Dos Passos's *USA Trilogy*. Like Rouch, Fredric Jameson ties the modern closely to its colonial conditions of possibility: see Fredric Jameson, *The Modernist Papers* (New York: Verso, 2007), 152–69.

25 It is perhaps only fitting to observe that in certain respects it appears as if Rouch were imagining what Walter Benjamin's reading of Baudelaire might look like if it were translated into the colonial African city of the late 1950s. Benjamin and Baudelaire, of course, jointly inspired this chapter's title, and we might say, like Benjamin, that Rouch's African flaneur is "abandoned in the crowd." For Rouch, though, this abandonment has nothing to do with alienation or isolation. Instead, it heralds the distinct pleasures to be had from being left to one's own devices in the modern colonial city: see Walter Benjamin, "The Paris of the Second Empire in Baudelaire," in *The Writer of Modern Life: Essays on Charles Baudelaire*, ed. Michael W. Jennings, trans. Howard Eiland, Edmund Jephcott, Rodney Livingstone, and Harry Zohn (Cambridge, MA: Harvard University Press, 2006), 85.

26 This is a brilliant bit of cinematic self-referentiality. Lemmy Caution is a fictitious FBI agent created by the British crime writer Peter Cheyney in the 1930s. Eddie Constantine was the American actor who made a name for himself in French cinema by playing Caution on the big screen in the 1950s.

27 As Sasha Newell points out in his ethnography of mimesis and modernity in contemporary Abidjan, Treichville was always conceived by its residents as a more cosmopolitan version of the rural African village. As he puts it, Treichville's "muddy, garbage strewn streets" still have an "aura of glamour": see Sasha Newell, *The Modernity Bluff: Crime, Consumption, and Citizenship in Côte d'Ivoire* (Chicago: University of Chicago Press, 2012), 24–25.

28 Robinson's boastful declaration of modernity mobilizes here a rhetoric and aesthetic of "trash," a cinematic category in African film whose conceptual genealogy Kenneth Harrow has recently and provocatively traced. Rouch does not figure in Harrow's study of mostly contemporary African films, yet the proliferation of

"trash" and disused, dilapidated objects abounds in *Moi, un Noir*, which should hardly come as a surprise since one of Rouch's goals in the film is to highlight the run-down underside of idealized dreams of modernity in almost-postcolonial West Africa: see Kenneth W. Harrow, *Trash: African Cinema from Below* (Bloomington: Indiana University Press, 2013), 1–6.

29 See Paul Gilroy, *The Black Atlantic: Modernity and Double Consciousness* (Cambridge, MA: Harvard University Press, 1993), 30.

30 Paul Gilroy, *Against Race: Imagining Political Culture beyond the Color Line* (Cambridge, MA: Harvard University Press, 2000), 58.

31 Fredric Jameson, *A Singular Modernity: Essay on the Ontology of the Present* (New York: Verso, 2002), 6.

32 As Jameson puts it, "The trope of 'modernity' is always in one way or another a rewriting, a powerful displacement of previous narrative paradigms. Indeed, when one comes to recent thought and writing, the affirmation of the 'modernity' of this or that generally involves a rewriting of the narratives of modernity itself which are already in place and have become conventional wisdom": see Jameson, *A Singular Modernity*, 36.

33 Jameson, *A Singular Modernity*, 40.

34 Indeed, important readings of Rouch's film have been carried out with this convergence in mind, although they generally do not seek to theorize Rouch's ethnofiction or look beyond readings of individual texts to broader connections on the level of genre with other figures who have also been torn between fiction and anthropology/documentary: see, e.g., Jean-André Fieschi, "Slippages of Fiction," in *Anthropology, Reality, Cinema: The Films of Jean Rouch*, ed. Mick Eaton (London: British Film Institute, 1979), 67–77. Peter Loizos, for his part, places Rouch's interest in fiction in relation to the conventionally realist aesthetic of much ethnographic filmmaking. See Peter Loizos, *Innovation in Ethnographic Film: From Innocence to Self-Consciousness, 1955–1985* (Chicago: University of Chicago Press, 1993). More recently, Maxime Scheinfeigel pays special attention in her monograph on Rouch to his method of inventing fiction and uses *Moi, un Noir* as a chapter-long case study. See Maxime Scheinfeigel, *Jean Rouch* (Paris: CNRS, 2008). Alan Cholodenko, Michael Laramee, and William Rothman have all written essays dealing more or less directly with the fictional elements of several of Rouch's films in William Rothman, ed., *Three Documentary Filmmakers* (Albany: State University of New York Press, 2009). From a different perspective, Alexandra Juhasz and Jesse Lerner point to the ways in which *Moi, un Noir* uses fiction to gain access to the realities of everyday life as they situate Rouch as a provocative figure in the prehistory of what they call the "fake documentary." See Alexandra Juhasz and Jesse Lerner, eds., *F Is for Phony: Fake Documentaries and Truth's Undoing* (Minneapolis: University of Minnesota Press, 2006), 29.

35 *Les Maîtres fous* (1955) is, of course, an exception in this regard. Readings of the film have stressed Rouch's ability to explore how ordinary Africans confront their own alienation through mimicry of European social norms and creative sorts of

wish-fulfillment. See Laura U. Marks, *The Skin of the Film: Intercultural Cinema, Embodiment, and the Senses* (Durham, NC: Duke University Press, 2000), 100–1; Michael Taussig, *Mimesis and Alterity: A Particular History of the Senses* (New York: Routledge, 1993), 241–43. See also Paul Stoller, "Jean Rouch and the Power of the Between," in *Three Documentary Filmmakers*, ed. William Rothman (Albany: State University of New York Press, 2009), 125–37. Peter Bloom gestures in a more general way toward this problem in his *French Colonial Documentary: Mythologies of Humanitarianism* (Minneapolis: University of Minnesota Press, 2008).

36 Benjamin writes that "'Modernity' in Baudelaire . . . gives expression to extreme spontaneity," and given the pleasures of spontaneous narrative creation on offer in Rouch's ethnofiction, we can say the same for him: see Benjamin, *The Writer of Modern Life*, 139.

37 Pascale Casanova, *The World Republic of Letters*, trans. M. B. DeBevoise (Cambridge, MA: Harvard University Press, 2004), 1–6.

38 Also, like many of his voice-overs, this comment in particular simply and playfully does not give the viewer the whole story. Rouch omits the fact that his protagonist's haunting, improvised introspection was born of a formal innovation that was itself brought about through technical limitations and frustrations.

39 Gilles Deleuze, *Cinema 2: The Time-Image*, trans. Hugh Tomlinson and Robert Galeta (Minneapolis: University of Minnesota Press, 1989), 129.

40 The Shakespearean reference here is Deleuze's, as he highlights in his short book on Kant. See Gilles Deleuze, *Kant's Critical Philosophy*, trans. Hugh Tomlinson and Barbara Habberjam (Minneapolis: University of Minnesota Press, 1984), vii.

41 Deleuze, *Cinema 2*, 130–31.

42 Rouch was a close friend of Nkrumah's and made another film in 1957, *Baby Ghana*, dealing with Nkrumah's election.

43 Viewers of Rouch's work who have developed some familiarity with his approach will take note of moments such as this one, since there is often precious little work of ethnographic or historical contextualization that takes place in his films.

44 Of course, when the film's three heroes cross into the Gold Coast, we as viewers are certainly aware that they are crossing a colonial frontier, but their improvised narrative skirts any explicit discussion of the matter. Likewise, when they are turned away because they do not have passports, Damouré, Lam, and Illo simply walk around the border crossing, skirting the very materiality of the colonial border, and continue on their way.

45 Henley, *The Adventure of the Real*, 84. See also Stoller, *The Cinematic Griot*, 46. The word *zazouman* is thrown around on several occasions in *Jaguar*, and the term is synonymous with *jaguar*.

46 Rouch, *Ciné-Ethnography*, 140.

47 Scheinfeigel, *Jean Rouch*, 158. Scheinfeigel points out that this fictional move of Rouch's (which is little more than an inside joke of post-production) continues the neorealist tradition of dubbing a character's voice with that of another actor. In addition, in another move linking Rouch to Godard, we might observe that, in

Charlotte et son Jules (1960), Godard substituted his own voice for that of Jean-Paul Belmondo during the dubbing process because Belmondo had been called away to serve in the army.

48 The producer Pierre Braunberger insisted that Rouch be accompanied by a professional crew during the shooting of the film. This explains who was behind the camera during Rouch's time on-screen: see Henley, *The Adventure of the Real*, 94.

49 See Fredric Jameson, *Signatures of the Visible* (London: Routledge, 1992), 273–74.

50 James Clifford famously called for such polyvocal approaches to anthropological text making in 1983, more than three decades after Rouch dove into these questions of the multiplicity of voices in ethnographic cinema: see James Clifford, *The Predicament of Culture: Twentieth-Century Ethnography, Literature, and Art* (Cambridge, MA: Harvard University Press, 1988), 51.

51 See Jean Rouch, *Alors le Noir et le Blanc seront amis: Carnets de mission 1946–1951*, ed. Marie-Isabelle Merle des Isles (Paris: Mille et Une Nuits, 2008), 114–15.

52 See Damouré Zika, *Journal de route* (Paris: Mille et Une Nuits, 2007 [orig. 1956]).

53 This story is fairly widely cited in scholarship on Rouch: see, e.g., Rouch, *Ciné-ethnography*, 42, 157; Scheinfeigel, *Jean Rouch*, 108; Stoller, *The Cinematic Griot*, 43.

54 Dziga Vertov, "Kinoks: A Revolution," in *Kino-Eye: The Writings of Dziga Vertov*, ed. Annette Michelson, trans. Kevin O'Brien (Berkeley: University of California Press, 1995), 20.

55 Jean Rouch, "On the Vicissitudes of the Self: The Possessed Dancer, the Magician, the Sorcerer, the Filmmaker, and the Ethnographer," in Rouch, *Ciné-Ethnography*, 99. See also Rouch's genealogy of his relationship to cinéma vérité (to Vertov, of course, but also to Flaherty) in Jean Rouch, "Le vrai et le faux," in Rouch, *Jean Rouch*, 112–15.

56 Ginsburg argues that the "parallax effect" for which Rouch strove involved including cinematic subjects in the process of cinematic production. Rouch's shared anthropology offers an early example of how "the object (the filmed image of a culture) appears to change in different films, depending on the position of the observer/filmmaker. When these different images are considered together, a more dialogical understanding results": see Faye Ginsburg, "The Parallax Effect: The Impact of Indigenous Media on Ethnographic Film," in *Collecting Visible Evidence*, ed. Jane M. Gaines and Michael Renov (Minneapolis: University of Minnesota Press, 1999), 159. Relatedly, although in a different register, Slavoj Žižek has highlighted the Kantian genealogy of such "parallax" positions, identifying in Kant "the irreducibly antinomic character of our experience of reality." Rouch would appreciate such a formulation, since for him the documentary reality of everyday life is situated at the vanishing point at which the perspectives of cinematic subjectivity and objectivity appear to converge: see Slavoj Žižek, *The Parallax View* (Cambridge, MA: MIT Press, 2006), 20–28.

57 Henley, *The Adventure of the Real*, 210–17.

58 Diawara was Rouch's student in Paris, and his compelling short film asks questions of the vestiges of colonialism that haunt Rouch's work while he engages with

Rouch on his own terms. What results is a filmic text that mobilizes a thoroughly Rouchian form in order to interrogate problems in the content of Rouch's best-known works.

59 Scheinfeigel, *Jean Rouch*, 162. Scheinfeigel's analysis of *Moi, un Noir* focuses on several dream sequences in the film in order to highlight the relationship between documentary and fiction. Another of these, for example, is when Robinson imagines that he and Dorothy Lamour are married as Rouch's camera constructs fictional shots of Dorothy playing the dutiful, seductive wife in Robinson's fantasy: see Scheinfeigel, *Jean Rouch*, 159–60.

60 Scheinfeigel, *Jean Rouch*, 158.

61 Rouch, *Ciné-ethnography*, 165.

62 James Clifford and George Marcus, eds., *Writing Culture: The Poetics and Politics of Ethnography* (Berkeley: University of California Press, 1986); Talal Asad, ed., *Anthropology and the Colonial Encounter* (New York: Humanities, 1973).

63 See Casanova, *The World Republic of Letters*, 115–16.

64 Casanova, *The World Republic of Letters*, 116.

65 See Manthia Diawara, *African Cinema: Politics and Culture* (Bloomington: Indiana University Press, 1992), 24, 160; Nwachukwu Frank Ukadike, *Black African Cinema* (Berkeley: University of California Press, 1994), 50, 77–79.

66 Henley, *The Adventure of the Real*, 328–29.

67 Rouch, *Ciné-ethnography*, 160.

68 Diawara also staunchly refuses to write Rouch out of the history of African cinema, which is often a Sembene-centric narrative: see Manthia Diawara, *African Film: New Forms of Aesthetics and Politics* (Munich: Prestel, 2010), 68, 232.

69 Deleuze, *Cinema 2*, 223.

70 From this point of view, Deleuze might have done better to think through Rouch's work in terms of immanence rather than in terms of a "break."

Chapter 3. Ethnographic Nation Building

1 See Michel-Rolph Trouillot, *Haiti: State against Nation. The Origins and Legacy of Duvalierism* (New York: Monthly Review, 1990), 25–26.

2 For his early point, see Benedict Anderson, *Imagined Communities*, rev. ed. (New York: Verso, 1991), 1–7.

3 See Melville J. Herskovits, *Life in a Haitian Valley* (Princeton, NJ: Markus Wiener, 2007 [orig. 1937]), 1.

4 Gérarde Magloire and Kevin A. Yelvington, "Haiti and the Anthropological Imagination," *Gradhiva* 1 (2005), accessed July 28, 2014, http://gradhiva.revues.org/335.

5 Hurston studied anthropology at Columbia University, working with Franz Boas and Ruth Benedict. While her writing on Haitian Vodou does not entirely avoid the sort of primitivism found in many pseudoscientific or sensationalist travel narratives on Haiti at the time, it at the very least begins from disciplinary training in anthropology and thus proceeds according to different epistemological aspirations:

see, e.g., the chapter "Voodoo and Voodoo Gods" in Zora Neale Hurston, *Tell My Horse: Voodoo and Life in Haiti and Jamaica* (New York: Harper Perennial, 1990 [orig. 1938]), 113–31.

6 On this point, see Kate Ramsey, "Prohibition, Persecution, Performance: Anthropology and the Penalization of Vodou in mid-20th-century," *Gradhiva* 1 (2005), accessed July 28, 2014, http://gradhiva.revues.org/352; J. Michael Dash, *Haiti and the United States: National Stereotypes and the Literary Imagination* (New York: St. Martin's, 1988), 87–88. Foreign anthropologists working in Haiti around this time also noted the Catholic Church and Haitian government's attempts to rid the country of Vodou: see Herskovits, *Life in a Haitian Valley*, 292–95; Alfred Métraux, *Le vaudou haïtien* (Paris: Gallimard, 1958), 12–13.

7 Martin Munro, *Exile and Post-1946 Haitian Literature: Alexis, Depestre, Ollivier, Laferrière, Danticat* (Liverpool: Liverpool University Press, 2007), 2–3. All of the figures I study in this chapter (Price-Mars, Roumain, Alexis, Depestre, and Laferrière) spent significant periods of their lives away from Haiti, although Price-Mars lived in Paris and traveled through the United States long before the rise to power in 1946 of the *noiristes*, the pro-black group that played on popular resentment of Haiti's mulatto and US-backed political elite.

8 For a detailed historical account of the foundation, evolution, and decline of the Bureau d'Ethnologie in Haiti, see Rachelle Charlier-Doucet, "Anthropologie politique et engagement social: L'expérience du Bureau d'ethnologie d'Haïti," *Gradhiva* 1 (2005), accessed July 28, 2014, http://gradhiva.revues.org/313.

9 René Depestre, "Parler de Jacques Roumain (1907–1944)," in *Jacques Roumain: Oeuvres complètes*, ed. Léon-François Hoffmann (Paris: Allca XX, 2003), xxvii.

10 See Jacques André, *Caraïbales: Études sur la littérature antillaise* (Paris: Éditions Caribéennes, 1981), 21–50.

11 On the ambiguities of an "organic community" in *Gouverneurs* that reforms and renews itself through external intervention, see Celia Britton, "'Common Being' and Organic Community in Jacques Roumain's *Gouverneurs de la rosée*," *Research in African Literatures* 37, no. 2 (2006): 164–75.

12 Jacques Roumain, *Gouverneurs de la rosée*, in *Jacques Roumain: Oeuvres complètes*, ed. Léon-François Hoffmann (Paris: Allca XX, 2003 [orig. 1944]), 363.

13 This distinction is fundamental for Trouillot, who writes against the derisiveness inherent in undue stressing of Haiti's radical exceptionality: see Michel-Rolph Trouillot, "The Odd and the Ordinary: Haiti, the Caribbean, and the World," *Cimarrón* 2, no. 3 (1990): 3–12.

14 Dash, *Haiti and the United States*, 37. See Mary A. Renda, *Taking Haiti: Military Occupation and the Culture of U.S. Imperialism, 1915–1940* (Chapel Hill, NC: University of North Carolina Press, 2001), 62; Magdeline W. Shannon, *Jean Price-Mars, the Haitian Elite and the American Occupation, 1915–1935* (New York: St. Martin's, 1996), 38–44.

15 Trouillot, *Haiti*, 132. See also Jacques Carméleau Antoine, *Jean Price-Mars and Haiti* (Washington, DC: Three Continents, 1981), 190–91. On the relationship be-

tween indigenism and the Griot movement, see Michel-Rolph Trouillot, "Jeux de mots, jeux de classe: Les mouvances de l'indigénisme," *Conjonction* 197 (1993): 29–44.

16 Joseph Anténor Firmin, *De l'égalité des races humaines (anthropologie positive)* (Montreal: Mémoire d'Encrier, 2005 [orig. 1885]), xxxix.

17 See Magloire and Yelvington, "Haiti and the Anthropological Imagination."

18 Jean Price-Mars, *Ainsi parla l'Oncle* [*suivi de* Revisiter l'Oncle] (Montreal: Mémoire d'Encrier, 2009 [orig. 1928]), 7.

19 Price-Mars, *Ainsi parla l'Oncle*, 7.

20 On these primitivist writings and Haitian reactions to them, see Magloire and Yelvington, "Haiti and the Anthropological Imagination"; Dash, *Haiti and the United States*, 22–44; Steven Gregory, "Voodoo, Ethnography, and the American Occupation of Haiti: William B. Seabrook's *The Magic Island*," in *Dialectical Anthropology: Essays in Honor of Stanley Diamond*, vol. 2, ed. Christine Ward Gailey (Gainesville: University Press of Florida, 1992), 169–207.

21 René Depestre, "Jean Price-Mars et le mythe de l'Orphée noir ou les aventures de la négritude," *L'Homme et la Société* 7 (1968): 171. For another essay on Price-Mars and Haitian Negritude, see Romuald Blaise Fonkoua, "Jean Price Mars ou les débuts scientifiques de la négritude en Haïti," in Price-Mars, *Ainsi parla l'Oncle*, 329–36.

22 As Charlier-Doucet points out, from its inception in the early 1940s, Haiti's Bureau d'Ethnologie set itself the task of promoting "native anthropology" many years before the question arose in other Anglo-American academic circles: see Charlier-Doucet, "Anthropologie politique et engagement social." Suzanne Comhaire-Sylvain is one native anthropologist who took up this project. Born in Port-au-Prince at the turn of the twentieth century, she studied under Paul Rivet and Marcel Mauss at the Institut d'Ethnologie in Paris and went on to publish collections of Haitian and African folktales based on fieldwork in her home country and throughout Africa. In the preface to her anthology *Le roman de Bouqui* (1940), she argues that even though many of the book's tales were "invented" outside Haiti, the text incontestably has "folkloric value" and "philosophical value": the collection is "a national monument in which the spirit of the people has unconsciously left the trace of its ideas and its aspirations": see Suzanne Comhaire-Sylvain, *Le roman de Bouqui* (Ottawa: Editions Leméac, 1973 [orig. 1940]), 11. On Comhaire as a student in Paris, see Alice L. Conklin, *In the Museum of Man: Race, Anthropology, and Empire in France, 1850–1950* (Ithaca, NY: Cornell University Press, 2013), 243–44.

23 Price-Mars, *Ainsi parla l'Oncle*, 14.

24 See René Depestre, *Bonjour et adieu à la négritude* (Paris: Robert Laffont, 1980), 43–57.

25 In terms of this book's argument more generally, these weaknesses are often discussed in relation to Haiti's dual French and American colonial encounter. For example, in *Une etape de l'évolution haïtienne*, Price-Mars identifies a "crisis" in Haitian society and observes that "the foreign Occupation sowed such disarray

in our consciences that the leaders of the nation are, in a large majority, in a state of mental impairment and [it is] there that we must seek out a sign of regression": see Jean Price-Mars, *Une etape de l'évolution haïtienne* (Port-au-Prince: La Presse, 1929), 15.

26 Price-Mars, *Ainsi parla l'Oncle*, 26.

27 Price-Mars, *Ainsi parla l'Oncle*, 13.

28 Price-Mars, *Ainsi parla l'Oncle*, 26.

29 See J. Michael Dash, "Jean Price-Mars et l'image d'Haïti," in *Ainsi parla l'Oncle* [*suivi de Revisiter l'Oncle*], by Jean Price-Mars (Montreal: Mémoire d'encrier, 2009), 339–40.

30 See Price-Mars, *Ainsi parla l'Oncle*, 203.

31 Both of these quotations are from Price-Mars, *Ainsi parla l'Oncle*, 202–3.

32 Price-Mars, *Ainsi parla l'Oncle*, 203.

33 Price-Mars, *Ainsi parla l'Oncle*, 250.

34 Quoted in Jean Price-Mars, *Formation ethnique, folk-lore et culture du peuple haïtien* (Port-au-Prince: V. Valcin, 1939), 1.

35 Jacques Stephen Alexis, *Compère général soleil* (Paris: Gallimard, 1955), 36. I read this dual movement in Alexis's work as one of national rewriting informing humanist desire, but one could also view it in historical terms, as a sense of socialist futurity complementing and pulling against a grounding in a national past: see Munro, *Exile in Post-1946 Haitian Literature*, 38.

36 And, as Elisabeth Mudimbe-Boyi has pointed out, the novel turns to local vernaculars in reproducing the speech of rural Haitians over and against that of the bourgeoisie: see M. Elisabeth Mudimbe-Boyi, *L'œuvre romanesque de Jacques-Stephen Alexis: Une écriture poétique, un engagement politique* (Montreal: Humanitas-Nouvelle Optique, 1992), 72–76.

37 For an ethnohistorical account of this campaign, see the chapter "Cultural Nationalist Policy and the Pursuit of 'Superstition' in Post-Occupation Haiti" in Kate Ramsey, *The Spirits and the Law: Vodou and Power in Haiti* (Chicago: University of Chicago Press, 2011), esp. 200–204, 211–13.

38 Price-Mars, *Formation ethnique*, 147.

39 Jacques Stephen Alexis, "Jacques Roumain vivant," preface in *La Montagne ensorcelé*, by Jacques Roumain (Paris: Les Editeurs Français Réunis, 1972 [orig. 1957]), 11–12. My translation of this phrase follows Langston Hughes's translation of Roumain's *Gouverneurs*.

40 Jacques Stephen Alexis, "Du réalisme merveilleux des Haïtiens," *Présence Africaine* 165–66 (2002 [orig. 1956]): 91, 96. On Alexis's literary (and partially unacknowledged) debt to Carpentier, see J. Michael Dash, *The Other America: Caribbean Literature in a New World Context* (Charlottesville: University of Virginia Press, 1998), 94–97.

41 Jacques Stephen Alexis, *Les arbres musiciens* (Paris: Gallimard, 1957), 154.

42 Alexis, *Les arbres musiciens*, 39.

43 Alexis, *Les arbres musiciens*, 102–3.

44 Alexis, *Les arbres musiciens*, 239–40.

45 Jacques Stephen Alexis, "Le Sous-lieutenant enchanté," in *Romancero aux étoiles* (Paris: Gallimard, 1960), 201, 206.

46 Alexis, "Le Sous-lieutenant enchanté," 205.

47 Alexis, "Le Sous-lieutenant enchanté," 206.

48 For another reading of this story, see Dash, *Haiti and the United States*, 99–100.

49 Alexis, *Les arbres musiciens*, 273.

50 Alexis, *Les arbres musiciens*, 344–45.

51 Alexis, *Les arbres musiciens*, 392.

52 Alexis, "Le Sous-lieutenant enchanté," 213.

53 See Jacques Stephen Alexis, *L'espace d'un cillement* (Paris: Gallimard, 1959).

54 J. Michael Dash makes a similar point when describing how in *Gouverneurs* Roumain (through his protagonist, Manuel) wants to found a new sociality in the clearing of a more or less ahistorical Haiti in which a "lost paradise" makes space for a "Caribbean heterocosm." This use of "heterocosm," I think, is not only apt but might playfully push us toward reading Roumain's novel as a site where ethnographic fiction meets science fiction, insofar as science fiction creates new worlds through cognitive estrangement: see Dash, *The Other America*, 76–80.

55 Depestre, *Bonjour et adieu à la négritude*, 218.

56 See Munro, *Exile and Post-1946 Haitian Literature*, 80–85.

57 René Depestre, *Le mât de cocagne* (Paris: Gallimard, 1979), 157. Achille Mbembe echoes this thematic when he discusses the "spectral function" of the phallus in "games of power and subordination" in contemporary African autocracy: see Achille Mbembe, *Sortir de la grande nuit: Essai sur l'Afrique décolonisée* (Paris: La Découverte, 2010), 217.

58 Depestre, *Le mât de cocagne*, 12.

59 Both quotations are from Depestre, *Le mât de cocagne*, 9.

60 See Munro, *Exile and Post-1946 Haitian Literature*, 81–83.

61 On Breton's and Mabille's surrealist ethnographic writing, see two essays by J. Michael Dash: "Caraïbe Fantôme: The Play of Difference in the Francophone Caribbean," *Yale French Studies* 103 (2003): 93–105, and "Le Je de l'autre: Surrealist Ethnographers and the Francophone Caribbean," *L'Esprit Créateur* 47, no. 1 (2007): 84–95.

62 See Dash, "Le Je de l'autre," 88–89.

63 René Depestre, *Hadriana dans tous mes rêves* (Paris: Gallimard, 1988), 17.

64 On Haitian marvelous realism, see Depestre, *Bonjour et adieu à la négritude*, 236–46.

65 Depestre, *Hadriana dans tous mes rêves*, 51.

66 See Jacques Derrida, *Specters of Marx: The State of the Debt, the Work of Mourning, and the New International*, trans. Peggy Kamuf (New York: Routledge, 1994), 10.

67 For more on this valorization of local knowledge and, especially, zombisme, see Kaiama L. Glover, "Exploiting the Undead: The Usefulness of the Zombie in Haitian Literature," *Journal of Haitian Studies* 11, no. 2 (2005): 105–21.

68 Depestre, *Hadriana dans tous mes rêves*, 101–2. For a philosophically minded account of certain features of zombisme and Vodou, see Roberto Strongman, "Transcorporeality in Vodou," *Journal of Haitian Studies* 14, no. 2 (2008): 4–29.

69 Depestre, *Hadriana dans tous mes rêves*, 134–36.

70 In a contemporary postcolonial context, discussing millennial capitalism and the proliferation of zombies in South Africa, the anthropologists Jean and John Comaroff cite Depestre decrying colonialism as "a process of man's general zombification": see Jean Comaroff and John L. Comaroff, *Theory from the South: Or, How Euro-America Is Evolving toward Africa* (Boulder, CO: Paradigm, 2012), 168.

71 This citation and the preceding one are from Depestre, *Hadriana dans tous mes rêves*, 142.

72 As Joan Dayan has written, Depestre "inhabits" Haiti when he is living and writing in France. This formulation is somewhat similar to the move his character Patrick makes in *Hadriana*: see Joan Dayan, "France Reads Haiti: René Depestre's *Hadriana dans tous mes rêves*," *Yale French Studies* 83, no. 2 (1993): 155.

73 On these biographical details, see Munro, *Exile and Post-1946 Haitian Literature*, 178–83.

74 Laferrière's character cites primitivist Haitian painters such as Hector Hippolyte and Micius Stéphane and refers to himself as a "primitive writer" in the first and last chapters of the novel: see Dany Laferrière, *Pays sans chapeau* (Paris: Serpent à Plumes, 2001 [orig. 1996]), 11–14, 177–78, 275–76.

75 Georg Stanitzek points out that paratextuality signals a "*simultaneous distinction and nondistinction* between *literary work* and *text*." Along these lines, but referring more specifically to paratextuality, my argument here is that the paratext in ethnographic fiction simultaneously speaks to or addresses the genre of the literary work to which it is appended and obscures it or blurs its distinguishing features: see Georg Stanitzek, "Texts and Paratexts in Media," trans. Ellen Klein, *Critical Inquiry* 32, no. 1 (2005): 28.

76 Laferrière, *Pays sans chapeau*, 8.

77 This process is part and parcel of what Piotr Sadkowski refers to as an "Odyssean" model of self-writing, which includes both self-narration as well as a readjustment to cultural contexts from which one was hitherto estranged: see Piotr Sadkowski, "Les écritures migrantes et le récit odysséen: *Pays sans chapeau* de Dany Laferrière," *Francofonia* 57 (2009): 102.

78 Laferrière, *Pays sans chapeau*, 11.

79 In Laferrière's *L'énigme du retour* (2009), a novel whose narrator returns to Haiti after the death of his father in exile, the narrator explains his absorption of experiential data in much more poetic terms: "I no longer want to think. / Only see, hear, and feel. / And note everything down before losing my head, / intoxicated by this explosion of colors / smells and tropical flavors. / For so long I have not / been part of such a landscape." Laferrière's narrator dissolves poetically here into pure sensible receptivity in a formulation that stands in marked contrast to the hyperor-

ganized enumeration of sensorial and experiential data in *Pays sans chapeau*: see Dany Laferrière, *L'énigme du retour* (Paris: Bernard Grasset, 2009), 82.

80 Glissant's poems in this book offer impressionistic sketches of phenomenologies of the Caribbean natural world, pointing at the same time to another, internally articulated land ("We breathe in this country that dries up inside us"): see Édouard Glissant, *Pays rêvé, pays réel* (Paris: Seuil, 1985), 14.

81 Laferrière, *Pays sans chapeau*, 46–47. The image of two countries walking side by side without ever intersecting calls to mind China Miéville's novel *The City and The City*, about two city-states that are geographically and topographically coextensive but geopolitically distinct and, indeed, mutually exclusive (indeed, the citizens of one country must "unsee" citizens of the other as they come across each other in everyday life): see China Miéville, *The City and The City* (New York: Del Rey, 2009).

82 Carlo Avierl Célius, "La création plastique et le tournant ethnologique en Haïti," *Gradhiva* 1 (2005), accessed April 2, 2015, http://gradhiva.revues.org/301.

83 Munro sees *Pays sans chapeau* as a broader rewriting of *Gouverneurs*, among other texts, given the parallel between Vieux Os's return from exile and Manuel's return home from the Cuban plantation. These structural similarities are striking, but I am interested more narrowly in ethnographic fiction as intertextual referentiality—a strategy and thematic to which I return in chapter 4 with Chamoiseau and the créolistes: see Munro, *Exile and Post-1946 Haitian Literature*, 188–93.

84 These zombie-like presences from the past are not just autobiographical but also literary-historical apparitions: see Jean L. Prophète, "Dany Laferrière and the Autobiography of Disorderly Past Times," trans. Carrol F. Coates, *Callaloo* 22, no. 4 (1999): 947–49; Martin Munro, "Ethnography, Exile, and Haitian Literary History in Dany Laferrière's *Pays sans chapeau*," *Journal of Haitian Studies* 9, no. 2 (2003): 74–88.

85 Carrol F. Coates and Dany Laferrière, "An Interview with Dany Laferrière," *Callaloo* 22, no. 4 (1999): 910.

86 Laferrière, *Pays sans chapeau*, 269.

87 Laferrière, *Pays sans chapeau*, 271.

88 Haitian indigenism morphed into a static black nationalism for the members of the Griot movement, including François Duvalier. He would go on to base his noiriste ideology on an essentialized Africanist authenticity that resonated perversely with Price-Mars's anthropological work, which significantly influenced the future dictator. Duvalier maintained ties with anthropology throughout his life. As Rachelle Charlier-Doucet points out, he was honorary director of the Bureau d'Ethnologie until his death in 1971, although his ethnographic publications may have been largely the work of his collaborator, the anthropologist Lorimer Denis. Even after his death, the bureau was known for its proximity to Duvalierism: see Charlier-Doucet, "Anthropologie politique et engagement social"; Antoine, *Jean Price-Mars and Haiti*, 171–73; Munro, *Exile and Post-1946 Haitian Literature*, 16–19, 25–26; Paul Christopher Johnson, "Secretism and the Apotheosis of Duvalier," *Journal of the American Academy of Religion* 74, no. 2 (2006): 420–45.

Chapter 4. Creole Novels

1 Édouard Glissant, "Michel Leiris: The *Repli* and the *Dépli*," trans. Cynthia Mesh, *Yale French Studies* 81 (1992): 23.

2 Glissant, "Michel Leiris," 23.

3 Glissant, "Michel Leiris," 23, 27.

4 Cited in Christina Kullberg, "Crossroads Poetics: Glissant and Ethnography," *Callaloo* 36, no. 4 (2013): 968.

5 Édouard Glissant, *Poetics of Relation*, trans. Betsy Wing (Ann Arbor: University of Michigan Press, 1997 [orig. 1990]), 11. For the slightly modified book version of his essay on Leiris, see Édouard Glissant, *Traité du tout-monde* (Paris: Gallimard, 1997), 128–38.

6 Michel Leiris, *Contacts de civilisations en Martinique et en Guadeloupe* (Paris: Gallimard and United Nations Educational, Scientific and Cultural Organization, 1955), 9. See also J. Michael Dash, "Caraïbe Fantôme: The Play of Difference in the Francophone Caribbean," *Yale French Studies* 103 (2003): 95. Perhaps because of this concern for the French "national community," Leiris's work in the Caribbean has often been seen in France as having brought that part of the world into anthropology's disciplinary consciousness, as Sally Price has argued. Such a narrative, she continues, misses the contributions of Caribbeanist (and Caribbean) scholars of the region from other national backgrounds: see Sally Price, "Michel Leiris, French Anthropology, and a Side Trip to the Antilles," *French Politics, Culture and Society* 22, no. 1 (2004): 31–32.

7 Leiris, *Contacts de civilisations en Martinique et en Guadeloupe*, 104.

8 Leiris, *Contacts de civilisations en Martinique et en Guadeloupe*, 111.

9 Leiris, *Contacts de civilisations en Martinique et en Guadeloupe*, 111.

10 Jean Bernabé, Patrick Chamoiseau, and Raphaël Confiant, *Éloge de la créolité*, bilingual ed., trans. M. B. Taleb-Khyar (Paris: Gallimard, 1993 [orig. 1989]), 75. My modifications to the English translation are noted.

11 Bernabé et al., *Éloge de la créolité*, 75.

12 Dash, "Caraïbe Fantôme," 94. For the purposes of this book it is crucial to point out that Dash situates *L'Afrique fantôme* (1934) as the index case for the Surrealists' "exemplary sensitivity" to the cultural particularities the Caribbean offered.

13 Christina Kullberg, *The Poetics of Ethnography in Martinican Narratives: Exploring the Self and the Environment* (Charlottesville: University of Virginia Press, 2013), 3. Kullberg points out that Glissant, writing in *Poetic Intention*, both critiques ethnography's reifying gaze and insists that it can teach Martinicans to look at metropolitan France and themselves in new ways. The créolistes heed his advice, as this chapter shows.

14 However, in a 2009 "address to Barack Obama" that Glissant co-wrote with Chamoiseau, the recently elected US president's Creoleness is celebrated as emblematic of politics in the *tout-monde* and as an eminently visible example of the relationship between créolité and *identité relation*. In a short text that reads as immeasur-

ably optimistic in the fractiously hostile political climate of the United States at the time of this book's writing, Glissant and Chamoiseau laud the fact that the US has finally caught up with the history of its own racial-cultural multiplicity: see Édouard Glissant and Patrick Chamoiseau, *L'intraitable beauté du monde: Adresse à Barack Obama* (Paris: Galaade, 2009), 15.

15 See Kristen Stromberg Childers, *Seeking Imperialism's Embrace: National Identity, Decolonization, and Assimilation in the French Caribbean* (New York: Oxford University Press, 2016), 2.

16 See Childers, *Seeking Imperialism's Embrace*, 179–80.

17 Patrick Chamoiseau, *Chronique des sept misères* (Paris: Gallimard, 1986), 118.

18 Édouard Glissant, *Poétique de la relation* (Paris: Seuil, 1990), 103.

19 On the latter point, see Chris Bongie, *Islands and Exiles: The Creole Identities of Post/Colonial Literature* (Stanford, CA: Stanford University Press, 1998), 63–64.

20 Bernabé et al., *Éloge de la créolité*, 76.

21 Roberto Bolaño, *2666*, trans. Natasha Wimmer (New York: Picador, 2008 [orig. 2004]), 339.

22 On this point, see David Scott, "Preface: Islands of *Créolité*?" *Small Axe* 13, no. 3 (2009): viii.

23 Romuald Blaise Fonkoua, "Édouard Glissant: Naissance d'une anthropologie antillaise au siècle de l'assimilation," *Cahiers d'Études Africaines* 35, no. 140 (1995): 803–4.

24 Édouard Glissant, *Soleil de la conscience* (Paris: Seuil, 1956), 15.

25 Françoise Lionnet borrows from and pays homage to Glissant in her bilingual *Le su et l'incertain: Cosmopolitiques créoles de l'océan indien/The Known and the Uncertain: Creole Cosmopolitics of the Indian Ocean* (La Pelouse, Mauritius: L'Atelier d'Écriture, 2012). Like my approach in this chapter, Lionnet acknowledges a debt to Glissant and investigates the relationship between créolité (understood broadly) and lived experience, although in her case she is interested in cosmopolitanism and *le vécu* in Mauritius and La Réunion. In another fortuitous parallel, the work of Amitav Ghosh, which I briefly discussed in chapter 1, is the subject of her first chapter: see Lionnet, *Le su et l'incertain/The Known and the Uncertain*, 13–14, 27–54.

26 Édouard Glissant, *Caribbean Discourse: Selected Essays*, trans. J. Michael Dash (Charlottesville: University of Virginia Press, 1989), vii. Given the partial nature of the English edition of *Discours*, I will generally give my own translation when quoting from it, unless noted otherwise.

27 Nick Nesbitt translates this question of "erasure" into a thematics of "forgetting" in Glissant's fictional texts, referring to the "poetification of historical experience" in the rehabilitation of experiential narratives of suffering and struggle. This approach certainly constitutes a literary-fictional response to the question Glissant asks in his fourth introduction to *Discours*: see Nick Nesbitt, *Voicing Memory: History and Subjectivity in French Caribbean Literature* (Charlottesville: University of Virginia Press, 2003), 182–84.

28 These quotations are all from Édouard Glissant, *Le discours antillais* (Paris: Gallimard, 1997 [orig. 1981]), 20. I translate the French verb *crier* here as "to speak" because this is how the verb is often used in French-language writing from the Caribbean. *Crier* might more literally be translated as "to call out," "to shout," or "to cry," and the frequent use of this verb in Francophone Caribbean letters certainly hints at semantic slippage in all of these directions.

29 Glissant, *Le discours antillais*, 157.

30 Glissant, *Le discours antillais*, 197.

31 Glissant, *Le discours antillais*, 289.

32 Glissant, *Le discours antillais*, 313.

33 Glissant, *Le discours antillais*, 315–16. For an extended analysis, see Glissant, *Le discours antillais*, 728–59.

34 Glissant, *Le discours antillais*, 283.

35 These quotations are from Glissant, *Le discours antillais*, 283.

36 Glissant, *Le discours antillais*, 759. See also Jacques Rancière, *The Politics of Aesthetics*, trans. Gabriel Rockhill (New York: Continuum, 2004 [orig. 2000]), 22.

37 Glissant, *Le discours antillais*, 346.

38 Bernabé et al., *Éloge de la créolité*, 108. On critiques of the créolistes writing in French, see Bongie, *Islands and Exiles*, 346. Here Bongie brings to a culmination his reading of Annie Le Brun's strong critique of the créolité movement in her *Statue cou coupé* (Paris: Jean-Michel Place, 1996). As I have insisted, and as will become clearer in what follows, the critiques of créolité are well taken but fall somewhat outside the argument I elaborate in this chapter—namely, that the créolistes rewrite Caribbean literary history by making space for ethnographic fiction. That they do so problematically does not detract from my broader point.

39 Bernabé et al., *Éloge de la créolité*, 89.

40 Patrick Chamoiseau and Raphaël Confiant, *Lettres créoles: Tracées antillaises et continentales de la littérature, Haïti, Guadeloupe, Martinique, Guyane, 1635–1975* (Paris: Gallimard, 1999 [orig. 1991]), 257.

41 Bernabé et al., *Éloge de la créolité*, 94. Italics in original.

42 See, e.g., Bongie, *Islands and Exiles*, 341–47. Bongie also points out how Glissant himself likened créolité to a "prison," opposing it to radically open-ended processes of creolization: quoted in Bongie, *Islands and Exiles*, 65. Other scholars have examined how the créolistes articulated créolité by attributing to Césaire positions he never actually (or only temporarily) held, anachronistically trying him for crimes against their movement. On this point, see Richard D. E. Burton, "Two Views of Césaire: Négritude and créolité," *Dalhousie French Studies* 35 (1996): 135–52. Richard Watts, for his part, argues against critiques of Chamoiseau's créolité that would unduly reduce it to an essentialist atavism: see Richard Watts, "The 'Wounds of Locality': Living and Writing the Local in Chamoiseau's *Ecrire en pays dominé*," *French Forum* 28, no. 1 (2003): 111–29.

43 Bernabé et al., *Éloge de la créolité*, 101. Italics in original.

44 Bernabé et al., *Éloge de la créolité*, 100.

45 Bernabé et al., *Éloge de la créolité*, 101.

46 Bernabé et al., *Éloge de la créolité*, 109.

47 Raphaël Confiant, "Foreword," in *Two Years in the French West Indies*, by Lafcadio Hearn (New York: Interlink, 2001 [orig. 1890]), xii.

48 Confiant, "Foreword," x.

49 It is outside the genealogical scope of this discussion to go into much detail on Hearn's writing. For a fuller analysis of Hearn and his ethnographic approach to Creoleness, see Mary Gallagher, "Lafcadio Hearn's American Writings and the Creole Continuum," in *American Creoles: The Francophone Caribbean and the American South*, ed. Martin Munro and Celia Britton (Liverpool: Liverpool University Press, 2012), 19–39. For a reading of the creolized relationship between Hearn and Glissant, see Chris Bongie, "Resisting Memories: The Creole Identities of Lafcadio Hearn and Édouard Glissant," *SubStance* 26, no. 3 (1995): 153–78.

50 Lafcadio Hearn, *Two Years in the French West Indies* (New York: Interlink, 2001 [orig. 1890]), 78.

51 Hearn, *Two Years in the French West Indies*, 78.

52 Chamoiseau and Confiant, *Lettres créoles*, 51.

53 Chamoiseau and Confiant, *Lettres créoles*, 159. The créolistes' relationship to Césaire is nothing if not ambivalent: see, e.g., Christopher L. Miller, *The French Atlantic Triangle: Literature and Culture of the Slave Trade* (Durham, NC: Duke University Press, 2008), 325–30; Raphaël Confiant, *Aimé Césaire: Une traversée paradoxale du siècle* (Paris: Stock, 1993), 65–100. Chamoiseau, Césaire, Glissant, and Perse form a single "entity" in his affective-aesthetic bibliography, although the three figures do not thereby dissolve into one another: see Patrick Chamoiseau, *Césaire, Perse, Glissant: Les liaisons magnétiques* (Paris: Philippe Rey, 2013), 13, 17.

54 Patrick Chamoiseau, *Écrire en pays dominé* (Paris: Gallimard, 1997), 24.

55 Chamoiseau, *Écrire en pays dominé*, 110.

56 Chamoiseau, *Écrire en pays dominé*, 114.

57 Chamoiseau, *Écrire en pays dominé*, 222–23.

58 Chamoiseau, *Écrire en pays dominé*, 233.

59 Raphaël Confiant, *Le Nègre et l'Amiral* (Paris: Grasset, 1988), 93–105. For the corresponding episode as recounted by the anthropologist himself, see Claude Lévi-Strauss, *Tristes Tropiques*, trans. John and Doreen Weightmann (New York: Penguin, 1992), 29–36.

60 For a detailed text that examines the riots and relies (ethnographically) on first-hand testimonies, see Louis-Georges Placide, *Les émeutes de décembre 1959 en Martinique: Un repère historique* (Paris: L'Harmattan, 2009).

61 Roy Caldwell Jr. views this and other aspects of Confiant's formalism as indicating the "decidedly non-Western aesthetic" operating in the novel. I suggest that this aesthetic is predicated more on demonstrating how Creole literary production is in, but not necessarily of, Western artistic and literary traditions: see Roy Chandler Caldwell Jr., "*Créolité* and Postcoloniality in Raphaël Confiant's *L'allée des soupirs*," *French Review* 73, no. 3 (1999): 303.

62 Raphaël Confiant, *L'allée des soupirs* (Paris: Gallimard, 1994), 172. At the end of *Nadja* (1928), Breton writes, "Beauty will be convulsive or will not be at all": André Breton, *Nadja*, trans. Richard Howard (New York: Grove Press, 1960 [orig. 1928]), 160. And in an article for the journal *Tropiques*, Suzanne Césaire writes, "Martinican poetry will be cannibal or will not be at all": Suzanne Césaire "Misère d'une poésie: John Antoine-Nau," *Tropiques* 4 (1942): 50.

63 James Clifford, "On Ethnographic Allegory," in *Writing Culture: The Poetics and Politics of Ethnography*, ed. James Clifford and George E. Marcus (Berkeley: University of California Press, 1986), 98.

64 See Lawrence Venuti, *The Scandals of Translation: Towards an Ethics of Difference* (New York: Routledge, 1998), 75–82.

65 For the authors of *Éloge*, Negritude represents one form of literary exteriority among others: see Bernabé et al., *Éloge de la créolité*, 79–83. J. Michael Dash, however, has rightfully warned of the dangers of placing Césairean Negritude in too stark an opposition to a Glissantian-inspired creolized poetics of global relationality: see J. Michael Dash, "Hemispheric Horizons: Confinement, Mobility, and the 'Bateaux-Prisons' of the French Caribbean Imaginary," *Contemporary French and Francophone Studies* 15, no. 1 (2011): 20.

66 Confiant, *L'allée des soupirs*, 113.

67 Confiant, *L'allée des soupirs*, 113.

68 Confiant, *L'allée des soupirs*, 113.

69 Confiant, *L'allée des soupirs*, 115.

70 Confiant, *L'allée des soupirs*, 110.

71 Confiant, *L'allée des soupirs*, 306.

72 Confiant, *L'allée des soupirs*, 315.

73 Confiant, *L'allée des soupirs*, 315.

74 Confiant, *L'allée des soupirs*, 315.

75 Confiant, *L'allée des soupirs*, 239.

76 This is an allegorical rendering of Emily Apter's point that créolité allows the novel to narrativize its own literariness: see Emily Apter, *The Translation Zone: A New Comparative Literature* (Princeton, NJ: Princeton University Press, 2006), 180–82, 189–90.

77 See, e.g., Raphaël Confiant, *Le meurtre du Samedi-Gloria* (Paris: Gallimard, 1997).

78 See Kullberg, *The Poetics of Ethnography in Martinican Narratives*, 103–21. This is the fullest treatment of the relationship in question, integrated as it is into Kullberg's study of narrative, environment, and ethnography in Martinican literature. See also Celia Britton's reading of *Texaco*: Celia Britton, *The Sense of Community in French Caribbean Fiction* (Liverpool: Liverpool University Press, 2008), 93–110. On *Solibo Magnificent*, see, e.g., Wendy Knepper, "Remapping the Crime Novel in the Francophone Caribbean: The Case of Patrick Chamoiseau's *Solibo Magnifique*," *PMLA* 122, no. 5 (2007): 1431–46; Marie-Agnès Sourieau, "Patrick Chamoiseau, *Solibo Magnifique*: From the Escheat of Speech to the Emergence of Language," *Callaloo* 15, no. 1 (1992): 131–37.

79 As Lydie Moudileno has argued, Chamoiseau's characterological sketch of himself in this novel functions as a way to wrestle with the role of the contemporary Caribbean writer in the face of French assimilation: see Lydie Moudileno, *L'écrivain antillais au miroir de sa littérature: Mises en scène et mise en abyme du roman antillais* (Paris: Editions Karthala, 1997), 84–85.

80 See Chamoiseau, *Chronique des sept misères*, 217.

81 Patrick Chamoiseau, *Solibo Magnificent*, trans. Rose-Myriam Réjouis and Val Vinokurov (New York: Vintage, 1997 [orig. 1988]), 21. In what follows, I quote from the English translation and note any modifications.

82 Chamoiseau, *Solibo Magnificent*, 21, translation slightly modified.

83 Chamoiseau, *Solibo Magnificent*, 166.

84 James Joyce, *Ulysses* (New York: Vintage, 1990), 783.

85 Vincent Debaene, *Far Afield: French Anthropology between Science and Literature*, trans. Justin Izzo (Chicago: University of Chicago Press, 2014), 91, 93.

86 Chamoiseau, *Solibo Magnificent*, 158–59. On "atmosphere" and indigenous literature in French anthropology, see Debaene, *Far Afield*, 67–110.

87 Letchimy made waves in the Metropole in 2012 when he sharply rebuked the right-wing politician Claude Guéant, then the minister of the interior, in the Assemblée Nationale after Guéant said in a speech that "all civilizations are not equal": see François Krug, "Point Godwin contre Guéant: Qui est Serge Letchimy?" *L'Obs*, February 7, 2012, accessed August 2 2018, https://www.nouvelobs.com/rue89 /rue89-politique/20120207.RUE7706/point-godwin-contre-gueant-qui-est-serge -letchimy.html#/news/229166.

88 Patrick Chamoiseau, *Texaco*, trans. Rose-Myriam Réjouis and Val Vinokurov (New York: Vintage, 1997 [orig. 1992]), 220. I quote from this English translation and note any modifications.

89 Chamoiseau, *Texaco*, 257.

90 Chamoiseau, *Texaco*, 298.

91 Chamoiseau, *Texaco*, 315.

92 See the French edition of Patrick Chamoiseau, *Texaco* (Paris: Gallimard, 1992), 493. The English translation offers "Source" as a rendering of the French *Informatrice*, and while this word choice captures the signifying spirit of Chamoiseau's original, it misses the ethnographic resonance of the French that harks back to *Solibo Magnificent* and to the anthropological underpinnings of créolité.

93 Chamoiseau, *Texaco*, 360.

94 Chamoiseau, *Texaco*, 321.

95 Chamoiseau, *Texaco*, 322.

96 For Benítez-Rojo's original Deleuzian definition of this phrase, see Antonio Benítez-Rojo, *The Repeating Island: The Caribbean and the Postmodern Perspective*, 2d ed., trans. James Maraniss (Durham, NC: Duke University Press, 1996), 3. As he points out, the analytic "exploration" of the Caribbean involves potentially infinite repeating islands wherein repetition always instills new differences at each

instantiation. My more humorous spin on this formulation simply involves the temporary bracketing of "difference."

97 On this point, see J. Michael Dash, "Remembering Édouard Glissant," *Callaloo* 34, no. 3 (2011): 673. As Dash goes on to state, this is another instance of rapprochement between Glissant and Leiris, a crucial connection with which I opened the chapter.

Chapter 5. Speculative Cityscapes

1 Jean-Paul Colleyn, "Fiction et fictions en anthropologie," *L'Homme* 175–76 (2005): 156.

2 Jean Jamin, "Fictions haut régime: Du théâtre vécu au mythe romanesque," *L'Homme* 175–76 (2005): 195.

3 Jean Comaroff and John L. Comaroff, *The Truth about Crime: Sovereignty, Knowledge, and Social Order* (Chicago: University of Chicago Press, 2016), xiv–xv.

4 They also read *The Wire* as "grand storytelling in the mode of realist ethnography": see Comaroff and Comaroff, *The Truth about Crime*, 80–81, 102–3.

5 Comaroff and Comaroff, *The Truth about Crime*, xvi.

6 Nasiali begins her study of postwar housing in Marseille by asking, "Why didn't Marseille burn?" during the 2005 riots: see Minayo Nasiali, *Native to the Republic: Empire, Social Citizenship, and Everyday Life in Marseille since 1945* (Ithaca, NY: Cornell University Press, 2016), ix.

7 "Contempt" is the word Alèssi Dell'Umbria uses to describe the *longue durée* view held by outsiders of Marseille. "Reconquer" is a paraphrase of official discourses of urban renewal in the 1990s: see Alèssi Dell'Umbria, "The Sinking of Marseille," *New Left Review* 75 (2012): 69, 84.

8 See Dell'Umbria, "The Sinking of Marseille," 83; Michel Peraldi and Michel Samson, *Gouverner Marseille: Enquête sur les mondes politiques marseillais* (Paris: La Découverte, 2006), 245–61. Euromed is still going strong, and at the time of writing the project's website has webcams and live videos that give visitors a real-time look at current construction work: see http://www.euromediterranee.fr/telechargements /suivi-chantiers.html.

9 See Dell'Umbria, "The Sinking of Marseille," 81, 86.

10 Teju Cole, *Open City* (New York: Random House, 2011), 59.

11 Peraldi and Samson, *Gouverner Marseille*, 264.

12 Romantic impotence and failed idea(l)s of masculinity are particularly strong thematic concerns of Izzo's. Montale constantly bemoans his lack of success in love but, by the same token, seems to have little trouble attracting female companionship, as it were. In *Total Khéops* he has a brief affair with a Caribbean prostitute in addition to a more sustained connection with Leila, whom he was incapable of loving. In *Solea*, the narrative proceeds via the killing of a woman Montale has just met but whom he is nonetheless sure he loves, and he ends up falling for a female police officer who helps him investigate her murder.

13 See Michel de Certeau, *The Practice of Everyday Life*, trans. Steven Rendall (Berkeley: University of California Press, 2011 [orig. 1984]), 91.

14 On urban renewal in premillennial Marseille, see Alèssi Dell'Umbria, *Histoire universelle de Marseille: De l'an mil à l'an deux mille* (Marseille: Agone, 2006), 583–674. See also Peraldi and Samson, *Gouverner Marseille*, 175–206. These questions of urban renewal have antecedents tied to histories of immigration in Marseille. Mary Dewhurst Lewis addresses urban life, immigration, and French republican universalism in *The Boundaries of the Republic: Migrant Rights and the Limits of Universalism in France, 1918–1940* (Stanford, CA: Stanford University Press, 2007), 1–16. Izzo's utopian Marseille, by contrast, is based on a limitless universalism that stands in palimpsestic tension with urban phenomenologies of marginalization, exclusion, and xenophobia.

15 Gilles Deleuze, *Difference and Repetition*, trans. Paul Patton (New York: Columbia University Press, 1994 [orig. 1968]), xx.

16 For the well-known discussion of anthropology's "crisis," see George E. Marcus and Michael M. J. Fischer, *Anthropology as Cultural Critique: An Experimental Moment in the Human Sciences* (Chicago: University of Chicago Press, 1999 [orig. 1986]), 7–16.

17 Marcus and Fischer, *Anthropology as Cultural Critique*, xviii–xix.

18 Johannes Fabian, *Memory against Culture: Arguments and Reminders* (Durham, NC: Duke University Press, 2007), 50.

19 Jean-Claude Izzo, *Chourmo*, in *La trilogie Fabio Montale* (Paris: Gallimard, 2006 [orig. 1996]), n.p. (author's note). Hereafter, cites of Izzo's novels *Total Khéops*, *Chourmo*, and *Solea* refer to this anthology; I give the novel title, followed by the page number.

20 Izzo, *Total Khéops*, n.p. (author's note).

21 George E. Marcus, "The Modernist Sensibility in Recent Ethnographic Writing and the Cinematic Metaphor of Montage," in *Visualizing Theory: Selected Essays from V. A. R., 1990–1994*, ed. Lucien Taylor (New York: Routledge, 1994), 42.

22 Marcus, "The Modernist Sensibility in Recent Ethnographic Writing and the Cinematic Metaphor of Montage," 44.

23 Izzo, *Total Khéops*, 257.

24 This point about moving through and tying together fragmented social sites echoes Jameson's reading of Raymond Chandler's fiction: see Fredric Jameson, "On Raymond Chandler," in *The Critical Response to Raymond Chandler*, ed. J. K. Van Dover (Westport, CT: Greenwood, 1995), 72–73. Kristen Ross begins from a related observation about "the detective as social geographer" and goes on to investigate how French noir authors negotiate alternative historiographies: see Kristen Ross, "Parisian Noir," *New Literary History* 41, no. 1 (2010): 95. Also illuminating is her earlier essay, "Watching the Detectives," in *Postmodernism and the Re-reading of Modernity*, ed. Francis Barker, Peter Hulme, and Margaret Iversen (Manchester, UK: Manchester University Press, 1992), 46–65. Several critical essays on Izzo and the trilogy also point in this direction. Edmund Smyth argues that Marseille and social space for Izzo do not just constitute what he calls a "noir cityscape" in the style

of Chandler's Los Angeles or Montalbán's Barcelona, they also allow for "a sustained inquiry into the sociology and political culture of this alternative French capital": see Edmund J. Smyth, "Marseille *Noir*: Jean-Claude Izzo and the Mediterranean Detective," *Romance Studies* 25, no. 2 (2007): 111. Other work discussing Izzo focuses on the relationship between his representation of Marseille and the detective as a psychologizable figure: see David Platten, "Polar Positions: On the Theme of Identity in Contemporary Noir Fiction," *Nottingham French Studies* 41, no. 1 (2002): 5–18; Françoise Grauby, "Force mentale; Fabio Montale: *Total Khéops* au risque de la psychanalyse," *Australian Journal of French Studies* 43 (2006): 80–93. Nicholas Hewitt departs from this trend to analyze the twinned thematics of departure and diaspora in the trilogy. This formulation gestures toward my reading, but my argument here is broader and much more closely related to postcolonial generic overlapping as it emerges from written forms of urban overlapping: see Nicholas Hewitt, "Departures and Homecomings: Diaspora in Jean-Claude Izzo's Marseille," *French Cultural Studies* 17, no. 3 (2006): 257–68.

25 Izzo, *Total Khéops*, 254.

26 Gilles Deleuze, "Philosophie de la Série Noire," in *L'île déserte et autres textes: Textes et entretiens 1953–1974.* (Paris: Editions Minuit, 2002 [orig. 1966]), 116.

27 Izzo, *Chourmo*, 443.

28 Deleuze, "Philosophie de la Série Noire," 117. Some of the ideas in this early article receive fuller treatment in Deleuze's later text, *Proust and Signs*, in which he argues that the search for truth cannot proceed from any "benevolence of thought" that predisposes us toward a truth whose existence is pre-established and must simply be uncovered. Proust's novelty, then, is that he renders the search for truth contingent on random encounters that force thought to occur: see Gilles Deleuze, *Proust and Signs*, trans. Richard Howard (Minneapolis: University of Minnesota Press, 2000), 16–17.

29 Claire Gorrara, *The Roman Noir in Post-War French Culture* (Oxford: Oxford University Press, 2003), 15.

30 Andrea Goulet and Susanna Lee gesture in this direction in their introduction to a special issue of *Yale French Studies* devoted exclusively to crime fiction: see Andrea Goulet and Susanna Lee, "Editors' Preface," *Yale French Studies* 108 (2005): 1–7.

31 Izzo, *Total Khéops*, 71.

32 Dominic Thomas outlines a different type of textual production of marginalized social space in his analysis of a manifesto called "Qui fait la France?" written in 2007 by a group of artists, writers, and music performers. These figures, Thomas suggests, "[provide] a kind of blueprint . . . an explicit and unambiguous call for social inclusion and belonging. The common denominator among these young artists and activists . . . is that they are for the most part residents of the *banlieues*." As I show in this chapter's final section, for Izzo this "unambiguous call" takes the form of presentist utopian desires that actually avoid appearing like blueprints for alternative cultural futures: see Dominic Thomas, *Africa and*

France: Postcolonial Cultures, Migration, and Racism (Bloomington: Indiana University Press, 2013), 192.

33 Didier Fassin, *Enforcing Order: An Ethnography of Urban Policing* (Malden, MA: Polity Press, 2013), xviii.

34 Fassin, *Enforcing Order*, 11.

35 Izzo, *Total Khéops*, 86.

36 Izzo, *Total Khéops*, 86.

37 Izzo, *Chourmo*, 351.

38 Izzo, *Total Khéops*, 92.

39 Izzo, *Total Khéops*, 92–93.

40 Izzo, *Total Khéops*, 94.

41 Izzo, *Total Khéops*, 55.

42 Izzo, *Total Khéops*, 96.

43 Izzo, *Chourmo*, 346.

44 Jacques Rancière, *Disagreement: Politics and Philosophy*, trans. Julie Rose (Minneapolis: University of Minnesota Press, 1999), 29. On the distribution of the sensible, see Jacques Rancière, *The Politics of Aesthetics*, trans. Gabriel Rockhill (New York: Continuum, 2004), 12–45.

45 Izzo, *Total Khéops*, 88.

46 Izzo, *Total Khéops*, 88.

47 Izzo, *Total Khéops*, 89.

48 This idea of opportunism is part of Douglas Holmes's argument about Jean-Marie Le Pen's Front National: the party takes advantage of "ruptures in the experience of belonging" brought about by both globalization and European Union integration: see Douglas R. Holmes, *Integral Europe: Fast-Capitalism, Multiculturalism, Neofascism* (Princeton, NJ: Princeton University Press, 2000), 5. Holmes also analyzes a speech delivered by Le Pen in 1997. He highlights how Le Pen taps into "a resounding politics of the present" that aligns itself provocatively with this chapter's alternative renderings of presentist social forms: see Douglas R. Holmes, "Society Lost, Society Found," in *Zeroing In on the Year 2000: The Final Edition*, ed. George E. Marcus (Chicago: University of Chicago Press, 2000), 167.

49 Izzo, *Total Khéops*, 279. Indeed, cultural hybridization for Izzo is what Marseille has to offer France and the French language. For instance, although we meet the character Leila in *Total Khéops* only after her murder, in Montale's recollections of her, she appears as the embodiment of this idealized, utopian version of the city—Marseille's hybridized Marianne, as it were. Before her death Leila was completing a master's thesis on poetry and identity, and Montale tells us that her conclusion specifically touched on questions of hybridity. "For her, a child of the East, the French language became the place where the migrant pulled together all his lands and could finally put down his suitcases. The language of Rimbaud, of Valéry, of Char would be able to hybridize (*se métisser*), she argued. . . . In Marseille, a curious French was already being spoken, a mixture of Provençal,

Italian, Spanish, Arabic, with a dash of slant and a touch of *verlan*": Izzo, *Total Khéops*, 98.

50 Both of these citations are from Édouard Glissant, *Introduction à une poétique du divers* (Paris: Gallimard, 1996), 14–15.

51 Étienne Balibar, "Citizenship without Community?" in *We, the People of Europe? Reflections on Transnational Citizenship*, trans. James Swenson (Princeton, NJ: Princeton University Press, 2004), 63.

52 Arjun Appadurai, *The Future as Cultural Fact: Essays on the Global Condition* (New York: Verso, 2013), 5–6, 299.

53 Izzo, *Chourmo*, 436.

54 Izzo, *Chourmo*, 437.

55 Fredric Jameson, *The Seeds of Time* (New York: Columbia University Press, 1994), 75. Jameson is referring in this passage to the "epistemological value" of the idea that utopias are inextricably linked to their own failures as imaginative projects. While the failure of utopian projects is slightly outside the scope of my discussion, I think that the presentist temporality of Izzo's utopian imaginings in his trilogy performs the same sort of diagnostic epistemological work.

56 Izzo, *Total Khéops*, 253.

57 Izzo, *Total Khéops*, 253.

58 At the beginning of this novel, in one of the author's notes mentioned earlier, Izzo includes a literary disclaimer indicating that a good amount of what he writes in *Solea* is based on official documents from the US and newspapers such as *Le Monde* and *Le Canard Enchaîné*. Izzo leaves it up to us to speculate on just how much these fictionalized citations rely on real-world journalism. But I think the more compelling problem lies elsewhere—namely, in the ways in which these citations allow us to see how the text blurs temporal distinctions between a corrupt present and a dystopian near-future.

59 My point here emerges from my understanding of Izzo's sense of temporality, but it also responds to a claim Jameson makes about utopias more generally— that "utopia as a form is not the representation of radical alternatives; it is rather simply the imperative to imagine them": see Fredric Jameson, *Archeologies of the Future: The Desire Called Utopia and Other Science Fictions* (New York: Verso, 2005), 416.

60 Izzo, *Total Khéops*, 257.

61 Izzo, *Total Khéops*, 257.

62 If this were the case, though, we would then need to wonder why a utopian dimension in the trilogy is necessary for this political universalism to be fully realized and whether the existence of this dimension itself implies a critique of republican universalist ideology.

63 See Marcus, "The Modernist Sensibility in Recent Ethnographic Writing and the Cinematic Metaphor of Montage," 44.

64 Izzo, *Solea*, 597–98.

65 Izzo, *Solea*, 598.

66 Izzo, *Total Khéops*, 131.

67 Thomas More, *Utopia*, trans. Paul Turner (New York: Penguin, 1963), 50.

68 We could formulate this idea slightly differently. Peter Geschiere points out that autochthony has become a "global" and "free-floating" phenomenon due to its "capacity to emerge at completely different points in our globalizing world." Izzo's utopian, radically open belonging in premillennial Marseille suggests that we might repurpose Geschiere's argument. For him, autochthony is "global" because of the unexpectedly multilocal sites of its discursive and political articulation. For Izzo, however, autochthony's globality is an ontological a priori, a condition from which utopian belonging proceeds, since those who "belong" to his rewriting of the port city live Marseille's role in global histories of exile: see Peter Geschiere, *The Perils of Belonging: Autochthony, Citizenship, and Exclusion in Africa and Europe* (Chicago: University of Chicago Press, 2009), 6.

69 Izzo, *Chourmo*, 394.

70 "I decided to be what crime made of me," Sartre quotes Genet as saying early in *Saint Genet*. He goes on to elaborate on the philosophical consequences of such an apparently simple statement in a formulation that coincides (to use the Sartrean term) with my point in this paragraph. "To be is to throw oneself into one's being in order to coincide with it. The word ["be"] suggests a compromise between the calm coinciding of an object with its essence and the storm-tossed development whereby a man fulfills himself. . . . In that case, it can be said, not without a certain impropriety, that I have become what I was, that is, that my life has gradually realized certain gifts which existed in me in a virtual state. . . . Thus, the paradoxical expression 'to want to be what one is' can be meaningful: it may refer to the efforts we make to coincide with our being": see Jean-Paul Sartre, *Saint Genet: Actor and Martyr*, trans. Bernard Frechtman (New York: Pantheon, 1963), 59–60.

71 Izzo, *Chourmo*, 434.

72 Balibar, "Citizenship without Community?," 77.

73 To return briefly to Marcus here, this is where he stops short of declaring his modernist strategy to be utopian in the strict sense of the word. As he sees it, these thought experiments "might be thought to border on the utopian or the nostalgic if [they] were not dependent, first of all, on a documentation that these traces do have a life of their own, so to speak." Marcus's sense of empiricism seems to hold him back from embracing more properly utopian possibilities, and yet this is precisely what Izzo's palimpsest accomplishes in the trilogy, since it responds to and deploys ethnographic concepts and strategies in the inherently experimental realm of fiction: see Marcus, "The Modernist Sensibility in Recent Ethnographic Writing and the Cinematic Metaphor of Montage," 44.

74 Elizabeth A. Povinelli, *Economies of Abandonment: Social Belonging and Endurance in Late Liberalism* (Durham, NC: Duke University Press, 2011), x.

Conclusion

1 On these points, see, respectively, Michael Hardt and Antonio Negri, *Assembly* (New York: Oxford University Press, 2017), 200–6; Wendy Brown, *Undoing the Demos: Neoliberalism's Stealth Revolution* (New York: Zone, 2015), 215–218; Achille Mbembe, *Politiques de l'inimitié* (Paris: La Découverte, 2017), 7–15.

2 Gary Wilder, *The French Imperial Nation-State: Negritude and Colonial Humanism between the Two World Wars* (Chicago: University of Chicago Press, 2005), 29–36, 63–75.

3 The speculative Atlantic is thus distinct from what Ian Baucom calls the "speculative culture" of finance capital underpinning Britain's colonial domination: see Ian Baucom, *Specters of the Atlantic: Finance Capital, Slavery, and the Philosophy of History* (Durham, NC: Duke University Press, 2005), 106.

4 See Judith Butler, *Bodies That Matter: On the Discursive Limits of "Sex"* (New York: Routledge, 1993), 3.

5 Emily Apter, *Against World Literature: On the Politics of Untranslatability* (New York: Verso, 2013), 3.

6 Apter, *Against World Literature*, 4.

7 Achille Mbembe, *Sortir de la grande nuit: essai sur l'Afrique décolonisée* (Paris: La Découverte, 2010), 203–37, esp. 221–29.

8 Achille Mbembe, "L'Afrique qui vient," in *Penser et écrire l'Afrique aujourd'hui*, ed. Alain Mabanckou (Paris: Seuil, 2017), 28.

9 Mbembe, "L'Afrique qui vient," 28.

10 Achille Mbembe, "Penser le monde à partir de l'Afrique: Questions pour aujourd'hui et demain," in *Ecrire l'Afrique-Monde*, ed. Achille Mbembe and Felwine Sarr (Paris: Philippe Rey, 2017), 383, 386.

11 Mbembe, "Penser le monde à partir de l'Afrique," 383, 392.

12 All quotations in this paragraph are from Mbembe, "Penser le monde à partir de l'Afrique," 393.

13 Eric W. Weisstein, "Orthogonal Curves," *MathWorld*, accessed January 12, 2018, http://mathworld.wolfram.com/OrthogonalCurves.html.

14 Hardt and Negri, *Assembly*, xv.

15 See Hardt and Negri, *Assembly*, xiv–xv.

16 Hardt and Negri, *Assembly*, 233.

17 Hardt and Negri, *Assembly*, 97.

18 Hardt and Negri, *Assembly*, 248.

19 Hardt and Negri, *Assembly*, 25.

20 Hardt and Negri, *Assembly*, 38. As I hint here, Hardt and Negri are well aware of the colonial and postcolonial reach of their argument since they cite Wilder's work on Aimé Césaire and Léopold Sédar Songhor and their attempts to think decolonization outside the boundaries of state sovereignty.

21 Hardt and Negri, *Assembly*, 289.

22 Mbembe, *Politiques de l'inimitié*, 42.

23 Mbembe, *Politiques de l'inimitié*, 10.
24 Mbembe, *Politiques de l'inimitié*, 10.
25 Mbembe, *Politiques de l'inimitié*, 8.
26 Hardt and Negri, *Assembly*, 265; see also, more generally, Hardt and Negri, *Assembly*, 263–67. On cosmopolitanism and the violence of "perpetual war," see Bruce Robbins, *Perpetual War: Cosmopolitanism from the Viewpoint of Violence* (Durham, NC: Duke University Press, 2012), 1–30.
27 Mbembe, *Politiques de l'inimitié*, 173, 177.

Bibliography

Aggarwal, Kusum. *Amadou Hampâté Bâ et l'africanisme: De la recherche anthropologique à l'exercice de la fonction auctoriale.* Paris: L'Harmattan, 1999.

Albers, Irene. "Mimesis and Alterity: Michel Leiris's Ethnography and the Poetics of Spirit Possession." *French Studies* 62, no. 3 (2008): 271–89.

Alexis, Jacques Stephen. *Les arbres musiciens.* Paris: Gallimard, 1957.

Alexis, Jacques Stephen. *Compère général soleil.* Paris: Gallimard, 1955.

Alexis, Jacques Stephen. "Du réalisme merveilleux des Haïtiens." *Présence africaine* 165–66, 2002 (orig. 1956): 91–112.

Alexis, Jacques Stephen. *L'espace d'un cillement.* Paris: Gallimard, 1959.

Alexis, Jacques Stephen. "Jacques Roumain vivant." Preface in *La Montagne ensorcelé*, by Jacques Roumain, 11–30. Paris: Les Editeurs Français Réunis, 1972 (orig. 1957).

Alexis, Jacques Stephen. "Le Sous-lieutenant enchanté." In *Romancero aux étoiles*, 181–213. Paris: Gallimard, 1960.

Anderson, Benedict. *Imagined Communities*, rev. ed. New York: Verso, 1991.

André, Jacques. *Caraïbales: Études sur la littérature antillaise.* Paris: Éditions Caribéennes, 1981.

Antoine, Jacques Carmeleau. *Jean Price-Mars and Haiti.* Washington, DC: Three Continents, 1981.

Appadurai, Arjun. *The Future as Cultural Fact: Essays on the Global Condition.* New York: Verso, 2013.

Apter, Emily. *Against World Literature: On the Politics of Untranslatability.* New York: Verso, 2013.

Apter, Emily. *The Translation Zone: A New Comparative Literature.* Princeton, NJ: Princeton University Press, 2006.

Asad, Talal, ed. *Anthropology and the Colonial Encounter.* New York: Humanities, 1973.

Attwell, David. "Coetzee's Estrangements." *Novel: A Forum on Fiction* 41, nos. 2–3 (2008): 229–43.

Austen, Ralph. "From a Colonial to a Postcolonial African Voice: *Amkoullel, l'enfant peul.*" *Research in African Literatures* 31, no. 3 (2000): 1–17.

Balibar, Étienne. *We, the People of Europe? Reflections on Transnational Citizenship*, trans. James Swenson. Princeton, NJ: Princeton University Press, 2004.

Baucom, Ian. *Specters of the Atlantic: Finance Capital, Slavery, and the Philosophy of History*. Durham, NC: Duke University Press, 2005.

Benítez-Rojo, Antonio. *The Repeating Island: The Caribbean and the Postmodern Perspective*, 2d ed., trans. James Maraniss. Durham, NC: Duke University Press, 1996.

Benjamin, Walter. "The Paris of the Second Empire in Baudelaire." In *The Writer of Modern Life: Essays on Charles Baudelaire*, ed. Michael W. Jennings, trans. Howard Eiland, Edmund Jephcott, Rodney Livingstone, and Harry Zohn, 46–133. Cambridge, MA: Harvard University Press, 2006.

Benjamin, Walter. "The Storyteller: Reflections on the Works of Nikolai Leskov." In *Illuminations: Essays and Reflections*, ed. Hannah Arendt, trans. Harry Zohn, 83–109. New York: Schocken, 1969.

Bernabé, Jean, Patrick Chamoiseau, and Raphaël Confiant. *Éloge de la créolité*, bilingual ed., trans. M. B. Taleb-Khyar. Paris: Gallimard, 1993 (orig. 1989).

Bloom, Peter. *French Colonial Documentary: Mythologies of Humanitarianism*. Minneapolis: University of Minnesota Press, 2008.

Bolaño, Roberto. *2666*, trans. Natasha Wimmer. New York: Picador, 2008 (orig. 2004).

Bongie, Chris. *Islands and Exiles: The Creole Identities of Post/Colonial Literature*. Stanford, CA: Stanford University Press, 1998.

Bongie, Chris. "Resisting Memories: The Creole Identities of Lafcadio Hearn and Édouard Glissant." *SubStance* 26, no. 3 (1995): 153–78.

Breton, André. "A Great Black Poet." In *Notebook of a Return to the Native Land*, by Aimé Césaire, ed. and trans. Clayton Eshleman and Annette Smith, ix–xix. Middletown, CT: Wesleyan University Press, 2001.

Breton, André. *Nadja*, trans. Richard Howard. New York: Grove Press, 1960 (orig. 1928).

Brink, André. *Rumors of Rain*. Naperville, IL: Sourcebooks Landmark, 2008 (orig. 1978).

Britton, Celia. "'Common Being' and Organic Community in Jacques Roumain's *Gouverneurs de la rosée.*" *Research in African Literatures* 37, no. 2 (2006): 164–75.

Britton, Celia. *The Sense of Community in French Caribbean Fiction*. Liverpool: Liverpool University Press, 2008.

Brown, Wendy. *Undoing the Demos: Neoliberalism's Stealth Revolution*. New York: Zone, 2015.

Burton, Richard D. E. "Two Views of Césaire: Négritude and Créolité." *Dalhousie French Studies* 35 (1996): 135–52.

Butler, Judith. *Bodies That Matter: On the Discursive Limits of "Sex."* New York: Routledge, 1993.

Caldwell, Roy Chandler, Jr. "*Créolité* and Postcoloniality in Raphaël Confiant's *L'allée des soupirs*." *French Review* 73, no. 3 (1999): 301–11.

Casanova, Pascale. *The World Republic of Letters*, trans. M. B. DeBevoise. Cambridge, MA: Harvard University Press, 2004.

Célius, Carlo Avierl. "La création plastique et le tournant ethnologique en Haïti." *Gradhiva* 1 (2005). Accessed April 2, 2015. http://gradhiva.revues.org/301.

Césaire, Aimé. *Cahier d'un retour au pays natal*. Paris: Présence Africaine, 1956 (orig. 1939).

Césaire, Aimé. *Notebook of a Return to the Native Land*, ed. and trans. Clayton Eshleman and Annette Smith. Middletown, CT: Wesleyan University Press, 2001.

Césaire, Suzanne. "Misère d'une poésie: John Antoine-Nau." *Tropiques* 4 (1942): 48–50.

Chakrabarty, Dipesh. *Provincializing Europe: Postcolonial Thought and Historical Difference*. Princeton, NJ: Princeton University Press, 2000.

Chamoiseau, Patrick. *Césaire, Perse, Glissant: Les liaisons magnétiques*. Paris: Philippe Rey, 2013.

Chamoiseau, Patrick. *Chronique des sept misères*. Paris: Gallimard, 1986.

Chamoiseau, Patrick. *Écrire en pays dominé*. Paris: Gallimard, 1997.

Chamoiseau, Patrick. *Solibo Magnificent*, trans. Rose-Myriam Réjouis and Val Vinokurov. New York: Vintage, 1997 (orig. 1988).

Chamoiseau, Patrick. *Texaco*. Paris: Gallimard, 1992.

Chamoiseau, Patrick. *Texaco*, trans. Rose-Myriam Réjouis and Val Vinokurov. New York: Vintage, 1997 (orig. 1992).

Chamoiseau, Patrick, and Raphaël Confiant. *Lettres créoles: Tracées antillaises et continentales de la littérature, Haïti, Guadeloupe, Martinique, Guyane, 1635–1975*. Paris: Gallimard, 1999 (orig. 1991).

Charlier-Doucet, Rachelle. "Anthropologie politique et engagement social: L'expérience du Bureau d'Ethnologie d'Haïti." *Gradhiva* 1 (2005). Accessed July 28, 2014. http://gradhiva.revues.org/313.

Childers, Kristen Stromberg. *Seeking Imperialism's Embrace: National Identity, Decolonization, and Assimilation in the French Caribbean*. New York: Oxford University Press, 2016.

Chow, Rey. *Not Like a Native Speaker: On Languaging as a Postcolonial Experience*. New York: Columbia University Press, 2014.

Clifford, James. "Feeling Historical." In *Writing Culture and the Life of Anthropology*, ed. Orin Starn, 25–34. Durham, NC: Duke University Press, 2015.

Clifford, James. "Introduction: Partial Truths." In *Writing Culture: The Poetics and Politics of Ethnography*, ed. James Clifford and George E. Marcus, 1–26. Berkeley: University of California Press, 1986.

Clifford, James. *The Predicament of Culture: Twentieth-Century Ethnography, Literature, and Art*. Cambridge, MA: Harvard University Press, 1988.

Clifford, James. "On Ethnographic Allegory." In *Writing Culture: The Poetics and Politics of Ethnography*, ed. James Clifford and George E. Marcus, 98–121. Berkeley: University of California Press, 1986.

Clifford, James. "Tell Me about Your Trip: Michel Leiris." In *The Predicament of Culture: Twentieth-Century Ethnography, Literature, and Art*, by James Clifford, 165–74. Cambridge, MA: Harvard University Press, 1988.

Clifford, James, and George Marcus, eds. *Writing Culture: The Poetics and Politics of Ethnography*. Berkeley: University of California Press, 1986.

Coates, Carrol F., and Dany Laferrière. "An Interview with Dany Laferrière." *Callaloo* 22, no. 4 (1999): 910–21.

Coetzee, J. M. *Summertime: Fiction*. New York: Viking, 2009.

Cole, Teju. *Open City*. New York: Random House, 2011.

Colleyn, Jean-Paul. "Fiction et fictions en anthropologie." *L'Homme* 175–76 (2005): 147–63.

Comaroff, Jean, and John L. Comaroff. *Theory from the South: Or, How Euro-America Is Evolving toward Africa*. Boulder, CO: Paradigm, 2012.

Comaroff, Jean, and John L. Comaroff. *The Truth about Crime: Sovereignty, Knowledge, and Social Order*. Chicago: University of Chicago Press, 2016.

Comhaire-Sylvain, Suzanne. *Le roman de Bouqui*. Ottawa: Leméac, 1973 (orig. 1940).

Confiant, Raphaël. *Aimé Césaire: Une traversée paradoxale du siècle*. Paris: Stock, 1993.

Confiant, Raphaël. *L'allée des soupirs*. Paris: Gallimard, 1994.

Confiant, Raphaël. "Foreword." In *Two Years in the French West Indies*, by Lafcadio Hearn, ix–xii. New York: Interlink, 2001 (orig. 1890).

Confiant, Raphaël. *Le meurtre du Samedi-Gloria*. Paris: Gallimard, 1997.

Confiant, Raphaël. *Le nègre et l'amiral*. Paris: Grasset, 1988.

Conklin, Alice L. *In the Museum of Man: Race, Anthropology, and Empire in France, 1850–1950*. Ithaca, NY: Cornell University Press, 2013.

Coundouriotis, Eleni. *Claiming History: Colonialism, Ethnography, and the Novel*. New York: Columbia University Press, 1999.

Dash, J. Michael. "Caraïbe Fantôme: The Play of Difference in the Francophone Caribbean." *Yale French Studies* 103 (2003): 93–105.

Dash, J. Michael. *Haiti and the United States: National Stereotypes and the Literary Imagination*. New York: St. Martin's, 1988.

Dash, J. Michael. "Hemispheric Horizons: Confinement, Mobility, and the 'Bateaux-Prisons' of the French Caribbean Imaginary." *Contemporary French and Francophone Studies* 15, no. 1 (2011): 19–25.

Dash, J. Michael. "Le Je de l'Autre: Surrealist Ethnographers and the Francophone Caribbean." *L'Esprit Créateur* 47, no. 1 (2007): 84–95.

Dash, J. Michael. "Jean Price-Mars et l'image d'Haïti." In *Ainsi parla l'Oncle [suivi de Revisiter l'Oncle]*, by Jean Price-Mars, 337–42. Montreal: Mémoire d'Encrier, 2009.

Dash, J. Michael. *The Other America: Caribbean Literature in a New World Context*. Charlottesville: University of Virginia Press, 1998.

Dash, J. Michael. "Remembering Édouard Glissant." *Callaloo* 34, no. 3 (2011): 671–75.

Dayan, Joan. "France Reads Haiti: René Depestre's *Hadriana dans tous mes rêves*." *Yale French Studies* 83, no. 2 (1993): 154–75.

Debaene, Vincent. "Ethnographie/Fiction: A propos de quelques confusions et faux paradoxes." *L'Homme* 175–76 (2005): 219–32.

Debaene, Vincent. *Far Afield: French Anthropology between Science and Literature*, trans. Justin Izzo. Chicago: University of Chicago Press, 2014.

De Certeau, Michel. *The Practice of Everyday Life*, trans. Steven Rendall. Berkeley: University of California Press, 2011 (orig. 1984).

Deleuze, Gilles. *Cinema 2: The Time-Image*, trans. Hugh Tomlinson and Robert Galeta. Minneapolis: University of Minnesota Press, 1989.

Deleuze, Gilles. *Difference and Repetition*, trans. Paul Patton. New York: Columbia University Press, 1994.

Deleuze, Gilles. *Kant's Critical Philosophy*, trans. Hugh Tomlinson and Barbara Habberjam. Minneapolis: University of Minnesota Press, 1984.

Deleuze, Gilles. "Philosophie de la Série Noire." In *L'île déserte et autres textes: Textes et entretiens 1953–1974*, 114–19. Paris: Minuit, 2002 (orig. 1966).

Deleuze, Gilles. *Proust and Signs*, trans. Richard Howard. Minneapolis: University of Minnesota Press, 2000.

Dell'Umbria, Alèssi. *Histoire universelle de Marseille: De l'an mil à l'an deux mille*. Marseille: Agone, 2006.

Dell'Umbria, Alèssi. "The Sinking of Marseille." *New Left Review* 75 (2012): 69–87.

Depestre, René. *Bonjour et adieu à la négritude*. Paris: Robert Laffont, 1980.

Depestre, René. *Hadriana dans tous mes rêves*. Paris: Gallimard, 1988.

Depestre, René. "Jean Price-Mars et le mythe de l'Orphée noir ou les aventures de la négritude." *L'Homme et la Société* 7 (1968): 171–81.

Depestre, René. *Le mât de cocagne*. Paris: Gallimard, 1979.

Depestre, René. "Parler de Jacques Roumain (1907–1944)." In *Jacques Roumain: Oeuvres complètes*, ed. Léon-François Hoffmann, xxi–xxx. Paris: Allca XX, 2003.

Derrida, Jacques. *Specters of Marx: The State of the Debt, the Work of Mourning, and the New International*, trans. Peggy Kamuf. New York: Routledge, 1994.

Devey, Muriel. *Hampâté Bâ: L'homme de la tradition*. Dakar: LivreSud, 1993.

Di Iorio, Sam. "Total Cinema: *Chronique d'un été* and the end of Bazinian Film Theory." *Screen* 48, no. 1 (2007): 25–43.

Diawara, Manthia. *African Cinema: Politics and Culture*. Bloomington: Indiana University Press, 1992.

Diawara, Manthia. *African Film: New Forms of Aesthetics and Politics*. Munich: Prestel, 2010.

Dos Passos, John. *The Big Money*. New York: Mariner, 2000 (orig. 1936).

Dubreuil, Laurent. *Empire of Language: Toward a Critique of (Post)colonial Expression*, trans. David Fieni. Ithaca, NY: Cornell University Press, 2013.

Edwards, Brent Hayes. "Introduction." In *Phantom Africa*, by Michel Leiris, trans. Brent Hayes Edwards, 1–56. New York: Seagull, 2017.

Edwards, Brent Hayes. *The Practice of Diaspora: Literature, Translation, and the Rise of Black Internationalism*. Cambridge, MA: Harvard University Press, 2003.

Equilbecq, François-Victor. *Contes populaires d'Afrique occidentale*. Paris: G.-P. Maisonneuve et Larose, 1972.

Fabian, Johannes. *Memory against Culture: Arguments and Reminders*. Durham, NC: Duke University Press, 2007.

Fassin, Didier. *Enforcing Order: An Ethnography of Urban Policing*. Malden, MA: Polity, 2013.

Feld, Steven. "Introduction." In *Ciné-Ethnography*, by Jean Rouch, ed. and trans. Steven Feld, 1–25. Minneapolis: University of Minnesota Press, 2003.

Fieschi, Jean-André. "Slippages of Fiction." In *Anthropology, Reality, Cinema: The Films of Jean Rouch*, ed. Mick Eaton, 67–77. London: British Film Institute, 1979.

Firmin, Joseph Anténor. *De l'égalité des races humaines (anthropologie positive)*. Montreal: Mémoire d'Encrier, 2005 (orig. 1885).

Fonkoua, Romuald Blaise. "Édouard Glissant: Naissance d'une anthropologie antillaise au siècle de l'assimilation." *Cahiers d'Études Africaines* 35, no. 140 (1995): 797–818.

Fonkoua, Romuald Blaise. "Fonkoua Price-Mars ou les débuts de la négritude scientifique en Haïti." In *Ainsi parla l'Oncle [suivi de Revisiter l'Oncle]*, by Jean Price-Mars, 329–36. Montreal: Mémoire d'Encrier, 2009.

Fortun, Kim. "Foreword to the 25th Anniversary Edition of *Writing Culture*." In *Writing Culture: The Poetics and Politics of Ethnography*, ed. James Clifford and George E. Marcus, vii–xxii. Berkeley: University of California Press, 2011 (orig. 1986).

Foucault, Michel. *The Archeology of Knowledge and The Discourse on Language*, trans. A. M. Sheridan Smith. New York: Pantheon, 1982 (orig. 1972).

Gallagher, Mary. "Lafcadio Hearn's American Writings and the Creole Continuum." In *American Creoles: The Francophone Caribbean and the American South*, ed. Martin Munro and Celia Britton, 19–39. Liverpool: Liverpool University Press, 2012.

Geertz, Clifford. *Works and Lives: The Anthropologist as Author*. Stanford, CA: Stanford University Press, 1988.

Genette, Gérard. *Fiction and Diction*, trans. Catherine Porter. Ithaca, NY: Cornell University Press, 1993 (orig. 1991).

Geschiere, Peter. *The Perils of Belonging: Autochthony, Citizenship, and Exclusion in Africa and Europe*. Chicago: University of Chicago Press, 2009.

Ghosh, Amitav. *In an Antique Land: History in the Guise of a Traveler's Tale*. New York: Vintage, 1992.

Ghosh, Amitav. *Sea of Poppies*. New York: Picador, 2008.

Gilroy, Paul. *Against Race: Imagining Political Culture beyond the Color Line*. Cambridge, MA: Harvard University Press, 2000.

Gilroy, Paul. *The Black Atlantic: Modernity and Double Consciousness*. Cambridge, MA: Harvard University Press, 1993.

Ginsburg, Faye. "The Parallax Effect: The Impact of Indigenous Media on Ethnographic Film." In *Collecting Visible Evidence*, ed. Jane M. Gaines and Michael Renov, 156–75. Minneapolis: University of Minnesota Press, 1999.

Glissant, Édouard. *Caribbean Discourse: Selected Essays*, trans. J. Michael Dash. Charlottesville: University of Virginia Press, 1989.

Glissant, Édouard. *Le discours antillais*. Paris: Gallimard, 1997 (orig. 1981).

Glissant, Édouard. *Introduction à une poétique du divers*. Paris: Gallimard, 1996.

Glissant, Édouard. "Michel Leiris: The *Repli* and the *Dépli*," trans. Cynthia Mesh. *Yale French Studies* 81 (1992): 21–27.

Glissant, Édouard. *Pays rêvé, pays réel*. Paris: Seuil, 1985.

Glissant, Édouard. *Poétique de la Relation*. Paris: Seuil, 1990.

Glissant, Édouard. *Poetics of Relation*, trans. Betsy Wing. Ann Arbor: University of Michigan Press, 1997 (orig. 1990).

Glissant, Édouard. *Soleil de la conscience*. Paris: Seuil, 1956.

Glissant, Édouard. *Traité du tout-monde*. Paris: Gallimard, 1997.

Glissant, Édouard, and Patrick Chamoiseau. *L'intraitable beauté du monde: Adresse à Barack Obama*. Paris: Galaade, 2009.

Glover, Kaiama L. "Exploiting the Undead: The Usefulness of the Zombie in Haitian Literature." *Journal of Haitian Studies* 11, no. 2 (2005): 105–21.

Godard, Jean-Luc. "L'Afrique vous parle de la fin et des moyens." *Cahiers du Cinéma* 94 (1959): 19–22.

Goody, Jack. "From Oral to Written: An Anthropological Breakthrough in Storytelling." In *The Novel, Volume 1: History, Geography, and Culture*, ed. Franco Moretti, 3–36. Princeton, NJ: Princeton University Press, 2006.

Gorrara, Claire. *The Roman Noir in Post-War French Culture*. Oxford: Oxford University Press, 2003.

Goulet, Andrea, and Susanna Lee. "Editors' Preface." *Yale French Studies* 108 (2005): 1–7.

Grauby, Françoise. "Force mentale; Fabio Montale: *Total Khéops* au risque de la psychanalyse." *Australian Journal of French Studies* 43 (2006): 80–93.

Gregory, Steven. "Voodoo, Ethnography, and the American Occupation of Haiti: William B. Seabrook's *The Magic Island*." In *Dialectical Anthropology: Essays in Honor of Stanley Diamond*, vol. 2, ed. Christine Ward Gailey, 169–207. Gainesville: University Press of Florida, 1992.

Hampâté Bâ, Amadou. *Amkoullel, l'enfant peul*. Paris: Actes Sud, 1991.

Hampâté Bâ, Amadou. *L'empire peul du Macina (1818–1853)*. Paris: Éditions de l'École des hautes études en sciences sociales, 1984 (orig. 1955).

Hampâté Bâ, Amadou. *L'étrange destin de Wangrin*. Paris: 10/18, 1973.

Hampâté Bâ, Amadou. *Oui mon commandant!* Paris: Actes Sud, 1994.

Hardt, Michael, and Antonio Negri. *Assembly*. New York: Oxford University Press, 2017.

Harrow, Kenneth W. *Trash: African Cinema from Below*. Bloomington: Indiana University Press, 2013.

Hazoumé, Paul. "Foreword." In *Doguicimi*, by Paul Hazoumé, 13–14. Paris: G.-P. Maisonneuve et Larose, 1978 (orig. 1938).

Hearn, Lafcadio. *Two Years in the French West Indies*. New York: Interlink, 2001 (orig. 1890).

Heckmann, Hélène. "Annexe I, Genèse et authenticité des ouvrages *L'étrange destin de Wangrin* et la série des *Mémoires*." In *Oui mon commandant!*, by Amadou Hampâté Bâ, 479–84. Paris: Actes Sud, 1994.

Henley, Paul. *The Adventure of the Real: Jean Rouch and the Craft of Ethnographic Cinema*. Chicago: University of Chicago Press, 2009.

Herskovits, Melville J. *Life in a Haitian Valley*. Princeton, NJ: Markus Wiener, 2007 (orig. 1937).

Hewitt, Nicholas. "Departures and Homecomings: Diaspora in Jean-Claude Izzo's Marseille." *French Cultural Studies* 17, no. 3 (2006): 257–68.

Holmes, Douglas R. *Integral Europe: Fast-Capitalism, Multiculturalism, Neofascism*. Princeton, NJ: Princeton University Press, 2000.

Holmes, Douglas R. "Society Lost, Society Found." In *Zeroing In on the Year 2000: The Final Edition*, ed. George E. Marcus, 161–90. Chicago: University of Chicago Press, 2000.

Huggan, Graham. *Interdisciplinary Measures: Literature and the Future of Postcolonial Studies*. Liverpool: Liverpool University Press, 2008.

Hurston, Zora Neale. *Tell My Horse: Voodoo and Life in Haiti and Jamaica*. New York: Harper Perennial, 1990 (orig. 1938).

Irele, F. Abiola. *The African Imagination: Literature in Africa and the Black Diaspora*. New York: Oxford University Press, 2001.

Izzo, Jean-Claude. *La trilogie Fabio Montale*. Paris: Gallimard, 2006.

James, Alison. "Thinking the Everyday: Genre, Form, Fiction." *L'Esprit Créateur* 54, no. 3 (2014): 78–91.

James, Regina. "'Writing without Authority': J. M. Coetzee and His Fictions." *Salmagundi* 114–15 (1997): 103–21.

Jameson, Fredric. *Archeologies of the Future: The Desire Called Utopia and Other Science Fictions*. New York: Verso, 2005.

Jameson, Fredric. *A Singular Modernity: Essay on the Ontology of the Present*. New York: Verso, 2002.

Jameson, Fredric. *The Modernist Papers*. New York: Verso, 2007.

Jameson, Fredric. "On Raymond Chandler." In *The Critical Response to Raymond Chandler*, ed. J. K. Van Dover, 65–87. Westport, CT: Greenwood, 1995.

Jameson, Fredric. *The Seeds of Time*. New York: Columbia University Press, 1994.

Jameson, Fredric. *Signatures of the Visible*. London: Routledge, 1992.

Jamin, Jean. "Fictions haut régime: Du théâtre vécu au mythe romanesque." *L'Homme* 175–76 (2005): 165–201.

Jamin, Jean. "Objets trouvés des paradis perdus: A propos de la Mission Dakar-Djibouti." In *Collections passion: Exposition du 5 juin au 31 décembre 1982*, ed. Jacques Hainard and Roland Kaehr, 69–100. Neuchâtel, Switzerland: Musée d'Ethnographie, 1982.

Jamin, Jean. "Présentation de *L'Afrique fantôme*." In *Miroir de l'Afrique*, by Michel Leiris, ed. Jean Jamin, 65–85. Paris: Gallimard, 1996.

Jézéquel, Jean-Hervé. "Grammaire de la distinction coloniale." *Genèses* 69 (2007): 4–25.

Jézéquel, Jean-Hervé. "Voices of Their Own? African Participation in the Production of Colonial Knowledge in French West Africa, 1910–1950." In *Ordering Africa: Anthropology, European Imperialism, and the Politics of Knowledge*, ed. Helen Tilley and Robert J. Gordon, 145–72. Manchester, UK: Manchester University Press, 2007.

Johnson, Paul Christopher. "Secretism and the Apotheosis of Duvalier." *Journal of the American Academy of Religion* 74, no. 2 (2006): 420–45.

Joyce, James. *Ulysses*. New York: Vintage, 1990.

Juhasz, Alexandra, and Jesse Lerner, eds. *F Is for Phony: Fake Documentaries and Truth's Undoing*. Minneapolis: University of Minnesota Press, 2006.

Julien, Eileen. "The Extroverted African Novel." In *The Novel, Volume 1: History, Geography, and Culture*, ed. Franco Moretti, 667–700. Princeton, NJ: Princeton University Press, 2007.

Kabanda, Théophiste. "Théâtralité et formes parodiques dans *En attendant le vote des bêtes sauvages*." In *L'imaginaire d'Ahmadou Kourouma: Contours et enjeux d'une esthétique*, ed. Jean Ouédraogo, 245–67. Paris: Karthala, 2010.

Knepper, Wendy. "Remapping the Crime Novel in the Francophone Caribbean: The Case of Patrick Chamoiseau's *Solibo Magnifique*." *PMLA* 122, no. 5 (2007): 1431–46.

Kourouma, Ahmadou. *En attendant le vote des bêtes sauvages*. Paris: Points, 2000.

Krug, François. "Point Godwin contre Guéant: Qui est Serge Letchimy?" *L'Obs*, February 7, 2012. Accessed August 2, 2018. https://www.nouvelobs.com/rue89 /rue89-politique/20120207.RUE7706/point-godwin-contre-gueant-qui-est-serge -letchimy.html#/news/229166.

Kullberg, Christina. "Crossroads Poetics: Glissant and Ethnography." *Callaloo* 36, no. 4 (2013): 968–82.

Kullberg, Christina. *The Poetics of Ethnography in Martinican Narratives: Exploring the Self and the Environment*. Charlottesville: University of Virginia Press, 2013.

Laferrière, Dany. *L'énigme du retour*. Paris: Bernard Grasset, 2009.

Laferrière, Dany. *Pays sans chapeau*. Paris: Serpent à Plumes, 2001 (orig. 1996).

Le Brun, Annie. *Statue cou coupé*. Paris: Jean-Michel Place, 1996.

Leiris, Michel. *L'Afrique fantôme*. Paris: Gallimard, 1934.

Leiris, Michel. *L'âge d'homme*. Paris: Gallimard, 1939.

Leiris, Michel. *Biffures*. Paris: Gallimard, 1948.

Leiris, Michel. *Cinq études d'ethnologie*. Paris: Denoël, 1969.

Leiris, Michel. *Contacts de civilisations en Martinique et en Guadeloupe*. Paris: Gallimard and United Nations Educational, Scientific and Cultural Organization, 1955.

Leiris, Michel. "L'ethnographe devant le colonialisme." In *Cinq études d'ethnologie*, by Michel Leiris, 83–112. Paris: Denoël, 1969 (orig. 1950).

Leiris, Michel. *Fibrilles*. Paris: Gallimard, 1966.

Leiris, Michel. *Frêle bruit*. Paris: Gallimard, 1976.

Leiris, Michel. *La Possession et ses aspects théâtraux ches les Éthiopiens de Gondar*. Paris: Librairie Plon, 1958.

Leiris, Michel. *Scratches*, trans. Lydia Davis. Baltimore: Johns Hopkins University Press, 1997.

Lévi-Strauss, Claude. *Tristes Tropiques*, trans. John and Doreen Weightmann. New York: Penguin, 1992.

Lewis, Mary Dewhurst. *The Boundaries of the Republic: Migrant Rights and the Limits of Universalism in France, 1918–1940*. Stanford, CA: Stanford University Press, 2007.

Lionnet, Françoise. *Le su et l'incertain: Cosmopolitiques créoles de l'océan indien/The Known and the Uncertain: Creole Cosmopolitics of the Indian Ocean*. La Pelouse, Mauritius: L'Atelier d'Écriture, 2012.

Loizos, Peter. *Innovation in Ethnographic Film: From Innocence to Self-consciousness, 1955–1985*. Chicago: University of Chicago Press, 1993.

Magloire, Gérarde, and Kevin A. Yelvington. "Haiti and the Anthropological Imagination." *Gradhiva* 1 (2005). Accessed July 28, 2014. http://gradhiva.revues.org /335.

Majumdar, Saikat. *Prose of the World: Modernism and the Banality of Empire*. New York: Columbia University Press, 2013.

Malinowski, Bronislaw. *A Diary in the Strict Sense of the Term*. Stanford, CA: Stanford University Press, 1989.

Maran, René. *Batouala*. Paris: Albin Michel, 1921.

Marcus, George E. "The Modernist Sensibility in Recent Ethnographic Writing and the Cinematic Metaphor of Montage." In *Visualizing Theory: Selected Essays from V. A. R., 1990–1994*, ed. Lucien Taylor, 37–52. New York: Routledge, 1994.

Marcus, George E., and Michael M. J. Fischer. *Anthropology as Cultural Critique: An Experimental Moment in the Human Sciences*. Chicago: University of Chicago Press, 1999 (orig. 1986).

Marks, Laura U. *The Skin of the Film: Intercultural Cinema, Embodiment, and the Senses*. Durham, NC: Duke University Press, 2000.

Mbembe, Achille. "L'Afrique qui vient." In *Penser et écrire l'Afrique aujourd'hui*, ed. Alain Mabanckou, 17–31. Paris: Seuil, 2017.

Mbembe, Achille. "Penser le monde à partir de l'Afrique: Questions pour aujourd'hui et demain." In *Ecrire l'Afrique-Monde*, ed. Achille Mbembe and Felwine Sarr, 379–93. Paris: Philippe Rey, 2017.

Mbembe, Achille. *Politiques de l'inimitié*. Paris: La Découverte, 2017.

Mbembe, Achille. *Sortir de la grande nuit: Essai sur l'Afrique décolonisée*. Paris: La Découverte, 2010.

Métraux, Alfred. *Le vaudou haïtien*. Paris: Gallimard, 1958.

Miéville, China. *The City and The City*. New York: Del Rey, 2009.

Miller, Christopher L. *The French Atlantic Triangle: Literature and Culture of the Slave Trade*. Durham, NC: Duke University Press, 2008.

Miller, Christopher L. *Theories of Africans: Francophone Literature and Anthropology in Africa*. Chicago: University of Chicago Press, 1990.

More, Thomas. *Utopia*, trans. Paul Turner. New York: Penguin, 1963.

Moretti, Franco. *Graphs, Maps, Trees: Abstract Models for Literary History*. New York: Verso, 2007.

Moudileno, Lydie. *L'écrivain antillais au miroir de sa littérature: Mises en scène et mise en abyme du roman antillais*. Paris: Karthala, 1997.

Moura, Jean-Marc. "Textual Ownership in *L'étrange destin de Wangrin* (*The Fortunes of Wangrin*) by Amadou Hampâté Bâ." *Research in African Literatures* 37, no. 1 (2006): 91–99.

Mudimbe-Boyi, M. Elisabeth. *L'oeuvre romanesque de Jacques-Stephen Alexis: Une écriture poétique, un engagement politique*. Montreal: Humanitas-Nouvelle Optique, 1992.

Munro, Martin. "Ethnography, Exile, and Haitian Literary History in Dany Laferrière's *Pays sans chapeau*." *Journal of Haitian Studies* 9, no. 2 (2003): 74–88.

Munro, Martin. *Exile and Post-1946 Haitian Literature: Alexis, Depestre, Ollivier, Laferrière, Danticat*. Liverpool: Liverpool University Press, 2007.

Nasiali, Minayo. *Native to the Republic: Empire, Social Citizenship, and Everyday Life in Marseille since 1945*. Ithaca, NY: Cornell University Press, 2016.

Nesbitt, Nick. *Voicing Memory: History and Subjectivity in French Caribbean Literature*. Charlottesville: University of Virginia Press, 2003.

Newell, Sasha. *The Modernity Bluff: Crime, Consumption, and Citizenship in Côte d'Ivoire*. Chicago: University of Chicago Press, 2012.

Parks, Tim. "The Education of 'John Coetzee.'" *New York Review of Books*, February 11, 2010. Accessed August 1, 2018. http://www.nybooks.com/articles/archives/2010/feb/11/the-education-of-john-coetzee.

Pavel, Thomas. "Literary Genres as Norms and Good Habits." *New Literary History* 34, no. 2 (2003): 201–10.

Peat, Amanda. *Travel and Modernist Literature: Sacred and Ethical Journeys*. New York: Routledge, 2010.

Peraldi, Michel, and Michel Samson. *Gouverner Marseille: Enquête sur les mondes politiques marseillais*. Paris: La Découverte, 2005.

Placide, Louis-Georges. *Les émeutes de décembre 1959 en Martinique: Un repère historique*. Paris: L'Harmattan, 2009.

Platten, David. "Polar Positions: On the Theme of Identity in Contemporary Noir Fiction." *Nottingham French Studies* 41, no. 1 (2002): 5–18.

Poe, Edgar Allan. "The Poetic Principle." In *Essays and Reviews*, by Edgar Allan Poe, ed. G. R. Thompson, 71–94. New York: Library of America, 1984.

Povinelli, Elizabeth A. *Economies of Abandonment: Social Belonging and Endurance in Late Liberalism*. Durham, NC: Duke University Press, 2011.

Price, Sally. "Michel Leiris, French Anthropology, and a Side Trip to the Antilles." *French Politics, Culture and Society* 22, no. 1 (2004): 23–35.

Price-Mars, Jean. *Ainsi parla l'Oncle* [*suivi de* Revisiter l'Oncle]. Montreal: Mémoire d'Encrier, 2009 (orig. 1928).

Price-Mars, Jean. *Une etape de l'évolution haïtienne*. Port-au-Prince: La Presse, 1929.

Price-Mars, Jean. *Formation ethnique, folk-lore et culture du peuple haïtien*. Port-au-Prince: V. Valcin, 1939.

Prophète, Jean L. "Dany Laferrière and the Autobiography of Disorderly Past Times," trans. Carrol F. Coates. *Callaloo* 22, no. 4 (1999): 947–49.

Ramsey, Kate. "Prohibition, Persecution, Performance: Anthropology and the Penalization of Vodou in Mid-20th-century." *Gradhiva* 1 (2005). Accessed July 28, 2014. http://gradhiva.revues.org/352.

Ramsey, Kate. *The Spirits and the Law: Vodou and Power in Haiti*. Chicago: University of Chicago Press, 2011.

Rancière, Jacques. *Disagreement: Politics and Philosophy*, trans. Julie Rose. Minneapolis: University of Minnesota Press, 1999.

Rancière, Jacques. *The Politics of Aesthetics*, trans. Gabriel Rockhill. New York: Continuum, 2004 (orig. 2000).

Renda, Mary A. *Taking Haiti: Military Occupation and the Culture of U.S. Imperialism, 1915–1940*. Chapel Hill, NC: University of North Carolina Press, 2001.

Riesz, János. *De la littérature coloniale à la littérature africaine: Prétextes-contextes-intertextes*. Paris: Karthala, 2007.

Riesz, János. "From Ethnography to the African Novel: The Example of *Doguicimi* (1938) by Paul Hazoumé (Dahomey)." *Research in African Literatures* 35, no. 4 (2004): 17–32.

Robbins, Bruce. *Perpetual War: Cosmopolitanism from the Viewpoint of Violence*. Durham, NC: Duke University Press, 2012.

Rohdie, Sam. *Promised Lands: Cinema, Geography, Modernism*. London: British Film Institute, 2008.

Ross, Kristen. "Parisian Noir." *New Literary History* 41, no. 1 (2010): 95–109.

Ross, Kristen. "Watching the Detectives." In *Postmodernism and the Re-reading of Modernity*, ed. Francis Barker, Peter Hulme, and Margaret Iversen, 46–65. Manchester, UK: Manchester University Press, 1992.

Rothman, William, ed. *Three Documentary Filmmakers*. Albany: State University of New York Press, 2009.

Rouch, Jean. *Alors le Noir et le Blanc seront amis: Carnets de mission 1946–1951*, ed. Marie-Isabelle Merle des Isles. Paris: Mille et Une Nuits, 2008.

Rouch, Jean. *Ciné-Ethnography*, ed. and trans. Steven Feld. Minneapolis: University of Minnesota Press, 2003.

Rouch, Jean. "Des films ethnographiques." *Positif* 14–15 (1955): 145–49.

Rouch, Jean. "On the Vicissitudes of the Self: The Possessed Dancer, the Magician, the Sorcerer, the Filmmaker, and the Ethnographer." In *Ciné-Ethnography*, by Jean Rouch, ed. and trans. Steven Feld, 87–101. Minneapolis: University of Minnesota Press, 2003.

Rouch, Jean. *Jean Rouch: Cinéma et anthropologie*, ed. Jean-Paul Colleyn. Paris: Cahiers du Cinéma-Institut National de l'Audiovisuel, 2009.

Rouch, Jean. "Questions de méthode: Entretien avec Éric Rohmer et Louis Marcorelles." In *Jean Rouch: Cinéma et anthropologie*, ed. Jean-Paul Colleyn, 123–36.
Paris: Cahiers du Cinéma-Institut National de l'Audiovisuel, 2009.

Rouch, Jean. "The Situation and Tendencies of the Cinema in Africa." In *Ciné-
ethnography*, by Jean Rouch, ed. and trans. Steven Feld, 47–86. Minneapolis:
University of Minnesota Press, 2003.

Rouch, Jean. "Le vrai et le faux." In *Jean Rouch: Cinéma et anthropologie*, ed. Jean-Paul
Colleyn, 111–21. Paris: Cahiers du Cinéma-Institut National de l'Audiovisuel,
2009.

Roumain, Jacques. *Gouverneurs de la rosée*. In *Jacques Roumain: Oeuvres complètes*,
ed. Léon-François Hoffmann, 267–396. Paris: Allca XX, 2003 (orig. 1944).

Rushdie, Salman. *Joseph Anton*. New York: Random House, 2012.

Russell, Catherine. *Experimental Ethnography: The Work of Film in the Age of Video*.
Durham, NC: Duke University Press, 1999.

Saada, Emmanuelle. *Empire's Children: Race, Filiation, and Citizenship in the French
Colonies*, trans. Arthur Goldhammer. Chicago: University of Chicago Press,
2012.

Sadkowski, Piotr. "Les écritures migrantes et le récit odysséen: *Pays sans chapeau* de
Dany Laferrière." *Francofonia* 57 (2009): 101–19.

Said, Edward W. "Representing the Colonized: Anthropology's Interlocutors." *Critical
Inquiry* 15, no. 2 (1989): 205–25.

Sartre, Jean-Paul. *Saint Genet: Actor and Martyr*, trans. Bernard Frechtman. New
York: Pantheon, 1963.

Sartre, Jean-Paul. *"What Is Literature?" and Other Essays*. Cambridge, MA: Harvard
University Press, 1988.

Scheinfeigel, Maxime. *Jean Rouch*. Paris: CNRS, 2008.

Scott, David. *Conscripts of Modernity: The Tragedy of Colonial Enlightenment*. Durham,
NC: Duke University Press, 2004.

Scott, David. "Preface: Islands of *Créolité*?" *Small Axe* 13, no. 3 (2009): vii–x.

Shannon, Magdeline W. *Jean Price-Mars, the Haitian Elite and the American Occupation,
1915–1935*. New York: St. Martin's, 1996.

Shelton, Marie-Denise. "Primitive Self: Colonial Impulses in Michel Leiris's *L'Afrique
fantôme*." In *Prehistories of the Future: The Primitivist Project and the Culture of
Modernism*, ed. Elazar Barkan and Ronald Bush, 326–28. Stanford, CA: Stanford
University Press, 1995.

Singaravélou, Pierre. *Professer l'empire: Les "sciences coloniales" en France sous la IIIe
République*. Paris: Publications de la Sorbonne, 2011.

Smyth, Edmund J. "Marseille *Noir*: Jean-Claude Izzo and the Mediterranean Detective."
Romance Studies 25, no. 2 (2007): 111–21.

Snyder, Carey. "The Possibilities and Pitfalls of Ethnographic Readings: Narrative
Complexity in *Things Fall Apart*." *College Literature* 35, no. 2 (2008): 154–74.

Sourieau, Marie-Agnès. "Patrick Chamoiseau, *Solibo Magnifique*: From the Escheat
of Speech to the Emergence of Language." *Callaloo* 15, no. 1 (1992): 131–37.

Stanitzek, Georg. "Texts and Paratexts in Media," trans. Ellen Klein. *Critical Inquiry* 32, no. 1 (2005): 27–42.

Stankiewicz, Damien. "Anthropology and Fiction: An Interview with Amitav Ghosh." *Cultural Anthropology* 27, no. 3 (2012): 535–41.

Starn, Orin. "Introduction." In *Writing Culture and the Life of Anthropology*, ed. Orin Starn, 1–24. Durham, NC: Duke University Press, 2015.

Stocking, George W., Jr. "Empathy and Antipathy in *Heart of Darkness*." In *Readings in the History of Anthropology*, ed. Regna Darnell, 85–98. New York: Harper and Row, 1974.

Stoler, Ann Laura. *Along the Archival Grain: Epistemic Anxieties and Colonial Common Sense*. Princeton, NJ: Princeton University Press, 2009.

Stoler, Ann Laura. *Duress: Imperial Durabilities in Our Times*. Durham, NC: Duke University Press, 2016.

Stoler, Ann Laura. "Introduction: 'The Rot Remains.'" In *Imperial Debris: On Ruins and Ruination*, ed. Ann Laura Stoler, 1–35. Durham, NC: Duke University Press, 2013.

Stoller, Paul. *The Cinematic Griot: The Ethnography of Jean Rouch*. Chicago: University of Chicago Press, 1992.

Stoller, Paul. "Jean Rouch and the Power of the Between." In *Three Documentary Filmmakers*, ed. William Rothman, 125–37. Albany: State University of New York Press, 2009.

Strongman, Roberto. "Transcorporeality in Vodou." *Journal of Haitian Studies* 14, no. 2 (2008): 4–29.

Taussig, Michael. "Excelente Zona Social." In *Writing Culture and the Life of Anthropology*, ed. Orin Starn, 137–51. Durham, NC: Duke University Press, 2015.

Taussig, Michael. *Mimesis and Alterity: A Particular History of the Senses*. New York: Routledge, 1993.

Thomas, Dominic. *Africa and France: Postcolonial Cultures, Migration, and Racism*. Bloomington: Indiana University Press, 2013.

Trouillot, Michel-Rolph. *Haiti: State against Nation. The Origins and Legacy of Duvalierism*. New York: Monthly Review, 1990.

Trouillot, Michel-Rolph. "Jeux de mots, jeux de classe: Les mouvances de l'indigénisme." *Conjonction* 197 (1993): 29–44.

Trouillot, Michel-Rolph. "The Odd and the Ordinary: Haiti, the Caribbean, and the World." *Cimarrón* 2, no. 3 (1990): 3–12.

Ukadike, Nwachukwu Frank. *Black African Cinema*. Berkeley: University of California Press, 1994.

Venuti, Lawrence. *The Scandals of Translation: Towards an Ethics of Difference*. New York: Routledge, 1998.

Vertov, Dziga. "Kinoks: A Revolution." In *Kino-Eye: The Writings of Dziga Vertov*, ed. Annette Michelson, trans. Kevin O'Brien, 11–21. Berkeley: University of California Press, 1995.

Watts, Richard. "The 'Wounds of Locality': Living and Writing the Local in Chamoiseau's *Ecrire en pays dominé*." *French Forum* 28, no. 1 (2003): 111–29.

Webster, Steven. "Ethnography as Storytelling." *Dialectical Anthropology* 8, no. 3 (1983): 185–205.

Weisstein, Eric W. "Orthogonal Curves." *MathWorld* website. Accessed January 12, 2018. http://mathworld.wolfram.com/OrthogonalCurves.html.

Wilder, Gary. *Freedom Time: Negritude, Decolonization and the Future of the World.* Durham, NC: Duke University Press, 2015.

Wilder, Gary. *The French Imperial Nation-State: Negritude and Colonial Humanism between the Two World Wars.* Chicago: University of Chicago Press, 2005.

Wulff, Helena. "An Anthropological Perspective on the Literary Arts in Ireland." In *A Companion to the Anthropology of Europe*, ed. Ullrich Kockel, Máiréad Nic Craith, and Jonas Frykman, 537–50. Chichester, UK: Wiley-Blackwell, 2012.

Zika, Damouré. *Journal de route.* Paris: Mille et Une Nuits, 2007 (orig. 1956).

Žižek, Slavoj. *The Parallax View.* Cambridge, MA: MIT Press, 2006.

Index

ethnographic fiction (continued)
and, 127; and readers, 19, 22, 24, 54;
Rouch and, 55–97; shared anthropology
and, 83–95; speculation and, 172, 196;
and time, 13; utopia and, 200; virtuosity
and, 45–52

ethnographic film, 1–2, 56, 94, 96; fiction
and, 59. *See also* documentary film

ethnographic realism. *See* realism

ethnography, 6–7, 9, 17; Chamoiseau
and, 150–51, 160, 167; as collaborative,
55; Confiant and, 152–58, 167; créolité
movement and, 146; Glissant and, 135;
Leiris and, 22, 38–40, 43–44, 48–52;
policing and, 173, 184, 188, 190–91;
Price-Mars and, 105, 109; reverse ethnography, 87–90, 230n20; style and, 29;
translation and, 154

Euroméditerranée project, 172, 248n8

exile: Depestre and, 119, 121, 124–25;
Haitian writers and, 101, 132, 236n7;
Laferrière and, 126, 240n79; Marseille
and, 198–99

experimentation, 6–7, 11, 15, 170; Chamoiseau and, 150; créolité movement and,
139; empire and, 9, 12–13, 203–5, 216;
ethnographic film and, 59, 64; Haitian
literature and, 100, 103, 111, 132; Rouch
and, 55–56, 58–61, 63, 72; social forms
and, 203

Fabian, Johannes, 177

Fabio Montale trilogy, 169–202; fieldwork
in, 175–83; form in, 185; masculinity in,
248n12; policing in, 184–86; realism in,
188; utopia in, 171–72, 191–202. *See also
individual works*

Fanon, Frantz, 7, 207, 214

Fassin, Didier, 184

fiction, 9, 222n9; anthropology and, 2, 4–7,
26, 96, 115; documentary and, 72–74;
fieldwork and, 178; folklore and, 100, 109;
genre and, 21–23, 27; Hampâté Bâ and,
17; Leiris and, 22, 41, 44–45, 47, 50–52; in

Moi, un Noir, 57; nation and, 132; powers
of the false, 77–78; realism and, 1; Rouch
and, 55, 59, 62, 66, 73–75; speculation
and, 201–2; translation and, 154

fictionality. *See* fiction

fieldwork, 19–20, 25, 29, 83; aesthetics
of, 175–83, 201; Chamoiseau and, 159;
fiction and, 178; Hampâté Bâ and, 17, 24;
Leiris and, 26, 43–45, 48–49; novel and,
171; Rouch and, 56, 59–60, 86, 94; and
time, 177

Firmin, Anténor, 104

Fischer, Michael, 176

folklore, 98–133, 142; Alexis and, 111–19;
Chamoiseau and, 159; Depestre and,
119–26; fiction and, 100; history and,
117; humanism and, 111–19; Laferrière
and, 127, 129–30; literature and, 108;
nation and, 112, 132; Price-Mars and,
105, 108, 110; Roumain and, 101, 103

form, 5, 6; anthropology and, 100, 132–33;
in Confiant, 152; crime fiction and, 171,
180; in Depestre, 120, 124; empire and,
8–11; politics and, 103; Rouch and, 56,
58–61

*Formation ethnique, folk-lore et culture du
peuple haïtien* (Price-Mars), 110, 112

Foucault, Michel, 14

France, 3, 19, 58, 78, 80–81, 170; citizenship in, 173, 193; créolité movement and,
146; cultural influence in Haiti, 100,
104–5, 126; national identity and, 196;
postcolonial departmentalization and,
137–38; race in, 184, 189; social sciences
in, 52–53, 222n7; 2005 riots in, 172

French Atlantic. *See* Atlantic

Front National (FN), 3, 172, 174, 178–79,
184, 251n48

futurity, 13–14; in Alexis, 117; in Chamoiseau, 164; créolité movement and, 146;
crime fiction and, 171; democracy and,
213–16; dystopia and, 195–96; in Glissant, 141, 143, 145; nation and, 101; in
Roumain 103; utopia and, 193–94, 196

Gaisseau, Pierre-Dominique, 59

Ganda, Oumarou, 1, 62, 67, 76, 82, 93

Gaoudel, Illo, 62, 65

Geertz, Clifford, 29, 32

Genette, Gérard, 45

genre, 1–2, 6, 15, 23, 58, 204, 217n9; Africa
and, 21–28; anthropology and, 56;
Caribbean literature and, 139; créolité
movement and, 151; crime fiction and,
183–91; empire and, 12–13; ethnography
as, 176; in Laferrière, 127; of *L'Afrique
fantôme*, 27; in *Le discours antillais*,
140–41, 144; Rouch and, 73–74

geography: countermapping and, 11–14, 19,
173, 220n34; in Fabio Montale trilogy,
198–99; literature and, 101; modernity
and, 72, 96

Geschiere, Peter, 253n68

Ghosh, Amitav, 13, 220n37, 243n25

Ginsburg, Faye, 87, 234n56

Gilroy, Paul, 35, 71, 207

Glissant, Édouard, 4, 15, 106, 128, 136, 139–45,
164, 192, 207; and Caribbean writing,
142–44; in Chamoiseau, 150; and créolité,
137, 146, 167; on discourse, 143–44, 147;
on Leiris, 134–35; and lived experience,
141, 142, 145; on Relation, 134–35, 138–39,
242n14; social sciences and, 135, 137–40,
147, 208; and temporality, 141, 143

globalization, 6, 214

Gobineau, Arthur de, 104

Godard, Jean-Luc, 58, 65, 95, 233n47

Gold Coast, 59, 62, 65–66, 74

Goody, Jack, 226n46

Gouverneurs de la rosée (Roumain), 101–4,
111, 119, 129, 239n54; history in, 102

Griaule, Marcel, 3, 22–23, 25, 37, 49, 59–60,
150, 162

Guadeloupe, 135, 137

Hadriana dans tous mes rêves (Depestre),
120–26

Haiti, 4, 5, 15, 98–133, 213; African survivals
in, 4, 99, 106, 135; American occupation

of, 98–100, 104, 109, 116; Duvalierism
in, 98, 104; folklore and, 112; French
influence in, 100, 105, 126; in Laferrière,
128; as nation, 99, 132; in Roumain, 102;
zombisme in, 119–26

Hamidou, Moussa, 93

Hampâté Bâ, Amadou, 8, 13–14, 17–54,
57–60, 65, 169, 203; career of, 23, 222n8,
223n20, 224n22, 226n49; as character,
17, 21–22, 27, 32, 35, 121, 127, 220n37; didacticism in, 28–35, 42, 102, 184; fiction
in, 21, 23, 223n20; knowledge project
of, 20–21, 29, 35, 206, 211–12, 226n51; as
storyteller, 17, 19, 22, 24–25, 28–36, 47;
virtuosity in, 30, 42, 45–53, 191

Hardt, Michael, and Antonio Negri, 204,
209–12, 214, 254n20

Harrow, Kenneth, 231n28

Hazoumé, Paul, 4, 223n20, 225n33

Hearn, Lafcadio, 148–49

Heckmann, Hélène, 21

Henley, Paul, 229n1

Herskovits, Melville, 98–100, 129, 132

Hewitt, Nicholas, 249n24

Holmes, Douglas R., 251n48

humanism, 132, 193; Alexis and, 111–19;
créolistes and, 145, 147; Glissant and,
145; Roumain and, 101–2

Hurston, Zora Neale, 99, 235n5

hybridity, 146, 149

immigration, 172–76, 179, 181, 183, 185, 187,
192; French politics and, 188

improvisation, 1–2, 55, 58–59; in *Jaguar*,
62, 64; in *La pyramide humaine*, 64, 65;
modernity and, 56, 72, 96; in *Moi, un
Noir*, 57, 64, 76; narrative and, 73–83,
233n44; shared anthropology and, 84;
storytelling and, 57

In an Antique Land (Ghosh), 220n37

insularity, 167–68

intertextuality, 15, 30, 159–67

introspection, 26–27, 36–44, 49, 64, 140; in
Moi, un noir, 69, 76

literary history, 134–68; anthropology and, 133, 138–39, 167–68; créolistes and, 138, 145–51

literature, 11; anthropology and, 4, 9, 15, 101, 154; as documentary, 9–10; epistemology and, 101, 105; folklore and, 108–9; national literature, 138, 143–44; speculation and, 206; world literature, 93, 205–6

Loizos, Peter, 232n34

Lumière noire (Daeninckx), 181–82

Mabille, Pierre, 121–22, 136, 219n22

Magic Island, The (Seabrook), 99, 123

Mali, 55, 59–60

Malinowski, Bronisław, 27, 51–52

Maran, René, 9–10, 20

Marcus, George, 176–78, 197, 227n56, 254n73

Marseille, 170–202, 251n49; gentrification of, 172, 175–76; space of, 175, 198; as utopia, 172, 178, 192–93, 197–201

Martinique, 4, 10, 106, 115, 134–68; in Glissant, 138, 141–43; Hearn in, 148–49; 1959 riots in, 152–53

Maurras, Charles, nationalism of, 108–10, 114

Mbembe, Achille, 29, 35, 204–6, 215, 239n57; on Africa World, 207–9; on democracy, 213–14

Métraux, Alfred, 101–2

Meurtres pour mémoire (Daeninckx), 181–82

Miéville, China, 241n81

Miller, Christopher L., 217n4, 219n22

Mission Dakar-Djibouti, 3, 17–54, 217n5

modernism, 178, 197, 227n56

modernity, 1, 13, 36, 40, 53, 68; in Alexis, 118–19; colonialism and, 56, 62, 67, 69–70, 78; créolité and, 153; in *Jaguar*, 63, 65–66, 70, 92; in *La pyramide humaine*, 69–70; in *Moi, un noir*, 63, 67–70, 78, 83, 92, 231n28; as narrative category, 56–57, 63, 65, 70–73; race and, 71–72, 83;

Rouch and, 55–56, 58, 61–73, 96, 207, 212; shared anthropology and, 83–95

Moi, un Noir (Rouch film), 1, 8, 55, 58, 61; improvisation in, 57, 76; modernity in, 63, 67–70, 78, 83, 92; narrative in, 75–78, 82–83, 90–91; production of, 62–64; race in, 82–83; shared anthropology in, 87, 90–91, 94

Monod, Théodore, 23, 60

More, Thomas, 198–99

Moretti, Franco, 13, 220n34

Moudileno, Lydie, 247n79

Mudimbe-Boyi, Elisabeth, 238n36

Munro, Martin, 101, 241n83

narrative: in Chamoiseau, 161, 166; crime fiction and, 170, 176, 182; Deleuze and, 77; democracy and, 215; Depestre and, 121; improvisation and, 73–83; in Izzo, 171, 174, 177, 182, 184–86; in *Jaguar*, 74–75, 77–80; in *L'Afrique fantôme*, 225n29; in *L'allée des soupirs*, 153; in *La pyramide humaine*, 80; modernity and, 56–57, 61, 63, 65, 70–73; in *Moi, un Noir*, 75–76, 82, 90–91; nation and, 103, 110, 112; in *Pays sans chapeau*, 129; Rouch and, 63, 70, 79, 95–96

Nasiali, Minayo, 172, 248n6

nation: as aesthetic, 99–100; Alexis and, 111–19; anthropology and, 100, 105, 110; Depestre and, 119–26; epistemology of, 100; ethnographic fiction and, 101; folklore and, 101; human and, 111; literary nationalism, 108–10; narrative and, 103; as palimpsest, 128; Price-Mars and, 100, 103–11, 131; rewriting of, 98–133

Nausea (Sartre), 175

Negritude, 20, 104, 135–36, 219n22; versus Antillanité, 143; créolité movement and, 147, 154, 246n65; Price-Mars and, 106; Sartre and, 228n64

neoliberalism, 204

Nesbitt, Nick, 243n27

New Caledonia, 137

Ross, Kristen, 249n24
Rouch, Jean, 4, 6, 13–15, 23, 55–97, 102, 120, 205, 215; ethnofictional turn, 56–57, 59, 74, 96, 229n1, 230n14, 231n23, 232n34; experimentation in, 55, 58–61, 203, 233n38; on fiction, 1–2, 55; fieldwork and, 56, 86, 230n9; modernity in, 56, 61–73, 207, 212, 231n25; narrative in, 73–83, 233n44; shared anthropology and, 62, 72, 83–95, 96, 206, 234n56
Roumain, Jacques, 5, 101–4, 114, 132, 135; Alexis and, 111–1; and Price-Mars, 101–2, 110; Laferrière and, 130; Vodou and, 102
Rushdie, Salman, 11
Russell, Catherine, 229n4

Saada, Emmanuelle, 228n70
Sadkowski, Piotr, 240n77
Said, Edward, 7
Samson, Michel, 174
Sartre, Jean-Paul, 41, 45, 175, 199, 253n70; on Negritude, 228n64
Scheinfeigel, Maxime, 232n34, 233n47, 235n59
Scott, David, 13, 220n36
Seabrook, William, 99, 123
Sea of Poppies (Ghosh), 220n37
selfhood: in *L'Afrique fantôme*, 25, 37–38, 40–42, 49–52
Sembene, Ousmane, 94–95
Senghor, Léopold Sédar, 57, 223n20
Série Noire, 173–74, 178
shared anthropology. *See* anthropology
Shelton, Marie-Denise, 227n56
Singaravélou, Pierre, 218n19
singularity, 54
Sissoko, Fily Dabo, 223n20
Smyth, Edmund, 249n24
socialism, 103, 111, 116, 132
Solea (Izzo), 174, 184, 201; anxiety in, 195–96; utopia in, 198. *See also* Fabio Montale trilogy
Soleil de la conscience (Glissant), 140, 168

Solibo Magnificent (Chamoiseau), 159–63, 165–66, 168, 171
South Africa, 58, 80–81, 240n70
sovereignty, 203, 209, 212, 254n20; autonomy and, 210; epistemology and, 213; nonsovereign knowledges, 211–13
space: cinematic, 77; of city, 172–73; in colonial Africa, 19; crime fiction and, 170–71, 249n24; in Izzo, 183; utopia and, 193, 201
speculation, 2, 19, 97, 196, 201–2, 204, 210; Atlantic and, 204–6; geography and, 12–14; Haitian literature and, 103, 111; in Izzo, 172, 192; knowledge production and, 207–8, 220n36; in Laferrière, 127; narrative and, 58
Stanitzek, Georg, 240n75
Starn, Orin, 218n13
Stoler, Ann Laura, 10, 12–13
Stoller, Paul, 60
storytelling, 18–19, 21, 24–25, 71; Chamoiseau and, 159–67; cinema and, 56, 61, 97; improvisational, 57, 65; in *Oui mon commandant!*, 28–36; Rouch and, 65, 73; virtuosity and, 30, 32, 47
style, 5, 11, 14, 19, 27; as documentary, 10, 162; virtuosity and, 30, 32, 44–52
synchronized sound, 56, 60, 62, 64, 231n22; postsynchronization, 64–65, 73–75, 77, 80

Taussig, Michael, 6
Tell My Horse (Hurston), 99–100
teleology, 145–51
Texaco (Chamoiseau), 159, 162–68
Thomas, Dominic, 250n32
time, 15; in cinema, 77; geography and, 13; politics of, 177; Rouch and, 75, 77
Total Khéops (Izzo), 174, 177–80, 182; dystopia in, 194–95; policing in, 184–86, 189–91; politics in, 188; speculation in, 192; utopia in, 196. *See also* Fabio Montale trilogy
Traité du tout-monde (Glissant), 135

translation, 34, 152–58, 206
Treichville. *See* Abidjan
Trouillot, Michel-Rolph, 98–100, 132, 236n13
Two Years in the French West Indies (Hearn), 148–49

United States, 58, 68–70, 113; occupation of Haiti, 98–100, 104, 109, 116
universalism, 19, 33–36, 53–54, 163, 212, 215; in Alexis, 111–12; in France, 176, 189, 197; utopia and, 252n62
Ulysses (Joyce), 161, 231n24
utopia, 8, 15, 34, 51–52, 71, 89, 215; citizenship and, 193, 199–201; créolité and, 153; in Fabio Montale trilogy, 191–202; film and, 94; futurity and, 194; geography and, 171, 173; Izzo and, 172–73, 175, 187, 203, 211, 252n55; Marseille as, 172, 192–93, 197–99; present and, 193–94, 196; race and, 63, 81–82

Venuti, Lawrence, 154
Vertov, Dziga, 64, 86–87, 230n21

Victory (Conrad), 50–52
virtuosity, 30, 32–33, 42, 44, 53, 191; epistemology and, 45–52
Vodou, 4, 99; Alexis and, 111–19; campaign against, 100, 111–12, 114, 236n6; in Depestre, 123; in Laferrière, 131; Price-Mars and, 105–6; Roumain and, 101–2

Watts, Richard, 244n42
West Africa, 1, 25, 37, 55, 58, 94; French West Africa, 17, 19, 24, 26, 28, 30, 205; literature in, 219n22; modernity in, 56, 61, 63, 71, 73; race in, 56, 63, 73
Wilder, Gary, 11, 19, 205, 218n18, 226n40, 254n20
wish fulfillment, 126–33, 144
Writing Culture (ed. Clifford and Marcus), 5, 6, 92
Wulff, Helena, 2

Zika, Damouré, 62, 65, 86, 189, 230n9
Žižek, Slavoj, 234n56
zombies: in Laferrière, 129–30; zombisme, 119–26